Introducing Judaism

Eliezer Segal's book is an excellent introduction to the history of Judaism as religion and as religious practice from its Biblical origins through the Middle Ages to the contemporary scene of today. In its comprehensiveness and lucidity, there is no other textbook quite like it on the market. It is perfect for both beginners with no previous knowledge of Judaism and a valuable resource for students with more background.

David Stern, University of Pennsylvania

Eliezer Segal has done an extremely impressive job of providing a broad introduction to Judaism within the scope of a single volume. Segal knows his subject matter thoroughly and writes with authority. What is more, Segal writes engagingly and in an accessible fashion. This book will surely be welcomed warmly by readers from a variety of backgrounds, both Jewish and non-Jewish, who wish to learn about the many facets of the Jewish religion as seen through the eyes of an expert and sympathetic "insider." Segal has done a great service to his readers and to contemporary Judaism.

Robert Brody, Hebrew University of Jerusalem

Introducing Judaism is the ideal starting point for students beginning their studies of this fascinating religion. Segal takes a historical approach, focusing on religious aspects of Judaism, and introducing themes as they emerge from authentic Jewish documents. Students will gain an understanding of how Judaism is lived by its adherents and the historical and geographical diversity of Jewish beliefs and practices.

Throughout the book, Segal stresses the diversity of interpretations that have been generated by historical circumstances, differing theological and ideological outlooks, and the spiritual creativity of the religious community. Attention is paid to various models of piety, mysticism, scholasticism and folk religion, including the impact of Judaism on the daily life of believers and the experiences of Jewish women.

Illustrated throughout, *Introducing Judaism* includes text boxes, a glossary, and a list of further reading to aid students' understanding and revision, providing a thorough overview of one of the first recorded monotheistic faiths and one of the oldest religions still practiced today.

Eliezer Segal is Professor of Western Religions at the University of Calgary, Canada.

World Religions series

Edited by Damien Keown and Charles S. Prebish

This exciting series introduces students to the major world religious traditions. Each religion is explored in a lively and clear fashion by experienced teachers and leading scholars in the field of world religions. Up to date scholarship is presented in a student-friendly fashion, covering history, core beliefs, sacred texts, key figures, religious practice and culture, and key contemporary issues. To aid learning and revision, each text includes illustrations, summaries, explanations of key terms, and further reading.

Introducing Judaism
Eliezer Segal

Introducing Buddhism
Charles S. Prebish and Damien Keown

Introducing Christianity
James R. Adair

Introducing Hinduism
Hillary P. Rodrigues

Introducing Japanese Religion
Robert Ellwood

Forthcoming:

Introducing American Religions
Introducing Chinese Religions
Introducing Daoism
Introducing Islam
Introducing New Religious Movements
Introducing Tibetan Buddhism

Introducing Judaism

Eliezer Segal

 Routledge
Taylor & Francis Group

LONDON AND NEW YORK

First published 2009
by Routledge
2 Park Square, Milton Park, Abingdon, Oxon OX14 4RN

Simultaneously published in the USA and Canada
by Routledge
270 Madison Ave, New York, NY 10016

Routledge is an imprint of the Taylor & Francis Group, an informa business

© 2009 Eliezer Segal

Typeset in Jenson and Tahoma by
HWA Text and Data Management, London
Printed and bound in Great Britain by
CPI Antony Rowe, Chippenham, Wiltshire

Every effort has been made to trace copyright holders, but in a few cases this has not been
possible. Any omissions brought to the publishers' attention will be remedied in future
editions.

British Library Cataloguing in Publication Data
A catalogue record for this book is available from the British Library

Library of Congress Cataloging-in-Publication Data
Segal, Eliezer.
Introducing Judaism / Eliezer Segal. – 1st ed.
    p.   cm. (World religions)
Includes bibliographical references and index.
1. Judaism–History. 2. Judaism–Customs and practices. 3. Judaism–Doctrines.
I. Title.
BM155.3.S44 2008
296–dc22   2008003877

ISBN10: 0–415–44008–4 (hbk)
ISBN10: 0–415–44009–2 (pbk)

ISBN13: 978–0–415–44008–0 (hbk)
ISBN13: 978–0–415–44009–7 (pbk)

This book is dedicated to the beloved memory of my father-in-law Pal Romer (1923–2008)

Contents

Illustrations

Acknowledgments

The author and publisher thank the following for permission to reproduce the illustrations:

Figure 3.1: Ken Welsh/The Bridgeman Art Library
Figure 7.1: Private Collection/The Bridgeman Art Library
Figure 13.1: Bibliothèque Nationale, Paris/The Bridgeman Art Library
Figure 13.2: Library of the Hungarian Academy of Sciences, Budapest/The Bridgeman Art Library
Figure 18.2: Private Collection/Lauros/Giraudon/The Bridgeman Art Library
Figure 18.5: Leslie Scott Antiques, London, UK/The Bridgeman Art LibraryFigure
Figure 19.2: The Israel Museum, Jerusalem, Israel/The Stieglitz Collection/The Bridgeman Art Library

Introduction

In this chapter

Certain assumptions are built into the conventional vocabulary and concepts used to describe Judaism, and some of these terms can produce misunderstandings unless they are explained precisely. This chapter discusses some of these misunderstood terms and explains in what ways Judaism is a religion. Because of the close connection between the Jewish religion and the Jewish people, it is easy to confuse the religion with the historical, cultural or ethnic dimensions. Nevertheless, this book will try to confine itself to topics related to religion, and will avoid discussions of Jewish political and national history. The various terms used for designating the Jews are explained.

Main topics covered

- The word Judaism and its significance
- Jewish religion and nationality
- Different names for Jews and Judaism

The word Judaism and its significance

The English word "Judaism," although it appears to designate a clearly recognizable religion, is in fact a problematic term for a number of reasons. There is no real equivalent to it in the traditional vocabulary of the Jewish religion itself.

To begin with, the normal use of the English "-ism" suffix is to designate an ideological system. Though it applies well to religions that define themselves principally by their dogmas and doctrines, as is true of many forms of Christianity, it cannot be applied without qualifications to other kinds of traditions.

As we shall be noting frequently in this book, whether a person is a member of the Jewish religious community has rarely been determined by their adherence to specific doctrines. There have been attempts to formulate official lists of Jewish beliefs, such as Moses Maimonides's "Thirteen Articles of Creed" in the twelfth century—but none of these have ever achieved universal acceptance. Even Maimonides's list has been used primarily in order to define heretical deviations from acceptable norms; and yet, a person who subscribes, however passionately or sincerely, to all the articles of the creed could hardly be considered Jewish on that basis.

For rather different reasons, the "Juda-" part of "Judaism" is also problematic. As we shall be learning shortly, the term reflects a proper name, Judah (Yehudah in Hebrew), that was originally one of twelve tribes constituting the nation of "Israel." Although historical circumstances created a situation in which the province of Judea was the only one to survive the conquests and exiles that destroyed the other original tribes, the traditional religious literature of the Jewish people almost invariably refers to their community as "Israel." The terms "Judean" and its English variants "Jew" or "Jewish" were imposed on them by outsiders. This vocabulary choice can have theological implications, and it is probable that the common English usage reflects an old Christian desire to differentiate between the ideal theological category of "Israel" (which they claimed to have inherited) and the inferior status of the fragmented and rejected "Jews."

In spite of the problems outlined here, the word "Judaism" has become so entrenched in English discourse that it would be jarring and futile to avoid it in an introductory textbook written for an English-speaking audience. Nevertheless, the airing of the issues can serve a helpful purpose in raising our sensitivities to a variety of potential stumbling blocks that might otherwise prevent us from achieving an accurate understanding of the Jewish religion as it has been experienced by its own community. The achievement of such an understanding is the main objective of the present book.

In some respects, it would be much easier to present an accurate description of Judaism if it could be presumed that the readers were entirely unfamiliar with the subject. What complicates the matter considerably is precisely the fact that the Jews and their heritage, and especially the Bible, are a fundamental pillar of "western civilization." Because that civilization has been a predominantly Christian one, the portrayals of Judaism have generally been filtered through Christian perspectives, even for people who are not actual Christians. It will require a concerted mental effort to avoid this tendency.

Jewish religion and nationality

A further source of potential confusion in presentations of Judaism is the interplay between religious, national and ethnic elements. Because Judaism developed as the religion of a particular nation, terms like "Jewish" or "Israel" can be used to designate a system of rituals or beliefs, a cultural or linguistic heritage, a political unit, and more. Clearly, not all these topics are relevant to a book about the *religion* of Judaism;

though it is more difficult than it appears initially to declare that any of them are completely irrelevant to the book's main subject. In studying the religious expression of a national group, it is necessary to know something about that group's historical and national aspects. Judaism is a decidedly "historical" religion, both in the sense that it considers history to have spiritual significance, and in the fact that it has been affected decisively by historical developments. Therefore, considerable attention will be devoted to providing historical background for the religious phenomena being described and discussed. Nevertheless, there are many topics that belong properly to the national history of the Jewish people, but which will be omitted from the present book because their relevance to the Jewish religion is marginal or non-existent.

A peculiarity of many books about Judaism is their overwhelmingly passive perspective. That is to say, a disproportionate amount of space is devoted to what non-Jews have thought about or done to Jews and Judaism, particularly to instances of anti-Jewish prejudice (anti-Semitism) and persecution. A variety of theological and ideological suppositions contribute to this situation. Though extensive treatment of Jewish victimization might be justified in a conventional national or political history, phenomena like philo-Semitism and anti-Judaism are not really aspects of Judaism so much as they are features of the religions or ideologies where they appear. For this reason, they will be mentioned here only to the extent that they contribute to our understanding of Judaism itself.

A few specific examples should help clarify these theoretical programmatic and methodological statements. Based on the criteria that I have set out, this book will not include accounts of the wars and intrigues of the Hasmonean kings of Judea, nor of the diplomacy and military events involved in the Zionist movement and the creation of the State of Israel. Nor will it chronicle the Crusader massacres in the medieval Rhineland or the Nazi Holocaust in modern Europe. It will, however, note the Jewish religious responses to these historical events and movements, and the impact that the events exerted on the development of Judaism as a religion.

Most of the preceding discussion has been of a relatively negative character, focusing on what Judaism is *not* or on what should be excluded from a book about Jewish religion. I have not said anything substantial about what does legitimately fall within the legitimate purview of "religion" in general or "Judaism" in particular.

As regards a working definition of "religion," the immense diversity of human confrontations with the absolute or the divine have made it very difficult to arrive at a definition that adequately reflects that variety without imposing a partisan religious or ideological outlook on the data. No doubt there are borderline phenomena, such as "non-theistic religions" or the identification of God with the impersonal totality of nature or science, regarding which it is legitimate to ask whether they can be properly classified as religious.

As regards Judaism, however, the phenomena that we will be describing here, with some rare exceptions, are so obviously "religious" by the most minimal definition of the term that it seems superfluous to argue about theoretical nuances. For the most part, the Jewish tradition includes such features as the worship of a personal supernatural deity, a revealed scripture, a divinely ordained code of laws, and an assortment of institutions and communal structures in which the religion is observed. To be sure, the religious credentials of some varieties of Judaism, especially in recent years, might be open to question (for instance, certain types of Humanistic Judaism), but such borderline cases are too rare to concern us at this stage.

For the most part, then, I shall include within the domain of "Judaism" all religious phenomena that have found expression within the Jewish community in its diverse historical and geographical manifestations. Clearly, this definition will have to be applied with a measure of selectivity. Not every belief or ritual that has been associated with a person who is ethnically Jewish deserves to be classified as "Jewish," and there are complex questions raised by phenomena like multi-religious identity, or unaffiliated Jews (concepts that would once have been considered an absurdity, but are now quite widespread).

Different names for Jews and Judaism

The people, or religious community, whom we will be describing in this book have been known by a number of different names. Each of them originated in a particular historical context, and is most appropriate for certain purposes. The following glossary summarizes the origins, meanings and most common uses of the English terms. The biblical or other historical references that are mentioned here will be explained in greater detail later in this book.

Hebrew

Original meanings:

- The name of the language in which the Bible and other works of Jewish literature were composed.
- The name "Hebrew" appears in the Bible as a description of Abraham (Genesis 14:13), without any explanation. Some possible meanings that have been proposed include:
  - Foreigner ("from the other side of the river")
  - A descendant of Eber, a figure mentioned in Genesis 10:21–25.

Normal usage:

- To designate the people from the era of the "Patriarchs" (Abraham, Isaac and Jacob) until the conquest of the Promised Land.

Israel

Original meaning:

- This name was bestowed upon Abraham's grandson Jacob, father of the twelve tribes, after Jacob's struggle with a supernatural being, as described in Genesis 32:29. It is explained enigmatically as meaning "thou hast striven with God and with men, and hast prevailed."
- The designation "Children of Israel" (or: "Israelites") is therefore applied to Jacob's descendants.
- During the era of the "Divided Monarchy," when the nation was divided into two separate states, the northern kingdom was known as Israel. It was composed of ten tribes, as distinct from the southern kingdom that was dominated by the tribe of Judah.
- Jews always refer to their homeland as "the land of Israel" (Erez Yisra'el).

Normal usage:

- This term is the one that has been used most often by the Jews to refer to themselves in their own texts written in the Hebrew language.

Jews (←Judeans)

Original meanings:

- After the fall of the Israelite kingdom, when the ten northern tribes were exiled by the Assyrians, only the Judeans survived captivity in Babylonia to carry on their history and religion. Under the Persian, Greek and Roman empires, their country was known as the province of "Judea." This term was used primarily by non-Jews.

Normal usage:

- This is the most commonly used English term for designating the religious and ethnic community.

(Semites)

Original meaning:

- In the Bible, the Middle-Eastern peoples, including Jews, Arabs and others are traced to Shem, son of Noah. Hence they are all "S(h)emites."
- "Semitic" is also used to denote a language family to which Hebrew, Aramaic, Arabic and other Near Eastern languages belong.

- The term "anti-Semitism" was coined by Wilhelm Marr in 1879 as a more "polite" term for Jew-hatred.

Normal usage:

- The word "anti-Semitism" is the only context in which the term "Semite" refers specifically to Jews as a nation, race or religious community.

Based on this survey, it is clear that certain names are more appropriate for certain historical contexts. For example, it would be factually incorrect to refer (as do many Jewish writers) to the enslavement of the "Jews" in Egypt, because at that time Judah was only one of the twelve tribes who were subjected to slavery. On the other hand, some writers who insist that the term "Judaism" cannot be applied correctly to the biblical era are really trying to make a theological point, questioning whether the Jews of later generations are true heirs to the religious tradition of biblical Israel.

The fine distinctions between the names have lost much of their original relevance, and they have become almost interchangeable. In modern times, especially, one or another term has acquired negative associations in the non-Jewish culture, causing Jews to prefer a different one. This pattern has varied in different localities. "Israelite" has enjoyed popularity in France, whereas "Hebrew" has been preferred in Italy and among liberal Jews in nineteenth-century America.

Key points you need to know

- The presentation of the Jewish religion in the English language can lead to potential misunderstandings because of differing cultural and theological assumptions.
- Religion and national identity have usually overlapped in the history of Judaism. This book will try as much as possible to restrict itself to religious topics, however broadly that is defined. It is not a history of the Jewish nation.
- The religious community that is studied in this volume is known by several different names. These names and their implications are briefly explained.

Discussion questions

1. Based on the considerations mentioned in this chapter, in what ways (if any) do you think that it is relevant to include a discussion of the Nazi genocide of the Jews (Holocaust, Sho'ah)?
2. Traditional Jews often refer to biblical heroes as "Jews" even though they lived before the rise of the Judean state, or were not members of the tribe of Judah. What might this reveal about how they relate religiously to their ancient history?

Further reading

Baron, Salo Wittmayer, *A Social and Religious History of the Jews*, 19 vols. New York: Columbia University Press, 1952–83.

Ben-Sasson, Haim Hillel, and Samuel Ettinger, *Jewish Society through the Ages*. New York: Schocken Books, 1971.

Eisen, Arnold M., *Rethinking Modern Judaism: Ritual, Commandment, Community*, Chicago Studies in the History of Judaism. Chicago, IL: University of Chicago Press, 1998.

Seltzer, Robert M., *Jewish People, Jewish Thought: The Jewish Experience in History*. New York: Macmillan, 1980.

Sharot, Stephen, "Judaism and the Secularization Debate." *Sociological Analysis* 52 (1991): 255–75.

Part I
The historical framework

1 *The biblical legacy*

In this chapter

This chapter will describe the Hebrew sacred scriptures and their importance for subsequent eras of Judaism. It will describe the works included in the Bible, how they are arranged and their importance to Jewish life. It will survey the three main divisions—Torah, Nevi'im and Ketuvim—and summarize their contents and historical narratives.

Main topics covered

- The Hebrew scriptures and their structure
- Torah
- Nevi'im (prophetic books)
- Ketuvim (sacred writings)

The Hebrew scriptures and their structure

The main foundation for all subsequent incarnations of Judaism is its body of sacred scriptures. According to conventional English (that is, Christian) usage, the Jewish holy books constitute the "Old Testament" of the "(Holy) Bible" (which also contains a "New Testament" of later, specifically Christian writings). Although the Jewish scriptures consist of the same works that are included in the Christian "Old Testament," the differing nomenclature is crucial to any discussion of how those works function in a Jewish context.

As to the external form, the books are all written in the Hebrew script. Like other languages in the Semitic family, the root meaning of words is contained in the consonants, and most of the vowels were not originally written down, so that the proper pronunciation had to be memorized. Early in the medieval era, written notations were introduced to indicate vowels, punctuation, syntax and musical cantillation; and one of those systems, the Tiberian, emerged as the standard.

Figure 1.1 The Scroll of Esther

Nevertheless, for ritual readings in the synagogue it is still expected that the Bible be read from a handwritten scroll without written vowels or cantillation signs.

In academic discourse, it is common to refer to the Jewish scriptures by the theologically neutral term "Hebrew Bible," referring to the language in which the books are written (a very few sections are written in a similar language called Aramaic). The term used to designate this corpus in traditional Jewish sources is *Mikra*, a Hebrew term that has no precise equivalent in English, and which carries the connotation of "that which is read aloud." This tells us a great deal about how Judaism envisioned the importance of its scriptures: their importance lay primarily in the fact that they were ordained to be read before the community.

The use of the singular form "Bible" can be misleading. Although it may come bound in a single volume, it is a veritable library or anthology of works that were composed over many centuries and in several different localities.

If we confine ourselves here to the "Jewish Bible," we may make the following observations about its general literary structure: According to the traditional Jewish division, it consists of twenty-four books, though it is extremely rare to find an edition, even one published under Jewish auspices, that preserves that division. Printed versions normally follow the familiar Christian system of division into books with conveniently numbered chapters and verses; and this system divides several of the longer books into two separate sections; or divides the single Hebrew volume of twelve "Minor" Prophets ["minor" in the sense that they consist of shorter books] into twelve distinct works.

The Jewish division divides the Bible into three main sections.

- Torah (5 books).
- Nevi'im (8 books)
- Ketuvim (11 books)

It has become common for Jews, especially in recent decades, to refer to the Hebrew Bible as the TaNaKh, a word made from the Hebrew initials of those three parts.

Torah

The Hebrew word "Torah" means "teaching" or "instruction." As a section of the Bible, it is sometimes referred to as the "five books of Moses," reflecting the traditional Jewish belief about its authorship. In reality, though Moses is unquestionably the dominant figure from the beginning of the second book through to its end (the Torah's final chapter describes his death and its aftermath), the attribution is not stated explicitly in the Torah itself, and Moses is always referred to in the third person. It was once common to designate the Torah as the Pentateuch, from the Greek expression for "five books." Some older Christian works (including the New Testament) refer to the Torah as "Law," a usage that often carries negative connotations as the Law is contrasted unfavorably with faith or grace. The usage, though it may be inaccurate as a translation, preserves an ancient usage that goes back to Hellenistic times, and correctly reflects the centrality of the Torah's laws and precepts in traditional Jewish religion.

The Torah consists chiefly of two types of material.

- Much of it is a narrative, tracing the history of the world, humanity, and then focusing on a particular nation.
- The other type consists of laws, in the form of divine commandments.

Most academic Bible scholars believe that the Torah was assembled from a number of separate documents that were composed and modified by different circles representing diverse religious ideologies. It acquired its current form during the

Babylonian exile, in the fifth century BCE or later. The dominant view of traditional Judaism has always been that the Torah was revealed in precisely its present version by God through Moses at Mount Sinai.

Although all the books of the Hebrew scriptures are considered divinely inspired and holy, the Torah is more holy than any of the others. The exception to this generalization is the Karaite movement, who treat all the books of the Bible as having equal sanctity.

Nevi'im

The original meaning of this title was evidently something like "divinely revealed works" (*nevi'im* is the plural form of a noun whose singular is *navi*). This section of the Hebrew Bible includes a number of works whose sacred status was accepted by Jews at about the same time that the Torah was given its authoritative literary form.

The *Nevi'im* are known in English as "the Prophets." The section contains two main literary genres.

1. As in the Torah, there is a historical component. The historical works are often referred to as the "Former Prophets" because they appear at the beginning of the section.
2. Several of the books in the *Nevi'im* section of the Bible contain transcripts of the teachings ascribed to particular prophets. Generally, such works can be identified by the fact that their titles consist of the prophets' names, such as Isaiah, Jeremiah or Ezekiel. Most prophets spoke in powerful and vivid poetry, full of memorable imagery, and according to the poetic and rhetorical conventions of the time; especially "parallelism," in which the same content is expressed twice in different words.

The thrust of most prophetic teachings is to chastise Israel for its failures to live up to its religious and moral obligations. The people, and especially its rulers, are accused of unfaithfulness when they turn to fertility gods such as Baal and Astarte. The priests are taken to task for their reliance on ritual and cultic worship that is not combined with true devotion and moral sensitivity. The prophets were social critics who were constantly accusing the rich of injustice or indifference in their treatment of the poor: if the people do not return to God's ways they will be punished by drought, famine, invasion, carnage, and exile from their land. When these threats were eventually carried out, in the Assyrian and Babylonian conquests of Israel and Judah, the post-exilic prophets took it upon themselves to reassure the people that all was not lost. Israel was being deservedly punished for their offenses; but the relationship between God and Israel is eternal, and after they have suffered for their crimes, and learned their lesson, they will be restored to divine favor under the leadership of their legitimate kings and priests.

Ketuvim

The third section of the Jewish Bible consists of miscellaneous works that were admitted into the body of sacred scripture after the first two sections had already been consolidated. The Hebrew word *ketuvim* means "writings," "scriptures," and is a shortened form of "holy writings"; this is the meaning of the Greek term "Hagiographa" by which they are often designated in English.

> Evidently, one of the criteria for acceptance into the Jewish Bible required that the works be composed during the era of prophetic revelation; that is, no later than the time of the building of Second Temple in Jerusalem by the returned exiles from Babylonia. Evidently, one of the issues that divided Jewish sects during the era of the Second Commonwealth (see below) was the question of which books should be included in or excluded from their Bibles.

Biblical narrative: covenantal history

The Bible's historical narrative opens with an account of God's creation of the world in six days, culminating in the creation of the first man and woman (Adam and Eve) on the sixth day, and God's ceasing from creation on the seventh day, commemorated by Jews thereafter as a weekly day of rest, the Sabbath (*Shabbat*). It then proceeds to relate in schematic terms the early saga of humanity as they diffuse into nations during twenty generations. Humans committed grave sins that had to be punished—by means of a great flood in the generation of Noah; and by being divided into different languages after an attempt to challenge God by erecting the tower of Babel.

At this point, the narrative narrows its focus to a single individual, the righteous Hebrew Abram (his name will later be changed to Abraham) who, with his wife Sarai (later: Sarah), was commanded by God to leave his ancestral birthplace "Ur of the Chaldeans" in Mesopotamia and travel to an undefined destination that turns out to be in the land of Canaan. God enters into a covenant (a pact) with Abraham. In a striking symbolic ceremony described in Genesis Chapters 15 and 16, God appears to Abraham, who is at this point aged and childless, and assures him he will have descendants as numerous as the stars in the heavens. However, God also informs Abraham:

> … Your descendants will be sojourners in a land that is not theirs, and will be slaves there, and they will be oppressed for four hundred years; but I will bring judgment on the nation which they serve, and afterward they shall come out with great possessions. … And they shall come back here in the fourth generation …

The covenant ceremony concludes with a promise that God will afterwards give the land in which Abraham now dwells to his descendants, "from the river of Egypt to the great river, the river Euphrates"; and it is sealed by an everlasting command to circumcise Abraham and his male descendants. The story now traces the lives of Abraham and Sarah, the birth of their son Isaac and his wife Rebecca, and the lives of their son Jacob and his wives, and their twelve sons and daughter. The latter sections of Genesis are devoted primarily to the story of how dysfunctional relationships within Jacob's family led to a situation in which their young brother Joseph was sold to Egypt, where he rose to prominence and managed the resources of the country through a period of international famine. The outcome of this fascinating drama was that Jacob and his household ended up as sojourners in Egypt. These generations of the nation's founding ancestors are often referred to as the "Patriarchal" era.

The slavery foretold in Abraham's covenant took place in the early chapters of Exodus, the second book of the Torah. A new Pharaoh subjected the Hebrews to cruel slavery, a situation that lasted for more than two centuries. A leader emerged in the person of Moses, a Hebrew who was brought up in the Egyptian royal court. Moses was forced to flee to the desert nation of Midian after he slew an Egyptian who was mistreating a Hebrew slave. During this period, at Mount Horeb, he encountered a burning bush whose fire would not be consumed. God spoke from the bush and ordered Moses to lead the Hebrews to freedom, in which task his elder brother Aaron would assist him. Reluctantly, Moses returned to Egypt, where the new Pharaoh stubbornly refused to free his slaves, until Egypt was ravaged by ten terrible plagues, and by the loss of his army when the Red Sea miraculously parted to allow the Hebrews to pass through safely, and subsequently closed up to drown their pursuers.

The Israelites were now led to Mount Sinai, the same Mount Horeb where Moses had first been called by God, and there God publicly revealed the Torah to the assembled populace. In Jewish tradition, the revelation that took place at Sinai was not confined to the "ten words" ("Decalogue"; usually translated as the "ten commandments"). The divine revelation encompassed all the laws and precepts that are set out in detail through the remaining four books of the Torah, totaling 613 according the generally accepted view. According to the view that would later become the prevalent one among Jews, there was also revealed at Sinai an elaborate oral tradition. It is through their devoted observance of the laws of the Torah that Israel are to uphold their side of a national covenant with God.

From the middle of the book of Exodus, through the books of Leviticus, Numbers and Deuteronomy, the Torah alternates between continuations of the story of Israel in the desert—a sojourn to the "promised land" that is punctuated by constant complaints and rebellions against God and Moses—and hundreds of precepts and prohibitions. The people's faithlessness and their lapses into idolatry provoke God to

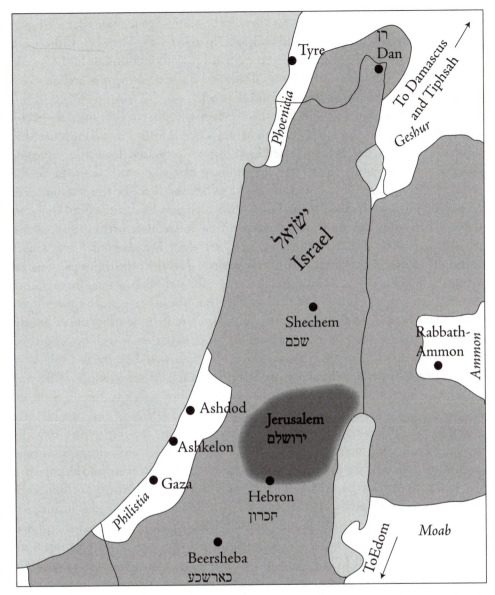

= A rough approximate map of the lands inhabited by Israelites or under direct central royal administration during the United Monarchy (according to the Bible). This was basically what is referred to by the recurring Biblical phrase "from Dan to Beersheba."

= The central core of ancient Judea. This area was part of a Jewish kingdom, or a Jewish province within a larger empire, almost continuously from the days of King David down to 135 CE.

Figure 1.2 Map of biblical Israel

keep them in the desert for forty years so that the original generation that left Egypt will die out. Even Moses is declared undeserving to enter the land. He is allowed to view it from a mountain, but he dies at the age of 120 without fulfilling his life's great longing. The Torah ends with Moses's death and his appointment of Joshua as his successor to lead the people into the land of Israel.

The second section of the Bible, the Nevi'im (Prophets), continues the story, beginning where the Torah left off, with Moses' disciple Joshua assuming leadership after his teacher's death. The Israelites enter the promised land and overcome the current inhabitants in a ferocious military campaign, and then divide the territory among the tribes. Later, the books of Samuel describe the beginnings of an institutionalized monarchy. As Israel's first monarch God chose Saul from the tribe of Benjamin, but he was ultimately driven to self-destructive paranoia and perished in a battle with the Philistines. Saul's successor, David of Judah, was a more successful leader. In his personality were combined qualities of religious piety, moral virtues, military heroism, musical and literary genius—though he was also subject to severe failings in his romantic and family lives that would bring much misery upon him and his household during his later years. David united the tribes under Judean leadership, and founded the new national capital of Jerusalem, which he designated as the site of a holy Temple. The magnificent Temple would be erected only after David's death by his heir, Solomon, as described in the Books of Kings. Following Solomon's reign, the northern ten tribes seceded from Judah to form a separate kingdom of Israel. The books of Kings chronicle the affairs of the two Hebrew states, largely from a religious perspective; that is to say, the respective monarchs are judged according to whether or not they followed God's word and eradicated the pagan cults. The northern kingdom eventually fell to the Assyrians, and its populace was exiled from their homeland, where they were lost to Judaism. The Kingdom of Judah was afterwards conquered by the Babylonians under Nebuchadnezzar, who destroyed the Jerusalem Temple and sent the Jews into captivity to Babylonia. From the perspective of the biblical authors, the political and military defeats were punishments for Israel's failure to uphold their covenant with God. When Babylonia fell to Persia, the Jews were invited by king Cyrus to return to their homeland and rebuild their sanctuary. The book of Ezra-Nehemiah describes the return from the captivity and the building of the Second Temple in Jerusalem. This was the point at which the Bible's narrative ceases.

A brief survey of the Ketuvim demonstrates the diverse range of its contents:

- Psalms: a collection of poetic prayers, ascribed to King David, but also including contributions by other authors and from later times.
- Wisdom literature: these works represent a worldview that emphasized the achievement of practical success in life, through wisdom achieved by observation of the world. The biblical Wisdom books include:

- Proverbs: advice on choosing the prudent course in life, avoiding temptations, and acting wisely.
- Job: a dramatic exploration of suffering and evil, built around a story in which God inflicts horrible afflictions on an innocent man in order to test his faith.
- Ecclesiastes (Kohelet): a discourse on the futility of human striving in the face of death; advising people to enjoy life and not always take themselves too seriously.
- Song of Songs: a sensual and erotic collection of love poetry. It was included in the Bible because it was interpreted as a symbolic portrayal of the relationship between God and Israel.
- Ruth: an idyllic rustic romance describing the courtship of the Moabite Ruth and the Judean Boaz, who would become the ancestors of King David.
- Lamentations: a collection of poems mourning the destruction of Jerusalem by the Babylonians.
- Esther: an account of an attempt by the wicked minister Haman to kill all the Jews of the Persian Empire (around 483 BCE), and how the plot was averted through the efforts of Esther, a Jewish queen of Persia, and her cousin, the courtier Mordecai.
- Daniel: most scholars agree that this work was composed in the mid-second century BCE and reflects a time of religious persecution at the hands of the Syrian Hellenists. However, it claims to describe events in the court of the Babylonian King Nebuchadnezzar in the sixth century BCE. Daniel is depicted as a pious Jew who is capable of interpreting signs and visions that symbolically foretell the rise and fall of a succession of evil pagan empires, until God personally establishes a righteous dominion over the world.
- Historical chronicles: the historical works included in the Ketuvim were probably originally a single work. Chronicles (conventionally divided into two books) retells the historical material contained in the Torah and Nevi'im, often with major or minor differences, and with additional interpretations. Ezra (conventionally divided into Ezra and Nehemiah) describes the return of the Babylonian exiles to Jerusalem with the authorization of King Cyrus of Persia, the building of the Second Temple, and the acceptance by the people of the Torah as the basis of their community.

In the Jewish religion, the Bible serves as the ultimate source of sacred history, laws, beliefs and values. All these topics will be discussed in subsequent chapters of this book.

Key points you need to know

- The central document of Judaism is the Hebrew Bible.
- The Hebrew Bible is written in Hebrew and includes many diverse works.
- The traditional Jewish classification divides the scriptures into three main sections, Torah, Nevi'im and Ketuvim. These are made up of twenty-four books, according to the accepted division.
- The Torah is the most authoritative section of the Bible. Its core is a body of commandments believed to have been revealed by God at Mount Sinai.
- The Bible defines the relationship between God and Israel in terms of a covenant, a contractual agreement. Biblical history is largely a chronicle of how the people fulfilled their covenantal obligations.

Discussion questions

1. What difference does it make whether one thinks of the Jewish scriptures as "Hebrew Bible" or "Old Testament"?
2. Why did God's plan for Israel require that they should undergo enslavement?
3. The main targets of the exhortations in the *Nevi'im* are worship of idols and social injustices. What can this imply about the biblical understandings about God and religious life?

Further reading

Jewish Publication Society, *Tanakh = JPS Hebrew-English Tanakh: The Traditional Hebrew Text and the New JPS Translation*. 2nd ed., Philadelphia, PA: Jewish Publication Society, 1999.

Leiman, Shnayer Z., *The Canonization of Hebrew Scripture: The Talmudic and Midrashic Evidence*. 2nd ed., New Haven, CT: Connecticut Academy of Arts and Sciences, 1991.

Scherman, Nosson, Yaakov Blinder, Avie Gold, and Meir Zlotowitz, *Torah, Nevi'im, Ketuvim: Tanakh = Tanach: The Torah, Prophets, Writings: The Twenty-Four Books of the Bible*. 1st ed., Artscroll. Brooklyn, NY: Mesorah Publications, 1996.

2 *The Second Temple era*

In this chapter

The transition from the scriptural saga of Israel to the Jewish religion took place under the dominion of two great empires. The Persians allowed the exiled Judeans to return to Judea and rebuild their Temple. From this time Judaism was characterized by a tension between the historical homeland and a large diaspora where most of the people usually lived. The Persian era marked a schism between Jews and the Samaritans. Two models of religious leadership, the hereditary Zadokite priests and the scholarly scribes, evolved at this time. Features of Babylonian and Persian religion were absorbed into Jewish thought and practice.

The conquests of Alexander the Great produced a synthesis of Greek and Middle Eastern cultures known as "Hellenism," which had a profound impact on the Jews, both in Judea and in diaspora communities. In Judea, tensions arose between those who wanted to reform their religion along Hellenistic lines, and those who were determined to preserve their ancestral ways intact. In diaspora centers like Alexandria in Egypt, a new synthesis of Jewish and Greek traditions was created, based on the Greek translation of the Bible known as the Septuagint. Thinkers like Philo Judaeus of Alexandria employed the allegorical method to interpret the Torah as a statement of Greek philosophy.

In the early second century BCE, the Emperor Antiochus IV Epiphanes decreed the introduction of Hellenistic rites in Jerusalem, provoking an uprising under the leadership of the priestly Hasmonean family. The uprising was successful, but it produced acute internal conflicts among diverse Jewish religious ideologies. The Jewish historian Josephus Flavius described three principal sects: the Sadducees, representing the values of the old aristocratic high priesthood; the Pharisees, known for their thorough study of the scriptures and their reverence for ancestral traditions; and the exotic Essenes who lived a simple life of holiness and purity in the Judean wilderness. Our knowledge of these groups, especially of the Essenes, has been enriched significantly by the discovery of the remains of an ancient library at Qumran in the Judean desert, known as the Dead Sea Scrolls. An additional Jewish movement, followers of the charismatic teacher Jesus of Nazareth, later evolved into a separate religion, Christianity.

Main topics covered

- Homeland and diaspora
- Jews and Samaritans
- Priestly and scholarly leadership
- Hellenism in the Middle East
- The Greek-Jewish synthesis of Alexandria
- The anti-Jewish decrees of Antiochus Epiphanes and the Hasmonean uprising
- Sectarian divisions in the wake of the Hasmonean victory
- The Pharisees, Sadducees and Essenes, and the Qumran library
- The Jesus movement

Homeland and diaspora

At the conclusion of the historical narrative of the Hebrew Bible, only a small segment of the original nation of Israel, as it existed in the glorious monarchy of David and Solomon, had survived the ravages of conquest and exile. The northern kingdom of Israel was displaced by the Assyrians, as they became the "ten lost tribes" whose descendants were indeed lost to the Jewish community. However, an unexpected development in international politics allowed the Judean captivity in Babylon to continue and develop. In 539 BCE, the mighty Babylonian empire was overthrown by the Persians, whose king Cyrus the Great sought to gain the loyalty of his subject nations by allowing them to return to the homelands from which they had been exiled under the prevailing Babylonian policy. By this time, many Jews had become comfortable in their new land; so that only a portion of them answered Cyrus' call and returned to Jerusalem to reestablish their religious and national life. The story of these returning exiles is described in the biblical book of Ezra-Nehemiah, named for the two most prominent leaders of that community. With encouragement and material support from the Persian government, they succeeded in building a new Temple, more modest than the one that had been built by Solomon. This structure was later replaced by a more magnificent one that was built during the reign of King Herod the Great around the turn of the millennium. In keeping with the teachings set out in the Bible (primarily in the book of Deuteronomy and in passages ascribed to its school of authorship), no Jewish Temple was allowed other than the one in Jerusalem—though we do know of temples where Jews worshipped in Egypt, at which sacrifices were offered.

Whereas the Judaism of biblical times was concentrated, with a few significant exceptions, in one geographic area, the land of Israel, from now on the Jewish communities would be scattered in numerous lands, some of which would be more prominent than others in their contributions to the collective body of Jewish traditions. It was natural that the community in the traditional homeland usually had a more central position in the nation's religious life, but other important, and often more populous, centers arose in places like Babylonia (Mesopotamia), Egypt, Italy, Asia Minor and elsewhere. Although the Bible had often portrayed exile from the holy land as a particularly severe and dreaded form of retribution, a catastrophic departure from the ideal situation of the Jewish people, the existence of a *diaspora* was to remain a permanent fixture of Jewish life.

Jews and Samaritans

Historians acknowledge that the forms of Judaism that became normative for subsequent generations were influenced decisively by the experience of the Babylonian captivity. When Ezra, Nehemiah and their flocks returned to Zion (Jerusalem), they were confronted by communities of their coreligionists who had managed to evade the exile, and to remain on their native soil. Such communities remained unaffected by the far-reaching religious developments that had taken place in Babylon, and were understandably hostile to what they viewed as unwarranted tampering with the ancient religious traditions of Israel. The book of Ezra-Nehemiah tells that these groups interceded with the Persian authorities and were able to prolong the rebuilding the Temple.

A peculiar ambivalence characterized the relationships between the Jews and the community known as the Samaritans. According to the account in the Bible, the Samaritans originated as foreigners, from a land called Kutha, who were brought in by the Assyrians to inhabit the region of Samaria (on the west bank of the Jordan River) after its Israelite natives were exiled. They found that they were subject to terrible disasters, including being eaten by lions, until an Israelite elder explained to them that the land would not tolerate any inhabitants who did not observe Israelite traditions. For these questionable motives, the Samaritans agreed to follow the commandments of the Torah. Their scriptures consist of the Torah (in a version that differs slightly from the standard Jewish one); and they consider Mount Gerizim in Samaria (near Nablus/Shechem) as their holy city, instead of Jerusalem.

The Samaritans themselves reject the biblical story of their origins and insist that they are the descendants of the northern kingdom of Israel who were able to remain on their land. They claim (and some scholars take their claim seriously) that their religion preserves the authentic beliefs and practices of ancient Israel that were not adulterated by the innovations introduced in Babylonia. Although reduced now to a few hundred followers, they constituted a large community in ancient times. Relations between them and mainstream Judaism tended to waver between extremes of hostility and mutual respect. During the talmudic era, Jewish sages debated whether or not the Samaritans should be treated as sincere converts to Judaism. Ultimately, they were dismissed as idol-worshippers, as a separate religion that lies outside the boundaries of "normative" Judaism.

Priestly and scholarly leadership

Judea remained under Persian rule for some two and a half centuries (from about 550 to 300 BCE), but we have almost no documented records of this era. This in itself indicates that it was a relatively peaceful and uneventful time. Therefore, when historians try to reconstruct the events and religious developments that took place during this era, they are generally forced to resort to circumstantial evidence or conjecture. For the most part, they compare the situation at the beginning of the era, as described in the Bible, with the situation at its end, for which there is more extensive documentation, and try to visualize the most likely path that would lead from the one to the other. Sometimes, they rely on more imaginative speculation to suppose how the people or their leadership would have responded to hypothetical situations. Such historical reconstructions are, of course, very tentative.

As a province of a larger empire, Judea did not have the status of a real nation-state. They did not formulate their own political positions or foreign relations. The biblical tradition speaks of a political leadership, embodied in the person of Zerubabel, a descendant of the Davidic royal dynasty who was appointed as the Persian governor of Judea; however, the (admittedly, limited) historical and literary evidence indicates that real authority during the Persian era was vested in the priesthood, particularly the High Priestly family that claimed descent from Zadok, King David's priest. In the absence of true political independence or autonomy, Jerusalem evolved into a true holy city dominated by the Temple, its worship and the priesthood. This is an impression that is confirmed by testimonies from early Greek travelers to Judea.

Ezra himself is described in the Bible as both a priest (that is, a descendant of Moses's elder brother Aaron; the Torah assigns priestly functions exclusively to this family) and a "scribe." While it is possible that the latter title refers to the position he held within the Persian administration, Jewish tradition has generally understood it as an allusion to his role as a scholar with expertise in the understanding and interpretation of the Torah. At any rate, once the Torah and prophetic works had been accepted by the people as the authoritative source for their religious guidance and instruction, it was natural that intensive efforts should be devoted to the study and exposition of the Bible. While we possess no real explicit documentation of the scholarly achievements of the Jewish scribes and biblical interpreters during the Persian or Greek eras, the vast and variegated literature that emerges after this historical "dark age" attests to the fact that Jews were cultivating serious examination of the holy scriptures during these times. The differing interpretations that were proposed for biblical texts, particularly the laws and commandments of the Torah, would provide frequent occasions for sectarian controversies.

It is generally accepted that certain important concepts penetrated Jewish religious thought from the Persian environment, particularly from Zoroastrianism. These ideas include the belief in angels, or at least a more vivid interest in them; the image of a supernatural personification of evil, Satan; interest in an afterlife, including the belief in bodily resurrection. These ideas are virtually unknown to the earlier books of the Bible, but achieve prominence in later ones, or in post-biblical works. We will discuss them in greater detail in subsequent chapters.

Hellenism

From the beginning of the third century BCE, with the triumphal expansions of Alexander the Great of Macedon, the former Persian possessions in the Middle East fell under Greek dominion. Alexander conquered Judea in 333 BCE. After his death in 323, the empire was divided up among his generals. Seleucus founded a dynasty (the Seleucids) that ruled the provinces north of Judea, while Ptolemy's dynasty ruled Egypt. Judea, on the borderline between the two superpowers belonged first to the Ptolemies, and later (from 200 BCE) to the Seleucids. Alexander, as student of Aristotle, was convinced of the absolute superiority of Greek civilization over the primitive "barbarians"; and was therefore determined to spread Greek culture throughout his domains. A keystone of Greek life was the city-state, *polis*, the civic structure in which their society operated; therefore they attached great importance to the establishment of Greek-style cities throughout their empire, such as Alexandria in Egypt and Antioch in Syria. Involvement in the civic affairs in the polis was usually associated with religious rites.

Although Alexander may have envisioned a unidirectional spread of Greek enlightenment to the barbaric frontiers, the actual historical process known as "Hellenism" was a far more complex phenomenon. For one thing, the native cultures were not really crude barbarians who immediately recognized the superiority of the dominant culture. Quite the contrary, many of them, like the Jews, had their own ancient traditions that they held in great reverence. Furthermore, the Greeks continued to constitute a small demographic minority in the colonies. The Greeks who took up long-term residence in the Middle East were not usually the representatives of the highest ideals of Athenian art or philosophy, but simple merchants or pensioned soldiers. Such individuals were at least as likely to be influenced by the native culture as vice versa, especially when they intermarried with local woman. The resulting phenomenon of Hellenism was, in fact, a synthesis of Greek and local cultures, one that was more readily apparent in the material culture than in the domain of ideas.

For Jews and other native populaces, the attractions of Hellenism were most strongly felt among the wealthier classes. Hellenism took on the status of an international, global ethos; therefore, people who aspired to be true citizens of the world, especially the wealthy classes who wished to cultivate international economic connections, often believed that it was necessary to adopt the prevailing norms in order to avoid being relegated to a parochial backwater. On the whole, Hellenism did not seek to force itself on the native peoples, especially in the realm of religion. The various polytheistic religions had similar deities, representing the basic forces of nature or moral virtues; so it was convenient to equate the Greek pantheon with those of the local cults and claim that they were worshipping the same gods under different names. The monotheism of the Jews presented an awkward exception to this pattern. Biblical religion was uncompromising in its utter refusal to tolerate the worship of any deity other than the one God. This situation created some discomfort for both the gentiles and the Jews who sought fuller participation in the broader culture. The Hellenistic societies demonstrated a readiness to exempt Jews from activities that would conflict with their religious beliefs or observances; such as the ceremonies and sacrifices that normally accompanied civic councils; or military service that might require violation of the Sabbath restrictions.

The Greek–Jewish synthesis of Alexandria

The Greek-speaking Jewish communities, especially that of Alexandria, produced their own impressive synthesis of Hellenism and Judaism. Central to the religious life of the Alexandrian Jews was a Greek translation of the Bible that became increasingly crucial, as fewer members of the community were able to read scripture in its original language. The Greek word "Septuagint" means "seventy," alluding to the widespread tradition about how the Emperor Ptolemy II Philadelphus commissioned the translation of the Torah, which was done by seventy-two elders of Israel (six from each of the twelve tribes). Later elaborations of the story (which appears initially in a work called the Letter of Aristeas) introduced new legendary elements, such as the claim that the translators, though working independently and in isolation from one another, were able to arrive at word-for-word agreement. Stories of this sort achieved the purpose of endowing the translation with an aura of sanctity: the Septuagint was not merely an accurate rendering of the divinely revealed scriptures, but the translation was composed under supernatural guidance. This allowed Greek-speaking Jewish preachers and commentators to interpret the words of the Septuagint text with a degree of precision that was comparable to the methods that were in force for interpreting the Hebrew Torah. The Alexandrian Greek translation was extended to other books in the Bible, and even some that were not ultimately included in the official canon of the Jewish sacred scriptures. It is common to extend the term "Septuagint" to cover the entire corpus of the Bible translations. Books, or parts of books, that were included in the Greek version but not in the standard Jewish biblical canon, are known as the "Apocrypha" (Greek for "hidden books").

Easily the most magnificent literary work to survive from the religious world of Hellenistic Judaism was the oeuvre of Philo Judaeus of Alexandria (*c.* 20 BCE to *c.* 50 CE). Philo composed an extensive series of commentaries to passages from the Torah, in which he demonstrated that the Jewish Scriptures express the most refined philosophical concepts and moral values of Greek philosophy, especially those of Plato and the Stoa. In order to arrive at these interpretations, Philo read the Bible according to the *allegorical* method; that is to say, he claimed that, in addition to the obvious literal meaning of the text, each element had a symbolic meaning. Thus, the Hebrew patriarchs and matriarchs, apart from being people who lived and participated in the events described in the Bible, were the embodiments of certain abstract philosophical concepts: thus, Abraham represents virtue acquired by learning; Isaac represents innate virtue; and Jacob represents virtue acquired by practice.

Underlying Philo's interpretations is the widespread assumption that monotheism serves as a unifying force between traditional Judaism and the most prominent forms of Greek philosophical thought. Although the literature and official cults of the Greek and Roman world involved the worship of innumerable deities, the reasoning of Socrates, Plato, Aristotle and other great thinkers had succeeded in effectively discrediting any literal belief in multiple gods and goddesses, and in demonstrating that the existence of our world could be traced back to a single, unified author. Notwithstanding some serious contradictions that existed between philosophy and traditional biblical religion, Jewish rationalists through the ages would continue to be guided by the assumption that philosophy provided decisive proof for the revealed faith of Judaism.

The anti-Jewish decrees of Antiochus Epiphanes and the Hasmonean uprising

As noted previously, the prevailing policy of the Hellenistic rulers, one that had been initiated by Alexander himself, was to allow the Jews to uphold their own religious traditions. This privilege was reconfirmed by the Seleucid ruler Antiochus III in 198 BCE. However, for reasons that are not entirely clear, the tolerant policy was rescinded in 175 BCE by Antiochus IV Epiphanes. Antiochus took aggressive measures to establish a full-fledged Greek *polis* in Jerusalem; and to that end, he imposed edicts prohibiting some of the most sacred of Jewish religious practices, such as the observance of the weekly Sabbath, circumcision of males, and traditional religious study. A *gymnasium* was established in Jerusalem, in which the Greek admiration of the human body was expressed in public nudity, a practice that was anathema to traditional Jewish ideals of modesty. Furthermore, Antiochus instituted reforms in the Jerusalem Temple itself, including the mandatory sacrifice of swine to Zeus, a practice that would clearly offend any Jew who was even minimally devoted to the Torah and the ancestral tradition.

So unprecedented was this departure from the long-established policy of Hellenistic religious tolerance that some historians have proposed that the reforms must have been initiated from within the Jewish community itself, from groups who saw the uniqueness of Jewish ritual as an obstacle to their full participation in the cosmopolitan civilization that had been embraced by the rest of the world. It is likely that the pagan cult that was being introduced in the Temple was not outright worship of the Greek Zeus, but rather a more palatable Middle Eastern synthesis that equated the Greek God with the Syro-Phoenician deity Baal Shamin ("Lord of the Heavens"). Whatever the precise details may have been, the edicts of Antiochus IV were viewed as unacceptably sacrilegious by most Jews of that generation; though the military might of the Seleucid Empire seemed invincible.

This situation probably provides the historical context for understanding the biblical Book of Daniel, whose author was convinced that the only way to save the Torah from continued profanation was if God himself would take an active hand in the events.

The Hellenistic religious persecution provoked what was probably the first known war that was fought in the name of religious liberty. The first group that is reported to have taken up arms against the persecutors was known as the "Hasidim" (pious). However, their military effectiveness was offset by their refusal to wage war on the weekly day of rest, the Sabbath. It did not take long for their enemies to catch on, subjecting the Hasidim to terrible massacres. The turning point came when the leadership of the rebellion was taken over by the priest Mattathias and his five sons. When an apostate Jew consented to participate in the offering a pig to Zeus in the village of Modiin, the aged Mattathias, of the priestly Hasmonean family, killed the apostate; and then fled to the mountains with his five sons and a band of followers. They became the nucleus of a guerrilla army that would pursue a victorious military campaign against the hellenizers. Their readiness to defend themselves on the Sabbath increased their prospects of success. On Mattathias's death in 166 BCE, the leadership fell to Judah Maccabee (the name means "hammer," and might be either an allusion to his military power, or to the shape of his head). Judah captured Jerusalem in 165 BCE, and proceeded to purify the Temple from all traces of heathen worship and to rededicate it to God. The anniversary of the rededication of the Temple was now proclaimed a religious holiday that would be celebrated for eight days each year: Ḥanukkah, the Feast of Dedication. By the time of his death in battle in 161 BCE, Judah had succeeded in expanding the tiny borders of the Judean territory and to score several triumphs against the Seleucid forces.

Sectarian divisions in the wake of the Hasmonean victory

For the first time in centuries, the Jews had their own independent state. As often happens with successful wars of liberation, the victory contained the seeds of eventual political and religious divisions. Under the Hasmonean leadership, several diverse Jewish movements had rallied to fight against an obvious threat to the survival of their traditional faith and way of life. The coalition included supporters of the established priestly aristocratic leadership (the house of Zadok), remnants of the Hasidim (who withdrew from the campaign after achieving the initial objectives of purifying the Temple and restoring traditional worship), advocates of the scholarly study of the Torah, along with proponents of other Jewish ideologies. As long as they were all fighting against a common enemy, the differences between these groups appeared insignificant; and each of them probably expected that their own particular vision of an ideal Jewish society would be implemented after the elimination of the extreme hellenizers. However, after their triumph, and after the Hasmoneans installed themselves as the political and religious leaders of the nation, cracks became evident in the original alliance that would have far-reaching repercussions for the character of Jewish religious life.

The political constitution of the post-rebellion government was itself questionable according to the criteria of traditional Jewish religious concepts. Judea prior to the Hellenistic era had been led by the high priesthood, and the Hasmoneans themselves were a priestly family. On the surface, therefore, it would appear perfectly appropriate that the leaders of the insurrection should assume the dual mantles of political and priestly leadership. However, from the standpoint of Jewish religious tradition, this policy was doubly controversial. As regards the political leadership, the Bible had spoken of a divine covenant with King David according to which the Israelite monarchy would permanently remain in the hands of his descendants. Because David belonged to tribe of Judah, whereas the priests stemmed from the tribe of Levi, it was clear that the Hasmoneans could not make a legitimate claim to the crown. Regarding their claims to the high priesthood, the Hasmoneans also encountered fierce opposition. Since biblical times, this office had been limited to a single family within the priestly tribe, that of the descendants of Zadok who had served as priest in King David's time. It would appear that members of that family, as well as other conservatives who insisted on a return to the situation that had prevailed before the rebellion, now consolidated themselves into a separate religious

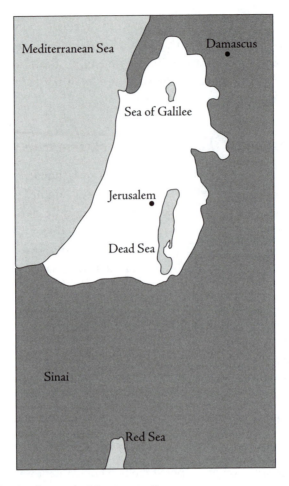

Figure 2.1 Map of Judea during the Hasmonean Era

and political movement known as the Sadducees (that is: Zadokites) to promote the authority and values of the established priestly aristocracy that had been supplanted by the Hasmoneans.

The upshot of this complex situation is that the latter part of the Second Temple era is characterized primarily by its deep sectarian division. While sharing a common commitment to the Torah, the Temple and many time-honored values, each movement was passionately committed to its own interpretations of the Bible and other religious traditions, insisting that its own approach was the only correct one; and that anyone who espoused a different Jewish outlook was guilty of deceiving the people and of disseminating heresy. The opposing sects strove to influence the political leaders of their day, even to the extent of urging them to kill adherents of rival ideologies.

The Pharisees, Sadducees and Essenes, and the Qumran library

The classic statement of Second-Temple sectarianism comes from the works of Josephus Flavius.

> Josephus, actually Joseph son of Matthiah (*c.* 37–*c.* 100 CE), was a priest who served as a general in the Jewish revolt against Rome in 66–73 CE (see below), but defected to the Roman side before the Jewish defeat. Under the patronage of the emperor, Josephus composed several works, including an autobiography, a detailed history of the recent rebellion (*The Jewish Wars*), and a survey of Jewish history *(The Jewish Antiquities)*. Josephus claimed to have personally tried out the important Jewish religious sects, and therefore his descriptions of them have a particular claim to authenticity as eyewitness testimonies.

Josephus tells of three main sects (though he refers elsewhere to a "fourth philosophy" defined by its zealous resistance to any subjection to foreign domination). The three groups are:

- Sadducees
- Pharisees
- Essenes.

His descriptions of them were tailored to Greek and Roman readers, and he therefore referred to the sects as "philosophies," focusing on their doctrines concerning the kinds of standard philosophical controversies that were argued in the Greek or Roman philosophical schools, such as: determinism and free will, the fate of the soul after death, and the existence of angels. When we supplement Josephus' descriptions with other records, we discover that the situation was considerably more variegated than his schematic three-fold arrangement might suggest. Among the most important sources for our knowledge of late Second Temple Judaism are the many ancient scrolls and manuscript fragments that were preserved in the caves near Qumran (the Dead Sea Scrolls). Many other works from that period have survived, most of them Hebrew works that were preserved in translations to Greek or other languages. Such works are referred to as Apocrypha or Pseudepigrapha ("falsely attributed," because they usually took the form of works falsely ascribed to figures from the Bible). Similarly, the literature of the Jewish rabbis (see below) contains much information that is useful in reconstructing beliefs, institutions and exegetical traditions that were current during the Second Temple era. The Christian New Testament also preserves some interesting and useful information related to this topic.

The Sadducees are the Jewish movement about which we know the least. Virtually all the information that we possess about them was transmitted by their opponents, a fact that requires us to be very cautious when interpreting and evaluating those reports. Apart from the specific theological positions that Josephus ascribes to them—belief in human free will and denial of an afterlife—they appear primarily as a social or political group associated with the aristocracy, sympathetic to Hellenism, and in competition with the Pharisees. This picture is confirmed in part by the rabbinic traditions; though the Sadducees are also associated there with certain positions and interpretations in matters of Jewish religious law. For the most part, the disputes between the Sadducees and the Pharisees do not seem to be qualitatively different from the many disputes that took place among the rabbis themselves. Several of the Sadducee legal positions—but not all of them—can be regarded as "literalist"; that is to say, they are based on an unsophisticated reading of the words of the Torah, or on simple logical reasoning. The association with the priesthood is suggested by their name, which derives from Zadok, the family of the pre-Hasmonean high priesthood.

The second sect described by Josephus was that of the Pharisees. The meaning of the name, which is also attested in rabbinic sources (as "*Perushim*"), is not entirely clear; but it most likely has the connotation of "those who are separate." This likely reflects the fact that they took on special stringencies with regard to certain purity and dietary laws that prevented them from full social interaction with Jews who did not keep the same stringencies. The title *Perushim* appears rarely in rabbinic literature, usually in quotations attributed to Sadducees, or with negative connotations; for example, as stereotypes of people who are so concerned with the minutiae of purity and ritual that they lose sight of larger moral demands. This suggests that the title might have originated in insults hurled at them by their ideological opponents, though it was afterwards accepted as a neutral name for their sect.

Central to Josephus's account of the Pharisaic ideology—and confirmed by passages in the Qumran scrolls, New Testament and rabbinic literature—was their belief in an unwritten law, or ancestral tradition, alongside the authority of the scriptures. From a theological perspective, this allowed them to adopt ideas like the belief in bodily resurrection of the dead, in spite the Bible's general reticence about the afterlife. They could also invoke the ancestral tradition in order to justify customs and institutions that had developed among the common folk or were borrowed from Babylonian and Persian cultures. Josephus states that the Pharisees were considered the most accurate interpreters of the law, and he suggests that they were influential enough to impose their own interpretations even on those who did not really accept them. To the extent that we may reconstruct a picture of Pharisaism based on the later evolution of rabbinic Judaism (and this must be done with much scholarly caution), it is evident that the Pharisees cultivated intensive study of the Bible and other sources of their religious tradition, and that they believed that religious authority was founded on a person's scholarly credentials. Ultimately, this served as a democratizing principle, at least when it is compared with the priestly model of leadership, which was determined entirely by genealogical pedigree. Scholarly attainments, on the other hand, may be achieved by all those who devote themselves to profound study, whatever their tribe or social class.

The Pharisees' adoption of rigorous standards with respect to purity and the preparation of food may also be understood as a challenge to the priestly claims to authority. In biblical religion, the ideal of holiness was often expressed in the fact that holy things, places or objects could not be approached or touched by impure people or things. The Torah's detailed regulations governing purity and impurity were largely confined to the sanctuary and the priesthood, or to those who expect to be dealing with them. If scrupulous observance of these rules lent a special aura of sanctity to the priests, then their observance by Jews who were not of priestly birth served to diminish the authority of the priests. Evidently, the Pharisees chose to apply the laws of priestly purity to food that was technically non-sacred. They also did not trust people outside their own circles to properly tithe produce (that is, to set aside the portions of the food that the Torah designates for the priests, Levites, poor, or to be eaten in Jerusalem), and they therefore insisted on re-tithing food that was acquired from non-Pharisees. For some observers, these practices had the effect of investing the Pharisees with a quality of sanctity; others, presumably, saw them as an expression of snobbery and aloofness. If we are to believe Josephus on this matter, the Pharisees enjoyed widespread admiration and support among the general Jewish populace.

The third of Josephus's three sects were the Essenes. Scholars have so far been unable to reconstruct the Hebrew or Aramaic word that lies behind this Greek transliteration (*Essenoi*). His description of the Essenes, which is more sympathetic and more detailed than those of the other sects, mentions the great affection and hospitality that they extend to one another, their simple ascetic way of life, their rigid discipline over their emotions, their dedication to the study of sacred texts, their devout worship (including prayers directed to the sun), and their celibacy (a unique phenomenon in Judaism), which is based not on a rejection of sexuality, but on their distrust of women. Josephus describes their community as being without economic classes, because all of its members must forsake their private possessions and donate them to a communal fund. Their solemn common meals are eaten under conditions of purity, and outsiders are forbidden to participate.

Josephus also gives a detailed description of the procedures that are required before a person may be admitted to full membership in the Essene community, a process that includes several years of trial membership until the candidate is permitted to partake in the common meals and merges his property with that of the community. Those regulations bear an uncanny resemblance to one of the earliest documents to be published from the Qumran library, a work that has been given the English titles "Community Rule" or "Manual of Discipline." It is largely on the basis of this similarity that scholars have assumed that the community who lived in Qumran and created its library was that of the Essenes. Ancient writers mentioned an Essene settlement in the vicinity of Ein Gedi near the Dead Sea of Judea; though Josephus and others also state that Essenes were scattered throughout many towns.

> With the publication of more documents and archeological evidence, it has become evident that the relationships between the scrolls, the Qumran site and the Essenes are more complex and problematic than was originally supposed. Nevertheless, the prevalent scholarly view still maintains that Qumran housed an Essene settlement, though not all the scrolls in the library were necessarily of Essene sectarian origin. In some instances, the scrolls have required us to reinterpret the relevant passages from Josephus's descriptions of the Essenes.

There are texts among the Qumran scrolls that seem to allude to the history of the sect. Most of these texts appear in a particular type of work known as *pesher*, which consists of cryptic commentaries to books from the Bible in which the words of the ancient prophets are applied to recent events, though the protagonists of these events are referred to by epithets rather than by name. Several passages in the Pesher literature refer to a figure whom they call the "teacher of righteousness," probably a priest or even a high priest, who was uniquely endowed with the true understanding of the Torah and the divine will at a time when the rest of the world was being led astray by false teachings. The teacher of righteousness was persecuted and driven from Jerusalem by a "wicked priest," who is apparently to be equated with the "man of lies." The conventional theory holds that the teacher of righteousness went on to found the Qumran/Essene community in the Judean wilderness because of his conviction that the Jerusalem Temple was being not being run in the proper manner. There have been numerous attempts to identify the teacher, as well as the wicked priest, with known historical figures, but none of these has succeeded in becoming a consensus.

Some of the scroll fragments give reason to suppose that the interpretations of biblical laws that were current among the Dead Sea community were of Sadducee origin. Given the ceremonial prominence that is assigned to priests in the Manual of Discipline and other collections of Qumran regulations, this fact suggests that the Qumran community originated as an extremely conservative faction of the Sadducees. Perhaps the mainstream of the Sadducee movement was forced to compromise with the Pharisees whose interpretations determined most of the practices of the Jerusalem Temple. The Essenes, then, were Sadducees who refused to participate in what they regarded as an illegitimate form of worship. They dissociated themselves

Figure 2.2 Shrine of the book

from the Temple and created their own community in the isolation of the Judean desert where they could follow the authentic divine commandments—or, at least, as many of them as could be observed without a Temple.

Arguably, the most valuable contribution that the Qumran scrolls have made to the study of Second Temple Judaism was in forcing us to deal with the complex diversity of religious life that existed at that time. Even if we cannot always be certain that we fully understand a given text, or that we know from which religious sect it originated, we cannot avoid being impressed by the dazzling variety of opinions and interpretations that were being produced by Jews at that time, particularly in the area of religious law. It demands some effort to remind ourselves that all this diversity is founded, more or less, on the same corpus of sacred scriptures. Clearly, Josephus's three-fold scheme is too simplistic to account for the many variations and nuances that are attested in the literature that has survived from this era.

The Jesus movement

Another Jewish movement that arose at this time was that of the Christians. Insofar as Christianity evolved quite quickly into a rival religion, it will not be dealt with in any meaningful detail in the present book. At any rate, the earliest history of Jewish Christianity can serve as an instructive lesson in the complexities of sectarianism at that time. Evidently, the founder of the movement, Jesus (Joshua) from the Galilean town of Nazareth, was typical of many wonder-working preachers who were active in his time and whose exploits are described in rabbinic literature, Josephus, and elsewhere. Like those figures, Jesus was known as a charismatic healer who cured physical diseases and mental ailments, which he treated by exorcising demons.

Jesus's religious message incorporated many concerns that were common to Jews at that time. He was moved by an intense expectation that the world was on the verge of an apocalyptic transformation. Like the authors of Daniel, and of many apocalyptic visions that were being composed at that time, Jesus believed that God was about to overthrow the wicked Roman Empire and establish a new order in the world, the kingdom of God. Only those who have proven themselves righteous will be allowed to enjoy the wonders of the new world; all others will be excluded. Like his mentor John the Baptist, Jesus devoted his life to convincing his contemporaries of the urgency of preparing themselves to be worthy of admission to the kingdom of God. He conveyed his message through his skilful use of parables (simple stories that are meant to be understood symbolically) taken from the everyday realities of Galilean rural life. What was distinctive in his message was his dedication to bringing that message effectively to Jewish sinners who had been rejected by the mainstream leadership, such as criminals, prostitutes and collaborators with the Roman occupation forces.

In the accounts of Jesus' interactions with his contemporaries, as depicted in the New Testament, we may get a glimpse of the sectarian issues that interested and divided Jews during the late Second Commonwealth era. It would appear that Jesus himself was sympathetic to the Pharisees. He favors their positions on specific issues of doctrine (notably, the belief in resurrection) and religious law, though he criticizes them for a narrow focus on technical details that blinds them to the broader spiritual goals of the Torah. The issues that he dealt with were, in most cases, the same ones that were challenging other Jews of his generation.

Ultimately, the stream of Christianity that prevailed was the one espoused by Saul (Paul) of Tarsus who focused less on the teachings of Jesus than on the redemptive value of his crucifixion at the hands of the Romans. This was the model of Christian theology that rapidly became an influential force among gentiles in the Roman Empire. Evidently, the original Jesus movement had a relatively small following in the land of Israel, consisting of Jews who resembled their coreligionists in most other aspects of their commitment to the laws of the Torah and traditional beliefs; but were set apart by their conviction that Jesus was the promised redeemer. By the fourth century, Jewish-Christian groups like the Ebionites were considered nothing more than an anomalous curiosity. Jews could not fathom their devotion to a dead messiah, while Christians could not come to terms with their commitment to the obsolete Law of Moses.

Discussion questions

1. On what basis were some groups (like the Samaritans) excluded from Judaism while others are considered movements within Judaism?

2. How (if at all) is it possible to maintain an allegorical interpretation of the Bible without rejecting its literal meaning?

3. The Hasmoneans rose to power in an uprising against Hellenism, and yet they adopted many trappings of Hellenistic culture and politics. How can these facts be reconciled?

4. In what ways can the disputes over afterlife beliefs and oral traditions be viewed as aspects of the same basic controversy?

Key points you need to know

- When Babylonia fell to Persia, King Cyrus allowed the exiled Jews to rebuild Jerusalem and its Temple. Some accepted the invitation, returning to Judea under the leadership of Ezra and Nehemiah, and completing the construction of the Second Temple.

- As most Jews continued to live in Babylonia and other communities outside of Judea, the phenomenon of "diaspora" became a permanent feature of Jewish history.

- The Bible describes how the returning exiles formally accepted the law of Moses, the Torah, as their national law.

- Under Persian rule, several Persian ideas were absorbed into the Jewish religion.

- Out of the Second Temple era emerged two main models of Jewish religious leadership: the hereditary priesthood of the house of Zadok and a scribal tradition rooted in its scholarly mastery of the Torah and ancestral traditions. These were embodied in the Sadducee and Pharisee movements.

- Hellenism was a synthesis of Greek and Middle Eastern cultures. Jews differed in their receptiveness to the phenomenon.

- Greek-speaking diaspora Jewish communities, especially that of Alexandria, produced a remarkable synthesis of Hellenistic and Jewish civilizations, embodied in the Septuagint and the philosophical biblical expositions of Philo.

- Decrees against Judaism under the Seleucid emperor Antiochus IV provoked a successful Jewish revolt led by the Hasmonean family. This victory is celebrated annually as Ḥanukkah.

- The Hasmoneans installed themselves as high priests and kings of Judea, antagonizing traditionalist Jews who believed that they were not entitled to these positions.

- The Pharisees and Sadducees disagreed over several issues, including the status of the afterlife and the authority of oral tradition.
- The Qumran library, known as the Dead Sea scrolls, enriches our knowledge of Second Temple sectarianism, especially the Essenes.
- Christianity originated among the followers of a charismatic Jewish preacher who sought the repentance of Jewish sinners before the advent of the kingdom of God.

Further reading

Alon, Gedalia, *Jews, Judaism, and the Classical World: Studies in Jewish History in the Times of the Second Temple and Talmud*. Jerusalem: Magnes Press, 1977.

—— *The Jews in Their Land in the Talmudic Age: 70–640 CE* Translated by Gershon Levi. 2 vols. Jerusalem: Magnes Press, 1980.

Anderson, Robert T. and Terry Giles, *Tradition Kept: The Literature of the Samaritans*. Peabody, MA: Hendrickson Publishers, 2005.

Bickerman, E. J., *From Ezra to the Last of the Maccabees: Foundations of Post-Biblical Judaism*. New York: Schocken Books, 1968.

—— *The God of the Maccabees: Studies on the Meaning and Origin of the Maccabean Revolt*, Studies in Judaism in Late Antiquity. Leiden: Brill, 1979.

—— *Studies in Jewish and Christian History*. New ed. 2 vols, Arbeiten zur Geschichte des Antiken Judentums und des Urchristentums. Leiden: Brill, 2007.

Chazon, Esther G., Devorah Dimant and Ruth Clements, *Reworking the Bible: Apocryphal and Related Texts at Qumran*, Studies on the Texts of the Desert of Judah. Leiden and Boston, MA: Brill, 2005.

Cohen, Shaye J. D., *From the Maccabees to the Mishnah*. 2nd ed., Louisville, KY: Westminster John Knox Press, 2006.

Mason, Steve, *Flavius Josephus on the Pharisees: A Composition-Critical Study*. Boston, MA: Brill Academic, 2001.

Neusner, Jacob, *From Politics to Piety: The Emergence of Pharisaic Judaism*. 2nd ed., New York: Ktav Publishing House, 1979.

Nickelsburg, George W. E., *Jewish Literature between the Bible and the Mishnah: A Historical and Literary Introduction*. 2nd ed., Minneapolis, MN: Fortress Press, 2005.

Saldarini, Anthony J., *Pharisees, Scribes and Sadducees in Palestinian Society: A Sociological Approach*. Wilmington, DE: M. Glazier, 1988.

Sanders, E. P., *Judaism: Practice and Belief, 63 BCE–66 CE*. London and Philadelphia, PA: SCM Press and Trinity Press International, 1992.

Schenck, Kenneth, *A Brief Guide to Philo*. 1st ed. Louisville, KY: Westminster John Knox Press, 2005.

Schiffman, Lawrence H., *Reclaiming the Dead Sea Scrolls*. 1st Anchor Bible reference library ed, Anchor Bible Reference Library. New York: Doubleday, 1995.

—— *Understanding Second Temple and Rabbinic Judaism*. Jersey City, NJ: Ktav Pub. House, 2003.

Schürer, Emil, Géza Vermès and Fergus Millar, *The History of the Jewish People in the Age of Jesus Christ (175 B.C.–A.D. 135)*. Rev. ed. Edinburgh: Clark, 1973.

Stone, Michael E., *Jewish Writings of the Second Temple Period: Apocrypha, Pseudepigrapha, Qumran Sectarian Writings, Philo, Josephus*, The Literature of the Jewish People in the Period of the Second Temple and the Talmud. Assen and Philadelphia, PA: Van Gorcum and Fortress Press, 1984.

Talmon, Shemaryahu, *The World of Qumran from Within: Collected Studies*. Jerusalem and Leiden: Magnes Press and Brill, 1989.

Tcherikover, Victor, *Hellenistic Civilization and the Jews*. Translated by S. Applebaum. Philadelphia, PA: Jewish Publication Society of America, 1966.

Vermès, Géza, *The Complete Dead Sea Scrolls in English*. Rev. ed, Penguin Classics. London: Penguin, 2004.

3 Judaism of the Talmud and Midrash

In this chapter

The failure of the "Great Revolt" against Rome and the destruction of the Temple in 70 CE resulted in the disappearance of the Sadducees and Essenes, and the prevalence of a Pharisaic style of Judaism that we refer to as "rabbinic" because its leaders and teachers bore the title "Rabbi." The literature of the rabbis was largely concerned with academic questions of law and exegesis. The earlier portion of this era, known as "Tannaitic," produced diverse compendia of oral religious teachings. The later period, the "Amoraic," was largely devoted to the study of Tannaitic traditions, especially the Mishnah, a code of religious law compiled by Rabbi Judah the Patriarch. The diverse genres and topics of rabbinic learning are surveyed. The most important of these are: midrash (scriptural studies), mishnah (non-biblical traditions), halakhah (laws) and aggadah (non-legal topics). The Amoraic era produced two vast commentaries on the Mishnah, the Palestinian and Babylonian Talmuds, whose structure, contents and distinctive style of logical debate are described in this chapter.

Main topics covered

- The historical context of rabbinic Judaism
- The generations of the Tannaitic era: Yavneh, Usha, Tiberias
- The era of the Amoraim
- The genres of the oral Torah: midrash and mishnah, halakhah and aggadah
- The Talmuds: Palestinian and Babylonian

The historical context of rabbinic Judaism

Following the destruction of the Temple by the Romans in 70 CE, we no longer hear of the sectarian controversies that dominated the earlier generations. It is generally understood that the Pharisees were the only one of the sects to survive, and that the "rabbis" of the talmudic era were the heirs to Pharisaism. The influence of the

Figure 3.1 The Arch of Titus

Sadducees was so narrowly identified with the Temple and the priesthood that their ideology was largely irrelevant to a Judaism that was struggling to survive without its Temple. We know so little about the Essenes that it would be overly speculative to surmise what befell them after 70. At any rate, they had always been a small, exclusive community removed from the mainstream of Jewish life, so they were unlikely to play a major role in post-Temple Judaism.

The following centuries were largely a time of consolidation of ideas and institutions that had emerged from the previous eras. The religious developments of that time are known to us largely from works of literature that were redacted and became the foundation of Jewish life and thought in later times. These works, known as the Talmuds and the Midrash, will be described in greater detail further on in this chapter. The religious leaders who composed these works, and whose opinions are recorded in them, were known as "rabbis." The Hebrew word *rabbi* means "my master," and it is a term of respect that came into common use as a title for religious scholars towards the end of the first century CE. The use of the title became regulated as formal procedures were established for the ordination of authorities in the interpretation of Jewish religious law—which was the rabbis' main function. It is therefore common to refer to this era and its literature as "rabbinic."

Although Jewish communities could be found throughout the expanses of the Middle East and the Mediterranean basin, the religious literature that survived as authoritative was confined to two main geographical centers: the land of Israel (which the Romans named Palestine after the Philistines who had occupied its coastal plains in biblical times) and Babylonia (Mesopotamia, the fertile area between the Tigris and Euphrates Rivers).

This was a momentous era in both general and Jewish history. The destruction of Jerusalem left the Jews not only without their cherished center of worship, the holy Temple, but also resulted in immense loss of life and property, political repression, economic deprivation and social dislocation. It was the climax of a fierce insurrection against the the Roman empire that had broken out in 66, but it did not exhaust the determination of Jews to break the yoke of their conqueror. A garrison of Jewish Zealots held out until 73 at the desert fortress of Masada. Further revolts would break out, in 115 in Cyrene (Libya) and in Israel in 135. This last revolt, which was once known only from some vague allusions in rabbinic texts and in Roman historians, has been subject to major scholarly reevaluation in recent decades as the result of new archeological discoveries. From the new evidence we have learned much about the personality of the leader, Simeon bar Kuziba, known as Bar Kokhba, whose surviving letters reveal him as a forceful general with a strong religious commitment. The extensive networks of underground passages that have been discovered in Judea attest to the intense and widespread popular support that the revolt enjoyed. The archeological artifacts also tell us a story of extensive destruction that followed in the wake of the rebellion's suppression, as numerous Jewish villages in Judea became desolate.

This was also a time of important changes in the world at large. The Roman empire was facing threats, both from its far-flung frontiers and in the anarchy of its internal politics. A crucial turning point in world history, and one that had a major impact on the status of the Jews, was the emperor Constantine's adoption of Christianity in the early fourth century. In Babylonia, an important political transition occurred in 224 CE when the Hellenizing Parthian (Arsacid) dynasty, which had been tolerant of Jewish communal and religious autonomy, was overthrown by the centralist Sassanian dynasty whose aggressive advocacy of the dualistic Zoroastrian religion posed a threat to Judaism, sometimes erupting into outright persecutions.

The generations of the Tannaitic era: Yavneh, Usha, Tiberias

It is remarkable that the chronology of the major works of Jewish literature that were produced during this era has no substantial correlation with the political events that are of interest to historians. In spite of the determined efforts of historians to furnish historical explanations for literary or spiritual milestones, the evolution of rabbinic literature seems to follow an internal logic of its own, unconnected to historical events. Sometimes the incongruity appears so glaring that one is moved to suspect that the rabbis did this on purpose, in order to preclude the impression that the eternal truths of the Torah are subject to the vagaries of history.

As distinct from the important political milestones that marked the conventional history of the rabbinic era, the internal Jewish historiography of rabbinic literature speaks of two main divisions that were of religious significance to the development of Jewish religious tradition. They refer to the earlier division as the age of the *Tannaim*. The term derives from an Aramaic root (it is actually the Aramaic cognate to the Hebrew root that underlies *mishnah*). The term was coined by later scholars to express the fact that their knowledge of the earlier oral traditions reached them by means of human memorizers, who were known as *tannaim* and whose job was to recall and recite the oral texts that served as topics of discussion in the academy. Apart from a few individual passages in Tannaitic literature that are ascribed to Jewish sages from early in the Second Temple era, the oldest strata of substantial, organized rabbinic traditions seem to date from the generation preceding the destruction of the Temple, the middle of the first century CE. The end of the Tannaitic era is conventionally identified with the official oral publication of its most authoritative and influential literary product, the Mishnah. The precise date of this event cannot really be fixed with any certainty. It occurred some time around the end of the second or the beginning of the third century CE. In reality, there is no straightforward demarcation between the Tannaitic era and what follows, because several collections of Tannaitic teachings were redacted and published in the years following the completion of the Mishnah.

It is common among scholars of rabbinic history and literature to subdivide the Tannaitic era into generations whose names are derived from the towns that served as prominent scholarly centers, or as the homes of important scholars. In keeping with that convention, the decades immediately following the destruction of the Temple are referred to as the generations of Yavneh. Yavneh (also transliterated as Jabneh; or by the Greek form "Jamnia") was a town on the Mediterranean coast where, according to rabbinic tradition, an assembly of Pharisaic sages convened in order to continue the process of religious scholarship that had been carried on during the days of the Temple. A legend that is related in rabbinic traditions describes how Rabban Yohanan ben Zakkai, one of the great leaders of his time, was in Jerusalem while the city was being besieged by the Romans, and while Jerusalem's internal politics and institutions were under the control of extremist Zealots in whom the moderate Rabban Yohanan had no confidence. As it became clear that Jerusalem was doomed to destruction, he devised a desperate plan to have himself smuggled out of the city walls under the pretext that he had died and his corpse was being conveyed for burial. Once he had succeeded in reaching the enemy camp, he was able to impress the Roman general Titus by accurately predicting his imminent appointment to the Imperial throne, so that he could make some requests that would insure a future for Jewish religious life: He asked for Yavneh and its sages; and the safety of the Patriarchal dynasty (descendants of the great Pharisaic sage Hillel the Elder). Although there are many reasons to question the historicity of this story, it is nonetheless true that during the period of its operation, the assembly at Yavneh was a very important center whose activities had a lasting impact on the survival, vitality and character of Judaism.

The entire period between 70 and 133–5 CE is often designated the "Yavneh era," though we are obviously dealing with two or more generations. This was a momentous time in Jewish religious scholarship. The literary sources testify to a conscious endeavor to preserve the oral traditions, including the collection and sifting of dozens of disputes that were ascribed to the schools of Shammai and Hillel who were active during the preceding generation. It is generally understood that this was the beginning of the process that would culminate in the redaction of the major works of Tannaitic literature. Other issues that were dealt with by the scholars of Yavneh included: the redefinition of the festival calendar, deciding which rituals could be continued in the absence of the Temple; the establishment of a judiciary system, and the establishment of Yavneh itself as the replacement for the Jewish supreme court (Sanhedrin, Syhedrion) that had formerly been housed in the Temple; and dealing with the problem of Jewish property that had been expropriated and transferred illegally by the Roman authorities. With the loss of the Temple, new importance was attached to another institution, the synagogue. During this generation, there are reports in rabbinic literature that would indicate that the sages were arguing about whether certain books, such as Esther and Ecclesiastes mostly from the Ketuvim, had sacred status. Insofar as these reports are historically reliable, it is not clear that the question they were discussing was one of "canonization," whether they should be included among the sacred scriptures of the Bible.

The Yavneh stratum of rabbinic literature is distinguished by its structures of formal argumentation. When a question was posed to the scholars for which there was no straightforward answer, the rabbis argued the various positions, whether by elaborate logical interpretations of biblical texts or by appeal to received oral traditions, according to defined protocols; after which the question was settled by majority vote.

The latter segment of the Yavneh era was dominated by the figure of Rabbi Akiva ben Joseph. He is recognized as an important pioneer in the areas of biblical interpretation, where he developed a distinctive hermeneutical school; and in the topical organization of oral traditions. Rabbi Akiva died a martyr's death at the time of the Bar Kokhba rebellion for openly defying the Roman edicts against the practice and teaching of Judaism.

The middle decades of the second century CE are often designated as the generation of Usha, named for a village in the Galilee that was the home of one of its more distinguished sages, Rabbi Meir. Usha was also the place where some important legal enactments were issued, apparently in response to social crises that arose at that difficult time. The shift of the center of rabbinic activity from Judea (the southern region of the land of Israel, especially the area around Jerusalem) to Galilee (in the north) was an important consequence of the Bar Kokhba revolt. The uprising had provoked a systematic repression of the Judean Jewish community, including the razing of Jerusalem to the ground and its replacement by a new pagan city named Aelia Capitolina. From the time of Usha onwards, we witness a rapid decline in Hebrew as a spoken language. It had been a living vernacular in Judea, but was displaced by the Galilean dialect of Aramaic.

The final generation of the Tannaitic era, extending from the latter part of the second century to the beginning of the third, was marked by a gradual normalization of relations with the Roman administration. The rabbinic personality who dominated this generation was Rabbi Judah the Patriarch (Ha-Nasi). As remembered by the Jewish tradition, Rabbi Judah (he is usually referred to merely as "Rabbi" or "Rebbi"; or as "our holy rabbi") united in himself the virtues of scholarship, piety, wealth and political stature. Undoubtedly the achievement for which he is most reverently remembered was his redaction of the compendium of oral traditions known as the Mishnah, which will be discussed below, and which was regarded as the culmination of a major era in the development of Jewish religious literature.

The era of the Amoraim

Once the Mishnah was published, it appears that it was accepted almost immediately as an authoritative statement of Jewish law. Several additional collections of Tannaitic traditions were compiled during the early decades or the third century, and most of these—at least, in their final versions—presume the Mishnah's existence and compare their own teachings to those of the Mishnah. The authority of the Mishnah was such that, following the centuries that were devoted to the process of collecting and organizing its traditions, now that it existed as a completed work, it came to serve as the text that was studied and interpreted by the next generations of rabbinic scholars.

The scholars of these generations, who produced commentaries on the Mishnah, were known as the *Amoraim* [singular: *Amora*]. The Hebrew or Aramaic word refers to the special functionaries in their academies whose job was to recite aloud the statements of the leading rabbis so that they could be heard and understood by all those who were present—a kind of human loud-speaker system. By extension, the word came to be applied to the scholars themselves.

The time-period of the Amoraim is not easy to define with precision. At the beginning of the era, there was a period of transition in which some rabbis were treated as Tannaim and others as Amoraim; and some were believed to fit into both categories. More complex is the question of defining the end of the Amoraic era. Some traditional documents equate it with the deaths of the supposed redactors of major works, in the early or late fifth century. More recent academic scholarship has demonstrated that the redaction process was far more prolonged than any of those dates would allow for, and that major sections of the rabbinic corpus, especially in Babylonia, were being added well into the sixth and seventh centuries. This, of course, would require a reevaluation of how we define the extent of the "age of the Amoraim."

With the Amoraic era, the Babylonian rabbis emerged as a recognized force in Jewish religious scholarship. As far as we can tell, the literature of the Tannaitic era was produced entirely in the land of Israel. Although some of the individual rabbis who are cited in those works might have come from Rome or Babylonia, their inclusion in Tannaitic literature reflected their presence at discussions that took place in Israel. Another external difference between the two literary eras lies in the languages in which the literature was composed. Almost all the teachings of the Tannaim were composed and transmitted in rabbinic Hebrew. Amoraic works, on the other hand, contain extensive passages in Aramaic.

By the time we emerge into the medieval era, it is clear that the Mishnah, as interpreted in the Amoraic commentaries, had eclipsed all the other works of Tannaitic literature. Understandably, later authors, especially those who were writing from a traditionalist perspective, have tended to project this situation onto earlier generations. The truth is, however, that the Mishnah does not contain the entirety of the Jewish oral tradition. Many other compendia of oral law traditions have come down to us from the Tannaim.

The genres of the oral Torah: midrash and mishnah

The collections of ancient rabbinical teachings were all part of the oral Torah. Accordingly, they were not written down during the era of the Talmud and Midrash. Thus, when we refer to them as works of religious literature, it is important to bear in mind that we are using the word "literature" in a special sense, referring to texts that were memorized. Eventually these texts were set down in writing, though we are unable to date that development with any precision. Clearly, written texts of the Talmud were in use by the tenth century or earlier; though even at this stage, they were not cited in the discussions in the talmudic academies of Babylonia.

Although, as we shall see shortly, the rabbis produced an extensive and diverse body of teachings, almost all of those works can be reduced to four basic prototypes, based on their relationship to the Bible and to legal or non-legal subject matter.

Not surprisingly, much of the scholarly activity of the rabbis was devoted to the intensive study of the Bible, especially the Torah. The segment of their teachings and literature that is related to the Bible is referred to as *midrash*. The word is derived from a Hebrew root meaning "to seek out" or "to search." Early rabbinic (and presumably pre-rabbinic) scholarship formulated elaborate hermeneutical methods for interpreting biblical texts, methods that were probably influenced by the logical methods that the Hellenistic rhetors and jurists employed for the interpretation of Homer and of law codes; however, those methods were evolved in ways that were distinctive to rabbinic Judaism. Historically, the methods of midrashic interpretation were employed both to elicit new possibilities of meaning from the biblical texts, and to find *post facto* scriptural support for teachings that had been passed down on the authority of the oral traditions. In any given instance, it is not immediately obvious which of these possibilities is the correct one.

For example, one of the more common midrashic tropes is known in Hebrew as the *gezerah shavah* (roughly: comparison of equal things). In its simplest form, it is based on the premise that the meaning of an obscure word or expression can often be clarified by seeing how it is employed in other passages; this is a scientific principle that underlies much scholarly lexicography. However, the rabbis extended the use of the method so that the identification of words (even very common words) in virtually any two passages in the Bible could be used as a justification for applying the details of one verse to the other. The rabbis themselves acknowledged that the unrestrained use of this kind of *gezerah shavah* could allow a skillful interpreter to prove anything he wished; therefore they declared that it could not be used to derive new teachings, but only to support interpretations that had already been received as traditions.

The term *midrash* can be applied to a number of different phenomena. There are entire works of midrash that are organized to follow the sequence of a biblical work. It is also possible to find individual units of midrash, teachings that are derived from biblical verses, or at least attached to them in some manner, even though these units are embedded in larger literary settings that are not midrashic. "Midrash" can designate a particular interpretation that employs the rabbinic hermeneutical methods, or a literary genre.

Not all rabbinic teachings were derived from the Bible. The oral tradition included many components that were not mentioned at all in the Torah, such as the extensive elements of customary practice that were incorporated into rabbinic civil law. There were also frequent instances where a basic principle was derived from the midrashic study of a biblical text, but these principles were expanded to a degree that the biblical source was no longer apparent. For example, the Torah states repeatedly that it is forbidden to perform acts of labor on the weekly Sabbath, though it provides very few specific examples of which particular activities are included in the prohibition. Rabbinic tradition formulated a detailed list of thirty-nine archetypes of forbidden types of labor, each of which has its own minimum measure of how much a person has to do in order to be punishable. The detailed specifications of each type of labor rarely have any explicit connection to any text in the Torah; and an early rabbinic tradition observed, "the laws of the Sabbath… are comparable to mountains hanging on a hair, in that they consist of a small element of scripture and very many laws."

Therefore, some collections of rabbinic traditions were organized independently of the Bible. The term that refers to this material is *mishnah*, a Hebrew word whose basic meaning is "that which is memorized by rote." As with *midrash*, the term can be employed to designate either a complete collection, individual passages that conform to this format, or to the genre as a whole. The most obvious types of mishnah are organized logically by subject matter; however, the rabbis would also assemble units according to other criteria: for example, bringing together statements by a particular rabbi, or statements that follow a common literary format.

Halakhah and aggadah

The oral traditions of the rabbis were also subdivided into two categories according to their content: they can deal either with matters of law, or with other topics. The legal component is known in Hebrew as *halakhah*, probably in the sense of "the way in which one walks." The component that deals with other matters is known as *aggadah* (or *haggadah*), meaning "that which one says or tells." The distinction reflects the idea that halakhah, by its nature, establishes obligatory rules that must be observed in practice; whereas the aggadah consists of theoretical opinions, which may be expressed with relative freedom, and which are not usually subject to official regulation.

The definition of halakhah is relatively clear and precise. It can refer either to an individual law, or to the general category of legal discourse. The discussions of halakhic questions in rabbinic literature are usually very technical and precise in their scope. The rabbis dealt with how the various laws were derived, whether from the Torah, from oral traditions, or by logical inference. They discussed how to apply the laws to situations that were not mentioned in earlier sources, and especially about how to rule in cases where two different halakhic principles come into conflict. Statements about the theological or moral rationales for the laws were not usually regarded as belonging to the domain of halakhah, but to the aggadah.

Aggadah encompasses an enormous variety of subjects and literary formats. It encompasses interpretations of non-legal passages of the Bible; diverse types of stories, including hagiographic tales and legends about pious rabbis; miscellaneous information about the world, folklore, medical advice; moralistic observations and proverbs; parables; texts of prayers; and much more.

It would appear that the main setting for the creation of aggadah was in the preaching by rabbis to their communities when they gathered to hear the ceremonial reading of the Bible, especially on the Sabbaths and festivals. At those times, it was customary for the rabbis to deliver sermons, which were literary discourses in which the words of the scriptures were expounded to produce lessons that were directed to the audiences. The most frequent literary structure that is found in classical aggadah is what is known as a *petihah* or *petihta*; literally: an opening or introduction. The standard *petihta* begins with the citation of a verse from a section of the Bible other than the one that is supposed to be read on the present occasion. The preacher interprets that verse, developing the discourse until it reaches its culmination with the opening words of the day's designated biblical reading. The most plausible explanation for this peculiar structure is that it was designed to serve as a prelude to the congregational reading from the scriptures. This kind of rhetorical preaching was most common in the land of Israel, which is where most works of aggadic literature were composed. The Babylonian rabbis were less interested in the aesthetic dimensions of biblical expositions, and treated their aggadic interpretations as a more academic, analytical activity.

The era of the Tannaim produced quite a diverse legacy of works, all of them involving combinations of the four categories that were described previously. It is characteristic of rabbinic culture that it produced almost no literary works that can be ascribed to a single author, or even to a single generation. The normal pattern, insofar as we can reconstruct it from the structures and contents of the actual works, is of an ongoing process of collecting the traditions of previous generations, while adding new interpretations to the received corpus. Thus, the major works of rabbinic literature were produced by academies, or by schools of masters and disciples. We know very little about the institutional setting in which those works were composed, nor is it clear how they determined when these works had reached completion.

Halakhic mishnah

The classic instance of this combination was the collection known as the Mishnah that was redacted by Rabbi Judah the Patriarch. The Mishnah was composed in an elegant dialect of Hebrew, of the sort that was spoken at the time of its composition. Mishnaic Hebrew differs considerably from the Hebrew of the Bible. The process of collecting and organizing the oral teachings went on for several generations, at least from the time of Yavneh. The traditions contained in Rabbi Judah's Mishnah are predominantly from the school of Rabbi Akiva, as transmitted and interpreted by his chief students, especially Rabbi Meir. Rabbi Judah the Patriarch studied with most of Rabbi Akiva's main disciples.

What distinguishes the Mishnah among rabbinic works is its logical arrangement of the diverse traditions. It divides the whole body of Jewish law into six general sections, each of which is known in Hebrew as a *seder* (order):

1. *Zera'im* "Seeds" —laws relating to agriculture, especially to tithes and other portions that must be set aside from produce for religious use.
2. *Mo'ed* "Times"—laws related to the festival calendar, including the weekly Sabbath and annual holidays.
3. *Nashim* "Women"—family law, dealing with topics like marriage and divorce.
4. *Nezikin* "Damages"—civil and criminal law.
5. *Kodashim* "Holy things"—laws related to the Temple, sacrifices and the priesthood.
6. *Tohorot* "Purity"—the variegated situations in which people or things can contract ritual impurity; how the impurity is conveyed; how purification may be achieved; the restrictions that are created by the impurity.

The six orders of the Mishnah are further divided into individual treatises on specific topics, each of which is known as a *massekhet* (tractate). In all, there are sixty tractates in the Mishnah, though in standard use some of the longer ones are divided into two or three volumes. Each tractate is divided into numbered chapters, and the chapters are made up of numbered units, each of which is known as a *mishnah* or *halakhah*.

To take one example of the Mishnah's structure: the second *seder*, the one devoted to the sacred calendar, consists of the following tractates:

a) *Shabbat*: the Sabbath, concerned mostly with defining activities that are forbidden as "work" on that day.
b) *Eruvin*: this tractate deals with the prohibitions against carrying outside a private domain or traveling outside one's home on the Sabbath; and with various legal mechanisms that the rabbis devised for overcoming those prohibition, such as by treating a neighborhood as if it were a single property.
c) *Pesaḥim*: laws of the Passover festival.

d) *Shekalim*: laws related to the collection of funds for communal offerings and upkeep of the Temple. The collection was conducted at a set time of the year.

e) *Yoma* (or: *Kippurim*): Laws of the Day of Atonement.

f) *Sukkah*: laws of the feast of Tabernacles (*Sukkot*).

g) *Yom Tov* (or: *Bezah*): regulations governing activities that are forbidden or permitted on a festival (as distinct from the Sabbath).

h) *Rosh Ha-Shanah*: laws related to the Jewish New Year and New Moon.

i) *Ta'anit*: laws of fast days, especially those related to droughts and other calamities.

j) *Megillah*: laws related to the holiday of Purim (Feast of Esther).

k) *Mo'ed Katan*: laws governing the intermediate days of Passover and Tabernacles, which have a quasi-sacred status that is not as severe as full-fledged festival days.

l) *Hagigah*: laws relating to the pilgrimage festivals, with special reference to the sacrifices that should be offered in the Temple on those occasions.

Apart from some inconsistencies in the first order, the sequence of tractates in each order is according to the decreasing number of chapters.

The structure of a typical mishnah unit is "casuistic"; that is to say, it briefly describes a situation, and then determines whether it is permissible or forbidden, pure or impure, and so forth. Frequently, it will present conflicting views: "In such-and-such case, Rabbi X says: It is permitted; and Rabbi Y says: It is forbidden."

A peculiar feature of the Mishnah is that some opinions are attributed to named rabbis, whereas others are presented anonymously, or with the formula "and the sages say...". The prevailing rabbinic understanding was that the anonymous statements represent the majority positions, and are therefore to be accepted as binding law.

The range of generations represented in the Mishnah extends from the days of the Second Temple through to the late second century. For the most part, it does not include teachings of Rabbi Judah the Patriarch and his contemporaries. However, the bulk of the datable material comes from the generation of Rabbi Akiva's disciples, the "Usha" generation in the mid-second century.

Though the above description of the literary structure of the Mishnah represents its typical format, it should be noted that there are many exceptions. Thus, while each tractate is devoted to a particular topic, it is not unusual to find digressions. For example, the tractate Megillah discusses the major ritual observances of the Purim holiday, particularly the communal reading of the Book of Esther. However, the first chapter contains a series of mishnahs on a range of topics that include: festivals and the Sabbath, the Day of Atonement, vows, impurity from genital secretions and skin diseases, the writing of scriptural passages in scrolls and ritual objects, sacrifices, the status of altars and sanctuaries during the era before the building of the Temple. What all these diverse laws have in common is a literary format that follows the pattern "The only difference between X and Y is Z." It is likely that these mishnahs constituted a literary unit in an earlier collection of oral laws that was arranged according to common literary formats, and that a subsequent editor chose to keep them together when he incorporated them into his new collection, though only one of the passages was really relevant to the subject of the tractate. Such inconsistencies may be encountered quite frequently in the Mishnah.

> Another collection of Tannaitic halakhah that was composed in the mishnah format is known as the Tosefta. The word means "supplement" or "appendix"; meaning: supplements to the Mishnah. The Tosefta follows the sequence of the Mishnah's orders and tractates, and collects diverse kinds of supplementary materials, such as alternative versions of the Mishnah's sources, explanations of words in the Mishnah, or comparisons between different laws and concepts that were mentioned in the Mishnah. The Tosefta contains many traditions from contemporaries of Rabbi Judah the Patriarch, leading scholars to date its redaction a generation later than the Mishnah.

Halakhic midrash

The Tannaitic era produced an extensive literature of works that were devoted to the interpretation of the Torah's commandments of the Torah according to the methods of midrash. Traditionally, this genre has been known as "halakhic midrash" or "Tannaitic midrash." Most of the collections of Tannaitic midrash were redacted— at least, in their final versions—after the publication of the Mishnah. This is clearly evident from the many places where an exposition concludes: "Based on this, the rabbis have said…" at which point they cite a passage from the Mishnah.

Aggadic mishnah

The mishnah format was not often applied to aggadah. There are, however, exceptions to that rule, including a very significant one. A unique tractate in the Mishnah collects sayings about wisdom, Torah, theology and moral values. The tractate is found in the fourth order of Mishnah, *Nezikin*, among treatises on civil and criminal law. It is known in Hebrew as *Avot*, "Fathers," because it begins with an enumeration of the "fathers" of the oral tradition, from Moses through to the generations of the Tannaim. The opening chapters describe the sequence of transmission of the Torah;

and for each post-biblical authority, it adds several (usually, three) maxims that were associated with that sage. Later chapters are arranged by topics or by formal criteria.

> Avot has enjoyed a continuing popularity among traditional Jews. There is a widespread custom of studying it on Saturday afternoons, especially during the long days of summer. It is often published as a separate volume, or included in prayer books. It is also referred to as "*Pirkei Avot*": "the chapters of the fathers."

Aggadic midrash

As was mentioned previously, the main wellspring of rabbinic aggadah was in the sermons that were preached in the synagogues. While a great deal of aggadic midrash is included in the compendia of Tannaitic ("halakhic") midrash, the compilation of specialized works of aggadic midrash was a phenomenon associated with the Amoraic era. The "classical" age of aggadic midrash is usually dated to around the fourth century in the land of Israel. It is common to classify the aggadic midrash collections into two types:

1. Homiletical: consisting mostly of structured literary sermons on general themes.
2. Exegetical: containing line-by-line explanations of the biblical text.

Which type a work belongs to is usually determined by the nature of the biblical book to which the midrash is attached. To cite an obvious example, the technical laws of sacrifices and ritual purity that fill the pages of Leviticus do not lend themselves easily to aggadic interpretation; hence, the redactors of *Leviticus Rabbah* limited themselves to homilies on more general topics.

The literature of aggadic midrash is very extensive. The body of "classic" midrashic works produced in Amoraic Israel includes collections on Genesis, Leviticus, and several books of the Ketuvim that are designated for public reading during the liturgical year. A compendium known as the *Pesiqta deRav Kahana* consists of homiletical aggadic midrash for readings on festivals and special Sabbaths, when the assigned scriptural readings in the synagogues do not follow the sequential order of the Torah.

A separate family of aggadic midrashic works goes by the general name of "Tanhuma," after the name of a Rabbi Tanhuma whose name appears frequently in them. What distinguishes these collections from others is their tendency to merge the individual and discontinuous comments of the earlier works into a continuous presentation, which sometimes adds up to a sequential narrative. The dates of the

Figure 3.2 Hammat Tiberias synagogue

Tanhuma literature have not been determined with precision; the current theory argues that their composition began in the land of Israel during the Byzantine era, around the fifth century, and evolved for some time afterwards.

The Talmuds: Palestinian and Babylonian

In the Amoraic schools, a *tanna* (memorizer of earlier traditions) would recite passages from the Mishnah along with related material from other Tannaitic traditions. These would then be expounded by the head of the academy and submitted to the scholars for discussion and debate. The records of these discussions, creatively edited and elaborated over the generations, form the basis for the vast works known as the Talmuds. The word "talmud" derives form a Hebrew root meaning "study" or "learning." Two Talmuds have come down to us, from the land of Israel and from Babylonia, and their structures and purposes are basically similar. Both are organized as commentaries on the Mishnah.

The Talmud of the land of Israel was completed earlier, around 400 CE according to the general scholarly consensus (with some sections perhaps earlier than that). It is often referred to in English as the Palestinian Talmud or the Jerusalem Talmud. The latter name, which reflects a common Hebrew usage ("Talmud Yerushalmi"), is not technically correct, given that the city of Jerusalem had been demolished by the Romans prior to the Amoraic era. It covers (though not always completely) thirty-nine of the Mishnah's sixty tractates. Most of the missing tractates are from the orders dealing with sacrificial worship and purity.

The Babylonian Talmud, by way of comparison, covers 36 and a half tractates. Of the Mishnah's order Zera'im, concerned with agricultural regulations, the only tractate included in the Talmud is Berakhot, which deals with blessings and prayers. This situation is usually ascribed to the fact that most of the agricultural laws were not considered binding outside the land of Israel. Accordingly, it is not surprising that the Palestinian Talmud covers all these tractates. The absence of the order "Tohorot" (about rules of purity) from both talmuds can also be accounted for by the premise that most of the laws found there could not be observed following the destruction of the Second Temple. The single exception is the tractate "Niddah" which discusses the impurity of menstruating women. Several of those laws were still of practical relevance.

The discussions in the Talmuds deal with many aspects of the Mishnah, often going far beyond what would be necessary for an explanation or clarification. The discussions in the Babylonian Talmud are far more complex than in the Palestinian. This is often attributed to the fact that it underwent a prolonged period of redaction and reworking. Furthermore, it appears that the Babylonian rabbis generally had a more pronounced tendency towards logical virtuosity.

Some of the ways in which the Talmuds discuss the Mishnah include:

- demonstrating how the Mishnah's rulings or disputes derived from biblical sources and their interpretations.
- exploring the logical principles that underlie the Mishnah's statements. Once such principles have been proposed, it is normal to show how differing understandings of the Mishnah's reasons can lead to differences in applying the law to specific cases.

Figure 3.3 Talmud page

- resolving contradictions, whether perceived or actual, between different statements in the Mishnah, or between the Mishnah and other traditions. This can be done, for example, by stating that what appear to be two conflicting sources are actually speaking about differing circumstances; or that they represent the views of different rabbis.

The distinctive literary and intellectual flavor of the Talmuds derives largely from their intricate use of logical argumentation and debate. Some of these debates were actually conducted by the Amoraim; however, most of them were hypothetically reconstructed by the Talmuds' redactors, in the sense of "This is what Rabbi X could have argued had the objection been posed in his presence." As in the Mishnah, the talmudic rabbis encouraged multiple opinions and interpretations. Whereas the Mishnah usually limits itself to simple statements of the conflicting views, without explaining their underlying reasons, the Talmuds try to verify the integrity of the positions of the Tannaim and the Amoraim. Proof texts are adduced in order to corroborate or disprove the respective opinions. The process of inference that is required to derive a conclusion from a proof text is often logically complex and indirect. Every effort is made to uphold the logical consistency of the opinions ascribed to the rabbis, even if it requires forced and unconvincing interpretations of the evidence.

In addition to the Bible, Mishnah and the teachings of the Babylonian Amoraim, the talmuds cite and discuss several other kinds of sources.

These include:

- Teachings by the Tannaim that were not included in the Mishnah. Such sources are designated "external mishnahs" (in Aramaic: *baraita*).
- Many traditions of the Palestinian Amoraim were cited and incorporated into the Babylonian Talmud, and vice versa.
- Approximately one third of the Babylonian Talmud is devoted to aggadah, while the Palestinian Talmud contains only half that proportion. (In the land of Israel, separate compendia were created in which to collect the genre of aggadic midrash.)
- Records of legal rulings by the rabbis from cases over which they presided as judges.

Readers who have not been brought up in a traditional Jewish setting may find themselves wondering what Talmud study has to do with religion. The subject matter of these works usually consists of minute technical analysis of obscure legal questions, matters that modern society does not classify as religious pursuits. It must however be remembered that for Jews (as for several other religious communities), the ultimate expression of divine revelation is in the form of laws. This is certainly true for traditional Jews who believe that the most momentous event in history was when God revealed the Torah to the children of Israel at Mount Sinai. The Torah consists primarily of laws and commandments, and it has always been assumed that the intensive study of religious law is a fundamental act of religious devotion. Jewish religious law encompasses, not only matters of belief, liturgy and ritual, but also covers the full range of civil and criminal laws. For Jews, all these laws have their origin in a divine revelation, and their observance forms the basis of the eternal covenant between God and the people of Israel.

Key points you need to know

- Following the destruction of the Second Temple, the dominant form of Judaism was Pharisaic, as interpreted by the rabbis.
- The sages of Yavneh reinterpreted Jewish tradition to allow its continuation without the Temple and its sacrificial worship.
- Rabbinic literature assembled oral traditions and produced new teachings in the realm of halakhah (law) and non-legal matters (aggadah).
- The Tannaim developed sophisticated hermeneutics for expounding the Torah, known as *midrash*.
- The Mishnah, a topical arrangement of Jewish religious law, was regarded as the crowning achievement of Tannaitic Judaism.
- The Amoraim conducted elaborate analytical debates about the interpretation of the Mishnah. These debates are the basis of the Palestinian and Babylonian Talmuds.

Discussion questions

1. The compilation of the Mishnah is often presented as a response to the destruction of the Second Temple. Discuss some of the strengths and weaknesses of this approach.
2. In what ways can the rabbinic model of Judaism be considered more or less "democratic" than its rivals?
3. The surviving literature of the rabbis is limited to a relatively small number of genres and topics. What significant areas of Jewish religious life might thereby be excluded from our knowledge?
4. What reasons can you think of for insisting that part of the religious tradition not be written down?
5. The presentation in this chapter was largely restricted to the Jewish communities of Israel and Babylonia. Did developments in other lands have lasting significance for Judaism?

Further reading

Boyarin, Daniel, *Intertextuality and the Reading of Midrash*, Indiana Studies in Biblical Literature. Bloomington, IN: Indiana University Press, 1990.

—— *Sparks of the Logos: Essays in Rabbinic Hermeneutics*, Brill Reference Library of Judaism. Leiden and Boston, MA: Brill, 2003.

Cohen, Shaye J. D., "The Significance of Yavneh: Pharisees, Rabbis and the End of Jewish Sectarianism." *Hebrew Union College Annual* 55 (1984): 27–53.

——"The Place of the Rabbi in Jewish Society of the Second Century." In *The Galilee in Late Antiquity*, edited by Lee Levine, 157–73. New York: Jewish Theological Seminary of America, 1992.

—— *From the Maccabees to the Mishnah*. 2nd ed., Louisville, KY: Westminster John Knox Press, 2006.

Fraade, Steven D., *From Tradition to Commentary: Torah and Its Interpretation in the Midrash Sifre to Deuteronomy*, SUNY Series in Judaica. Albany, NY: State University of New York Press, 1991.

Halivni, David, *Midrash, Mishnah, and Gemara: The Jewish Predilection for Justified Law*. Cambridge, MA: Harvard University Press, 1986.

—— *Peshat and Derash: Plain and Applied Meaning in Rabbinic Exegesis*. New York: Oxford University Press, 1991.

Jaffee, Martin S., *Torah in the Mouth: Writing and Oral Tradition in Palestinian Judaism, 200 BCE–400 CE*. Oxford and New York: Oxford University Press, 2001.

Kadushin, Max, *The Rabbinic Mind. With an Appendix by Simon Greenberg*. 3rd ed., New York: Bloch Pub. Co., 1972.

Kalmin, Richard Lee, *The Sage in Jewish Society in Late Antiquity*. New York: Routledge, 1999.

—— *Jewish Babylonia between Persia and Roman Palestine*. New York: Oxford University Press, 2006.

Lieberman, Saul, *Hellenism in Jewish Palestine: Studies in the Literary Transmission, Beliefs, and Manners of Palestine in the I Century BCE–IV Century CE* 2nd improved ed., New York: Jewish Theological Seminary of America, 1962.

Rubenstein, Jeffrey L., *The Culture of the Babylonian Talmud*. Baltimore, MD: Johns Hopkins University Press, 2003.

Safrai, Shemuel, *The Literature of the Sages*. Assen and Philadelphia, PA: Van Gorcum and Fortress Press, 1987.

Satlow, Michael L., *Creating Judaism: History, Tradition, Practice*. New York: Columbia University Press, 2006.

Schechter, S., *Aspects of Rabbinic Theology*, Jewish Lights Classic Reprint. Woodstock, VT: Jewish Lights, 1993.

Strack, Hermann Leberecht and Günter Stemberger, *Introduction to the Talmud and Midrash*. 1st Fortress Press ed., Minneapolis, MN: Fortress Press, 1992.

Urbach, Efraim Elimelech, *The Sages, Their Concepts and Beliefs*. Cambridge, MA: Harvard University Press, 1987.

4 Medieval Judaism

In this chapter

Although the negative connotations of the "medieval" cultural decline do not apply to Judaism in the same way as to Christian Europe, there are several features of that time period that justify its designation as a separate era in the evolution of Judaism, when compared with what came before and after it: the surrounding cultures were no longer polytheistic, but monotheistic religions with roots in the Jewish scriptures. The oral tradition was submitted to writing and the Talmud came to be accepted as the authoritative voice of Jewish tradition. Rabbinic Judaism was eventually decentralized, spreading throughout the western world with no single center of hegemony; Judaism was being influenced by a new diversity of foreign cultures, while the authority of the land of Israel was increasingly marginalized. Works of religious scholarship were now being composed by individuals, no longer as collective expressions of the rabbinic leadership. New internal divisions became significant: between the Judaisms of Islamic and Christian lands (Sephardic or Ashkenazic); Rabbinites and Karaites; rationalists and kabbalists.

Main topics covered

- The significance of "medieval" in Judaism
- Differences between medieval and ancient Judaism
- Ashkenaz, Sepharad and Provence: general comments on medieval Jewish geography

The significance of "medieval" in Judaism

The concept of "medieval" or "middle age" was apparently coined by a fifteenth-century author to designate a historical epoch that was typified by cultural stagnation—a "dark age" that interrupted the flow of human progress, between the glory of classical antiquity and the rebirth of that glory in the beginnings of the modern world. In the sense that I have described it so far, the designation "medieval" is inappropriate to the Jewish context at this point in history. The period extending from the fifth through the fifteenth centuries, which is usually identified as the Middle Ages in Christian history, was an era of religious innovation, cultural enrichment and scientific advance for Jews and Muslims who lived outside the realms of Christendom. Although there were occasions when Judaism took on attitudes that were analogous to the ignorance and superstition of European medievalism, this also occurred during eras that we are accustomed to classify as "modern."

The Jews experienced no break with their cultural or religious heritage following the fall of Rome. Jewish religious scholarship during the Middle Ages was marked by its continuity with previous eras, and by a progressive deepening of their studies of the Bible, Talmud and other works of religious authority. The displacement of Roman domination over Jewish communities by the Muslim Arabs was welcomed by most Jews, because they had long suffered under the yoke of the rapacious "evil empire" of Rome, and even more under the anti-Jewish edicts of Christian Byzantium. This was also true for the Jews of Babylonia who, prior to the Arab invasion, had been persecuted by Persian Zoroastrians. The rediscovery of the heritage of Greece and Rome, which would be a chief component of the European Renaissance in the fifteenth century, occurred in the Arabic world in the eighth and ninth centuries, as the vibrant new empire rushed thirstily to translate into Arabic the writings of the ancient philosophers and scientists.

Given the essential continuity that linked the Judaism of that era to its earlier manifestations, it is fair to ask: Does it really make sense to single out the "medieval" era as a separate age?

In fact, there are a number of features that warrant singling out an age in Jewish history that coincides roughly with the centuries that are designated as medieval in conventional historiography. Depending on which of those criteria we consider most important, this can lead to several different options for assigning dates to the Jewish "Middle Ages."

Differences between medieval and ancient Judaism

There are a number of dates that mark significant turning points in the transition of Judaism from antiquity. These include:

The Christianization of the Roman Empire

With his Edict of Milan in 313, the Emperor Constantine the Great transformed Christianity from an illegal *superstitio* to a licit and tolerated religion. Quickly it became the favored religion of the Roman Empire, and it was actively promoted through the instrument of the Roman legal system. The ambivalent status of Judaism for Christian theology, as a religion that should have been superseded by the new faith but whose adherents blindly refused to acknowledge the "new covenant," led to official persecution of the Jews in the Roman Empire. The legal codices produced under Christian Roman emperors imposed severe restrictions on the Jewish community that were designed to perpetuate their inferior status. The principles established at this time remained more or less in force in most European lands until modern times. Many of those processes would be crucial to defining the status of Judaism in the coming centuries.

The fall of the Sassanian empire

Since the third century CE, Babylonia had been ruled by the Persian Sassanian dynasty. Although Jews in those times were not often subjected to overt restrictions on the practice of their religion and the community generally enjoyed autonomy, there were occasional flare-ups of officially sanctioned Zoroastrian intolerance that intensified in the declining years of the Sassanian emperors. By 637, the Arabs, inspired by their new religion of Islam, overthrew the Persian empire, bringing it under the influence of their own culture and religion. At around the same time, the Muslims were also taking control of other important Jewish centers, including the land of Israel. This milestone was to have far-reaching effects on most aspects of Jewish political, economic, cultural and religious life.

The redaction of the Talmud

Upon its completion, the Talmud (especially the Babylonian) came to be perceived as the definitive interpretation of Jewish religious tradition, to be consulted on all questions of ritual and legal observance. Subsequent generations of Jews would define their Judaism in terms of its conformity to the Talmud, and the best energies of Jewish scholarship would be devoted to explaining the Talmud and applying its teachings. Even those Jews who ultimately rejected the authority of the Talmud and of the rabbinic tradition that it embodied, such as the Karaite movement (see below), were being defined by their rejection of the Talmud.

Current scholarship has acknowledged that the Babylonian Talmud as we now possess it was the culmination of a long process of redaction that likely extended over centuries. An obscure group of scholars known as the "Savora'im," described by medieval chroniclers as being active during the sixth, or perhaps also the seventh century, were once believed to have exerted a negligible influence on Jewish tradition. Based on literary analysis of the Talmud's different strata, it is now widely thought that these Savora'im were actually responsible for the lion's share of the Talmud's redaction.

In some respects, it is much simpler to define the end of the Middle Ages, though this will lead us inevitably to dates that are considerably later than those used to demarcate the equivalent era in European Christian history, where the transition is usually located in the latter half of the fifteenth century.

There are several qualitative features that allow us to discern what was special about the Jewish Middle Ages, especially in contrast to what came before it. They give us some idea of the how medieval Judaism can be regarded as a distinctive phase in the development of the Jewish people and its religion.

Geographical distribution

The scholarly activity that produced the vast collections of talmudic and midrash literature were confined to two countries: the Land of Israel and Babylonia. What little has survived from the religious creations of other communities (for example, the work of Philo of Alexandria) was not transmitted to Jews of subsequent generations, and hence was functionally lost to the tradition. The supremacy of Israel and Babylonia continued to prevail until the tenth century, often in the guise of a rivalry for influence over the other diaspora communities. Shortly after the leaders of the Babylonian academies succeeded in achieving preeminence, there was a proliferation of religiously autonomous Jewish communities, each boasting its own renowned rabbis and talmudic academies, throughout North Africa and Europe, establishing a decentralization that would define the norm for Jewish life from that point onward.

The triumph of monotheism

In contrast to the ancient situation, where Judaism was the sole monotheistic religion confronting a polytheistic world, by the Middle Ages Judaism's main rival religions were now monotheistic "daughter" faiths.

Individual authorship

There was fundamental change in the character of rabbinic literature in the Middle Ages. The great creations of the Talmudic era did not have single authors, but rather represented the collective authority of rabbinic scholarship as it evolved over several generations. Even though names of editors have been attached to many of those compendia (such as the identification of Rabbi Judah the Patriarch as the redactor of the Mishnah), this fact does not significantly alter the shared or institutional quality of those works. This situation changed dramatically in the Middle Ages. In all the domains of Jewish religious scholarship, major works were being produced by individuals whose personalities were imprinted on their creations. This is true, whether we are dealing with biblical exegesis, philosophy, talmudic interpretation,

Hebrew grammar, liturgical poetry, or any of the many other areas that were pursued by the rabbis of the time.

A related innovation of the medieval era, whose precise significance is difficult to evaluate, was the putting of the "oral tradition" into writing. We do not know precisely when the ancient interdiction on writing down oral tradition was repealed, nor do we know the reasons for the change. The issue has been confused by the fact that influential medieval scholars, especially Saadiah and Maimonides, pushed the date back to the early third century with the publication of the Mishnah; a claim that is clearly contradicted by the evidence. In contrast to the previous situation, the medieval era was an age of books. The scholars studied the literature of the talmudic era from written manuscripts, and it was in this same manner that they published their own original works.

Foreign cultural influences

The character of Judaism in any specific historical setting was decisively influenced by the gentile culture that it was confronting. Just as earlier eras in Jewish history were shaped by encounters with the religions and cultures of Egypt, Babylonia, Persia, Greece and Rome, so was the character of medieval Judaism determined by the cultures among which most Jews were now living: the Arabic-speaking Islamic culture in the Middle East and southern Mediterranean, or the Christian peoples of central and western (and later: eastern) Europe.

Major schisms

Every era in the history of Judaism has had its own sectarian divisions. The major schism in medieval Judaism was between the Rabbinites, who accepted the "oral Torah" tradition embodied in the Talmud and its cognate works; and the Karaites, who accepted only the authority of the Bible. Apart from this fundamental sectarian split, in which each side denied the legitimacy of its opponents' religious stance, medieval Rabbinite Jews were also divided according to several other ideological or cultural lines. These were usually perceived as legitimate disagreements in that—except for a few rare outbursts of intolerance—adherents of one such group did not challenge the fundamental Jewishness of their rivals.

Though the communities in the Arab and Christian world (the Sephardim and Ashkenazim as they are respectively designated) differed in many important aspects of their Judaism (for example, the Sephardim favored systematic codification, whereas the Ashkenazim had a special reverence for ancestral custom), we find little evidence of systemic hostility between these communities during medieval times.

A more ambivalent attitude governed the relationships between champions of the philosophical and kabbalistic approaches to Jewish theology. As we shall be seeing, consistent identification with the theoretical doctrines of either school should logically have branded the other school as wrong, and likely heretical. In reality, however, the prevailing outlook among the Jewish populace was that the two streams could co-exist. This unexpected display of tolerance is exemplified in the theory of "the four levels of biblical hermeneutics" that advocated the coexistence of literal, midrashic, philosophical and kabbalistic interpretations of the same scriptural texts, on the understanding that, in some subtle way, all of them were simultaneously true.

Medieval Judaism as diaspora Judaism

The widespread cliché that the Jews of Israel were exiled by the Romans after 70 CE is plainly untrue, as can be easily established through archeological remains from the time, as well as from the rich literary legacy of talmudic and midrashic literature that were produced there, especially in Galilee. Nevertheless, matters were in a state of decline, whether on account of the general anarchy overtaking the Roman Empire or because of the anti-Jewish repression by the Byzantine government. As we enter the medieval era, the Jewish population of the Land of Israel was shrinking, and their spiritual creativity was diminishing. The Crusades brought a virtual end to autonomous Jewish life in the Land of Israel.

Thus, the Judaism of the Middle Ages was a religion of exile, and the anomalous situation of statelessness came to be thought of as normal. We can discern this attitude, for example, in the convention adopted by most medieval codifications of Jewish religious law, of limiting their scope to laws that were in force "at this time"; excluding thereby laws that applied only on the soil of the Holy Land. The consciousness of exile as a fundamental metaphysical state was most poignantly expressed in the symbolism of the Kabbalah, and in the yearning Hebrew poems of Zion by the Andalusian philosopher and poet Rabbi Judah Halevi (*c.* 1075–1141).

Ashkenaz, Sepharad and Provence

One of the most impressive features of medieval Jewish religion is the high degree of uniformity that was maintained among the scattered Jewish communities. Whether in Spain, Germany, Egypt or Yemen, the Jews acknowledged the authority of the same body of sacred books, practiced the same rituals, and recited prayers that were almost identical. In large measure, this was a result of their adoption of the approach implicit in the Babylonian Talmud, and perhaps more so among the *Geonim* who presided over the medieval Babylonian academies, of cultivating strict ritual uniformity at the expense of spontaneity or improvisation. In the end, this attitude produced a situation in which a Jew from Poland, entering a synagogue in Morocco, might feel quite comfortable with the prayers that were recited there. The phenomenon becomes even more extraordinary when we bear in mind the limited possibilities of international communication that existed in those technologically primitive times.

Nonetheless, there were important cultural differences that distinguished the major medieval Jewish communities from one another. Some of the most conspicuous cultural differences between the Jewish communities were reflections of the non-Jewish civilizations in which they dwelled.

It is customary to refer to the two main groupings of Jews as Ashkenazic and Sephardic. The former were those who lived in Christian Europe, while the latter dwelled in the Arabic-speaking Muslim lands. (When applied to modern times, the terms have a slightly different significance.) "Ashkenaz" is a name that appears in the Bible (Genesis 10:3 and elsewhere) to designate an ancient nation probably from central Asia, and medieval Jews adopted it as the Hebrew equivalent for Germany. Similarly, "the captivity of Jerusalem in Sepharad" is mentioned in Obadiah 1:20, and the name was understood in ancient Jewish sources (probably correctly) as a reference to far-off Spain.

The Arab civilization in which the Sephardic Jews were participating was a very "modern" one in many respects. It had recently made the acquaintance of the rationalist legacy of ancient Greece, and was deeply influenced by it. Educated individuals were expected to be acquainted with the rudiments of philosophy and natural science, including medicine and astronomy. Islam, the dominant religion of this culture, was a tradition that emphasized law and evolved an elaborate system of religious law based on its scripture, the Qur'an, and on its oral tradition, the *sunna* of the prophet Muhammad. Jews could feel at home with many of its religious values. The application of Greek-style rationalism to the study of religious law led to some remarkable and unique developments in Jewish religious scholarship. Probably the most conspicuous example was the Sephardic propensity for systematic codification of Jewish law. The classic Sephardic attitude to the Talmud valued it mainly as the source of normative religious law.

Although the Talmud itself seems more interested in the *process* of argumentation, the Sephardic tradition was often more interested in extracting from those debates a system of obligatory laws. During their "golden age," when Andalusian Jewry was producing masterworks in Hebrew poetry, science, philosophy and philology, their contribution to talmudic interpretation was limited. Academic study was left to a small elite, while most rabbis and educated laymen concentrated on mastering codified law.

The Ashkenazic Jews, though equally committed to the authority of the Talmud, had a diametrically different understanding of its importance. They lived in a society from which Greek learning and its rationalist ideals had been effectively lost. The intellectual climate of their Christian surroundings was characterized by a free flowing "scholasticism" that paralleled many features of traditional talmudic debate. The German respect for customary law was echoed in the Ashkenazic veneration of ancestral religious and liturgical customs, many of which had their roots in the land of Israel.

The Ashkenazic and Sephardic Jewish cultures developed differing nuances of their religion. The Ashkenazic flair for commentary and interpretation may be contrasted with the Sephardic genius for systematic codification; and the Sephardic leaning towards of a universalistic religion of reason differs from the deeply parochial character of German-Jewish pietism.

At the crossroads of these two civilizations was the region known to the medievals as "Provence" in south-eastern France along the Spanish border. Through most the Middle Ages, Provence was a frontier through which Islamic civilization found entry into northern Europe. From the perspective of Jewish religious history, Provence indeed had a very special role. Not only was it the home of the illustrious Ibn Tibbon dynasty of Marseilles who were responsible for translating the major works of philosophy into Hebrew, but it also produced a figure like Rabbi Menahem Meiri of Perpignan whose *Beit ha-Behirah* merged the finest elements of Sephardic codification and Ashkenazic textual commentary. It was in Provence that major clashes would arise over the orthodoxy of Maimonides's philosophy, and where we encounter the earliest teachings about the Kabbalah.

The Ashkenazic communities of the Rhineland and central Europe suffered a decline during the latter centuries of the Middle Ages. As their social situation deteriorated, and as new opportunities presented themselves elsewhere, migrations took place to Italy and to Poland, where they were courted because of their beneficial economic impact. By the sixteenth century, Poland had emerged as the foremost center of Ashkenazic Jewish scholarship.

Anti-Jewish measures in the fourteenth and fifteenth centuries, in the context of the Reconquista of the Iberian peninsula under Christian rule, forced many Jews to convert to Christianity, though many of them continued to live as Jews in secret. These Jews are known as "Conversos"; they were often referred to by the abusive epithet "marranos" (swine). As Christians, they were now placed under the jurisdiction of the Inquisition, whose task was to uproot all traces of heresy, such as judaizing. The Inquisitors did their work with efficiency, using torture to elicit confessions and accusations, and confiscating the property of their victims. With the final unification of Spain under the Christian monarchs Ferdinand of Aragon and Isabella of Castile, an edict was issued requiring all Jews who refused baptism to leave the country by 1492. Many found refuge in Portugal, but brutal persecutions were instituted there as well, often extending even to "New Christians" who were faithful to their new religion. Thousands of Jews found havens in other lands where their cosmopolitan culture and commercial connections were much appreciated. A thriving diaspora of Spanish and Portuguese Jewish refugees arose in the Ottoman empire (including the holy land), the Netherlands, Italy, Germany, the New World and elsewhere. Jews who remained in Iberia for a long time were usually denied access to any traditional Jewish texts other than the accepted Christian versions of the Bible. As a result, their familiarity with post-biblical Judaism was necessarily limited, and their eventual encounters with actual Jewish communities could be jarring, producing rootless individuals who were not fully at home in either Judaism or Christianity, though some continued to live in both worlds. This phenomenon may have contributed to the challenge to traditional religious values that manifested itself in the European Enlightenment.

Key points you need to know

- Medieval Judaism differed from ancient Judaism, in part because of the changed historical situation; for example, Jews were now living among monotheistic gentiles rather than pagans.
- There were also internal religious developments that were unique to medieval Judaism, such as the completion and acceptance of the Talmuds.

Discussion questions

1. In what ways might the relationships of Jews to Christians or Muslims be more problematic than with pagans?
2. Jews in Arabic lands composed works on religious law and philosophy in Arabic, but their coreligionists in Europe did not adopt Latin as a language for religious literature. What factors might account for this difference?

Further reading

General

Blumenthal, David R., ed., *Approaches to Judaism in Medieval Times*, 2 vols, Brown Judaic Studies. Chico, CA: Scholars Press, 1984.
Marcus, Jacob Rader, *The Jew in the Medieval World: A Source Book: 315–1791*, Harper Torchbooks. New York: Harper & Row, 1965.

Ashkenazic and Sephardic Judaism

Ashtor, Eliyahu, *The Jews of Moslem Spain*. Philadelphia, PA: Jewish Publication Society of America, 1973.

Halkin, Abraham S., "The Judeo-Islamic Age." In *Great Ages and Ideas of the Jewish People*. Edited by L. W. Schwarz. New York: Modern Library, 1956.

Roth, Cecil, "The European Age," in *Great Ages and Ideas of the Jewish People*. Edited by L. W. Schwarz. New York: Modern Library, 1956.

Zimmels, H. J., *Ashkenazim and Sephardim: Their Relations, Differences, and Problems as Reflected in the Rabbinical Responsa*. London: Oxford University Press, 1958.

5 Medieval Jewish philosophy

In this chapter

Jewish thinkers in Islamic lands became acquainted with the philosophical classics of ancient Greece, especially the works of Plato and Aristotle, through Arabic translations that became available early in the medieval era. For many Jews, these works provided an objective scientific justification for revealed teachings about monotheism and morality. Influential Jewish thinkers reinterpreted Judaism in the spirit of rationalist thought. This sometimes involved a transformation of priorities, in which the intellectual understanding of God was posited as the ultimate purpose of religious life. As in their Islamic environment, Jewish philosophers were divided into three main schools: (1) the Kalam employed reason to better understand the revealed traditions. Kalam thinkers, such as Saadiah Gaon, were particularly interested in demonstrating that physical or anthropomorphic descriptions of God that appear in the Bible should not be understood literally, and that humans have the freedom to choose between good and evil. (2) Neoplatonism encompasses an assortment of mystically oriented doctrines that are concerned with transcending material existence to achieve a spiritual state of metaphysical being. (3) Jewish Aristotelianism, as formulated by Moses Maimonides and his followers, offered a sophisticated model for a scientific explanation of the universe, and a program for attaining immortality by focusing one's intellect on the eternal truth of divine being.

Some Jewish thinkers do not fit neatly into the above classification. These include: Abraham Abulafia, who tried to experience prophecy by means of mystical discipline, not as an intellectual path; and Judah Halevi whose philosophical dialogue the *Kuzari* argued for the superiority of revelation and traditional faith over philosophical religion.

Main topics covered

- The rediscovery of Greek philosophy
- The three major schools of Islamic-Jewish rationalism

- Kalam
- Neoplatonism
- Aristotelianism
- Abraham Abulafia's mystical path

The rediscovery of Greek philosophy

When applied to the history of Jewish religious thought, the term "philosophy" has a rather narrow meaning, referring to a method and tradition of rationalistic inquiry that originated in ancient Greece. Therefore all examples of medieval Jewish philosophy will involve conscious confrontations with the works of Plato, \l, the Stoics and Pythagoreans, and other thinkers and schools who contributed to that world of discourse. There were of course other religious thinkers, Jewish and gentile, who gave serious thought to the eternal questions about God, humanity and morality. Nevertheless, those figures were not classified as "philosophers" in the medieval era unless they conducted their discussions according to the conceptual framework that had been developed by the Greek philosophers. For this reason, the Bible cannot properly be counted a philosophical work, even though the authors of books like Job and Ecclesiastes pondered basic issues of justice and the meaning of life. Similarly, though talmudic and midrashic texts reveal an elaborate world-view that embraces the tension between divine justice and mercy, the human potential for good and evil and the definition of the good life—as long as these topics are not dealt with from the perspective of the Greek rationalist tradition, they cannot be counted works of philosophy.

This is not to say that ancient Jews did not indulge in the pursuit of philosophical truth. Philo of Alexandria produced a monumental *oeuvre* of biblical interpretation, in which he explained the Torah as an allegorical exposition of philosophical ideas. The popularity of this approach among early followers of Christianity, many of whom were born Jews, suggests that there were large numbers of Jews, especially outside the land of Israel, who espoused a similar ideal of philosophical Judaism. The fact nevertheless remains that medieval Jews who were committed to the philosophical approach to Judaism could marshal little support for their views from the literary heritage of traditional Judaism. The works of Philo were not known directly to medieval Jewish scholars, even though he had dealt with many of the same issues that would later challenge the medieval Jewish philosophers.

This is not to say that the medieval Jewish rationalists would have agreed with our positing of a fundamental difference between traditional religion and philosophy. So convinced were they that the ultimate goal of Judaism lay in the philosophical knowledge of God that they reinterpreted the Bible and Talmud in order to read them as philosophical tracts. In fact, it was widely believed that the Greek thinkers had derived their ideas from Jewish mentors, from the prophets of ancient Israel who were the first to prove the existence and unity of the Creator and the principles of ethical behavior. Modern scholars have traced subtle influences of Hellenistic dialectic on the character of rabbinic discourse and hermeneutic methods, but these influences do not usually extend to the more conventional philosophical questions.

From the seventh century, as the Arabs commenced their swift expansion through North Africa, the Middle East and South Asia, this small and uneducated nation suddenly found itself in control of an immense geographic domain. In several places, such as Persia and India, the subject peoples were heirs to venerable civilizations, and the Arab Muslims had to rely on the literate natives to provide their administrative and political infrastructures. The leaders of the international Islamic community (known as the Caliphs) established a magnificent royal court in their new capital of Baghdad, Iraq that quickly became a renowned center of culture, scholarship and international trade. Many representatives of non-Muslim religious communities were able to rise to important positions in the court of the Caliph. When Islam expanded into Syria, the educated Syrian (Nestorian) Christians were able to achieve some influence in the administration of the Caliphate, especially as court physicians. The Arabs began to hear about the marvelous literary and intellectual treasures that had been preserved in Syriac translation from legendary Greek authors. They now commissioned Arabic translations of the more important ancient scientific and philosophical texts.

Notwithstanding their literal faithfulness to their exemplars, the medieval interpretations of the Greek philosophical texts often diverged in their contents from their original meanings. Certain discrepancies resulted from the manner in which the texts had been studied and transmitted:

- Certain works by the major philosophers were not available to the medieval students. For example, they did not possess Aristotle's *Politics*, and tried to fill in the gap by using Plato's *Republic* as if it were a statement of Aristotle's political theory, though it actually reflected a very different approach to the topic.
- Several works by other writers with vastly different philosophical systems were mistakenly attributed to Plato or Aristotle. In particular, works from the Neoplatonic and other mystical schools, such as the *Enneads* by the third-century philosopher Plotinus, were ascribed to Aristotle. This obviously led to a very different perception of Aristotelianism from the one that emerges from his authentic writings.

For Jews, the ancient philosophical texts were not only being read in Arabic translation, but the meanings of those texts had already been mediated by the interpretations of important Muslim Arab commentators, such as Alfarabi, Ibn Sina (known to Latin scholars as Avicenna) and Ibn Rushd (Averroes).

The initial Muslim and Jewish encounter with ancient philosophy was a very enthusiastic one, largely because it appeared to provide corroboration for the most important theological assumptions of their respective religions. All the major Greek philosophers had reached the conclusion that there exists a single deity who fashioned the universe. They also formulated systems of ethical and moral behavior that had much in common with the values espoused by the revealed religions. Because philosophy claimed to base its conclusions on completely objective criteria, including the empirical evidence of the senses and the self-evident principles of logic, it could be viewed as religiously neutral. Therefore, when representatives of different religious traditions argued with one another over the relative merits and drawbacks of their faiths, their claims could be measured against the standards of philosophy. Without such a neutral arbiter, the communities would be reduced to quoting scriptural verses and traditions at each other, when one group did not accept the authority of the other's revelation. As religious thinkers became increasingly committed to the teachings and methods of philosophical discourse, the relationships between philosophical doctrine and revealed faith became more complex. This is reflected to some extent in the emergence of the three major medieval philosophical schools in Islam, which were subsequently carried over into Jewish theological thought.

Jewish Kalam

The Arabic word "Kalam" (like its Greek cognate "logos") indicates both verbal speech and rational thought. Historians of religious thought often classify Kalam as a form of "theology" rather than a "philosophy." The difference between the two terms lies in the fact that *Kalam* is ultimately based on a revealed tradition, rather than on independent logical or scientific demonstration. For the theologian, Reason is not the final arbiter of truth. It is subordinated to the teachings of the revealed religion as they are embodied in the prophetic scriptures or oral traditions. After a person has acknowledged the truth of the traditional religious doctrines, the methods of rational and scientific analysis may be applied to them in order to clarify them, and in order to resolve apparent contradictions.

The most influential school of Muslim Kalam, known as the *Mu'atazila*, were known as "the people of unity and justice" because their works dealt with two central issues.

1. Divine unity as understood by medieval rationalists referred to the doctrine that, as a uniquely non-material and eternal being, God cannot be subdivided even conceptually into multiple components. Kalam theologians therefore had

to carefully study their scriptures, which ascribe numerous "attributes" to God, and explain how these attributes should not be understood as literally implying multiplicity in the deity.

2. The issue of divine justice, in the discourse of the *Mu'atazila*, was equated with the problem of human free will. Notwithstanding the many texts in the Qur'an or Bible that play down human power in the face of God's absolute power, they argued that belief in just retribution presupposes that humans have the ability to choose between good and evil.

The most eminent Jewish exponent of the Kalam school was Rabbi Saadiah Gaon (Cairo and Baghdad, tenth century). His theological treatise, *The Book of Doctrines and Opinions*, was composed in Arabic. In addition to the standard Kalamic sections about God's unity and attributes, and on divine justice and human free will, Saadiah provided systematic discussions of several cardinal Jewish beliefs, including prophecy, the divine origins of the Torah, creation out of nothing, the messianic era, the afterlife, and ethics. He was interested in the nature of human knowledge, and in justifying the application of reason to religious belief.

As a school of Jewish theology, Kalam was eventually superseded among Rabbinite Jews by Aristotelianism. However, it continued to enjoy popularity among the Karaites.

Neoplatonism

Though the word "Neoplatonism" contains the name of the ancient Greek philosopher Plato, the doctrines of this school are quite different from those expounded by Plato. The Neoplatonic school developed in the third century, under the influence of doctrines expounded in the *Enneads* by the Alexandrian philosopher Plotinus. Other influential Neoplatonists included Porphyry (*c.* 232–*c.* 304) and Proclus (*c.* 410–485). It was an otherworldly philosophy that attracted a large following in the early Christian church. The central concern of Neoplatonism was the relationship between the One spiritual deity, and the material, heterogeneous world. They found it all but impossible to account for how a God who is entirely abstract could have created a world that is so unlike himself in its nature. The difference was not only one of substance, but also of quality, because the Neoplatonists regarded all manifestations of physicality as essentially corrupt. Proponents of Neoplatonism leaned towards dualism, in the sense that they viewed life as an eternal battle between the spirit and the flesh.

Like most schools of ancient philosophy (and unlike most of our contemporary philosophy departments), Neoplatonism was more than a theoretical system. Out of its doctrines emerged a distinctive way of life and perspective towards the world. Its concern, which at times seems almost obsessive, with contemplating God's ultimate unity and spirituality made Neoplatonism into an intensely mystical world-view. Having mapped out intricate stages in the emanation of the divine radiance, the philosophers would also strive, through the regimen of contemplation, to return to that perfect source of light. As a religious way of life, Neoplatonism's dualistic outlook also made demands on the moral behavior of its adherents. It called for the liberation of the soul from the bonds of the physical body, in preparation for a spiritual ascent towards mystical union with absolute spirit. This kind of dualism was a departure from the normal attitudes of Jewish spirituality. In the Bible and Talmud, the material world is embraced as a divine creation that partakes of God's goodness. The centrality of law to Judaism presupposes involvement with the material and social worlds as a religious obligation, and not merely as a reluctant compromise with circumstances.

> The struggle between the spirit and the flesh became a popular theme of moralistic treatises, many of which were written from a Neoplatonic perspective. To some extent, all the medieval rationalistic streams, not only Neoplatonism, accepted a version of dualistic values, because they concurred in equating the ultimate goal of life with abstract intellectualism.

The Neoplatonic movement attracted a diverse assortment of Jewish exponents. The eleventh-century Spanish poet and thinker Solomon Ibn Gabirol composed an Arabic treatise entitled *Mekor Hayyim* (Hebrew for "source of life"), a Neoplatonic dialogue that became influential among Christian theologians in its Latin translation as *Fons Vitae*. The Arabic original was lost, and because the work was so universalistic in its tone, the author's Jewish identity remained unknown until the nineteenth century. Ibn Gabirol was best known to Jews for his moving religious and liturgical poetry in Hebrew. His *Keter Malkhut* (*Royal Crown*) is a deeply mystical praise of God that incorporates Neoplatonic themes.

The eleventh-century Spanish moralist and philosopher Bahya Ibn Paquda was the author of the Arabic treatise *Duties of the Heart* that became a classic of Jewish devotional literature. The title is based on the book's main theme, the contrast between the "duties of the limbs"—the physical performance of the commandments and regulations of Jewish law—and the "duties of the heart"—the proper beliefs and moral qualities that constitute the higher goal of a true religious life.

Though the Jewish Neoplatonic movement was largely displaced by Aristotelianism, many of its themes, particularly the detailed mapping of the emanations between the unknown God and the physical universe, would continue to exert an influence on Judaism in the guise of Kabbalah.

Aristotelianism

It is impossible to study the immense corpus of Aristotle's works without being astounded at both the breadth and depth of his accomplishment, which includes fundamental studies of science, logic, metaphysics and ethics. While he impresses us today as a diligent and brilliant scientist and thinker, in the eyes of the medievals Aristotle had a superhuman stature. It was believed that his philosophy embodied the ultimate intellectual achievement that can be attained without the aid of a supernatural revelation. For many European thinkers well into modern times, good science was measured more by its fidelity to Aristotle's writings than by the independent application of scientific methods. This is of course a deviation from Aristotle's own philosophy, which was firmly grounded in empirical observation and logical analysis.

Central to the Aristotelian world-view was his perception of the world as a combination of *matter* and *form*. Normally the two components cannot exist independently of one another. "Hylic" matter is a theoretical construction that refers to the generic substratum of all physical objects. In our world, matter never appears in its hylic stage, but is always stamped with a form. The form is what gives an object its distinctive qualities. Although in contemporary thought we are accustomed to think of matter as what is stable and permanent in the world, the Greek rationalist tradition took the opposite view: all matter is by definition ephemeral and transient, subject to degeneration and entropy. Ultimately, it is the realm of abstract ideas, which are not dependent on perishable matter, that is eternal. This approach permeates all the philosophical and religious writings of the medieval era.

As viewed by the medieval Aristotelians, the universe is a sequence of concentric spheres with our world at its center. Between the outermost sphere, the home of the "fixed stars" (the majority of stars visible in the night sky), and our world extends a series of "separate intelligences." These entities, consisting of form without matter, were identified with the sun, moon and planets, all of which were believed to orbit around our world. The separate intelligences are eternal disembodied minds that contemplate God free from the distractions to which material bodies are susceptible. In a manner similar to the Neoplatonists, the spirituality of the separate intelligences was believed to diminish in proportion to their distance from the divine source. The religious traditions believed that the separate intelligences are what the Bible was speaking of when it referred to "angels."

Aristotle believed that the universe was eternal, meaning that there was never a time in which matter did not exist. This doctrine conflicted with the traditional Jewish belief that God created the world out of nothing, at a particular point in time. This presented a major problem for the medieval Aristotelians, who also accepted the authority of their scriptures. Although the question was dealt with in diverse ways, the prevailing tendency among Jewish philosophers was to reject the Aristotelian position in favor of the traditional biblical view.

In the Aristotelian cosmological scheme, the lowest of the separate intelligences was identified with the moon, the heavenly body that is nearest to our world. Unlike any of the higher levels, our "sublunary" world is the domain of matter. It is made up of the four elements: air, fire, water and earth. It is through different combinations of the four basic elements that all material substances are created.

When we study the writings of the medieval Jewish philosophers, whether from the Neoplatonist or the Aristotelian streams, we become aware that a profound transformation has taken place in the relationship between philosophy and religion. In significant ways, it is philosophy that is now defining the goals and agendas of religious life. Whereas the Bible and Talmud emphasized that goodness and holiness lie in the scrupulous observance of God's law, as embodied in the Torah and the oral tradition, as an expression of loving devotion to "the holy one blessed be he," the philosophers were insisting that ultimate human perfection can be achieved only through the practice of philosophy. We are urged to pursue a course of intellectual development that proceeds through the natural sciences and logic, to bring us closer to an understanding of the universe's creator, who is eternal, perfect, and utterly dissimilar to the created world. The contemplation of abstract ideas will lead us to an understanding of the most sublime and abstract of all ideas, that of God himself. All of one's life should be directed to that single goal.

In this scheme, the acceptance of the Torah's laws was no longer an objective in its own right. Their purpose was only to provide a vehicle for the attainment of the higher, philosophical, goal. For Jewish Aristotelians, the Torah was the most effective means of achieving this perfection, by laying the groundwork for a peaceful society, by teaching us to discipline our physical appetites (which divert the mind from its proper intellectual pursuits), and by instilling a spiritual understanding of God.

Traditional Judaism imposes its demands on all segments of the community, setting expectations that are, in principle, attainable by everybody. The rationalist outlook was considerably less optimistic about most people's prospects for attaining spiritual perfection. Most medieval philosophical works are acutely conscious of an unbridgeable chasm between the small intellectual elite and the bulk of simple folk who are doomed to remain in their state of ignorance. Some writers merely dismiss these uneducated masses with disdain, while others note that they have a valuable role to play in providing the material conditions that allow the elite to pursue their philosophical studies. Medieval Aristotelians believed that those few who succeeded in purifying their intellects will be able to link their thoughts to the lowest of the separate intelligences, which is designated the "active intellect." At this point, the human "potential intellect" becomes transformed into the "acquired intellect." Some thinkers equated this state, characterized by the pure intellectual contemplation of eternal truths, with the traditional Jewish concept of the afterlife. Those individuals who are capable of reaching that state in their lifetimes are said to be gifted with the powers of prophetic revelation.

The first known medieval Jewish Aristotelian was the Spanish Rabbi Abraham Ibn Daud (1110–1180). However, the dominant figure in Jewish Aristotelianism was Moses Maimonides who also made such a magnificent contribution to the codification of Jewish religious law. Although he spent most of his life in Egypt, Maimonides was deeply rooted in the Jewish culture of Andalusia. His philosophical system, as found especially in his *Guide of the Perplexed*, became the standard statement of medieval Jewish rationalism, and most subsequent philosophical works were either commentaries or criticisms of Maimonides' system.

Maimonides included an outline of rational theology as the first section of his code of law, establishing thereby that the acquisition of correct doctrine was the most important goal of Judaism. This bold and unprecedented intrusion of philosophy into a compendium on rabbinic law angered many people. They protested, not without justification, that Maimonides was subordinating the God-given faith of Israel to Greek heresies.

Indeed, the philosophers had to justify their claims, not only that philosophy was not alien to Judaism, but also that it expressed the essential core values that underlie the biblical and rabbinic traditions. Maimonides addressed his *Guide of the Perplexed* to just such an individual, who was torn by the ostensible need to choose between Judaism and philosophy.

> The popular medieval legend held that Aristotle was a disciple of Jeremiah. The implication of such tales was that Greek philosophy was not a foreign ideology that had been artificially grafted onto authentic Jewish tradition; rather, Jewish rationalists claimed to be recovering a precious part of their own inheritance.

The question still remained, however: if philosophical speculation is really native to Judaism, then why do we not encounter traces of it in the classical texts of traditional Judaism? Maimonides responded to those objections by insisting that indeed, the doctrines of Aristotelian philosophy were well known to the talmudic sages, but they were not disseminated publicly.

Central to this argument is a passage in the Mishnah that singles out two bodies of teaching that may not be taught publicly. One of these is termed "the account of creation," and evidently deals with expositions of the opening chapters of Genesis, describing how God created the world. Another, called "the account of the chariot," focuses on the mystical vision of the prophet Ezekiel (found in the opening chapters of the book of Ezekiel) in which the prophet beheld an image of God seated on a magnificent throne borne aloft by a chariot of angelic beings. Because the Mishnah forbade the open teaching of these subjects, the ancient Jewish sources do not preserve much information about the contents of those teachings. The little that has been preserved from talmudic discussions about the "account of creation" indicates that the rabbis were interested in some of the same issues that crop up in medieval cosmology, such as whether the world was created out of nothing or out of some primordial matter. The "account of the chariot" was evidently a form of mystical experience in which the student tried to emulate the experience of Ezekiel in a spiritual ascent through the highest spiritual realms. Maimonides and other medieval Jewish philosophers insisted that the scientific and rationalistic teachings that they were including in their own works were identical with the "account of creation" and "account of the chariot." Maimonides identifies the "account of creation" as natural science, and "the account of the chariot" as metaphysics.

This argument invites the retort: if the Mishnah states that these topics are not to be taught publicly, what right do you have to publish books about it, and even to include it in your comprehensive code of Jewish religious law? The talmudic discussions imply that the study of these subjects presents tangible dangers to students who do not have the appropriate moral or spiritual qualifications. Rabbinic tradition told of students who lost their sanity or their lives, or abandoned Judaism, as a consequence of their pursuit of esoteric wisdom. The dangers of heresy or apostasy were particularly threatening to medieval Jews, and there were solid grounds for their fears that, by subjecting the Bible and the teachings of the rabbis to critical scientific and philosophical analysis, they would come to question the fundamental beliefs of Judaism.

Maimonides responded to these challenges by insisting that he was not really teaching these topics publicly. The snippets of cosmology and metaphysics that he included in his commentary to the Mishnah and in the *Mishneh Torah* were nothing more than a superficial introduction to the relevant teachings. As for the *Guide of the Perplexed*, Maimonides designed its format so that it would conform to the Mishnah's stricture: "The chariot may not be expounded even to a lone student, unless he is wise and capable of understanding on his own." The Talmud permitted the teacher to entrust to such a student the "chapter headings" of the account of the chariot. Accordingly, Maimonides claimed that his own work did not go beyond the minimal chapter headings, and that its full implications would not be appreciated or understood by the casual reader. Only those gifted students who approached the *Guide of the Perplexed* after a suitable apprenticeship in religious and scientific disciplines, and paid careful attention to every word, would be able to extract from it the full significance of its teachings. To others it would seem like cryptic nonsense, and they would soon lose interest.

The external structure of the *Guide* seems to substantiate Maimonides's claim. When we consider that Maimonides was arguably the most systematic author in Jewish history, the one who had succeeded in bringing logical order to the chaos of Jewish legal literature, the disorderly nature of the *Guide* strikes us as extraordinary. We often have the impression that Maimonides shuffled the chapters into an arbitrary order—and this is precisely the impression that he was trying to create. Because the presentation is not sequential, the readers will often find themselves reading about topics that have not yet been introduced.

The editorial policy of the *Guide* has been interpreted in varying ways by scholars. Some maintain that Maimonides was merely trying to get around the technical prohibitions against publicly teaching esoteric subjects, but once we have exerted ourselves to read and reread his text and to ponder its ideas, the *Guide* can be read in a relatively conventional way. Others, however, insist that Maimonides was aware that his philosophy could lead to subversive and heretical conclusions, and that he personally accepted those conclusions. Therefore, his true opinions are not stated explicitly in the book, but rather they must be deduced by the ingenious reader. The conservative religious society of the medieval era would not countenance open heresy of the kind that is immanent in Maimonides's philosophy, and therefore he was forced to conceal his true opinions under a veritable cloak of conventional religious language. Manuscript discoveries during recent generations have provided us with an intimate portrait of Maimonides's personality and communal involvement. The image that emerges from those documents, as well as from the years that he devoted to works on Jewish law, does not readily support the portrayal of Maimonides as a radical freethinker who was paying lip service to traditional Judaism. At any rate, the fact that the matter is still being argued in scholarly circles offers profound testimony to the enigmatic character of the *Guide of the Perplexed*.

Abraham Abulafia's mystical path

According to the medieval philosophical schools, it is by refining one's intellect, in order to allow it to contemplate concepts and ideas that are completely abstracted from physicality, that humans are able to connect to the angelic "intelligences" that serve as intermediaries between the material and spiritual realms. For the philosopher, this goal is achieved by pursuing a demanding regimen of moral discipline, scientific study and metaphysical speculation. The ultimate goal of such contemplation is knowledge of God, a being who is totally unlike anything that we experience on the physical plane, a being who is absolutely one, eternal and all-powerful. In the Aristotelian version of this theory, the select few who succeed in this spiritual and intellectual quest are deemed worthy of joining their minds with the "active intellect" and being filled with a supernatural wisdom that is the essence of prophecy.

Some students of Maimonides' philosophy became fixated on the achievement of the mystical objectives of his system, of arriving at an intimate encounter with God or the higher metaphysical forces. The thirteenth-century Spanish writer Abraham Abulafia developed an alternative route that could lead people to the experience of prophecy.

Abulafia concluded that metaphysical study was not the only path through which the mind could be liberated from the sensual and material thoughts that prevent us from knowing God. He believed that the same result could be accomplished, perhaps more effectively, by following the opposite course, by *emptying* the mind of any coherent thought, and thereby making it receptive to the divine influences that will flow into it. Towards this end, Abulafia formulated a mystical discipline that was founded chiefly on the contemplation of meaningless combinations of Hebrew letters. He referred to his system as the "science of combination." The focus of the contemplation was often the Hebrew names of God, though ultimately these names are deconstructed into individual letters that are reordered into endless permutations until that they are completely emptied of rational content.

We are not certain to what degree Abulafia's method was derived from earlier models. Some elements resemble those of various Jewish mystical schools. Possible non-Jewish influences on Abulafia might include the Muslim Sufi mystics, or the tradition of mystical contemplation known as Hesychasm that was cultivated by Byzantine Christian monks. Some scholars have remarked on the uncanny similarities between Abulafia's methods and those of yoga, which he could have known from the extensive oriental commerce that existed at that time. For all his eclecticism, Abulafia regarded himself as a loyal follower of Maimonides.

Judah Halevi

Rabbi Judah Halevi does not easily fit into the threefold classification of Kalam, Neoplatonist and Aristotelian. A native of Toledo Spain (*c.* 1075–*c.* 1141), his Arabic treatise on Judaism, the *Kuzari*, was a protest against the rationalist interpretation of Judaism, in spite of the fact that it was written by a scholar who had mastered that interpretation.

Outwardly, Halevi embodied all the skills and qualities that we normally associate with the "Golden Age" of Spanish Jewry in the eleventh and twelfth centuries. He had a prosperous medical practice, and was accomplished in the Arabic language (the language in which he composed his *Kuzari*), in philosophy, medicine and astronomy. In a culture that produced outstanding Hebrew poets, it is widely held that Judah Halevi was the finest Hebrew poet of the age, perhaps of all times.

During Halevi's lifetime, several crises were shaking the foundations of Jewish life in Spain and other lands. Andalusia was invaded by a militant Muslim dynasty known as the Almovarids, and the Crusader victories in the Holy Land had virtually eliminated the Jewish presence there. These events appear to have convinced him that there was something illusory about the prospect that Jews could enjoy long-term security or prosperity while they remained in the state of exile. The tolerant universalism of the Arab civilization was proving to be very fragile, and Jews ought to acknowledge the particularism of their religious beliefs, their homeland and their distinctive historical experience. Halevi's most moving poems were the "odes to Zion" in which his longing to tread the soil of the holy city is fed by the agony of exile. In the end, he abandoned his comfortable existence in Spain and set off to fulfill his dream. Recently discovered documents have confirmed that he did ultimately reach his destination.

Halevi's philosophical masterpiece, the *Kuzari: The Book of Argument and Proof in Defense of the Despised Faith*, was based on an intriguing episode in medieval Jewish history, the conversion to Judaism in the eighth century of the Khazars, a nation who lived in the Volga basin. The awareness that there existed an independent state of Jewish warriors was of immense importance for Jewish dignity, and kindled the people's imaginations. Not long before Halevi's time, a correspondence had taken place between the Spanish Jewish courtier Hisdai Ibn Shaprut and the Khazar King Joseph.

The *Kuzari* uses as its narrative basis the story of the original conversion of the Khazar monarch. It opens with the king's decision (inspired by a dream) to seek out the most acceptable religion. After consulting with a philosopher, a Christian and a Muslim he finds serious weaknesses in all three creeds. Because he observes that both the religious representatives claim to be rooted in the traditions of the Jews, the king calls in the Jewish scholar. The king is persuaded by the superiority of Judaism, and they conduct a lengthy and convivial discussion about aspects of the Jewish religion.

Unlike most Jewish philosophers of his time, who presented Judaism as the perfect embodiment of rational theology, Halevi stressed the importance of historical revelation, arguing that Judaism's superiority lies precisely in the fact that its prophetically revealed faith was transmitted accurately from generation to generation. By contrast, the philosophers' claims that they can attain irrefutable metaphysical knowledge are illusory, and Halevi subjects them to incisive criticism and ridicule.

Halevi rejected the philosophers' conviction that the goal of religion is an intellectual understanding of God. He believed that the primary religious urge is not expressed through the intellect, but through a distinctive religious faculty that has been implanted in humans. For Halevi, this spiritual spark, which was possessed by the very first man, was in the end inherited only by the Jewish nation. Its cultivation is at once the goal and the result of observing the precepts of the Torah, and is most successfully accomplished in the climate of the land of Israel.

Key points you need to know

- The translation of Greek philosophical texts into Arabic stimulated a new synthesis of rationalism and traditional Judaism. There were three principal schools of medieval Jewish rationalism: Kalam (theology), Neoplatonism and Aristotelianism.
- Abraham Abulafia formulated a mystical path based on Maimonidean premisses, but without the need for extensive intellectual preparation.

Discussion questions

1. If the philosopher (as distinct from the theologian) does not presuppose the truth of the revealed religious tradition, then does it really make sense to speak of "Jewish philosophy"?
2. For what reasons did some people fear that the study of philosophy could be hazardous if pursued by those with inadequate intellectual preparation?

Further reading

Philosophy: general

Guttmann, Julius, *Philosophies of Judaism: The History of Jewish Philosophy from Biblical Times to Franz Rosenzweig.* 1st Schocken paperback ed., New York: Schocken, 1973.

Husik, Isaac, *A History of Mediaeval Jewish Philosophy.* Jewish Publication Society Series, New York: Meridian Books and The Jewish Publication Society of America, 1960.

Katz, Steven T., ed., *Jewish Philosophers.* New York: Bloch, 1975.

Kellner, Menachem Marc, *Dogma in Medieval Jewish Thought: from Maimonides to Abravanel.* Oxford: Oxford University Press, 1986.

Sirat, Colette, *A History of Jewish Philosophy in the Middle Ages.* Cambridge, New York and Paris: Cambridge University Press and Editions de la Maison des Sciences de l'Homme, 1985.

Samuelson, Norbert M., "Medieval Jewish Philosophy," in *Back to the Sources: Reading the Classic Jewish Texts.* Edited by B. W. Holtz. New York: Summit Books, 1984.

Kalam

Cohen, Boaz, ed., *Saadiah Anniversary Volume, Artech House ITS Series.* New York: Jewish Publication Society of America, 1943.

Malter, Henry, *Saadiah Gaon: His Life and Works*. New York: Hermon Press, 1969.

Rosenblatt, Samuel, *The Book of Beliefs and Opinions, Yale Judaica Series*. New Haven, CT: Yale University Press, 1967.

Zeitlin, Solomon and Abraham A. Neuman, eds, *Saadiah Studies*. Philadelphia, PA: Dropsie College for Hebrew and Cognate Learning, 1943.

Neoplatonism

Bahya ben Joseph ibn, Pakuda, *The Book of Direction to the Duties of the Heart, from the Original Arabic Version of Bahya ben Joseph Ibn Paquda's al-Hidaya ila Fara'id al-Qulub*. Translated by M. Mansoor, Littman Library of Jewish Civilization. London: Routledge & Kegan Paul, 1973.

Goodman, Lenn Evan, *Neoplatonism and Jewish Thought, Studies in Neoplatonism*. Albany, NY: State University of New York Press, 1992.

Aristotelianism

Sarachek, Joseph, *Faith and Reason: The Conflict over the Rationalism of Maimonides, Oriental series*. Williamsport, PA: Bayard Press, 1935.

Silver, Daniel Jeremy, *Maimonidean Criticism and the Maimonidean Controversy, 1180–1240*. Leiden: E.J. Brill, 1965.

Maimonides

Davidson, Herbert A., "The Study of Philosophy as a Religious Obligation." In *Religion in a Religious Age*. Edited by S. D. Goitein, 53–68. Cambridge, MA: Association for Jewish Studies, 1974.

Dienstag, Jacob Israel, *Studies in Maimonides and St. Thomas Aquinas*. Bibliotheca Maimonidica; V. 1. [New York].

Faur, José, *Golden Doves with Silver Dots: Semiotics and Textuality in Rabbinic Tradition*, South Florida Studies in the History of Judaism. Atlanta, GA: Scholars Press, 1999.

Goodman, Lenn Evan, ed., *Rambam: Readings in the Philosophy of Moses Maimonides*, The Jewish Heritage Classics. New York: Viking, 1976.

Hartman, David, *Maimonides: Torah and Philosophic Quest*. Philadelphia, PA: Jewish Publication Society of America, 1977.

Heschel, Abraham Joshua, *Maimonides: A Biography*. Translated by Joachim Neugroschel. New York: Farrer Straus Giroux, 1982.

Maimonides, Moses, *The Guide for the Perplexed*. Translated by Michael Friedländer. 2nd, revised ed., London and New York: George Routledge & Sons and E. P. Dutton, 1904.

——— *The Guide of the Perplexed*. Translated by Shlomo Pines. Chicago, IL: University of Chicago Press, 1963.

Strauss, Leo, *Philosophy and Law: Essays Toward the Understanding of Maimonides and His Predecessors*. Translated by Fred Baumann. Philadelphia, PA: Jewish Publication Society, 1987.

Abraham Abulafia

Idel, Moshe, *The Mystical Experience in Abraham Abulafia*, SUNY Series in Judaica. Albany, NY: State University of New York Press, 1988.

Wolfson, Elliot R., *Abraham Abulafia—Kabbalist and Prophet: Hermeneutics, Theosophy and Theurgy*, Sources and Studies in the Literature of Jewish Mysticism. Los Angeles, CA: Cherub Press, 2000.

Judah Halevi

Hallevi, Judah, *The Kuzari (Kitab al Khazari): An Argument for the Faith of Israel*. Translated by H. Hirschfeld. New York: Schocken, 1964.

Strauss, Leo, "The Law of Reason in the Kuzari." *Proceedings of the American Academy for Jewish Research* 13 (1943): 47–96.

6 *Kabbalah*

In this chapter

The Kabbalah is an interpretation of Judaism that arose in medieval times, though it claimed to be an ancient teaching transmitted esoterically from biblical times. What set Kabbalah apart from other Jewish religious ideologies was not so much its mystical character as its distinctive doctrine of ten *sefirot*—emanated divine powers—that served as a key to understanding the secret meaning of the Bible, a way of understanding how God created and continues to govern the world, and as a practical guide for humans to influence the metaphysical realms through their observance of the Torah's commandments. Drawing from earlier Jewish movements, such as the talmudic Chariot mystics and the medieval German Jewish pietists, the first known kabbalistic text is the enigmatic *Bahir*, a small book composed in the style of an ancient midrash, which interprets biblical passages in a novel manner. We possess no evidence of the evolution of the *sefirot* system before its appearance in the *Bahir*.

The subtle kabbalistic hermeneutic technique allowed virtually every word in the Bible to be identified with one or other of the *sefirot*. Innocent-seeming nouns like "water," "silver" or "hand" were all candidates for this kind of interpretation. The upshot of this method is that, though the kabbalist and non-kabbalist were reading precisely the same scriptures, they understood them in radically different ways. For the kabbalist, the Bible is an intricately coded account of the metaphysical unfolding of the universe. This would apply equally to kabbalistic discourses on any verse in any book of the Bible.

During the generations following its publication, the ideas of the *Bahir* were elaborated by schools of esoteric scholars in Provence (southern France) and Gerona in Catalonia (Spain). The most revered classic of kabbalistic teaching was the *Zohar*, produced in the late thirteenth century by Rabbi Moses de Leon of Guadalajara, Spain. The *Zohar* takes the form of a rabbinic midrash composed by a circle of students attached to the Tanna Rabbi Simeon ben Yohai who delight each other with interpretations that uncover secret meanings in the Bible based on the symbolism of the ten *sefirot*. Subsequent authors composed similar works that were appended to the original core of the *Zohar*. Some of these works took a more aggressive stance in claiming that Kabbalah is the only legitimate system for understanding Judaism. In the sixteenth century, Rabbi Isaac Luria formulated a brilliant and complex version of kabbalistic teachings. The eschatological elements of Luria's doctrine inspired several kabbalistic messianic movements, of which the most important was that of Shabbetai Zevi in the seventeenth century. A popular version of Kabbalah was developed in Eastern Europe in the eighteenth century under the charismatic inspiration of Rabbi Israel Ba'al Shem Tov. The Ba'al Shem Tov advocated an intuitive mystical devotion based on awareness of God's love, as an alternative to the arid talmudic scholarship and meticulous adherence to Jewish law that defined religiosity for the conventional rabbinic leadership. Later generations of Hasidic teachers cultivated a model of charismatic leadership (*zaddik*), producing a fascinating range of powerful and individual personalities who served as foci for the simple Jewish masses.

Main topics covered

- The general character of Kabbalah as an esoteric interpretation of the Torah
- The sources of Kabbalah: Chariot mysticism, medieval German pietism (*Hasidut Ashkenaz*)
- The *Bahir*: the first known kabbalistic text
- The spread of the Kabbalah to Provence and Gerona
- The *Zohar*
- Supplements to the *Zohar*: the *Ra'aya Meheimna* and the *Tikkunim*
- The system of Rabbi Isaac Luria
- Shabbetai Zevi and kabbalistic messianic movements
- Rabbi Israel Ba'al Shem Tov and the Hasidic movement

The religious outlook known in Hebrew as Kabbalah was one of the most ambitious creations of medieval Jewish spirituality. Its elaborate symbolic restatement of Judaism was able to integrate within itself many elements from the other forms of Judaism, whether from the classical biblical and talmudic traditions or from contemporary trends in philosophy and exegesis.

The Hebrew word *Kabbalah* derives from a root meaning "receive." It is one of many Hebrew terms that can designate the process or content of tradition. "Kabbalah" was not the only term that was used to identify this particular set of esoteric doctrines, nor is it the one that is most frequently encountered in older texts. At any rate, the equation of Kabbalah with a received tradition calls our attention to one of the more intriguing and problematic aspects of the kabbalists' own self-image: they insisted that they were transmitting an ancient tradition—

indeed, the true and original tradition of how to correctly understand the revelations of the written and oral Torahs. Though the public appearance of the Kabbalah might have been delayed until the Middle Ages, the kabbalists claimed that its contents had been transmitted orally from teacher to student since the earliest times. Indeed, the kabbalists would insist that their teachings constituted the original understanding of revelation that had been given to Moses, if not to Adam. This attitude also accounts for the fact that central texts of the Kabbalah were pseudepigraphic, presented as ancient midrashic commentaries composed by the rabbis of the talmudic age.

> Like some of the medieval Jewish philosophers, the kabbalists justified their claim to historical authenticity by maintaining that their doctrines were the true embodiment of the "work of the chariot" and "work of creation" that were enigmatically mentioned in the Mishnah as topics of esoteric spiritual study.

German pietism (Hasidut Ashkenaz)

An influential pre-kabbalistic mystical stream that may have contributed to the emergence of Kabbalah was the movement known as *Hasidut Ashkenaz*. The Hebrew word *Hasid* (pious) has been applied to several different Jewish religious movements in ancient, medieval and modern times. The movement described here flourished in central Europe during the twelfth and thirteenth centuries. *Hasidut Ashkenaz* was not primarily a mystical movement. It had an eclectic quality that attempted to encompass diverse expressions of Judaism. Mysticism was one of several elements that the pietists incorporated into their variegated outlook.

For the most part, what distinguished the German Jewish pietists was their ideal of an uncompromising ascetic morality in which physical pleasures are rejected in favor of spiritual goals. They were distinguished by an intense sensitivity to impurity, and introduced severe strictures to Jewish religious practice based on their determination to avoid pollution related to sexual activity, menstruation, and so forth.

The main literary record of their ideals is the *Sefer Hasidim*, the *Book of the Pious*, composed by Rabbi Judah ben Samuel the Pious (died in 1217) and probably completed by others after his death. *Sefer Hasidim* is a kind of scrapbook that assembles hundreds of instructions, anecdotes and interpretations that were designed to illustrate the religious teachings of the movement. Its emphasis is not on theology or theoretical ideals, but on providing practical models for day-to-day behavior. Historians believe that their ideal of single-minded spiritual devotion inspired Jews to submit to martyrdom rather than abandon their ancestral faith in times of persecution, especially during the Crusades. Though the pietists regarded themselves as a spiritual elite and they imposed upon themselves demands that went beyond the norms of formal Jewish law, their influence among the broader Jewish public was nevertheless considerable, and several of their distinctive customs were incorporated into the mainstream practice of Ashkenazic Jewry. Indeed, *Sefer Hasidim* speaks very disdainfully of simple Jews who do not aspire to higher goals. Many of the most revered talmudic scholars in Germany were attached to the *Hasidut Ashkenaz* movement. On the other hand, there are features of the pietistic ideology that are critical of scholasticism, which they regarded as overly academic and not sufficiently concerned with moral and spiritual matters.

Much of the spiritual activity of the German pietists was devoted to meditations on the Hebrew liturgy. The recitation of uniform prayers several times each day can make it very difficult to concentrate on their meaning, and the *Hasidei Ashkenaz* labored hard to imbue the words with profound meaning. Towards that end, they made extensive use of number mysticism, carefully counting the words and the numerological values of the letters, in order to extract meaningful patterns and interrelationships between texts. They believed that the authors of the traditional prayers had carefully weighed and chosen every letter in accordance with their esoteric significance. A special tradition of mystical interpretation of the prayers was in the possession of the Kalonymus dynasty, a family of distinguished scholars who had branches in several Jewish centers in Germany, Italy and elsewhere. Several important Spanish rabbis of the fourteenth century pursued studies in Germany, resulting in a powerful influence of *Hasidut Ashkenaz* on Sephardic teachers. This influence found expression in the adoption by Spanish communities of German liturgical customs, as well as in the spread of mystical texts and doctrines.

There are indications that members of the movement were in possession of books, and perhaps oral traditions, of unknown origin, evidently from Babylonia, that preserved otherwise lost teachings about the process of divine emanation. It is possible that sometime during the latter half of the twelfth century, these traditions were brought from Germany to Provence, where they furnished the foundation of the earliest know work of the Kabbalah, the *Bahir*.

The **Bahir**

The small volume that is usually designated the *Bahir* (from a Hebrew word for brightness) takes the form of a midrashic exposition from the talmudic era. Like ancient midrashic compilations, it collects sayings by assorted rabbis. Some of the rabbis whose names appear in the *Bahir* are known from the Talmud, but several seem to have been invented. Medieval writers often referred to the work as "the Midrash of Rabbi Nehunya ben ha-Kanah."

Rabbi Nehunya was a rabbi who appears very occasionally in the Talmud, always in connection with conventional discussions of Jewish religious law. There is no indication that the original Rabbi Nehunya had any involvement with esoteric lore. The fact that he was given a prominent role in the *Bahir* probably derives from the unusual, even mysterious, character of his patronym, which translates literally as "son of the reed."

The text seems incomplete. It will often commence an exposition of a topic, move on to a digression, and never return to complete the argument. Our copies of the *Bahir* may derive from a fragmentary manuscript, or perhaps it was never completed by its author; however, the text was in the same state from as far back as we can trace it, and none of the medieval writers who cite it seem to have possessed a more complete version than we do.

The *Bahir* made its first known appearance in Provence where it was studied as a treatise on the account of the chariot, though its theoretical presentation of the process of creation by means of the sefirot was obviously very different from the mystical ascents that were the usual subject matter of the older Heikhalot texts that described ascents through celestial "palaces." Some of the *Bahir*'s themes are very close to those of Gnosticism. The affinity is particularly striking in matters involving the emanation of divine powers (which the Gnostics referred to as *aeons*) out of the supreme deity, and the belief that sparks of divinity are scattered among the lower realms, though, to be sure, the latter image is found in talmudic literature. The precise connection between Gnosticism and the Kabbalah cannot be determined with certainty. There is evidence that a Jewish gnostic tradition, originating in the Middle East, reached the circles of Hasidut Ashkenaz in the form of a work known as *Raza Rabba* (The Great Mystery) that is cited by some of the German Jewish mystics, and which resembles some passages in the *Bahir*. Scholars have also sought a link between early kabbalistic themes and the ideas of the Cathari, a dualistic Christian heresy that became very influential in southern France around the eleventh century, and was the object of a genocidal crusade by the Catholic church in the early thirteenth century; however, no substantial parallels have yet been discovered between the beliefs of the two movements. The kabbalists claimed that they were expounding an ancient Jewish doctrine that had been transmitted secretly over the generations; and while such claims must be treated with great suspicion, the possibility that Kabbalah originated in an older Jewish gnostic school cannot be dismissed entirely.

The earliest known schools of kabbalists were found in various centers in Provence in the middle and late twelfth century. The ideas and activities of these individuals have survived only in the most fragmentary form, a fact that testifies to the seriousness with which they observed the prohibitions against public dissemination of esoteric lore. Some of the names of these kabbalists are little more than legends that were preserved by later generations. One such figure was Rabbi Isaac the Blind, whose father was Rabbi Abraham ben David, the renowned Talmudist best known for his critical glosses on Maimonides' *Mishneh Torah*. From the little that has survived of his teachings, he appears to have attempted to synthesize the *sefirot* theory of the *Bahir* with the emanation theories of Neoplatonism.

Shortly afterwards, the center of kabbalistic activities shifted to Gerona in Catalonia. It is here that we find the first initiatives to publish their ideas, and the works produced by that community took a variety of forms, including commentaries on talmudic passages, treatises on specific topics (for example, the true significance of sacrifices), discourses on the proper intentions for prayers, and so forth. Their most prominent representative was Rabbi Moses Nahmanides (Ramban), who aroused controversy when he incorporated kabbalistic materials into his influential commentary to the Torah. Nahmanides' prestige as one of the leading authorities on Jewish law and talmudic interpretation, and as one of the foremost defenders of religious conservatism, went a long way toward facilitating the acceptance of Kabbalah as a legitimate expression of orthodox Jewish tradition.

The importance of the *Bahir* lies in the fact that it marks the first appearance of the distinctive kabbalistic doctrine of the ten *sefirot*. The theological significance of this doctrine will be discussed in later chapters in connection with Jewish beliefs about God. At this point we it will suffice to mention that the *sefirot* represent ten aspects of God, using terms that are familiar from traditional Jewish writings. The kabbalists understood these attributes as metaphysical entities, and their complex interrelationships are revealed in the words of the Bible, provided that one knows how to read the text according to its esoteric sense.

There now follows a list of the ten kabbalistic *sefirot* as they appear in the developed systems of Kabbalah, along with some of their most prominent symbolic associations:

Ein-Sof: the Infinite. This represents the true hidden essence of God, which is entirely unknown to humans and is rarely discussed in kabbalistic texts.

1. *Keter elyon*: the supreme crown, the uppermost aspect of the Sefirot that can be contemplated by humans. It is sometimes designated as "nothingness," the negation of all thought; and as "*Arikh Anpin*," the longsuffering (or: long-faced).
2. *Hokhmah*: wisdom; representing the contemplative, synthetic aspects of God's thought. It is the primordial point of creation from which all knowable reality originates, associated with the wise king Solomon and the divine will.
3. *Binah*: understanding, discernment; the analytic aspects of God's thought. This is the uppermost feminine element in the Godhead, symbolized as the mother of the Shekhinah. Having received the seed from Hokhmah, Binah conceived and gave birth to the seven lower Sefirot, often identified with the matriarch Leah or the celestial womb.

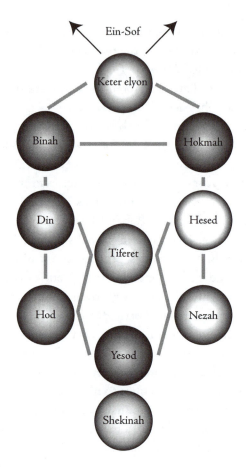

Figure 6.1 The ten *sefirot*

4. *Hesed* or *Gedullah*: loving kindness; the generous, benevolent side of God. It is often symbolized as God's right arm, and as the patriarch Abraham.

5. *Din* or *Gevurah*: judgment, power. This *sefirah* embodies the fearsome powers of divine punishment and wrath that are necessary to maintain order in the universe. It is symbolized as God's left arm, and associated with the biblical Isaac. The *sefirah* of Din contains the seeds of demonic evil, known as. the "Other Side" (sitra ahra).

6. *Tiferet*: glory, beauty. Tiferet represents the ideal balance of justice and mercy that is needed for the harmonious operation of the universe. It symbolically unites the nine upper *sefirot*, or the seven *sefirot* between Hesed and Hod. It is represented as the spine or torso of the divine body, as the Tetragrammaton (the four-letter divine name), and as the patriarch Jacob. In the guise of a king, prince or bridegroom, he yearns to be united with the Shekhinah (see below).

7. *Nezah*: eternity, endurance, victory. It represents divine grace in the world, symbolized as God's right leg, and as Moses.

8. *Hod*: majesty, the lower channel through which God's judgment descends into the world, associated with the power of prophecy; God's left leg.
9. *Yesod*: foundation (of the world), the channel through which Tiferet strives to unite with the Shekhinah and pass the creative and benevolent divine energy into the world. It is frequently represented as the male phallus, sanctified through the covenant of circumcision.
10. *Shekhinah* or *Malkhut*: divine presence, kingdom; God's immanence in the created world, identified with the "congregation of Israel," the personified spirit of the people of Israel. It is through the Shekhinah that humans may experience the divine. Kabbalistic symbolism often emphasizes the passivity and femininity of the Shekhinah as the recipient of forces from the higher *sefirot*. It is a bride, princess, the moon (reflecting the light radiated by *Tiferet*, the sun).

The Zohar

The most influential work of Kabbalah was the book known as the *Zohar*. Like the *Bahir*, its Hebrew title denotes shining light, and the title has been translated into English under such names as "The Book of Enlightenment," "The Book of Splendor" and the like. The resemblance between the *Zohar* and the *Bahir* extends to several features: both are pseudepigraphic, pretending to be midrashic compendia from the talmudic era. They both cite an assortment of fictitious rabbis, or fictitiously ascribe teachings to famous sages from the Talmud and Midrash. Neither work is concerned primarily with providing a systematic presentation of kabbalistic theory. Rather, they are homiletical compendia that make creative use of the Bible in order to derive original teachings. For the most part, the *Zohar*'s most original innovations, the doctrines and symbolic structures of the *sefirot*, are presupposed without being stated explicitly.

Whereas the key rabbinic protagonist of the *Bahir* was Rabbi Nehunya ben ha-Kanah, the *Zohar* chose as its hero Rabbi Simeon ben Yohai, a prominent second-century teacher who is not linked in talmudic literature with esoteric teachings. Before the title *Zohar* achieved currency, it was known to many as "the Midrash of Rabbi Simeon bar Yohai."

Presumably the *Zohar*'s author chose Rabbi Simeon as his spokesman on account of a legend in the Talmud about how the rabbi was forced into hiding because of his severe criticism of Rome, and spent twelve years concealed in a cave with his son. The Talmud goes on to tell that when he finally did emerge from hiding, he had reached such an uncompromising state of spiritual purity that he could not bear to see ordinary folk going about their day-to-day activities, and his fierce glances transformed them into piles of bones.

Philological analysis makes it very clear that the *Zohar* is a medieval creation, the main part of which was composed in the thirteenth century in Spain. Rabbi Moses de Leon of Guadalajara would release individual sections from it, claiming that he was copying it from an ancient manuscript that was in his possession. Following Rabbi Moses's death, his widow reported disdainfully that her husband had been lying about the ancient manuscript, and that the "midrash" was his personal creation.

The *Zohar* is a work of literary and theological genius. In order to lend it an air of mysterious antiquity, its author chose to compose it, not in Hebrew, the usual language of Jewish religious discourse, but in Aramaic, with which fewer people were familiar. The *Zohar*'s Aramaic is not the familiar dialect of the Babylonian Talmud, but an original idiom based largely on the Aramaic translations of the Bible, with admixtures of talmudic expressions, and even some new words designed to enhance the *Zohar*'s exotic aura. In contrast to the fragmentary and incomplete character of the *Bahir*, the *Zohar* demonstrates a high degree of literary polish. It crafts elaborate rhetorical constructions in imitation of midrashic models, and playfully introduces a cast of exotic characters, including a precocious infant and a learned camel-driver. The author displays an astounding erudition in the full range of talmudic and midrashic sources, medieval biblical exegesis, Maimonidean philosophy and earlier kabbalistic writers. The book embraces many aspects of traditional Jewish religious teaching, not just the Kabbalah. The *Zohar* would probably have been cherished as a masterpiece of moralistic homiletics even without its specifically kabbalistic contents.

The Ra'aya Meheimna *and* Tikkunei Ha-Zohar

The esoteric understanding of the Torah provided a powerful incentive for the performance of religious commandments and for maintaining traditional values. This was one of the chief reasons why Kabbalah proved so attractive to religiously conservative rabbis. The *Zohar* is filled with impassioned exhortations to be more meticulous in studying and observing the Torah.

It might have been objected that the straightforward reading of the Bible according to the traditional interpretations contradicted the *sefirot*-based hermeneutics of the Kabbalah. However, there is virtually no indication in the *Zohar* that its author perceived any contradiction, or that there was an antagonism between the kabbalistic and rabbinic versions of Judaism. Not all kabbalists saw the matter in that way. Even as Maimonides was ready to brand as heretical the simple Jews who understood the stories of the Bible and Midrash literally without submitting them to philosophical analysis, so too in kabbalistic circles there were figures whose commitment to their own doctrines led them to renounce the spiritual legitimacy of all others.

Remarks in this spirit may be found in the *Zohar* itself, in passages like this:

> Rabbi Simeon said: Woe to that person who says that the Torah comes only to tell mere stories and profane matters. For if that were so, then even in our times we are capable of composing a Torah consisting of profane matters, and it would even be superior. And if the Torah's purpose is to instruct us in worldly affairs, then we can find more elevated matters in those ordinary booklets. This being so, should we pursue them and make from them a Torah?!

An anonymous kabbalistic author who flourished at the close of the thirteenth century, or early in the fourteenth, advocated such a position. This individual composed works that claimed to be supplements to the *Zohar*, and which were subsequently incorporated into the standard editions of the *Zohar* as if they were parts of the original work. The two supplements are entitled *Ra'aya Meheimna* (the Faithful Shepherd) and *Sefer ha-Tikkunim*, or *Tikkunei Ha-Zohar* (The Book of Garments; the Garments of the *Zohar*). The title "*Ra'aya Meheimna*" refers to Moses, who appears in this work in the company of Rabbi Simeon ben Yohai and other talmudic sages, discoursing upon the inner meanings of the commandments. The author presents a systematic rationale for each one of the Torah's 613 commandments. The *Tikkunei ha-Zohar*, which is related in a similar narrative framework, is devoted largely to the author's original kabbalistic reading of the opening chapters of the book of Genesis.

Both these works are charged with a spirit of messianic imminence fueled by the author's conviction that the promulgation of kabbalistic teachings in the *Zohar* was an important stage in the unfolding of God's plan for redemption. This theme would be taken up in subsequent historical settings, especially after the expulsion of the Jews from Spain and Portugal, when Kabbalah and mystical messianism achieved influence among broad segments of the Jewish populace.

The *Ra'aya Meheimna* and *Tikkunim* declared that commitment to the rabbinic oral Torah as the authoritative interpretation of the Torah's precepts was a characteristic of the era of exile, a time when good is still pitted against evil. However, the ultimate redemption will completely eradicate evil from the world, restoring the state of innocence that existed prior to the sin of Adam and Eve, and the Torah will then be observed according to its kabbalistic significance. The anonymous author was outspoken in his denigration of the non-kabbalistic rabbinic culture. He frequently ridiculed simple orthodoxy as a fruitless pursuit of externals that remains blind to the innermost spiritual core. In reality, he insisted, it is the spiritual core that bestows religious significance on the Torah and its precepts.

The Kabbalah of Rabbi Isaac Luria

A spiritual revolution took place in the Jewish world during the sixteenth century that transformed the Kabbalah into an attractive and potent formulation of Jewish beliefs and values. In many respects, this transformation was an astounding and unlikely one.

For one thing, the author of the new system lived for a short time, dying at the age of 38. His public career as a kabbalistic teacher extended for only three years. He did not publish any of his thoughts, and he ordered his students to follow a similar policy. His theology was so intricate and abstract that only a select few would have the mental acumen, let alone the patience, to master its complexities His center of activity was an obscure town in the Galilee. In spite of all these factors, Rabbi Isaac Luria's interpretation of kabbalistic doctrine swept through the entire Jewish world, from Russia to Morocco, with astounding rapidity, and continues to be the definitive statement of Judaism for thousands of Jews.

Luria (1534–1572) was a scholar of Ashkenazic origin; he is usually referred to by his Hebrew acronym "the ARI (lion)", which stands for *Ashkenazi Rabbi Isaac*. He spent most of his early years in Egypt, but the main arena of his kabbalistic activity was Safed. Safed was an obscure, though picturesque, community situated on a hill overlooking the Sea of Galilee. Although it was barely mentioned in medieval records, it became a focus for Jewish refugee scholars from Spain and Portugal in the wake of the expulsion decrees at the end of the fifteenth century. Though it was home to some of the most erudite scholars of rabbinic and kabbalistic lore, Luria's spiritual personality made an immediate and profound impression. A wealth of hagiographic traditions evolved around him, and many of the stories told of his uncanny ability to fathom the depths of a person's soul after the most casual of acquaintances.

Many of his contemporaries believed that he must be the messiah. In keeping with the kabbalistic belief in reincarnation, Luria was able to identify remnants from the person's previous lives, usually as figures who had lived in the time of the Bible or Talmud. Luria's fertile mind overflowed with ideas and associations at such an unrestrained pace that he was unable to organize them into a systematic or sequential presentation.

In spite of Luria's reluctance to disseminate his teachings, versions of them were eventually put into writing by two of his students. The best-known collection was composed by Rabbi Hayyim Vital, who went a long way towards giving them a coherent formulation. Another one of Luria's disciples, Joseph Ibn Tabul, also tried to compose a statement of his master's teachings, and some scholars feel that his version constitutes a more authentic interpretation of Luria's thought. In the end, however, it was Vital's writings which achieved widespread prominence, and came to be equated with the Kabbalah of the "Ari."

As embodied in the numerous Hebrew folios of Vital's *Eẓ Ḥayyim*, we are struck—in fact overwhelmed—by the minute detail with which Luria mapped out the individual *sefirot*, their various combinations, the multiple levels of creation, the names of God and the words of the Jewish prayer book. The technical intricacy of his work is so overpowering that it is virtually impossible to translate it in a manner that would be understandable to the non-specialist reader. Out of that tangled mass of specific statements and interpretations, it is possible to discern an ambitious portrayal of cosmic history, reaching back to the deepest roots of the creation, and culminating in a vivid eschatological vision. Though much of Luria's terminology and imagery is taken from passages in the *Zohar*, he usually imbues them with radically new meaning.

Specific teachings from the Lurianic Kabbalah will be described in connection with Jewish beliefs about God, creation, evil and redemption.

Shabbetai Zevi

The messianic elements of the Lurianic Kabbalah attracted an immense audience among Jews throughout the world. The attraction was fed by a series of terrible disasters that Jews were experiencing in those days, chief among them being the swift expulsion of the magnificent Jewish communities of Spain and Portugal in 1492 and the dreaded persecution of "New Christians" (Jews who had accepted Christianity under duress) at the hands of the Spanish Inquisition. The teachings of Luria and his disciples generated an extensive "revivalist" movement in which Jews intensified their observance of religious precepts and mystical studies. The extent of the historical catastrophes and the high level of Jewish piety and penance convinced many people that redemption was imminent; and indeed, several messianic movements appeared on the scene at that time. The most significant of these was centered on the figure of Shabbetai Zevi (1626–1676), a Turkish kabbalist with an enigmatic personality that was prone to extremes of spiritual exaltation and dejection, which some historians have diagnosed as a bipolar disorder. Shabbetai Zevi's bizarre behavior, which often involved taking liberties with the norms of Jewish religious law, was viewed as a sign that he was ushering in a radically new, redeemed phase of history. The actions and teachings of Shabbetai Zevi were interpreted in this manner by the kabbalist Nathan of Gaza, who successfully spread the message of Shabbetai Zevi's messiahship. The Jewish world was receptive to this ideology, which was confirmed by many reports of wonders and miracles performed in his name. Youthful enthusiasts, dissatisfied with the staid respectability of the established leadership, rallied to the exciting Shabbatean cause as an expression of their rebellion. Shabbetai Zevi actually adopted the visible trappings of royalty, parading himself on horseback with a regal entourage of followers. Much of the mainstream rabbinic religious leadership of the time was swept up in the Shabbatean fervor; though intensive efforts were made afterwards to expunge the evidence of their participation.

Understandably, this kind of defiant behavior was regarded as subversive, and potentially dangerous, by the Turkish government. On September 15, 1666, the Sultan summoned Shabbetai Zevi before him, and offered him an ultimatum: either to convert to Islam, or be put to death. Shabbetai Zevi chose the former option, and he was given the honorary title of Keeper of the Palace Gates, with a modest pension, as he continued to hold court and entertain his followers and "subjects." For many of his followers, his act of apostasy—considered one of the cardinal offenses in Jewish tradition—was irrefutable proof of the falseness of his messianic pretensions. Nevertheless, his apostasy was given a theological interpretation in accordance with the symbolism of Lurianic Kabbalah: by committing the most terrible sin, the messiah was in fact completing the work of "elevating the sparks of holiness." Previous generations, through their devotion to religious observance, had been effective in sanctifying all the conventional manifestations of evil in the world. All that remained was to purify evil itself, and this could be accomplished only by indulging in sin with a pure mystical intention. This, they argued, was the momentous eschatological purpose of Shabbetai Zevi's apostasy. The same reasoning was used to justify other acts of ritual sin, including orgiastic behavior, that were performed by followers of Shabbetai Zevi.

In most communities, the Shabbateans were now discredited, and their opponents had the upper hand as they tried to purge the die-hard messianists from their midst. However, the movement could not be suppressed overnight, and many followers went "underground," concealing their sympathies under a mask of conventionality while continuing to await the reappearance of their redeemer. A community known as the Doenmeh has survived in Turkey, outwardly practicing Islam while secretly maintaining their faith in the return of Shabbetai Zevi. The charismatic Polish messianic pretender Jacob Frank (1726–1791) claimed to be Shabbetai Zevi's successor, and he himself converted to Christianity. His anti-rabbinic sect collaborated with Catholic authorities in promoting persecutions of the Jews, while indulging in rites marked by sexual licentiousness.

Hasidism

A remarkable formulation of kabbalistic teaching arose in eastern Europe in the second half of the eighteenth century, in the movement known as "Hasidism." As we have already seen, the Hebrew word *hasid* means "pious" and was employed in classical Jewish sources to designate one whose spiritual devotion extends beyond the technical requirements of Jewish religious law. The most familiar use of the name is in connection with the popular east European Jewish religious movement whose history and doctrines are outlined here.

The success of Hasidism is usually associated with a series of disastrous events that overcame the venerable Jewish settlements of Poland, Russia and the Ukraine during the seventeenth and eighteenth centuries, leaving them severely demoralized. Chief among these disasters were the 1648 Cossack massacres led by Bogdan Chmielnicki, in which thousands of Jews in Ukraine and Poland—about one half of the population—were murdered, bringing about the utter devastation of hundreds of Jewish communities that had existed for many centuries. In the space of a few decades, there were massacres by Poles who accused the Jews of collusion with the Swedes during the Swedish invasion of Poland. These were followed by church-instigated pogroms, and by Russian peasant revolts in 1668 that produced further riots and the deaths of thousands more Polish Jews. In addition to the death tolls, the impoverished Jewish communities had to cope with excessive taxation, the need to support widows, orphans and disabled; and extortion by bandits and Christian clergy.

These catastrophes brought about a decline in Jewish religious learning in Poland. The intellectual center of the community now shifted to Lithuania, as Polish Jewry fell into ignorance and superstition, and kabbalistic eschatological speculations gained in popularity. Like other Jewish communities throughout the world, Polish Jews were caught up in the enthusiasm for Shabbetai Zevi. His apostasy and death deepened the demoralization, as did the persecutions that were incited by Jacob Frank. The Polish Jewish communities at this time were rent by acute social divisions between the rich and the poor. The wealthier Jews and the talmudic scholars who led the communities used their power to maintain an inequitable distribution of the tax burden, imposing the heaviest obligations upon the poor. The rabbinic leadership was not vocal in protesting this situation, diminishing their credibility among the common people. The educated classes looked down on the ignorant Jewish masses. Rabbinic learning continued to focus on casuistic Talmud study (pilpul), which provided little spiritual nourishment or consolation for the common folk in their tribulations.

We possess very little reliable information about the founder of Hasidism, Rabbi Israel ben Eliezer Ba'al Shem Tov (c. 1700–1760). Most of the traditions about his life and personality come from hagiographic legends that have little historical value; and only a few probable facts can be salvaged about his life and original teachings. The Hebrew epithet *ba'al shem* translates as "master of the name" and refers to a person's ability to utilize the mysteries of God's names for magical purposes, especially for healing. The adjective *tov* means "good" and recognizes that Rabbi Israel was especially proficient as a shaman and as a practitioner of "practical Kabbalah." He is frequently designated by the Hebrew acronym: Besht. He was born in Okopy, Ukraine and lived in several different communities. His major activities took place in Medzibezh, in Podolia (southern Poland). While Hasidic legends describe him as a rebel who was (at least initially) dismissed as an ignoramus by the community leadership, there is evidence that he was in fact held in great esteem and even enjoyed financial support from the Jewish community. Later writers liked to depict him as a champion of the poor and illiterate against the established leadership; but this image is not borne out by the available evidence.

The religious ideal of "hasidism" was known to eastern European Judaism prior to the Besht's appearance, and it is not entirely obvious in what senses he may be characterized as the founder of a new sect. Much of his importance lies in the personal charisma that transformed the pietistic ideal from a quality found only in unique individuals into a popular movement with a large following among the Jewish masses.

A distinctive feature of the Ba'al Shem Tov's teachings was the priority of emotion over intellect. Hasidism taught that simple, sincere, intuitive devotion is preferable to the ideal of talmudic erudition that was commonly regarded as the hallmark of religious authority.

He cultivated an overwhelming consciousness of God's presence in all things, even in outwardly simple objects and actions ("sparks of holiness," according to the imagery of Lurianic Kabbalah). This included an appreciation of God's manifestations in nature. The experience of the Divine was therefore accessible to all, not only to the learned.

The continual awareness of a loving, ever-present creator should lead to a feeling of profound joy. Therefore the appropriate mood for worship is one of cheerfulness; whereas suffering impedes a proper relationship with God. Unlike the "fire-and-brimstone" preaching that was common in his time, the Ba'al Shem Tov eschewed asceticism and self-imposed deprivations as denials of faith in a loving Father. By encouraging joy as a primary religious virtue and teaching his followers to feel good about themselves and their relationships with God, the Ba'al Shem Tov was providing an effective antidote to the demoralizing forces that beset Polish and Russian Jewry. He encouraged the cultivation of joy through activities like singing, dancing, story telling, and even drinking alcohol.

Hasidic doctrine explained that the love songs and fairy tales of the gentile peasants were profoundly allegorical religious texts, perhaps the same songs that the Levites had sung in the Holy Temple of Jerusalem, and were expressing the mystical love between God and Israel. By singing or telling them now, with the proper spiritual intention, the Hassidim were, in effect, restoring them to their original purpose.

Hasidism, in a manner consistent with the characteristic approach of Ashkenazic Jewry, attached much importance to the preservation of popular customs. However they replaced the established Ashkenazic liturgical rite with a version of the Sephardic liturgy that had been sanctified by its use among the kabbalists, especially in the school of Rabbi Isaac Luria in Safed.

Subsequent development of Hasidism

The Ba'al Shem Tov himself does not appear to have defined a framework for the leadership of his movement following his death. After some disagreement among the circles of his disciples, one leadership model did emerge as the characteristic one of the movement: that of the *zaddik* ("righteous one"). Rooted in kabbalistic doctrines, the *zaddik* was a charismatic figure of extraordinary spiritual caliber. Because the common folk who made up the majority of Hasidim's following did not possess the material or spiritual means to pursue their own personal religious perfection, the *zaddik* provided them with vicarious fulfillment. By devoting oneself to a worthy *zaddik*, the individual *hasid* could benefit from the leader's spiritual guidance and merits.

The first generation of *zaddikim* consisted of actual disciples of the Ba'al Shem Tov, and included individuals of outstanding stature. The cultivation of personal charisma encouraged remarkable diversity among the individual Hasidic communities, as each was stamped with the imprint of its leaders and emphasized different aspects of religious piety.

Some of the better-known leaders include:

- Rabbi Dov Baer, the Maggid (Preacher) of Mezhirech:
  He was the most prominent of the Besht's original disciples, and was largely responsible for the organization of the movement after its founder's death.
- Rabbi Jacob Joseph of Polonoyye:
  He formulated the hasidic doctrine of the *zaddik*.
- Rabbi Shneur Zalman of Lyady:
  He founded the "Chabad" school in Lithuania that integrated a profound Hasidic theology with the traditional emphasis on talmudic scholarship.
- Rabbi Nahman of Braslav:
  He was a troubled, controversial and contentious figure with apparent messianic aspirations. He is known for his collection of allegorical "fairy tales." His followers, who never acknowledge a successor to Rabbi Nahman, were referred to as "the dead *hasidim*."
- Rabbi Levi Isaac of Berdichev:
  Renowned as the "advocate for Israel," he found virtue even among the Jewish sinners, boldly confronting God to argue in defense of the Jews.
- Rabbi Menahem Mendel of Kotsk:
  He was a kind of "anti-*zaddik*" who lost patience with his followers' reliance on him. He withdrew completely from public contact and spent his last twenty years secluded in a room.

Hasidic leadership evolved into a system of dynastic succession, in which the heirs to the title of *zaddik* did not always inherit their predecessors' spiritual qualifications.

Figure 6.2 Two Hasidim

Abuses of authority became widespread, as *zaddikim* established "courts" with trappings of royalty, to which their followers were expected to furnish generous gifts and make pilgrimages. Nevertheless, the movement continued to produce some remarkable leaders and religious models, as well as inspiring instances of devotion among the followers.

Although they suffered gravely from the devastation of the European Holocaust, many Hasidic groups continue to exist and thrive on the contemporary Jewish scene, especially in the United States and in Israel.

Discussion questions

1. Discuss how aptly the category "mysticism" can be applied to medieval Jewish philosophy, Kabbalah or to the teachings of Abraham Abulafia.
2. Why might kabbalistic teaching lend itself to publication in pseudepigraphic works?

Key points you need to know

- Kabbalah was a unique reinterpretation of Judaism that appeared in medieval Provence and Spain, and was based on a doctrine of ten *sefirot*, aspects of God. The doctrines provided the framework for a novel exegesis, theology and a motivation for religious observance.
- The kabbalistic system of Isaac Luria, with its strong eschatological component, achieved immense popularity among Jews. It also inspired messianic movements, such as those of Shabbetai Zevi and Jacob Frank.
- The hasidic philosophy of Rabbi Israel Ba'al Shem Tov was addressed to the unlettered masses, and encouraged an emotional devotion rooted in joyous awareness of a loving God. Hasidism evolved into diverse communities led by charismatic individuals known as *zaddikim*.

Further reading

German pietism

Dan, Joseph, "The Emergence of Mystical Prayer." In *Studies in Jewish Mysticism*. Edited by J. Dan and F. Talmage. New York: Ktav, 1982.

Marcus, Ivan G., *Piety and Society: the Jewish Pietists of Medieval Germany*, Études sur le Judaisme Médiévale. Leiden: Brill, 1981.

Marcus, Ivan G., "The Devotional Ideals of Ashkenazic Pietism." In *Jewish Spirituality: From the Bible through the Middle Ages*. Edited by A. Green. New York: Crossroads, 1987.

Soloveitchik, Haym, "Three Themes in the Sefer Hasidim." *AJS Review* 1 (1976): 311–57.

Kabbalah: general works

Blumenthal, David R., *Understanding Jewish Mysticism: A Source Reader*, The Library of Judaic learning; v. 2, 4. New York: Ktav Publishing House, 1978.

Fine, Lawrence, "Kabbalistic Texts." In *Back to the Sources: Reading the Classic Jewish Texts*. Edited by B. W. Holtz, New York: Summit Books, 1984.

Idel, Moshe, *Kabbalah: New Perspectives*. New Haven, CT: Yale University Press, 1988.

Idel, Moshe, *Messianic Mystics*. New Haven, CT: Yale University Press, 1998.

Idel, Moshe and Mortimer Ostow, eds, *Jewish Mystical Leaders and Leadership in the 13th Century*. Northvale, NJ: Jason Aronson, 1998.

Jacobs, Louis, *The Schocken book of Jewish Mystical Testimonies*. New York: Schocken Books, 1997.

Matt, Daniel Chanan, *The Essential Kabbalah: The Heart of Jewish Mysticism*. Edison, NJ: Castle Books, 1997.

Scholem, Gershom Gerhard, *Major Trends in Jewish Mysticism*, Schocken paperbacks, SB5. New York: Schocken Books, 1961.

Scholem, Gershom Gerhard, *On the Kabbalah and its Symbolism*. Translated by R. Manheim. New York: Schocken Books, 1965.

Scholem, Gershom Gerhard, ed., *Kabbalah, Library of Jewish Knowledge*. New York: Quadrangle/New York Times Book Co., 1974.

Wolfson, Elliot R., *Along the Path: Studies in Kabbalistic Myth, Symbolism, and Hermeneutics*. Albany, NY: State University of New York Press, 1995.

Wolfson, Elliot R., *Circle in the Square: Studies in the Use of Gender in Kabbalistic Symbolism*. Albany, NY: State University of New York Press, 1995.

The Bahir

Dan, Joseph and Ronald Kiener, eds, *The Early Kabbalah*. Edited by J. Farin, The Classics of Western Spirituality. New York, Mahwah, NJ and Toronto: Paulist Press, 1986.

Kaplan, Aryeh, *The Bahir*. York Beach, ME: S. Weiser, 1990.

Scholem, Gershom Gerhard, *Origins of the Kabbalah*. Translated by A. Arkush, 1st ed., Philadelphia, PA and Princeton, NJ: Jewish Publication Society and Princeton University Press, 1987.

The Zohar

Giller, Pinchas, *Reading the Zohar: The Sacred Text of the Kabbalah*. Oxford and New York: Oxford University Press, 2001.

Lachower, Yeruham Fishel and Isaiah Tishby, *The Wisdom of the Zohar: an Anthology of Texts*. Translated by D. Goldstein, *Littman Library of Jewish Civilization*. Oxford and New York: Oxford University Press, 1991.

Matt, Daniel Chanan, *Zohar, The Book of Enlightenment*, Classics of Western Spirituality. New York: Paulist Press, 1983.

Matt, Daniel Chanan, *The Zohar*. Pritzker ed. Stanford, CA: Stanford University Press, 2004.

Liebes, Yehuda, *Studies in the Zohar*. Translated by A. Schwartz, S. Nakache and P. Peli, SUNY series in Judaica. Albany, NY: State University of New York Press, 1993.

Segal, Eliezer, "The Exegetical Craft of the Zohar: Towards an Appreciation." *AJS Review* 17(1) (1992): 31–49.

Sperling, Harry, Maurice Simon and Paul Philip Levertoff, *The Zohar*. London: Soncino Press, 1978.

Lurianic Kabbalah and Shabbetai Zevi

Fine, Lawrence, *Physician of the Soul, Healer of the Cosmos: Isaac Luria and His Kabbalistic Fellowship*, Stanford Studies in Jewish History and Culture. Stanford, CA: Stanford University Press, 2003.

Freedman, Daphne, *Man and the Theogony in the Lurianic Cabala*, Gorgias Dissertations. Piscataway, NJ: Gorgias Press, 2006.

Scholem, Gershom Gerhard, *Sabbatai Sevi: The Mystical Messiah, 1626–1676*, Bollingen Series. Princeton, NJ: Princeton University Press, 1973.

Hasidism

Altshuler, Mor, *The Messianic Secret of Hasidism*, Brill's Series in Jewish Studies. Leiden and Boston, MA: Brill, 2006.

Ben-Amos, Dan, Jerome R. Mintz, and Samuel Dov Baer ben, *In Praise of the Baal-Shem Tov: The Earliest Collection of Legends About the Founder of Hasidism*. New York: Schocken Books, 1984.

Buber, Martin, *The Way of a Man According to the Teaching of Hasidism*. New York: Citadel Press, Kensington Publishing Corp., 1996.

Elior, Rachel, *The Mystical Origins of Hasidism*. Oxford and Portland, OR: Littman Library of Jewish Civilization, 2006.

Heschel, Abraham Joshua, and Samuel H. Dresner, *The Circle of the Baal Shem Tov: Studies in Hasidism*. Chicago, IL: University of Chicago Press, 1985.

Idel, Moshe, *Hasidism: Between Ecstasy and Magic*, SUNY Series in Judaica. Albany, NY: State University of New York Press, 1995.

Nigal, Gedalyah, *Magic, Mysticism, and Hasidism: The Supernatural in Jewish Thought*. Northvale, NJ: Jason Aronson, 1994.

Rosman, Murray Jay, *Founder of Hasidism: A Quest for the Historical Ba'al Shem Tov*, Contraversions. Berkeley, CA: University of California Press, 1996.

Weiss, J. G. and David Goldstein, *Studies in East European Jewish Mysticism and Hasidism*. London: Vallentine Mitchell, 1997.

7 The modern era

In this chapter

The admission of the Jews to individual citizenship in modern European nation-states is known as the Emancipation, and it required various forms of accommodation from the side of the Jews. The Jewish adaptation to modern values is known as the Enlightenment (*haskalah*). Proponents of Enlightenment and Emancipation sought to change features of traditional Judaism that were viewed as obstacles to the integration of Jews into European society, such as the enforcement of a separate legal system, or the beliefs that Jews constitute a separate nation and will be restored to their homeland in the future redemption. The most famous Jewish champion of Enlightenment ideals was Moses Mendelssohn of Dessau, a traditional Jew who distinguished himself as a philosopher and German author. Mendelssohn formulated a philosophy of Judaism that was consistent with modern values, while spearheading a program to educate Jews in European culture and vocational skills. The modernization of Jewish religion was known as Reform Judaism. In its earliest stages, it was a lay-driven phenomenon that focused on changing aspects of the tradition that were sources of embarrassment or served as obstacles to Jews who wanted to integrate into the local society. By the mid-nineteenth century they developed a systematic ideology and intellectual leadership. Zacharias Frankel, a moderate reformer who was upset by what he viewed as the Reformers' facile dismissal of folk religion and traditionalism, withdrew from the movement and established his own school of "Positive-Historical Judaism" that proposed an organic, evolutionary model of religion as the spiritual expression of the common folk. Samson Raphael Hirsch advocated a version of Judaism that was extremely conservative in its adherence to traditional beliefs about the literal truth of the Bible and oral tradition and its commitment to full observance of Jewish law, but encouraged involvement in European culture where it did not conflict with Jewish values. The failure of the Emancipation by the mid-nineteenth century led to a wave of Jewish immigration to America. Extreme Reformers established a brand of Judaism in America that was hostile to all manifestations of ritual or Jewish nationalism. The subsequent wave of millions of Jews from eastern

Europe, combined with ongoing persecutions and anti-Semitic agitation, led to a reassertion of traditionalism even in the Reform movement. The 1937 Columbus Platform was much more sympathetic to ritual observances and to solidarity with Jews of other lands, including the nascent Zionist enterprises in Palestine. Since then, American Reform has evolved in diverse directions. The successor to Frankel's Positive-Historical approach was called Conservative Judaism in America. Under the leadership of Solomon Schechter, the Jewish Theological Seminary of America became a distinguished center of Jewish scholarship. The Conservative movement achieved much popularity among middle-class and suburban Jews in the mid-twentieth century, but a discrepancy developed between the traditionalism of the movement's leadership and a general laxity in observance among the rank and file. By the beginning of the twenty-first century the movement was adopting halakhic policies that were strongly at variance with traditional Jewish law, making it difficult to differentiate between Conservative and Reform Judaism. New models of Jewish religious life have evolved, such as the Jewish Renewal movement, that are not linked to the established Jewish denominations.

Main topics covered

- The Emancipation of the Jews in modern Europe
- The Jewish Enlightenment
- Moses Mendelssohn, pioneer of Jewish Enlightenment
- Reform Judaism in Europe
- Zacharias Frankel and Positive-Historical Judaism
- Samson Raphael Hirsch and neo-Orthodoxy
- Reform Judaism in the New World
- The evolution of Conservative Judaism

Emancipation

The socio-political development that created the conditions for modern Judaism is known as the "Emancipation." It refers primarily to the legal process, which began in Europe with the French Revolution, of granting to the Jews equal civic rights in the countries in which they resided, and of abolishing discriminatory laws to which Jews had previously been subjected. Previous to this time, Jews lived in autonomous communities on the periphery of the majority Christian society, and were burdened with many religious, economic and social disadvantages. The Emancipation involved relating to Jews as individuals whose religious beliefs and observances were now considered private matters that were of no concern to the government. Similar transition occurred with respect to other segments of the society, such as the clergy and peasantry, whose identities during the medieval era were defined by the membership in a recognized social caste (known as a "corporation") and were now being granted citizenship as individuals. The primary push towards emancipation was motivated by economic factors, especially by the concentration of unprecedented wealth into the hands of European leaders from the New World and other new horizons in international commerce. This situation promoted the rise of powerful nation states and an entrepreneurial mercantilist ideology that was less concerned with people's faith or group identity than with the contributions they could make to the national prosperity as individuals. In a more general sense, the term Emancipation may be applied to the whole cultural and social movement that promoted, whether directly or indirectly, Jewish integration into the broader society. Corresponding to their acceptance of political equality, Jews were expected to give up their communal, cultural and national identities. This prospect presented a grave challenge to the traditional Jewish leadership, because the maintaining of a separate Jewish legal system had always been regarded as a sacred religious duty.

The economic and political processes were accompanied by momentous ideological changes that were occurring in European intellectual circles. This movement is known as the Enlightenment. The European Enlightenment, as it evolved in the seventeenth and eighteenth centuries, opposed the religious dogmatism that previously held sway over European life and had led to bloody wars between opposing Christian sects. Enlightenment philosophers advocated reason and science as more credible replacements for faith, especially in the public sphere. In theory, at least, this approach led to liberal views of human equality and to the extension of full civil rights to all— even to the Jews. In reality, however, the medieval legacy of anti-Jewish prejudice was so ingrained in the European mindset that many people doubted whether Jews could ever be absorbed into modern society. For this reason, the granting of civil rights to European Jewry was a protracted process that would be dragged out for many decades, and would continue to encounter strong opposition.

The Jewish Enlightenment

The term "Enlightenment" (or its Hebrew equivalent: *haskalah*) is standardly employed to designate an intellectual movement within the Jewish community. In some respects, it was merely a Jewish adaptation of the European Enlightenment, and its Jewish exponents sometimes allied themselves with liberal-minded Christian thinkers. The ideals of this movement included the elimination of medieval superstition and clericalism, the encouragement of rationalism, and the promotion of reason, tolerance, morality and a faith in human perfectibility. However, the concept "Jewish Enlightenment" is usually applied to the more specific task of providing theoretical rationales for the implementation of the Emancipation and modernizing Jewish life and thought. These changes were seen as necessary preconditions for achieving political and social integration. Insofar as these efforts were usually concentrated on the introduction of changes in the traditional religious outlook and observances, they took the form of "religious reform."

Certain beliefs that had long been central to traditional Judaism were perceived as incongruous, or at least problematic, to the quest for full participation in European society. For example, Jews who aspired to be loyal citizens of their current homelands could be embarrassed by the traditional Jewish eschatological visions that aspired to an eventual return from a tragic "exile" to the land of Israel and the restoration of the ancient Jewish monarchy. In keeping with the conceptions of evolution and progress that were current in historiographic thought, they portrayed Judaism as an evolving religion that had always been adapting to the advances in human culture.

> Enlightenment thinkers believed that there was a universal natural religion, consisting of a theology and morality, that all individual religions must conform to. Because liberal Protestant Christianity had taken to presenting itself as the embodiment of enlightened, universalistic faith, the very existence of Judaism as the religion of a separate nation was challenged; and Jews were faced with a tension between their commitment to universalism and their attachment to their own tradition.

As Jews became more open to the ideas of the surrounding environment, their perceptions of the role of religion increasingly corresponded to those of liberal Protestantism. Jews treated Judaism as primarily a matter of individual belief, while attaching less importance to observance and rituals. Like Christian priests and ministers, the main roles of rabbis now involved preaching, moral and theological guidance, and pastoral concerns, rather than being authorities on religious law. The synagogue, and especially the Sabbath worship service, now came to be viewed as the exclusive venue of communal religious activity. Because the Hebrew scriptures (as distinct from rabbinic writings) were still held in reverence by Christians, Enlightened Jews also cultivated a renewed interest in the Bible and tried to displace the Talmud as the main subject in the religious curriculum. They did so notwithstanding the fact that there was much in the Bible that was embarrassingly primitive according to modern sensibilities; such as the sacrificial cult and purity laws. Among the first reforms that were introduced into Jewish religious practice, several were designed to make Jewish worship conform to the esthetic standards of the host society.

Although the fundamental values of the European Enlightenment should, theoretically, have led to the immediate granting of full civil rights to Jews, the process was retarded by anti-Jewish assumptions and stereotypes that were prevalent in the society. Even in otherwise liberal circles, it was widely assumed by Christians that the Jews were by their very nature a backward, materialistic people, inherently lacking in culture and spirituality. In medieval Europe, Jews had been excluded from agriculture and crafts; and their economic activity was restricted to banking and money lending, professions that were forbidden to Christians under church law. The popular perception held that it was the Jewish religion that required its adherents to participate in money lending, and excluded them from economically productive occupations. For this reason, demands for the vocational retraining of Jews were often treated as proposals for religious reform. Some thinkers argued benevolently that those alleged flaws in the Jewish character had been a result of the Jews' forcible segregation, and that they would be remedied once Jews were permitted access to more advanced ideas and culture. Jews often accepted these stereotypes, and felt the obligation to improve themselves in order to prove themselves worthy of admission to the host society.

Moses Mendelssohn (1729–1786): pioneer of Jewish Enlightenment

To a significant extent, the earliest stages in the European Jewish Enlightenment are embodied in the life and works of a single individual, Moses Mendelssohn of Dessau. Mendelssohn was a traditionally observant Jew who also excelled as a philosopher and literary figure in the intellectual world of eighteenth-century Berlin. To his contemporaries, his importance lay not only in his ideas and writings, but in the very fact that a Jew was able to make a name for himself as a philosopher, man of letters, and as a morally sensitive human being.

Figure 7.1 Moses Mendelssohn

The Enlightenment thinker Gotthold Lessing was ridiculed for composing a drama in 1749 in which he suggested that Jews could possess nobility of character. When he subsequently met Mendelssohn in 1754, the two became close friends, and Lessing authored a play "Nathan the Wise" whose hero was modeled after Mendelssohn. Mendelssohn made important contributions to metaphysics, aesthetics, ethics and literary criticism, but they had no direct connection to Judaism.

Mendelssohn's personal approach to Judaism is evident on two different fronts. On the one hand, he was involved in defending the legitimacy of Judaism before the surrounding society. On the other hand, he instituted a program to reform Judaism in keeping with the values of the modern world.

He probably would not have consented to argue the case of Judaism before the gentile world had he not been provoked into a debate by the Swiss theologian Johann Lavater, who admired Mendelssohn so deeply that he was determined to convert him to Christianity. Lavater subscribed to the assumption that modern Christianity was the embodiment of rational, universalistic ideas, and that Judaism was the antithesis of enlightenment. He therefore challenged Mendelssohn that his posture of being an enlightened Jew was self-contradictory. If he was true to his noble ideals, then the only consistent path for him to take was either to refute Christianity or to convert. It was unsafe for a Jew to openly criticize the dominant religion. However, when he was left without an alternative, he responded by composing his work *Jerusalem*, published in 1783, advocating religious tolerance and freedom of conscience.

Mendelssohn argued aggressively that Judaism was, in fact, more universalistic than Christianity and more consistent with modern values. After all, a central tenet of enlightened theology was that true ideas about God, metaphysics and ethics can be derived through reason. If that is true, it makes little sense to speak of a revealed theology. Therefore, the traditional Jewish emphasis on practical commandments makes much more sense than the Christian focus on salvation through correct belief. What is distinctive about Judaism is its "revealed legislation," its body of laws and precepts. It makes no claim to a revealed theological message, because that would be a superfluous absurdity. Furthermore, it is Christianity that has historically made exclusivist claims that there is no salvation except through faith in Christ. This seems to be a cruel indictment of cultures who, through no fault of their own, have never been exposed to the saving truths. Judaism, on the other hand, maintains that while the Torah was addressed only to Israel, the rest of humanity may achieve salvation by observing the "seven laws of the children of Noah," the fundamental moral and religious obligations that constitute, according to the rabbinic understanding, the basic obligations of human society.

While coming to the defense of his religion against external attacks, Mendelssohn was also advocating extensive reforms and educational projects inside the Jewish community that were devised to bring it into conformity with the demands of the post-Emancipation realities. Mendelssohn fully accepted the Enlightenment theses that religion should be removed from the public arena, that matters of religion should be left to the individual conscience and cannot be enforced by coercive means. Under the medieval regimes, the rabbis possessed the power to enforce their decisions, primarily by placing noncompliant individuals under the *herem*, an order of ostracism or excommunication that would exclude them from the synagogue and other communal services, as well as forbidding others to socialize or do business with them. Mendelssohn urged the abolition of the *herem*.

Mendelssohn devised several projects in order to educate the Jewish masses along lines that would facilitate their absorption into European society. One of his most influential enterprises was a new translation of the Bible into literary German. This served several objectives, though the foremost among them was teaching Jews to read and communicate in proper literary German.

Most European Jews spoke a distinctive dialect of German, known as Yiddish, that combined substantial elements of Hebrew, Aramaic and other languages, and whose grammar was based on dialects that differed from what was accepted as the standard for literary German. Enlightened Jews looked with disdain on what they regarded as a vulgar and embarrassing "jargon." Recognizing that his target readership of unsophisticated Jews would be repelled by the German translation, or even unable to read it, Mendelssohn printed it in Hebrew letters, giving it a more conventional appearance. He claimed that this translation would keep Jews from having recourse to Christian translations that were inconsistent with Jewish tradition. Ultimately, Mendelssohn's stratagem proved very successful in accelerating the literacy of many European Jews in the German language.

Mendelssohn also initiated a new commentary on the Bible, entitled the *Bi'ur* (Hebrew for "explanation") most of which was composed by a circle of his collaborators. The *Bi'ur* differed considerably from the commentaries that were conventionally studied by Jews, in that it avoided the fanciful homiletical interpretations of the midrash in favor of a straightforward elucidation of the original Hebrew text. In the spirit of medieval exponents of literal interpretation, the *Bi'ur* was based on grammar, lexicography and sensitivity to literary aesthetics. The *Bi'ur* was composed in a Hebrew that was modeled on biblical precedents, which the authors considered more classical and elegant than the rabbinic style. To some extent, the use of Hebrew was a concession to the fact that potential readers were not sufficiently adept in

German. For similar reasons, the dissemination of the Enlightenment ideology was often done through Hebrew journals. Inadvertently, these writers were establishing the beginnings of a revival of Hebrew as a modern language, a phenomenon that would later play a role in the Hebrew nationalist movements and the creation of the state of Israel.

Historians speak of three different phases of Jewish Enlightenment:

1. The central European (primarily German) phase beginning in 1783 is the one that has been discussed here so far. It was dominated by Mendelssohn and his disciples. The German *Haskalah* was largely a middle-class phenomenon, propelled by Jews who needed to remove religious barriers that obstructed their enjoyment of the new economic and social opportunities.
2. A Galician *Haskalah* began around 1820. Galicia was a province of historic Poland that was joined to the Austro-Hungarian Empire. Galicia therefore produced an extraordinary synthesis of traditional Polish rabbinic learning and modern European culture. A central theme of the Galician *Haskalah* movement was its campaign against Hasidism, which it loathed as a manifestation of medieval superstition.
3. A branch of the Jewish Enlightenment was active in eastern Europe, especially from 1830 to 1882, though its influence was limited because of the resistance from the traditionalists and the competition from secular Jewish movements. The movement was severely discredited by the fact that the Czarist government exploited it as a vehicle for promoting Jewish assimilation with a view to religious conversion.

Religious reform in Europe

It was characteristic of the cultural patterns of central and western Europe that the main Jewish responses to the Enlightenment and Emancipation were directed towards modernizing religious beliefs and practices. This differs from comparable situations in eastern Europe. When the winds of modernity made themselves felt in Russia and Poland in the mid-nineteenth century and Jews felt unsatisfied with their traditional religious structures, it was more common for them to turn to forms of Jewish expression that lay outside the bounds of religion. Those who could not accept traditional Judaism were able to cultivate other kinds of ideological identification—social, political, nationalistic or cultural—usually in a Jewish guise. This was possible because Jewishness as it existed in Russia and Poland was as much a nationality as a religion, and the Jews were almost entirely segregated from the majority society. They spoke a different language, Yiddish, maintained distinctive dress and followed a different calendar. Therefore, even those who abandoned their traditional religion could never evade their Jewish separateness. An immense variety of secular expressions of Jewishness proliferated in eastern Europe that had no real equivalent in western lands.

In central Europe, especially in German-speaking territories, Jews quickly accepted the Enlightenment claim that religion was irrelevant to citizenship and was confined to matters of theological doctrine and morals. Ritual observances were largely restricted to the institutional house of worship and to particular sacred times. It followed naturally from this outlook that Jews who wished to maintain their Jewish identity in modern society were obliged to consider the introduction of changes in their religion.

An increasingly attractive alternative was to change one's religion. This had not been a serious option in the medieval milieu because gaping cultural and religious barriers separated Jews and Christians and the Jewish community was able to maintain the loyalty of its members. As knowledge of Judaism and its traditions diminished among German Jews, they were unable to provide compelling justifications for continuing their ancestral religion in the face of the inconveniences that it occasioned. Many followers of the Enlightenment or their children (including Mendelssohn's) converted to Christianity, a step that was widely considered to be a necessary "passport" to full acceptance into European society. Intermarriage with non-Jews, an option that had been unimaginable in medieval Jewish law and society, now became a practical option in secular Europe.

The first phase of Jewish religious reform (c. 1790–1830) was initiated by the laity. It did not consult rabbis or scholars, nor did it formulate coherent ideological positions. An important leader at this time was Israel Jacobson (1768–1828), a German philanthropist without theological or rabbinical training who founded a synagogue and school and published a modern prayer book. Most of the reforms were aimed at features of traditional Judaism that impeded the acceptance of Jews as individuals or as a group into European society. Because so much of Judaism was now confined to weekly synagogue worship, it was the liturgical texts and practices that bore the brunt of the changes. They sought to remove elements that were archaic, lengthy, incomprehensible, or embarrassing for esthetic or ideological reasons. The role of the rabbis was redefined to coincide with that of a Christian minister or priest—as a preacher and spiritual leader, rather than a judge and scholar of religious law.

The traditionalist camp was, on the whole, uncompromising in its resistance to any kind of change, and did not distinguish between minor and major reforms. In a pattern that repeated itself in several European communities, a wealthy community member would sponsor a synagogue (or temple, as the reformers preferred to call them) where changes were introduced and for which a new prayer book would be published. The traditionalist rabbis would immediately publish a collection of manifestos arguing that the proposed changes were illegitimate and must be resisted at all costs. In those days, the government maintained strict control over local religious institutions. Only one Jewish congregation was normally sanctioned in any given community, and the authorities were normally hostile to the creation of new religious movements because they threatened the stability of the society. Because of this situation, the traditionalists were often able to marshal state support for outlawing the Reform temples. However, because the reformers were often affluent and better connected to the government, they were at times able to persuade the authorities that their objectives dovetailed more closely with the needs of the state. This led to a polarization of positions that precluded any compromise or moderation.

The second generation of German Reform Judaism, which extended from about 1840 to 1880, was marked by the involvement of scholars and rabbis in the movement's leadership. These figures had academic training in Jewish tradition as well as sophistication in theological and philosophical discourse. During the 1830s and 1840s, a series of official conferences were convened (in Wiesbaden, 1837; Brunswick, 1844; Frankfurt, 1845; Breslau, 1846), in the hope of arriving at unified policies in matters of ideology and practice. These conferences attracted quite a broad range of non-traditionalist points of view; and they quickly abandoned their original project of formulating an official creed.

The reform ideologues found support for their policies in the historical accounts of Judaism that were being proposed in academic venues, which were demonstrating that development and evolution had been characteristic of Judaism (and of all religions) throughout history, and therefore there was nothing unprecedented about continuing to adjust to the progress of human culture and science. If the current reforms appeared to be more radical than the evolutionary changes of the past, that was only because of the radical novelty of the age of Enlightenment. They regarded the unprecedented proclamations of human equality and religious tolerance as quasi-messianic in their impact. Many reformers justified their departures from the tradition by arguing that what is eternal in the Jewish revelation is the system of core values, consisting of monotheistic theology and moral precepts; however, the specific implementations of these values were never meant to be permanent, and they may be legitimately changed and interpreted through the ages. Some saw themselves as belonging to a religion of "Mosaism": they accepted the authority of the Torah only with respect to the principles of monotheism and revelation, but not the vestiges of primitive sacrifices, rituals, nationalism and the like. They did not consider themselves bound by the teachings of the talmudic rabbis, though rabbinic literature could be profitably consulted as a source of general guidance.

The Reform synods tried to formulate official positions on the issues that had been bothering them. The more difficult questions were usually turned over to committees of scholars, who reported their findings at subsequent meetings. For example, the committee that was asked to look into the matter of messianic themes in the prayer book decided that messianism, as a vision of universal redemption and enlightenment, should be retained in the liturgy, though the expressions of nationalistic restoration should be removed. Similarly, although the doctrine of bodily resurrection was out of fashion in European theological circles, where a spiritual survival after death was considered a more refined idea, there was no perceived urgency in changing the text of the prayers, because the traditional wording could be interpreted as referring to the eternity of the soul. The movement had no difficulties in removing certain liturgical passages that were considered embarrassing or objectionable, such as the *Kol Nidrei* ceremony for annulling unfulfilled religious vows on the night of the Day of Atonement. This had occasioned anti-Semitic accusations that Jews could not be trusted to keep their promises. The halakhic obstacles to playing an organ or other musical instrument on holy days could also be dealt with within the general framework of traditional halakhic discourse. In order to shorten the lengthy reading from the Torah in Hebrew, which challenged the attention-span of congregants unfamiliar with the language, the reformers recommended the revival of the ancient Palestinian practice of reading the Torah over three years, in much smaller units, and of making extensive use of vernacular translation.

The attitude towards rituals was generally hostile, in keeping with the prevailing attitudes of a Protestant ideology that contrasted sharply between the "law" and the "spirit." The reformers singled out for elimination those rituals that impeded their participation in the general society (such as the dietary laws), as well as innocent liturgical customs that appeared strange to outsiders, such as the sounding of the ram's horn on Rosh Hashanah or the carrying of palm-fronds and citrons on Sukkot. The holiday of Purim was considered embarrassing because its traditional celebration often involved drinking and rowdy behavior. For similar reasons, the Jewish mourning practices, which require tearing garments out of grief and disregard for one's physical appearance, were opposed on the grounds that they are undignified.

The Reform leadership was also determined to remove the traditional disadvantages in the rights and duties of women. Whereas the Talmud had exempted them from time-defined negative precepts, the Reform movement declared that women's obligation was identical to that of men in all religious precepts, and that they were to be counted in the quorum of ten that was needed for communal prayer. Females were to be given the same type of education as males. Changes were introduced to the marriage laws to put an end to the tragic state of the *agunah*, the "anchored woman" who could not remarry because the death of her first husband could not be verified or because he refused to issue a religious divorce. They also rejected the biblical law of "levirate" marriage, according to which a childless widow must either marry her deceased husband's brother or undergo a ceremony of release.

Probably the most difficult issue that had to be dealt with by the Reform leadership was that of the Sabbath. The movement's constituency included many Jews who wished to participate in the economic life of the general society, especially in the civil service and liberal professions. Because a six-day week was in force universally at that time, their employment was rendered all but impossible by the fact that traditional Jewish law forbade them to write, travel, or carry objects outside the home. Those Jews looked to their scholarly authorities to find formulas that would permit them to perform those activities on the Sabbath. The committee that was assigned to deal with this question decided to base its decisions on a far-reaching theological reinterpretation of the Sabbath's purpose, rather than merely interpreting the technical details of permitted and prohibited activities as defined by rabbinic discourse. The seventh day was set aside as a day of spiritual elevation, prayer and meditation, and anything that advanced the religious character of the day should be permitted. On the basis of this premise, they could allow worshippers to travel in vehicles to the temple, as well as to play inspiring instrumental music to enhance the services.

Although this was undoubtedly a radical departure from the traditionalist model of Sabbath observance, it was not enough to satisfy the demands of Jews who were expecting permission to work at jobs on Saturday. The formulators of the policy stated explicitly that the Sabbath would not be forsaken as a day of rest, and they only made exemptions for workers in vital services, such as the government or military. Some later Reform authorities proposed a more radical solution: Because it was the principle and the spirit of the Sabbath that are of primary importance, it does not really matter on which day of the week it was observed. Accordingly, it was possible to observe the Sabbath on Sunday, the weekly day of rest in the civil calendar.

Over the latter half of the nineteenth century, the Reform movement veered farther away from established theology and observance, to the point where founding figures like Abraham Geiger, who had once been perceived as a radical anti-traditionalist, were now dismissed as hopelessly conservative. This brand of extreme liberalism would become the dominant one when the movement established itself in the New World.

Zacharias Frankel and Positive-Historical Judaism

The committee that was assigned to deal with the role of the Hebrew language in the prayers presented their report at the Breslau conference in 1846. They pointed out that traditional rabbinic law was quite flexible about permitting worship in the vernacular; and therefore they recommended the widespread use of the local language except for certain key passages that were most familiar in Hebrew. Although the technical issue was relatively straightforward, this decision was to have momentous importance as a line of demarcation between the extreme and moderate trends in the Reform movement. The distinguished scholar Zacharias Frankel (1801–1875) withdrew in indignation, claiming that the decision was indicative of systemic flaws in the movement's values. By relegating language to relative insignificance, Frankel contended, the Reformers were defining Judaism as a mere abstract theology that was unconnected to the experiences of the Jewish people, which were uniquely expressed in their language and culture. In his view, which was strongly influenced by the Romantic ideas that were current in European society at the time, Judaism is, above all, the natural religious expression of the historical Jewish people. As such, scholarly or rabbinic elites cannot introduce radical changes through *ex cathedra* pronouncements. Quite the contrary, Frankel understood Judaism as an organic entity that evolves gradually, and therefore any abrupt reforms that were out of harmony with the common Jewish folk (who at this time were mostly traditionalists) were to be rejected as illegitimate.

As an alternative to the extremes of inflexible traditionalism or radical reform, Frankel established a new program that he called "Positive-Historical Judaism" that combined a commitment to Jewish halakhah with openness to the rational analysis of religious and theological issues. Against the traditionalists, he argued that the authority of Jewish law rests not only on the supernatural revelation of the written and oral Torahs, but principally on its acceptance and observance by Jews over the generations. He was therefore willing to introduce aesthetic changes to synagogue liturgy and practices provided that they did not violate the norms of the halakhah. Unlike the Reformers, Frankel affirmed the fundamental human need for concrete religious symbols embodied in ritual. Consistent with his stress on the religious importance of Jewish history, Frankel, who possessed both traditional rabbinic training and a university degree, was a prolific and distinguished contributor to academic Judaic scholarship and produced important scholarly publications on rabbinic law and literature. As the head of the Jewish Theological Seminary in Breslau, he was able to train students who shared his approach and exerted a significant influence on the German Jewish communities. His *Introduction to the Mishnah* provoked an intense controversy with the traditionalists by denying the claim that the Mishnah and the oral law had been literally dictated to Moses at Mount Sinai. Nevertheless, Frankel was not ready to entertain the "documentary hypothesis" that was fashionable in liberal Christian scholarship and had been adopted by many Jewish Reformers, according to which the Torah was assembled in Exilic times from diverse documents and traditions.

Orthodoxy and Neo-Orthodoxy

Although the promise of equal rights was welcomed by most European Jews, many traditional Jews believed that the price of Emancipation was too high. Authentic Judaism, they felt, could not be squeezed into the confines of synagogues and theological doctrines, but must encompass areas of civil law and institutional structures. Oppressive as it might have been to the Jews inside their walls, Jewish segregation also functioned as a bulwark against the penetration of heretical or immoral values from the outside world. As their traditional beliefs and lifestyles were increasingly beleaguered and eroded, the rabbis were convinced that even minor concessions to modernity would introduce cracks into their venerable structures that would eventually result in the complete collapse of Judaism as it had evolved over the previous centuries. This perspective produced an tendency to automatically oppose every proposal for change, even ones that involved only minor breaches of local custom. The paradigmatic exponent of this approach was Rabbi Moses Schreiber, (1762–1839) (known in Hebrew as the *Hatam Sofer*) who served as rabbi in Pressburg (Bratislava). He was uncompromising in his resistance to all appearances of innovation or reform.

The term "Orthodoxy" is applied to Jewish traditionalist movements that have consciously resisted the influences of modernization. The word is not normally used to designate Jewish traditionalism prior to the eighteenth century, nor did the phenomenon arise in communities that were unaffected by the Reform movement, such as North Africa or in eastern Europe before the mid-nineteenth-century.

The adjective "Orthodox" ("correct belief") was taken from the conceptual world of Christianity, where it denotes a conservative and ritualistic religious outlook as viewed from the perspective of liberal Protestantism. Evidently, it was first applied derisively to Jewish conservatives by a Reform polemicist in an article published in 1795. Rabbi Samson Raphael Hirsch (who will be discussed below) commented bitterly in 1854: "...it was not 'Orthodox' Jews who introduced the word 'orthodox' into Jewish discussion. It was the modern 'progressive' Jews who first applied the name to 'old,' 'backward' Jews as a derogatory term. This name was at first resented by 'old' Jews." Yet so pervasive was the use of the term that in 1886, when Hirsch established an alliance of the traditionalist congregations in Europe, he named it the "Freie Vereinigung für die Interessen des Orthodoxen Judentums" (Free Union for the Interests of Orthodox Judaism)!

Of all the movements on the contemporary Jewish scene, Orthodoxy is the least centralized and the most varied. Whereas the Conservative and Reform movements in America each have a central seminary and institutional leadership, an association of rabbis and a synagogue union, the Orthodox world is fragmented into diverse institutional structures. Though they agree on basic issues of religious authority (such as the divine origins of the Bible and oral tradition) and share a commitment to the study and observance of Jewish law, Orthodox Jews diverge on a broad range of secondary issues, such as: the importance or legitimacy of mysticism, attitudes towards Zionism and Jewish nationalism, the eschatological status of the state of Israel, educational philosophies, leadership models, whether or not to cooperate with non-Orthodox Jews, differing ethnic styles and local customs.

The most influential attempt to formulate a traditionalist school in opposition to the reformist and modernist trends was that of Rabbi Samson Raphael Hirsch (1808–1888). Hirsch was born in Hamburg and raised in an "Enlightened" environment, including a full secular education at a German public school. He trained in philology at the University of Bonn, where he was friendly with the Reform leader Abraham Geiger and was profoundly influenced by German writers and thinkers like Schiller and Hegel. During Hirsch's first rabbinical post, as regional rabbi at Oldenburg (1830–1841), he published some of his most influential works. *The Nineteen Letters* (1836) was a fictitious exchange of letters between a teacher (the young rabbi-philosopher Naphtali) and a young intellectual (Benjamin), containing a well-argued case for the rationality of traditional Judaism. In 1838, he published *Choreb*, a rational explanation of the 613 commandments of the Torah.

Between 1841 and 1851, Hirsch served as rabbi to several German communities. He now turned his energies to an active campaign against the Reform movement, as well as formulating his doctrine of *"Torah im Derekh Erez,"* of integrating Torah with secular culture (see below). His moderate brand of traditionalism brought him acceptance by both traditionalists and modernists, though those at both extremes found him problematic.

An important turning point in his career occurred in 1851, when Hirsch resigned his prestigious office of chief rabbi of Moravia and Austrian Silesia to accept the leadership of the beleaguered traditionalist community (Adass Yeshurun) in Frankfurt-am-Main. In a controversial move, he brought about the withdrawal of the minority Orthodox community from the general Jewish organizational structure that was dominated by the Reform. From 1871 to 1873, he fought to have the Orthodox minority recognized by the Prussian government as a separate congregation, a policy that was opposed by some Orthodox leaders. His efforts bore fruit in 1876 when the Prussian parliament passed the "Law of Secession" allowing the creation of independent traditionalist communities. Hirsch's first priority was to establish religious schools to inculcate Jewish tradition. He erected beautiful modern buildings for schools and a synagogue. Hirsch's Frankfurt community became a model for similar projects in Mainz, Darmstadt, and Berlin.

Apart from his polemical and communal activities, Hirsch is best known for his doctrine of "Torah with *Derekh Erez.*" Taking his inspiration from a talmudic expression, Hirsch used the expression to refer to the integration of traditional Judaism with secular education, which he equated with German literature and culture. He maintained that the esthetic style and externals of Jewish practice could legitimately be changed, but (unlike the Reform and Positive-Historical schools) he did not tolerate extensive changes in religious law or traditional beliefs. The ideal product of Hirsch's educational model was the "Israel-Mensch," the enlightened religious personality who integrated the finest elements of both Jewish and humanistic values.

Hirsch was uncompromising in his conviction that the Torah, both the written and the oral components, originated in divine revelation, and hence the obligatory character of Jewish religious law is not subject to historical development or change. Israel is a religious community, and only the Torah is the ultimate purpose of Jewish peoplehood. In contrast to the historical model of religious development advocated by the reformers and the *Wissenschaft des Judentums* movement (see Chapter 13), Hirsch argued that Judaism was fundamentally impervious to change. Though the rest of humanity, who have not been favored with a supernatural revelation, are in need of a gradual historical process in order to evolve towards a recognition of truth, Israel was given the truth from the start.

The "Agudat Israel" movement

Unlike the situation in central or western Europe, where challenges to Jewish beliefs and institutions were dealt with through religious and theological reforms, or through conversion to another religion, in eastern Europe Jews were more likely to choose between traditional Jewish religion and a broad spectrum of secular Jewish ideologies. The result was that the influence of non-Orthodox Jewish religious movements was marginal in eastern Europe.

In 1912, an organization known as Agudat Israel (the Israelite Union) was established to serve as the political arm of traditional Orthodoxy, representing a wide range of anti-modern branches. Active in the Agudat Israel were several Hasidic groups, alongside advocates of Lithuanian-style yeshivahs (see below) and followers of German Orthodoxy. It even developed a Labor wing that called for the establishment of strictly religious agricultural settlements in Palestine outside the framework of the Zionist movement. The Agudat Israel in Europe wielded considerable political power, sending representatives to the Polish parliament.

Policy decisions of Agudat Israel must be ratified by their "Council of Torah Scholars," which consists of leading rabbis from the main constituent groups. When participating in Israeli government coalitions, they have generally refrained from accepting actual cabinet posts. Agudat Israel does not have clear positions on issues related to Israeli security or foreign policy. Because they do not attach eschatological or religious significance to the State of Israel, they generally approach such questions pragmatically.

The Agudat Israel established a broad assortment of religious institutions in Europe. Most of these institutions have been transplanted to Israel and America. In Israel they have maintained their separate school system (*Hinnukh 'Atzma'i*) outside the state-run religious school system.

Judaism in the New World

The promise of the Jewish Emancipation was not to be realized in nineteenth-century Europe. As the French armies were expanding the frontiers of the revolutionary cause, Napoleon made a special point of physically tearing down the walls of the Jewish ghettos in each city and of extending civil rights to the Jews. However, following Napoleon's defeat there was a re-entrenchment of conservative régimes that effectively rescinded the previous advances. During the early decades of the nineteenth century, there were occasional efforts to rekindle the liberal cause, culminating in a series of liberal uprisings throughout Europe in 1848. Ultimately, those uprisings failed, and the counterrevolutionary forces repressed the liberal cause with ruthlessness. Recognizing that this was a death knell for their dreams of acceptance into an enlightened Europe, many Jews decided that their only option was to emigrate to the New World. Religious traditionalists were less inclined to uproot themselves, whether because of their natural conservatism or because they feared the prospect of uncontrolled assimilation that would be posed in an open society. As a result, the wave of Jewish immigration that crossed the Atlantic in the mid-nineteenth century was made up largely of radical Reformers. Many of these belonged to the lower middle classes, and were able to fulfill the "American dream" by raising their economic status through hard work, rising from traveling peddlers to considerable affluence.

A tiny, mostly Sephardic Jewish community had resided in America since colonial times. In 1790, George Washington composed a letter to mark the opening of the new synagogue in Newport, Rhode Island, in which he expressed his hopes that "the children of the stock of Abraham who dwell in the land continue to merit and enjoy the goodwill of the other inhabitants." The nineteenth century witnessed initial attempts at organizing Jewish communities. A major force in this effort was Isaac Leeser (1806–1868), a Prussian-born rabbi with leanings towards the Positive-Historical approach who served in pulpits in Philadelphia. He pioneered the writing and publication of basic works on Judaism, including a new prayer book, for the American Jewish audience, and founded a monthly magazine, *The Occident*, devoted to Jewish issues. Leeser was involved in the founding of a Jewish publication society, a national organization of Jewish congregations, the first American Hebrew day schools, an advanced Hebrew college, and other enterprises.

A rabbinical conference was convened in 1886 in Pittsburgh, in order to formulate a unified platform for American Jewry. The resulting "Pittsburgh Platform" typified the most radical positions of German Reform, rejecting in principle most rituals and many traditional theological positions (such as resurrection of the dead), and defining Jews as a purely religious community without any national or ethnic component.

The wave of Jewish immigration from central Europe, significant though it was, was soon eclipsed by a much larger wave, mainly from Russia and Poland, which reached momentum in the 1870s. A campaign of discriminatory legislation and government-sanctioned pogroms in Czarist and Bolshevik Russia impelled some two million Jews to emigrate to America by 1924, when the United States adopted new policies restricting immigration. With the rise of Nazism in Germany, a new wave of Jewish refugees reached the New World, though these were limited by immigration restrictions.

By the time the Reform leadership convened, half a century later, to produce a new statement of principles, they were dealing with a world, and with a Jewish constituency, that differed significantly from the situation at the time of the Pittsburgh Platform. Jews from eastern Europe never doubted the ethnic dimension of their Jewish identity, and were unlikely to define their Judaism in terms of belief systems. Furthermore, the quasi-religious faith that an earlier generation may have had in the power of progress and enlightenment to overcome anti-Semitism had been decisively discredited by the policies of the European totalitarian régimes and the indifference of supposedly enlightened nations to the Jewish plight. The Zionist pioneers who were striving to create a refuge for persecuted Jews on the soil of the land of Israel earned the sympathies of many American Jews, even among the traditionally anti-Zionistic ranks of the Reform movement.

It is in this context that we must understand the radical reversal of positions that is so evident in the "Columbus Platform" that was adopted by the American Reform movement in 1937. Unlike the Pittsburgh Platform, the newer document expressed a most positive attitude towards religious observance and ritual in all its venues, as well as towards Zionism and solidarity with the Jewish people.

The evolution of Reform Judaism in the twentieth and twenty-first centuries has been so diverse as to defy simple summarization. As regards observances and rituals, the prevailing pattern follows that of the Columbus Platform, of encouraging them while not regarding them as binding or supernaturally revealed commandments in the traditionalist sense. There have even been efforts to develop Reform halakhah and responsa. To the extent that there is an interest in theology, it is likely to be more experiential and existential. In recent years there has been a pronounced interest in meditation and mysticism, and in the promotion of more intimate venues for worship and spiritual pursuits. Support for Israel has remained strong in the Reform ranks, as is the case in the American Jewish community as a whole.

Some of the more controversial issues that the movement has grappled with relate to the definitions of Jewish identity. While their official policies have discouraged marriages between Jews and non-Jews (as was confirmed in a 1973 resolution of the Central Conference of American Rabbis), many Reform rabbis actually preside at intermarriage ceremonies. In 1983, the movement decided to recognize as Jewish the children born to either a Jewish mother or father. This acceptance of "patrilineal descent" was a departure from the traditional Jewish stance that looked only at the status of the mother. While Reform Judaism has always professed full equality for men and women, it was only in the latter decades of the twentieth century that female rabbis became a familiar feature of the movement. In a similar vein, they have generally been vocal in calling for full acceptance of homosexuals in the Jewish community and in the general society.

Conservative Judaism in America

While the earlier wave of German-Jewish immigration to America included some scholars who identified with Frankel's Positive-Historical school, they constituted a small minority amid the Reformers. By 1880, only twelve out of 200 American congregations were not Reform. A number of the traditionalist Jews belonged to the older Sephardic communities concentrated on the eastern seaboard. In 1883, shellfish and other flagrantly non-kosher dishes were served at the dinner celebrating the first graduating class of the rabbinical seminary, the Hebrew Union College in Cincinnati. This episode, along with the adoption of the Pittsburgh Platform in 1885, made it clear to the traditionalist minority that they could not be accommodated in the existing Jewish institutions.

Attempts to establish a center of for the training of traditional American rabbis reached fruition in 1902 with the founding of the Jewish Theological Seminary of America in New York City, whose declared purpose was "for the preservation in America of the knowledge and practice of historical Judaism as ordained in the law of Moses expounded by the prophets and sages in Israel in Biblical and Talmudic writings." The seminary was, in fact, financed in part by established Reform Jews, who recognized that their own brand of Judaism would not be accepted by the immigrants from eastern Europe, and hoped that the moderate orthodoxy that would be professed in this seminary would contribute towards the "Americanization" of the new arrivals. At any rate, the Reform supporters assumed that they would be able to influence the institution's ideological direction. To head the new seminary, they invited Solomon Schechter, a traditionally trained rabbi from Romania with impeccable academic credentials who was then lecturing in Judaic Studies at Cambridge University. Schechter, who had been responsible for the discovery of the Cairo Genizah, succeeded in gathering into the seminary a team of the world's finest Judaic scholars, and under his leadership the Jewish Theological Seminary of America became one of the world's most prestigious centers of Jewish learning. Sephardic Jews also participated in the creation of the new institution.

The religious movement that was cultivated at the seminary was named "Conservative Judaism," indicating its determination to conserve (rather than reject or reform) the Jewish traditions. Like the other branches of American Judaism, Conservative Judaism evolved a variegated constellation of institutions for rabbis, cantors, synagogues, youth, women and men. They established schools for training cantors and teachers; religious schools and summer camps for children; and a Jewish museum. Although in the past, the influence of Conservative Judaism has been limited outside North America, it has made significant progress in recent decades. In Israel, it is known as the Masorti ("traditional") movement.

Many of the movement's specific features and policies arose from its place midway between the extremes of orthodoxy and liberalism. While acknowledging the potential for flexibility in the development of halakhah, Conservative Judaism insisted on justifying its departures from earlier norms by invoking the established methods of halakhic argumentation. In this respect it was distinct from the Orthodox approach that (at least in theory) rejected all change, and the Reform approach, which denied the binding character of religious law. As early as 1898, before there was an established Orthodox presence in America, European Orthodox rabbis repudiated the Conservative approach. The subtle balance maintained under Schechter's leadership is reflected in the fact that he defended the academic freedom of Mordecai M. Kaplan, whose book *Judaism as a Civilization* (1934) proposed a naturalist theology in which religion is a basically human invention and halakhah is reduced to the status of "folkways"; whereas he forbade the teaching of the "documentary hypothesis" of the compilation of the Torah.

During the 1940s and 1950s, Conservative congregations became the most attractive option for the second-generation American Jews who were moving from the inner cities into the suburbs. The movement's institutional expansion was not always accompanied by a corresponding commitment to standards of religious observance. Because the movement's leadership, especially the faculty of the Jewish Theological Seminary, were mostly traditionalist in their personal observance, there developed an ever-widening gap between them and the more liberal congregational rabbis and laity. It became common that in Conservative congregations, few individuals other than the clergy were observing basic Jewish practices, such as the Sabbath or the dietary regulations. As fewer congregants were competent to participate actively in the religious services, many Conservative synagogues adopted practices that served to reinforce the role of the worshipper as a passive observer, rather than an active participant; these included the widespread use of professional cantors, who often faced towards the congregation (unlike Orthodox services where they face in the same direction) and the positioning of the platform (*bimah*) at the front of the sanctuary, like a theatrical stage, rather than in the center.

Recognizing the broad diversity of views that coexisted within Conservative Judaism, the movement established a mechanism for allowing, or even encouraging, halakhic pluralism. The Committee on Law and Standards, which is responsible for defining official policies on matters of religious law, discusses the various positions and then votes on them. However, the committee also gives sanction to minority positions when they achieve significant support. These minority positions often reflect more liberal and permissive approaches; and are more likely to be adopted by the congregations. Conservative Jewish policy assigns considerable autonomy to the rabbis of individual synagogues.

> Many suburban Jews in the Conservative constituency lived beyond convenient walking distance of their synagogues. The Committee on Law and Standards issued a 1949 "Responsum on the Sabbath" in which they concluded that "the positive values involved in the participation in public worship on the Sabbath outweigh the negative values of refraining from riding in an automobile." The decision, in fact, defined very restrictive conditions under which driving, only to the synagogue, would be allowed if the local rabbi should decide to permit it. However, the perception rapidly arose among the laity that Conservative Judaism permits driving on the Sabbath.

Far-reaching tensions between traditional and Conservative religious law have been occasioned by the growing commitment of Americans, Jews included, to sexual egalitarianism, an ideal that runs counter to several features of traditional halakhah. Virtually from its beginnings, Conservative congregations adopted "family seating" rather than the separation of sexes that prevailed in Orthodox synagogues. In order to ameliorate the plight of women who were unable to obtain a religious divorce, they introduced in 1968 a controversial prenuptial agreement that would allow retroactive annulment of marriages under certain conditions. In 1973 they decided to count women in the prayer quorum (*minyan*), as well as to allow them to participate in the liturgical reading of the Torah. Though some of these changes involved drastic departures from the norms of halakhic decision-making, they were implemented without much controversy, probably because they did not directly affect the traditionalist practices of the faculty at the Jewish Theological Seminary. This was not the case with the decision to ordain women as rabbis (1977–1979). The Seminary faculty would now have to sign their names on the certificates of ordination; and therefore the debate and its aftermath produced a deeper split within the movement's leadership. By the turn of the millennium, the liberal stream dominated the movement. The standard criterion that differentiated Conservative from Reform Judaism, that of commitment to the authority of halakhah, was being questioned by leaders of the movement.

American "Centrist" Orthodoxy

The single most prominent branch of American Orthodoxy is based in the Yeshiva University with its main campus in New York City; and especially in its rabbinic school, the "Rabbi Isaac Elchanan Theological Seminary," (RIETS), which was established in 1896 as the first American Orthodox seminary. RIETS is the main institution for the training and ordination of Orthodox congregational rabbis in America. Unlike some of the more traditionalist yeshivahs, RIETS graduates are expected to hold academic degrees. The congregational organization of the movement is the Union of Jewish Orthodox Congregations, commonly referred to as the "Orthodox Union" or: "OU." Its rabbinic organization is the Rabbinical Council of America.

For much of the twentieth century, the spiritual mentor of the movement was Rabbi Joseph D. Soloveitchik. Rabbi Soloveitchik was heir to a chain of distinguished Lithuanian talmudic scholars. He adopted the analytical-conceptual method of Talmud study developed by his grandfather Rabbi Hayyim of Brisk (1853–1918), with a focus on Maimonides's systematic and philosophical presentation of Jewish religious law. Soloveitchik was also a distinguished philosopher, with a doctorate from the University of Berlin. He was an exponent of religious existentialism and was deeply influenced by Christian theologians like Karl Barth. Since arriving in the United States in 1932, he lived in Boston, and was involved in educational and communal activities. His influence was exerted largely through his position as a teacher at Yeshiva University and as head of RIETS, in which capacities he was mentor to several generations of the American Rabbinate. He also influenced the direction of Orthodox law as head of the Orthodox Union's "Halacha Commission."

Soloveitchik published very little during his lifetime, and most of the volumes that have been published under his name are transcriptions of classes that he gave. His best-known writings include:

- *Halakhic Man*, an analytical-anthropological study of the religious mentality of Lithuanian Judaism emphasizing the differences between Jewish "legalistic" piety and conventional religiosity. In this work he depicts the system of talmudic law as a means through which the Jewish scholar imposes a divinely founded conceptual order, analogous to a mathematical system, upon all aspects of day-to-day existence.
- *The Lonely Man of Faith*, an exploration of the tension between faith and reason, focusing on the biblical story of the "binding of Isaac."
- "The Voice of My Beloved is Knocking," on the religious significance of Zionism.
- *On Repentance*, discourses on Maimonides' "Laws of Repentance."

In recent decades, and especially since Rabbi Soloveitchik's death, the ideological direction of American Orthodoxy has moved away from his model of active engagement with modern society and philosophies, towards in a more traditionalist and insular approach. This has coincided with the renewed vitality of the Lithuanian Yeshivah culture that was transplanted to America after the Holocaust. Even at Yeshiva University and RIETS, the term "centrist" is often applied to the conservative Lithuanian approaches, while proponents of Soloveitchik's approach are referred to as "modern Orthodox."

Developments among Sephardic Jews

As in eastern Europe, the Sephardic and North African Jewish communities did not experience movements for religious reform like the ones in central and western Europe and in America. The main threat to their religious tradition came from the secular influences that they encountered under colonial rule, especially under the French regimes in Morocco, Tunisia and Algeria. At any rate, they did not produce an Orthodoxy on the European model.

With the establishment of the State of Israel in 1948, and the riots and persecutions that broke out against the Jews of Arab countries, massive numbers of Middle-Eastern Jews were brought to Israel. The Israeli leadership, consisting largely of secular Ashkenazic Jews, often viewed the religious lifestyles of their "oriental" cousins as vestiges of cultural primitiveness that would have to be shed as a precondition to their integration into a modern western society. Many of the immigrants were persuaded or forced to abandon the religious traditions they brought from their former homelands. During the early decades of Israeli statehood, many North African Jews were unable to establish their own political or religious movements or institutions, and most were absorbed into the established Ashkenazic structures. They were usually educated in the State Religious School system, though religious Ashkenazim often sent their children to private schools and yeshivahs. The religious political parties had few Sephardim among their leadership. By the mid-1970s the social inequities between Ashkenazic and Sephardic Israelis became a major social issue. In the religious sphere this led to the appearance of Sephardic versions of the mainstream religious parties. The most influential of these is known as "Shas."

Although considerable numbers of North African Jews had been educated at yeshivahs affiliated with the Agudat Israel movement, the movement continued to regard itself as an Eastern European constituency. Yiddish remained the language of discussions for its guiding "Council of Torah Scholars" and the Sephardic rabbinic authorities were often held in disdain. This was what led to the creation of a Sephardic equivalent to Agudat Israel, named "Shas," with its own Council of Torah Sages.

The principal spiritual leader of the party is the respected halakhic authority Rabbi Ovadiah Yosef. The Israeli government's refusal to extend Rabbi Yosef's term as Sephardic Chief Rabbi (Rishon le-Zion) had been one of the main reasons for the Shas party's establishment.

Havurat Shalom and Jewish Renewal

Two significant developments in recent Jewish religiosity have developed outside the mainstream of the institutional movements, and in reaction to them. Each of these can be viewed as a Jewish parallel to an American Christian cultural phenomenon.

The Havurah movement arose in the 1960s and 1970s in the cultural milieu that produced the Hippie movement and other forms of American counter-culture. Its membership consisted largely of students from the post-war "baby boomer" generation, many of them from the Conservative movement, who felt alienated from the impersonal suburban congregations in which their families were members. As an alternative, they chose to worship in intimate and unstructured settings, which were often modeled on experiences they had in Jewish summer camps, and they incorporated song and dance into their worship. Several figures from the movement, especially the branch at Brandeis University, went on to occupy important places in academic Jewish studies and in communal life.

Jewish Renewal evolved out of the Havurah movement, and has much in common with the New Age movement of the 1990s. Their most important spiritual mentors were two charismatic figures who emerged out of the Chabad-Lubavitch Hasidic movement and achieved prominence in the Jewish counter-culture in the 1960s. Shlomo Carlbach (1925–1994) was a guitar-playing rabbi whose lively renditions of traditional Hebrew texts continue to enjoy immense popularity even in the Jewish mainstream. Rabbi Zalman Schachter-Shalomi formulated his own synthesis of Hasidism and liberal American values, such as environmentalism, pacifism, sexual egalitarianism (including acceptance of homosexuality), Kabbalah and a discipline of meditation that draws on Jewish sources like Abraham Abulafia and Hasidic tradition. Jewish Renewal has avoided affiliation with any particular Jewish denomination, and has acquired significant followings from across the spectrum of the Jewish community.

Key points you need to know

- The Jewish Emancipation was the invitation to equal citizenship in modern nations. It was accompanied by a call to modernize Jewish life, ideas and practices, which is known as the Jewish Enlightenment.
- Moses Mendelssohn demonstrated in his life and person that it was possible for a Jew to participate in modern European intellectual and cultural life. He instituted a program to modernize the Jewish religion and society, and to treat Judaism as a matter of individual conscience.
- European Reform evolved from a lay movement seeking to facilitate their social integration, to an ideological movement led by rabbis and scholars.
- Zacharias Frankel's Positive-Historical school proposed an evolutionary model of Judaism that stressed the organic connection between Judaism and the historical Jewish people.
- The Reform presence in America was initially very untraditional, but with the absorption of many eastern European Jews, it adopted more traditional attitudes on issues like ritual and peoplehood.

- The Positive-Historical movement established itself in America as Conservative Judaism. Initially very traditional in its halakhic norms, it has become much less so in recent years, especially on issues related to egalitarianism.
- The Neo-Orthodoxy of Rabbi Samson Raphael Hirsch advocated strict adherence to traditional Jewish beliefs and practice, but encouraged engagement with modern culture and society.
- The defining figure of "centrist" Orthodoxy in America was Rabbi Joseph Soloveitchik, known for his integration of philosophical existentialism and the conceptual approach of Talmud study.
- As alternatives to the formal institutional structures of American Judaism, movements have arisen that stress the importance of intimate communal worship and a Hasidic-like mystical experience that encourages song, dance and communion with nature.

Discussion questions

1. Discuss why language became an important factor in the struggle between reformers and traditionalists.
2. Why do you think that the reformers preferred to have their houses of worship called "temples" instead of "synagogues"?
3. The intransigence of the traditionalists and the flexibility of the reformers were both prescriptions for the continuity of Judaism in modern society. From the perspective of historical hindsight, which approach proved most accurate?
4. Frankel and Hirsch both advocated the integration of modern culture into traditional Judaism. On what key principles did they differ?
5. Considering the extreme reversals in positions on key issues between the Pittsburgh and Columbus Reform platforms, how are we justified in conceiving of American Reform as a single movement?

Further reading

General

Blau, Joseph L., *Modern Varieties of Judaism*. New York: Columbia University Press, 1966.

Cohn-Sherbok, Dan, *Modern Judaism*. Basingstoke and New York: Macmillan and St. Martin's Press, 1996.

De Lange, N. R. M. and Miri Freud-Kandel, eds, *Modern Judaism: An Oxford Guide*. Oxford and New York: Oxford University Press, 2005.

Glatzer, Nahum Norbert, ed., *Modern Jewish Thought: A Source Reader*. New York: Schocken, 1977.

Mendes-Flohr, Paul R. and Jehuda Reinharz, eds, *The Jew in the Modern World: A Documentary History*, 2nd ed. New York: Oxford University Press, 1995.

Raphael, Marc Lee, *Approaches to Modern Judaism*, Brown Judaic Studies. Chico, CA: Scholars Press, 1983.

Emancipation and Enlightenment

Altmann, Alexander, *Moses Mendelssohn: A Biographical Study*. Tuscaloosa, AL: University of Alabama Press, 1973.

Baron, Salo Wittmayer, *Jewish Emancipation*. New York: Macmillan, 1932.

Feiner, Shmuel. *The Jewish Enlightenment*, Jewish Culture and Contexts. Philadelphia, PA: University of Pennyslvania Press, 2004.

Katz, Jacob, *Out of the Ghetto: The Social Background of Jewish Emancipation, 1770–1870*. New York: Schocken Books, 1978.

Sorkin, David Jan, *Moses Mendelssohn and the Religious Enlightenment*, Jewish Thinkers. London: P. Halban, 1996.

Reform Judaism

Borowitz, Eugene B., *Liberal Judaism*. New York: Union of American Hebrew Congregations, 1984.

Kaplan, Dana Evan, *American Reform Judaism: An Introduction*. New Brunswick, NJ and London: Rutgers University Press, 2003.

Koltun-Fromm, Ken, *Abraham Geiger's Liberal Judaism: Personal Meaning and Religious Authority*, Jewish Literature and Culture. Bloomington, IN: Indiana University Press, 2006.

Meyer, Michael A., *Response to Modernity: A History of the Reform Movement in Judaism*, Studies in Jewish History. New York: Oxford University Press, 1988.

Philipson, David, *The Reform Movements in Judaism*. A reissue of the new and rev. ed. New York: Ktav, 1967.

Positive-Historical and Conservative Judaism

Davis, Moshe, *The Emergence of Conservative Judaism: The Historical School in 19th Century America*, 1st ed. Philadelphia, PA: Jewish Publication Society of America, 1963.

Elazar, Daniel Judah and Rela M. Geffen, *The Conservative Movement in Judaism: Dilemmas and Opportunities*, SUNY Series in American Jewish Society in the 1990s. Albany, NY: State University of New York Press, 2000.

Scolnic, Benjamin Edidin, *Conservative Judaism and the Faces of God's Words, Studies in Judaism*. Lanham, MD: University Press of America, 2005.

Sklare, Marshall, *Conservative Judaism: An American Religious Movement*. New York: Schocken, 1972.

Wertheimer, Jack. *Jews in the Center: Conservative Congregations and Their Members*. New Brunswick, NJ: Rutgers University Press, 2000.

Neo-Orthodoxy

Grunfeld, Isidor, *Three Generations: The Influence of Samson Raphael Hirsch on Jewish Life and Thought*. London: Jewish Post Publications, 1958.

Hirsch, Samson Raphael and Jacob Breuer. *Timeless Torah: An Anthology of the Writings of Samson Raphael Hirsch*. New York: Feldheim, 1969.

Liberles, Robert, *Religious Conflict in Social Context: The Resurgence of Orthodox Judaism in Frankfurt-am-Main, 1838–1877*, Contributions to the Study of Religion. Westport, CT: Greenwood Press, 1985.

Rosenbloom, Noah H., *Tradition in an Age of Reform: The Religious Philosophy of Samson Raphael Hirsch*, 1st ed. Philadelphia, PA: Jewish Publication Society of America, 1976.

Centrist Orthodoxy and Soloveitchik

Bernstein, Saul, *The Orthodox Union Story: A Centenary Portrayal*. Northvale, NJ: Jason Aronson, 1997.

Diamond, Etan, *And I Will Dwell in Their Midst: Orthodox Jews in Suburbia*. Chapel Hill, NC: University of North Carolina Press, 2000.

Ferziger, Adam S., *Exclusion and Hierarchy: Orthodoxy, Nonobservance, and the Emergence of Modern Jewish Identity*, Jewish Culture and Contexts. Philadelphia, PA: University of Pennsylvania Press, 2005.

Freundel, Barry, *Contemporary Orthodox Judaism's Response to Modernity*. Jersey City, NJ: KTAV, 2004.

Geller, Victor B., *Orthodoxy Awakens: The Belkin Era and Yeshiva University*, 1st ed. Jerusalem and New York: Urim, 2003.

Gurock, Jeffrey S., *American Jewish Orthodoxy in Historical Perspective*. Hoboken, NJ: KTAV, 1996.

Heilman, Samuel C., *Sliding to the Right: The Contest for the Future of American Jewish Orthodoxy*, The S. Mark Taper Foundation Imprint in Jewish Studies. Berkeley, CA: University of California Press, 2006.

Rakeffet-Rothkoff, Aaron and Joseph Epstein, *The Rav: The World of Rabbi Joseph B. Soloveitchik*, 2 vols. Hoboken, NJ: KTAV, 1999.

Sokol, Moshe, *Engaging Modernity: Rabbinic Leaders and the Challenge of the Twentieth Century*. Northvale, NJ: Jason Aronson, 1997.

Weiss, Saul, *Insights of Rabbi Joseph B. Soloveitchik: Discourses on Fundamental Theological Issues in Judaism*. Lanham, MD: Rowman & Littlefield Publishers, Inc., 2005.

Havurah and Jewish Renewal

Prell, Riv-Ellen, *Prayer and Community: The Havurah in American Judaism*. Detroit, MI: Wayne State University Press, 1989.

Schachter-Shalomi, Zalman, *Paradigm Shift: From the Jewish Renewal Teachings of Reb Zalman Schachter-Shalomi*. Northvale, NJ: Jason Aronson, 1993.

Weissler, Chava, *Making Judaism Meaningful: Ambivalence and Tradition in a Havurah Community*, Immigrant Communities and Ethnic Minorities in the United States and Canada. New York: AMS Press, 1989.

Part II

Jewish beliefs and values

8   *Devotion to one God*

In this chapter

The religion of the Bible is solidly monotheistic, though God is referred to by different names and has a human-like personality. Later Jewish tradition tried to explain how humanity fell into the error of idolatry, and how Abraham alone realized that there must be a being who transcended all natural forces. Philo of Alexandria posited a non-physical rational force to serve as an intermediary between God and the physical universe. Medieval Jewish philosophers understood divine oneness in a more demanding sense, arguing that multiple attributes cannot be applied God, and he is not subject to change or anthropomorphic description. The kabbalists described God and his relationship with the world in terms of the *sefirot*, ten emanated aspects of divinity, the last of which is the Shekhinah, the divine presence in the world embodied in the Jewish people. Ancient Judaism had clearly demarcated boundaries between Jewish monotheism, legitimate "Noachide" religion and unacceptable idolatry. Medieval Judaism was unclear about how to apply those categories to Christianity and Islam, though modern Jewish movements are committed to interfaith tolerance.

Main topics covered

- The God of the Hebrew Bible
- Monotheism and idolatry
- Philo's Logos theology
- Divine unity in medieval Jewish philosophy
- The God of the Kabbalah
- Heathens and heretics

When attempting to present the Jewish religion to outsiders, it is all too easy to take a one-sided approach to beliefs and doctrines. Because Christianity, the dominant religion in western society, attaches great importance to beliefs, it is natural to also define Judaism as a system of theological doctrines. Conversely, many authors are persuaded to downplay the importance of theology precisely because they regard that approach as foreign to an authentic Judaism. Judaism, they remind us, is not an orthodoxy, but an orthopraxy, and Jews do not measure a person's religiosity by conformity to normative doctrine, but by how scrupulously they perform the divine commandments.

Though doctrine may function differently in Judaism than in Christianity, it is misleading to deny that ideas and values have been important for Judaism and served to distinguish Judaism from other religions. Still, it is not always obvious where we should look to find representative accounts of authentic Jewish beliefs. Revered works like the Talmud, the *Guide of the Perplexed* or the *Zohar* were produced by scholarly elites and their ideas were peculiar to their authors' ideologies or movements. They do not necessarily reflect a consensus, nor did they always determine the attitudes of the broad Jewish populace.

When choosing the topics to be discussed in this section, it was useful to consult the traditional Jewish prayer book. The major components of the liturgy were standardized in ancient times, lending them an official or normative status. They have shaped the religious sensibilities of Jews (not only the males) through daily recitation. The ideas that are expressed in the Jewish prayers cover a rich array of values, beliefs and doctrines related to theology, historiography, afterlife, mysticism, morality and ethics, eschatology, worship, and much more. These core themes were understood in diverse ways by Jews who lived in varied historical and cultural settings.

The God of the Hebrew Bible

In the Jewish liturgy, the central declaration of Jewish faith is the *Shema'*, the passage from the Torah that begins: "Hear, O Israel, the Lord is our God, the Lord is one." A number of important concepts are alluded to in this terse sentence (six words in the Hebrew).

For one thing, we observe in it a paradoxical tension between God's being at once the God of Israel and the Lord of the whole universe. This theme permeates all manifestations of Judaism. Although the Bible might preserve vestiges from earlier strata when the Israelite God was but the greatest among multiple deities, the dominant biblical belief was that the gods worshipped by the other nations are foolish fantasies, impotent creatures of wood and stone.

An explanation should be provided for the names that the Bible uses to designate God. Following the familiar precedent established by the translators of the King James English version, two names appear most prominently: "Lord" and "God." This reflects the ancient conventions for pronouncing the Hebrew text. The English word "God" is used to render Hebrew forms that are based on the word *el*. The most common of these forms is "Elohim." "Lord," on the other hand, is the conventional

English rendering of the "tetragrammaton," the four-letter name whose English equivalent would be YHVH. This enigmatic name, apparently related to the root for "to be," was generally understood to be God's proper name. At some point during the Second Temple era, Jews considered it too sacred to be pronounced, so they substituted for it the honorific *Adonai*, "my Lord." This practice is reflected as early as the Septuagint Greek translation of the Bible dating from the third century BCE, and some of the Qumran scrolls replace the tetragrammaton with four dots. Religious Jews still observe that convention—in fact, even the name *Adonai* is now considered too sacred to pronounce outside prayer or formal reading from the scriptures. Because Hebrew vowels were not written in ancient texts, the exact pronunciation of the Tetragrammaton is no longer known.

Academic biblical scholars generally agree that the duality of the names should be attributed to two different literary or local traditions that were merged in the final redaction of the Torah. However, traditional interpreters, who maintain that the Torah was revealed directly by God at Mount Sinai, explain that the different names relate to different aspects of God's personality or modes of relating to his creatures. The explanation favored by the rabbis was that the "God" name represents divine justice, whereas the "Lord" name represents God's mercy.

The assertion that there is only one God can be understood in numerous ways. The most obvious implication is the rejection of polytheism, which was the kind of religion practiced by virtually all other peoples in antiquity. Judaism generally understood that commitment to God's oneness also entailed rejection of dualism, the belief in absolute forces of good and evil; as well as of Christian trinitarian theology.

The ancient texts did not deal with theology in a theoretical manner. The familiar theological terminology of "omniscience," "omnipotence" and "omnipresence" is not to be found widely in traditional Jewish writings, though similar assumptions often underlie them. When they speak of belief in God, they were not speaking of adherence to a system of doctrines, but of an existential state of trust. Their authors were concerned with conveying a moral or spiritual message. Therefore, in reading those texts we should not expect to find rational demonstrations of theological claims.

The God of the Bible is distinctly lacking in mythical elements of the sort that were so central to the polytheistic faiths of the Near East and Mediterranean regions. The contrast is very marked in the creation stories. Pagan mythology usually described the creation of the world and its inhabitants as the outcome of epic battles between natural and supernatural forces, and the deities themselves were sexual beings subject to lusts, jealousies and betrayals. The opening verses of the Bible, on the other hand, are sublime in the simplicity of their narrative. On each day, God simply says, "Let there be…" and things come into existence. At the end of each day's creation, God sees that it is good; and at the conclusion of the process, he sees that it is very good.

Nonetheless, the biblical God is depicted as having a human-like personality, one that bears a strong resemblance to a conventional patriarchal father, or to a mighty monarch. All Hebrew nouns must be grammatically either masculine or feminine, and the masculine forms are usually employed to indicate indeterminate or generic genders; nevertheless, the use of masculine forms to describe God often strikes us as meaningful. He is capable of compassion, anger, satisfaction and other human-like emotions. The ancients did not question the reality of these character attributes, which were perhaps unavoidable if humans are to commit themselves to him.

Monotheism and idolatry

Many interpreters regarded the Hebrew patriarch Abraham as the first monotheist. According to this view, Abraham lived in a world that was steeped entirely in primitive idolatry, the worship of images and statues. Abraham was the first to recognize the folly of humans bowing before inanimate objects that they themselves had fashioned. After observing the movements of the heavenly bodies, he realized that none of those could be the true lord of the world, because the sun yielded to the moon at night, and the moon to the sun in the morning. There had to be a transcendent power above all the visible natural forces, and this insight was equivalent to the discovery of monotheism.

Based on traditions like this one, Maimonides proposed a reconstruction of early history that would account for how humanity, which is basically rational by nature and which had experienced divine revelation, could possibly have fallen into a state of irrational ignorance that led them to the worship of natural phenomena or manufactured objects. As the story was told by Maimonides, the dreadful error of idolatry can be traced to the generation of Enosh, the grandson of Adam. At that time it became acceptable to honor the heavenly bodies as agents and servants of the Creator. The gestures of respect that they demonstrated towards the sun, moon and stars included the erection of temples, the offering of sacrifices in their names, and other forms of verbal and non-verbal worship. At a later stage, however, false prophets arose and deceived the people, claiming that God had explicitly commanded the worship of the stars through the placement of images in the sanctuaries. Eventually, other charlatans began to teach that the stars were not merely representatives of the invisible God, but deserved to be treated as objects of worship in their own right. Out of these beginnings were born the elaborate idolatrous cults that persisted throughout the biblical era. As successive generations were brought up to believe in the divinity of physical objects, the memory of the original monotheism was all but forgotten from the world by the time Abraham appeared on the scene.

Elaborating on the midrashic legend, Maimonides described how Abraham, while still a small child, was able to arrive by scientific and logical reasoning at the conclusion that the prevailing idolatrous cults were based on lies. In Maimonides' retelling of the lives of the Hebrew patriarchs, the mission that was imposed on Abraham's descendants was to preserve the faint light of monotheistic faith in a world that was steeped in false heathenism. Israel is, in this sense, a nation of philosophers charged by God to bring truth to the world.

Philo's Logos theology

The first known thinker to attempt a synthesis between Judaism and the Greek philosophical tradition was the first-century writer Philo of Alexandria. One of the most important features of Philo's thought was his use of the Stoic doctrine of the "Logos" in biblical theology. In Greek, this word combines aspects of speech and of reason. The Stoic Logos is described as the underlying rational structure that governs the universe, and is the basis for the everlasting laws of logic and science. They can therefore posit a separation between the purely spiritual deity and the material, physical world that he created. It is the Logos that is responsible for the day-to-day running of the world and the interaction between God and his creatures, while God maintains a completely spiritual and self-contained existence. Philo made use of this theory in order to explain scriptural passages that appeared to portray God as directly involved with the physical world. For example, when the Bible portrays God as speaking to the people or to prophets, or responding to the words of humans, Philo explains that it is not God himself who is participating in such conversations, but the Logos.

Divine unity in medieval Jewish philosophy

The monotheistic principle of a single, non-material being who is the first cause of being is a premise regarding which an essential harmony seemed to exist between the traditional religions and the teachings of the Greek philosophers. However, as one explores the matter in greater detail, it becomes apparent that the philosophical understanding of "unity" is far more demanding than the traditional religious one. As understood in the medieval rationalist tradition, the doctrine of God's unity also implies that God is entirely one in the sense that he is not composed of multiple elements. This conception implied a rejection of belief in a deity who has a corporeal form. The medieval philosophers were certain that all matter is composite, and hence, in their view, subject to perishing when the components eventually decomposed. To deny that God is composite is therefore equivalent to denying that God has physical substance or human-like form (anthropomorphism).

The Muslim and Jewish advocates of the Kalam school of theology took that idea a step further. For them, the principle of divine unity also implied that God has no personal or emotional traits because they would be subject to changing moods. For them, to believe that God can be angry or compassionate is as much a violation of his unity as the belief that he has hands or eyes. Even attributes that seem honorable and praiseworthy, such as the assertion that God is "wise," "good," or "mighty," were unacceptable to the medieval theologians because the very multiplicity of attributes would also contradict God's fundamental unity.

Not only did such a refined view of God make it impossible for believers to maintain an emotional relationship with a personal God, but it also put them at odds with the plain meaning of the revealed scriptures and traditions whose authority they were claiming to uphold. After all, the God of the Bible has a very human-like personality that is capable of joy and wrath, sorrow and mercy. For this reason, most works of medieval Jewish theology or philosophy took on the task of carefully scanning the texts of the Bible, Talmud and midrash in order to reinterpret in a non-literal manner all those passages that seem to be ascribing personality traits to God.

Neoplatonic philosophy was constantly confronting the paradox of "the One and the Many": how could a perfectly spiritual and abstract being produce a universe that is material and diverse? The philosophers tried to resolve this contradiction, with varying degrees of success, by describing creation as a process consisting of subtle stages of emanation. Their most popular metaphor portrayed God as a pure, bright light whose rays lose their pristine clarity as they distance themselves from their source. The solution was rarely satisfactory, because it implied some compromising of the divine omnipotence in order to allow imperfections and multiplicity to gain entry into God's perfect radiance.

For Maimonides, as for many medieval Jewish philosophers, the ultimate goal of religious life is to attain a philosophical understanding of God. This requires that

A favorite exegetical principle that Maimonides employs in those discussions is "the Torah spoke in human language." The rule originated in talmudic literature where it was employed by Rabbi Ishmael. In the talmudic context it has a very narrow technical significance. However, in Maimonides' deft hands, the rule became a key to understanding the nature of revelation: once we have accepted that God chose to communicate with human beings, we must also acknowledge that that revelation had to be in human terms, through the vehicle of language. Language, as a human creation, reflects the realities of the human physical and social realities, and it is therefore inadequate for dealing with absolute metaphysical truths. For this reason, we cannot grasp the true meaning of scriptural passages until we have made allowances for the limitations imposed upon the discourse by language. When followed to its logical conclusion, this approach leads to the realization that all talk about God is inherently meaningless, because human language is inherently unequipped for discourse about the divine.

we overcome our normal human tendency to think in terms of sensory perception. Because God has no physical dimensions, and is outside the realms of time and space, he can only be grasped in abstract, conceptual terms. To achieve such a level of understanding requires long and arduous training. In his determination to purify people's conceptions of God from all elements of physicality and anthropomorphism, Maimonides was following in the lines of Saadiah and the Kalam theologians. Many chapters in the *Guide of the Perplexed* scan the Bible for expressions that appear to imply that God has physical characteristics or human emotions. Drawing upon his phenomenal erudition in biblical Hebrew, Maimonides is able to demonstrate in each case that the offending expression should be understood as a metaphor for an abstract concept.

Maimonides acknowledged only two ways in which biblical language can legitimately tell us about God:

1. *Attributes of action*: this is in evidence when we observe the effects of God on the world, and then metaphorically compare them with human acts that would produce analogous results. Thus, when we see a child benefiting from warmth and nourishment, we conclude that she has a mother who is loving. By way of analogy, when we witness humans or societies that are enjoying security and prosperity, we metaphorically describe this as an expression of divine love. However, Maimonides cautions that, when using that kind of language, we must not understand that God is motivated by any emotion that is comparable to the human feeling of love. God is not subject to changeable emotions, and ultimately humans are not capable of understanding why God acts as he does. The attributes of action are merely a way of describing things that happen in the world, and tell us nothing that is philosophically valid about God.

2. *Negative theology*: though it is impossible to use human language to say anything positive about God, because God's reality is so radically dissimilar to our own, it is nonetheless legitimate to deny that certain deficiencies apply to God. Thus, when the Bible speaks of God as being "wise," we cannot merely attribute the human quality of wisdom to God, even to an infinitely greater degree than human wisdom. God's omniscience is not just a more powerful version of the wisdom that is found in mortals, but a qualitatively different entity that utterly transcends our understanding. It is, however, correct to say that God is not subject to ignorance of any sort, and this is what the Bible is saying when it speaks of God's "wisdom": it is rejecting the attribution of any form of ignorance to God. Similarly, to say that God is "mighty" really means that we are denying all concepts of divine weakness. The words of scripture have been emptied of any meaningful content. Nevertheless, there is an indirect value to employing such language; because as we continue to delete inappropriate adjectives from our religious vocabulary, we will thereby be coming closer to a true understanding of the divine.

The philosophical understandings of God based on Greek models became less influential in the modern world as the Aristotelian system was consigned to obsolescence with the rise of modern experimental science. Many would argue that the key factor in this watershed was the philosophy of the Jewish heretic Baruch Spinoza (1632–1677). As an alternative to the Greek dualism of God and creation, Spinoza posited a pantheistic outlook in which God is equivalent to the totality of the universe.

The advances of science as an autonomous discipline have led religious thinkers in the western intellectual world to reject theologies in which God functions as a scientific principle. This has resulted to a large extent in a return to the idea of a personal deity, an existential absolute with whom the believer can maintain a subjective relationship.

Although remnants of the older rationalism still persist in some traditional Jewish writers for whom the medieval thinkers have an authoritative standing, Jewish theology in the twentieth and twenty-first centuries—as represented by figures like Abraham Isaac Kook, Martin Buber, Franz Rosenzweig, Mordecai M. Kaplan Abraham Joshua Heschel, Joseph Soloveitchik and Emil Fackenheim—have tended to avoid the older issues of proving God's existence, defining the divine attributes, or demonstrating the superior rationality of Judaism. These thinkers have, for the most part, begun from the subjective truth of confrontation with the absolute, and tried to describe the human–divine relationship from phenomenological and ethical perspectives, devoting their works to studies of the religious experience of humans in the world.

The God of the Kabbalah

It is the doctrine of the *sefirot* that defines the Kabbalah, and sets it apart from any other brand of Jewish theology, esotericism or mysticism. In the most influential books of early Kabbalah, the *Bahir* and the *Zohar*, the theory of the *sefirot* is not discussed at length, and the word itself makes only the rarest of appearances. The structure and symbolism of the *sefirot* are generally presupposed in the midrashic-style expositions that fill the pages of these works. Most of the names of the *sefirot* reflect conventional descriptions of God that appear in the Bible, in prayers and in other traditional texts: wise, understanding, glorious, just, and so forth. However, in non-kabbalistic usage, these words are adjectives that describe God, what the philosophers referred to as "divine attributes." In kabbalistic usage, on the other hand, each *sefirah* is a distinct and separate metaphysical entity, and is capable of interacting with the other *sefirot* or with the created world. Other symbolic motifs that are found in the Kabbalah involve balances or contrasts between male and female, parents and children, loving kindness and justice. The *sefirot* are perceived as a series of channels through which divine benevolence flows down to the earthly world.

Of course, there are many themes in the kabbalistic symbolism that originated in biblical and rabbinic writings. For example, the tension between the loving, compassionate God and the fearsome God of justice is integral to the Bible, and rabbinic literature created a special vocabulary in order to distinguish between God's "standard of justice" and "standard of mercy"—a distinction that they believed to be implicit in different divine names. However, there is no known precedent for the way in which the Kabbalah classified them into ten attributes that act as separate metaphysical entities.

Unique to the classic kabbalistic symbolic structures is its fascination with erotic and sexual imagery. This motif sets it apart from virtually every other interpretation of traditional Judaism from the Bible onwards, wherein God is depicted almost without exception in masculine imagery. Kabbalistic symbolism depicts a group of seven *sefirot* as constituting a single male figure whose torso is Tiferet (beauty, glory), usually portrayed as a king, prince or bridegroom. The object of his affections is the tenth sefirah, the Shekhinah (divine presence), who appears as a princess. The romantic longing between the prince and princess is never consummated, a tragic situation that serves as a celestial reflection of the state of disorientation and exile in which medieval Jews found themselves, an anomalous existence dominated by their exile from their homeland and their inability to worship in the proper manner at the Jerusalem Temple.

The kabbalistic Shekhinah incorporated several motifs from biblical and rabbinic religion. The ancient prophets often described the covenant between God and the Jewish people in terms of a marriage, with God as the husband and Israel as the wife. The Song of Songs was included in the Hebrew Bible because it was interpreted as such a metaphor. The male and female lovers are constantly longing for one another, but unfortunately, not usually at the same time, creating a powerful erotic tension that is rarely brought to its consummation. The imagery of the Song of Songs, understood as an account of turbulent relationship between God and the Shekhinah, figures prominently in the writings of the kabbalists.

The term Shekhinah is also taken from the rabbinic vocabulary where it was used initially as an abstract noun to express how the omnipresent God whose glory fills the universe could nevertheless be associated with specific localities, such as the Temple or a community of worshippers or of Torah scholars. Talmudic and midrashic sources, maintaining a respectful distance between God and the created world, preferred to employ a circumlocution, speaking of God's *presence* (rather than God himself) dwelling or acting in the world. Although the Hebrew word

Shekhinah is grammatically feminine (all Hebrew nouns must be either masculine or feminine), this fact did not usually affect the metaphoric usage of the term in rabbinic sources.

The term *sefirah* was not invented by the Kabbalah. It was borrowed from an earlier work entitled *Sefer Yezirah*, the Book of Creation. *Sefer Yezirah* is a remarkable little volume that made its appearance early in the Middle Ages, and inspired many commentaries and interpretations. It is not known when it was composed, and contemporary scholarship has been proposing increasingly early dates, extending as far back as the early talmudic era. The fundamental theory that is professed by *Sefer Yezirah* is that there is a close correlation between the physical world and the structures of language (meaning Hebrew) and mathematics. God created the universe by means of permutations and combinations of the ten decimal numbers and the twenty-two letters of the Hebrew alphabet. Most of the book deals with the linguistic aspect, expounding on the letter permutations. The first chapter, however, speaks of numbers: "Ten sublime numbers, like the count of the fingers, five opposite five…" The word that is translated here as "numbers" is *sefirot*, and that is one of the normal meanings of the Hebrew root *SPR*. The cosmological doctrine of *Sefer Yezirah* is a Jewish version of neo-Pythagoreanism, a Greek philosophical theory that glorified mathematical symmetry and found mystical significance in numbers. The kabbalistic *sefirot* as they appear in the *Bahir* and all subsequent works have almost no connection to numbers. The term has been transformed utterly into symbols of divine attributes. The particular names that were assigned to the *sefirot* were influenced to a large extent by the verse in 1 Chronicles 29:11: "Thine, O Lord is the greatness, and the power, and the glory, and the victory, and the majesty: for all that is in the heaven and in the earth is thine; thine is the kingdom, O Lord, and thou art exalted as head above all."

Although the *sefirot* demonstrate a subtle symbolic structure, their underlying theological or ontological status is far less transparent, and the kabbalists took a variety of different approaches to understanding what is the reality that the *sefirot* are symbolizing. One of the main points of contention is, not surprisingly, the question of the relationship between the *sefirot* and God. Do the *sefirot*, in combination with the unknowable *Ein-Sof*, constitute the totality of God; or do they issue *from* God without being part of him? In general, the earlier kabbalistic writers leaned towards the former view, whereas later writers (from the end of the thirteenth century) preferred the latter position, which is less vulnerable to accusations of heresy or polytheism.

Heathens and heretics

Although issues of dogma and correct doctrine might be less important for Judaism than for other religious traditions, Judaism has known its share of heretical schisms and has at times felt called to define the borders between orthodoxy and sacrilege. In this connection, it is useful to distinguish between the categories of heresy and of idolatry. The latter, which is repeatedly condemned in the Bible, involves the worship of deities other than God, the acknowledgement of multiple gods, or the portrayal of gods in a physical form, such as in statues or natural formations. It is clear that biblical religion rejected all manifestations of paganism as unacceptable. In later times, any Jew who chose to participate in the worship of Zeus or Odin might be considered an idol-worshipper—a follower of a foreign cult—not a heretic. The category of "heretic" can only be applied to someone whose illicit form of religion falls within the general circumference of the Torah and Judaism. During both the biblical and talmudic eras, the Jews were acutely conscious that they were unique in their devotion to a single and unique God, creator of the entire universe, who insisted that his worshippers live up to strict standards of ethics and morality. For all the diversity that existed in the religious beliefs of the surrounding nations, fundamentally all nations other than Israel were "heathens": worshippers of manifold deities, and followers of immoral lifestyles.

The distinction between foreign idolatry and internal heresy is not always easy to apply in actual historical situations. Though it is not very difficult to distinguish between the Jewish declaration "Hear, O Israel: The Lord our God is one Lord" and the innumerable gods and goddesses who populate the pantheons of ancient Greece and Rome, the question becomes more problematic when the numbers of deities are smaller. When Jews living under Persian rule made their first encounters with Zoroastrianism, many of them probably saw its beliefs and values as compatible with the tenets of their own ancestral traditions. True, Zoroastrianism is dualistic in that it believes that the universe is the scene of an eternal cosmic battle between supreme gods of good and evil. However, because the individual believers are expected to direct their exclusive devotion and worship to the good god, is this not practically equivalent to monotheism? What emerged as normative Judaism consciously rejected the belief in the "two powers in heaven"; nonetheless, features of dualistic religions continue to occupy a significant place in mainstream forms of Judaism. Thus, the malevolent supernatural figure of Satan, the accuser, appears in the book of Job and in classical rabbinic literature as a member of the heavenly court charged with entrapping and indicting humans. The Jewish Satan is a far cry from the rebellious fallen angel Lucifer of Christian tradition who acts in defiance of God, or from the Zoroastrian principle of evil, Ahriman. The Satan of Jewish folklore (who figures prominently in the literature of the midrash or Kabbalah) also seems to be a figure of willful evil who often acts in opposition to God. If we were to brand as heretics all Jews who adhere to such beliefs, then their ranks would include many respectable and venerated religious leaders.

A passage in the Mishnah stated that those who deny certain doctrines forfeit their share in the "world to come." The main heretical views that are enumerated in that Mishnah are:

1. The denial of resurrection
2. The denial of the heavenly origin of the Torah.
3. The "Epicurean"—probably to be understood as a denial that God takes an active interest in his creatures.

The beliefs that were selected for inclusion in that list were issues of controversy among rival Jewish movements during the late Second Temple era, and the positions advocated by the Mishnah were those professed by the Pharisees. When Josephus Flavius outlined the beliefs, institutions and general characters of the three Jewish movements of his time, it did not occur to him that any one of those movements was less authentic than the others in its interpretation of the tradition. The Mishnah, however, has taken a decisive step further by declaring the non-Pharisaic positions completely unacceptable for Jews who claim to be legitimate followers of their tradition.

One of the blessings in the "eighteen benedictions" prayer of the daily liturgy consists of a condemnation of heretics or traitors to the Jewish community. Early versions of that blessing mention quite a range of miscreants, including informers (collaborators with the Roman regime) and a category known as "*min*," a term for heretics that probably referred to some form of early Christians as well as to dualists.

It is crucial to bear in mind that the designation of a person as a heretic is not equivalent to their forfeiting their status as Jews. It is not clear whether a Jew born to a Jewish mother could ever be deprived of their Jewish identity. Although some authorities ruled that the acceptance of another religion would have that effect, others rejected that position, citing the dictum "an Israelite, even though he has sinned, remains an Israelite."

Ideological formulations of Judaism have often, especially in their initial and more aggressive stages, accused their opponents of heresy, and had the same accusations leveled against them. Thus, Maimonides claimed that anyone who accepted literally the Bible's anthropomorphic descriptions of God was a heretic; while many of his contemporaries hurled equivalent charges at Jewish rationalists who based their theologies on pagan Greek philosophers. Similar accusations were made about the kabbalists, the Ba'al Shem Tov's Hasidism—as well as to their opponents. In most cases, the very success of an ideology granted it legitimacy in the eyes of posterity, so that all those mutually contradictory versions of Judaism came afterwards to be regarded be authentic. Some schisms, however, like those between the Sadducees and Pharisees or the Karaites and the Rabbinites, remained irreconcilable.

Rabbinic Judaism formulated several lists of commandments that it considered obligatory for all human societies. It designated them the "seven Noachide commandments," and ostensibly derived them from verses in the early chapters of Genesis where they were addressed to the descendants of Noah, meaning the entire human race. The standard list of Noachide commandments is:

1. Prohibition of idolatry.
2. Prohibition of murder.
3. Prohibition of robbery.
4. Prohibition of incest and adultery.
5. Prohibition of blasphemy.
6. Prohibition of eating a limb from a living animal.
7. Obligation to maintain a judicial system.

The classic talmudic discussions of these precepts tend to assume that the heathens of their day were incapable of keeping even these elementary laws. The situation confronted by medieval Jews presents a radical contrast to the situation in ancient times. In the Middle East, North Africa, Asia Minor and Europe, paganism gave way rapidly to Christianity and Islam, religions that were fundamentally monotheistic and ethical in character. Both these religions were offshoots of Judaism, rooted in the traditions of the Jewish Bible and imbued with reverence for the patriarchs and prophets of the Hebrew past. Medieval and modern authorities, who were dealing with members of the monotheistic religions, took seriously the category of Noachide gentiles. Maimonides stated that a non-Jew who observed the seven commandments could qualify as one of the "righteous of the nations of the world." Moses Mendelssohn cited the institution as evidence of the fundamental universality and tolerance of the Jewish religion; and that approach has been adopted by most modern Jewish authorities.

The proliferation of monotheistic faiths was not always a positive development for the Jews. Both Islam and Christianity were claiming to be the true heirs to the legacy of biblical Israel, a claim that carried with it the accusation that the Jews themselves had somehow been untrue to their original mission. In many respects, this kind of "sibling rivalry" over a common spiritual heritage turned out far more acrimonious than the former antagonisms between monotheism and paganism. The ambivalences, or even contradictions, that were implicit in this situation made themselves felt in many ways. From both the Christian and Muslim perspectives, we can discern inconsistencies in the legal status that was assigned to the Jewish communities who lived in their respective domains. In both environments, there was usually enough reverence for the descendants of biblical Israel to prevent forced conversions. However, the Jewish "stubbornness" in the face of the manifest truth of the dominant religions had to be publicly acknowledged by placing severe restrictions on the Jews. Therefore, Jews could not be given positions of authority over Christians/Muslims; they had to bear a heavier burden of taxes and tributes; they might be required to wear distinguishing (that is, humiliating) clothing; and their synagogues must not be taller or more ornate than the churches or mosques.

Of course, people's attitudes could not always be dictated by official theological doctrines. There were situations when amicable personal relations between the gentiles and Jews of a given locality caused them to turn a blind eye to the discriminatory legislation. On other occasions, religious zeal or economic greed could ignite campaigns of forced conversion or vindictive massacres. Jewish attitudes towards the other religions could be determined more by the actual treatment they were receiving from their neighbors than by theological or halakhic principles.

Medieval Judaism was not always prepared to confront its changed situation as a tolerated minority in lands governed by her daughter religions. For example, Maimonides, usually a paragon of intellectual consistency, was generally much more sympathetic to Islam than to Christianity, because the monotheism of the former was purer than the problematic trinitarian beliefs of the latter. And yet, on one occasion he stated that Christians are to be preferred to Muslims because they acknowledge the literal authenticity of the Hebrew scriptures, whereas Islam incorporates biblical tradition only in a general and selective manner.

The Jewish sages of medieval France and Germany, less inclined to evaluate Christianity according to systematic theoretical criteria, looked to the Talmud for guidance. Virtually all they could find there were references to "gentiles" that had originally referred to the heathen Roman occupiers, a nation that was both an implacable political enemy and a model of moral depravity. Sidestepping the theological issues, most European rabbis transposed the talmudic laws governing heathen gentiles to the Christians of their own days; and then were compelled to create ingenious loopholes that would allow the people to interact on a day-to-day level the Christian environment.

The modern Jewish Emancipation brought with it a true commitment to religious toleration. Enlightenment ideas largely discredited the older notion that one's own religion is correct while the others are verifiably wrong; or that divine judgment will be based primarily on which faith a person espoused during their lifetime. Nevertheless, the medieval attitudes continue to exist among some Jews from communities that did not experience the Enlightenment, and these distrustful attitudes have been reinforced by the persistence of anti-Semitism and anti-Judaism in both European and Islamic environments.

Key points you need to know

- It was a central tenet of biblical and rabbinic religion that the God of Israel is the only God. This put Judaism at odds with majority of humanity who worshipped multiple deities. The worship of gods in physical form was condemned as idolatry.
- Philo applied to the biblical text the Stoic concept of the Logos, a rational principle that mediates between the purely spiritual creator and the physical universe.
- Medieval theology and philosophy insisted on a more restrictive understanding of the principle of divine oneness. God is completely beyond number, and not composed of multiple elements. This God is not subject to change, and hence the human-like imagery of the traditional texts must not be understood literally.
- Kabbalah is built on the doctrine of the ten *sefirot*, divine attributes whose complex interactions constitute the esoteric meaning of the Bible. It is not always clear whether they perceived the *sefirot* as emanations of God or as parts of the divinity itself.

Discussion questions

1. Is there a real contradiction in claiming that God is both the God of Israel and the sole deity of the universe?
2. Is the concept of "idols" really confined to the worship of physical objects, or can it be applied to other unworthy or false objects of adoration?
3. Can the philosophical quest to understand a God who is utterly self-contained and without personality be considered a "religious" experience?
4. Although Kabbalah is the Jewish theological school that has been most open to acknowledging a feminine aspect of God, there were no female kabbalists until very recently. How do you account for this paradox?

Further reading

Berger, David, *The Jewish-Christian Debate in the High Middle Ages: A Critical Edition of the Nizzahon Vetus*, 1st ed. Judaica: Texts and Translations. Philadelphia, PA: Jewish Publication Society of America, 1979.

Buber, Martin, *I and Thou*, 1st Scribner Classics ed. New York: Scribner, 2000.

—— *Two Types of Faith*, 1st Syracuse University Press ed. Syracuse, NY: Syracuse University Press, 2003.

Goitein, S. D., *Jews and Arabs: Their Contacts through the Ages*. New York: Schocken, 1955.

Jacobs, Louis, *A Jewish Theology*. New York: Behrman House, 1974.

—— *We Have Reason to Believe: Some Aspects of Jewish Theology Examined in the Light of Modern Thought*, 4th rev. ed. London: Vallentine Mitchell, 1995.

Katsh, Abraham Isaac, *Judaism in Islam: Biblical and Talmudic Backgrounds of the Koran and Its Commentaries*. New York: Bloch for New York University Press, 1954.

Katz, Jacob, *Exclusiveness and Tolerance: Studies in Jewish-Gentile Relations in Medieval and Modern Times*, Scripta Judaica. London: Oxford University Press, 1961.

Kaufmann, Yehezkel, *The Religion of Israel from Its Beginnings to the Babylonian Exile*. Translated by M. Greenberg. Chicago, IL: University of Chicago Press, 1969.

Kellner, Menachem Marc, *Dogma in Medieval Jewish Thought: From Maimonides to Abravanel*, Littman Library of Jewish Civilization. Oxford and New York: Oxford University Press, 1986.

—— *Must a Jew Believe Anything?* London and Portland, OR: Littman Library of Jewish Civilization, 1999.

Lasker, Daniel J., *Jewish Philosophical Polemics against Christianity in the Middle Ages*. New York: KTAV, 1977.

Novak, David, *The Image of the Non-Jew in Judaism: An Historical and Constructive Study of the Noachide Laws*, Toronto Studies in Theology. New York: Edwin Mellen Press, 1983.

Perlmann, Moshe, "The Medieval Polemics between Islam and Judaism." In *Religion in a Religious Age*, edited by S. D. Goitein, 103–38. Cambridge, MA: Association for Jewish Studies, 1974.

Schechter, Solomon, *Aspects of Rabbinic Theology*, Jewish Lights Classic Reprint. Woodstock, VT: Jewish Lights, 1993.

Scholem, Gershom Gerhard, *On the Kabbalah and Its Symbolism*. New York: Schocken, 1970.

Shapiro, Marc B., *The Limits of Orthodox Theology: Maimonides' Thirteen Principles Reappraised*. Oxford and Portland, OR: Littman Library of Jewish Civilization, 2004.

Steinberg, Milton, *Basic Judaism*. Northvale, NJ: Jason Aronson, 1987.

Talmage, Frank, *Disputation and Dialogue: Readings in the Jewish-Christian Encounter*. New York: KTAV, 1975.

Urbach, Efraim Elimelech, *The Sages: Their Concepts and Beliefs*. Cambridge, MA: Harvard University Press, 1987.

9 *God and the world*

In this chapter

Judaism is rooted in the consciousness that God is the creator and master of the physical world. Human dependence on nature, especially on rainfall in the Israeli climate, is an important contributor to biblical religiosity. Though the medieval Jewish philosophers proved the existence of God from the harmony of nature, they also had to confront disagreements between science and the Torah's creation story. Maimonides did this by allowing for a flexible interpretation of scripture. The kabbalists, especially Rabbi Isaac Luria, devised an elaborate mythical account of creation: the *Ein-Sof* withdrew himself from a portion of reality in order to create something other than himself upon which he might bestow his goodness, but the vessels that he prepared to receive the divine light could not hold it and shattered, producing a world in which good and evil are confused. Traditional Jewish religiosity has generally promoted belief in miracles as a way of reinforcing God's supremacy over natural laws. However, rationalists whose faith is founded on the unalterable natural order view miracles, interruptions of natural law, as challenges to divine omnipotence. Some modern Jewish thinkers have denied "supernaturalism" or any active involvement of God in the natural world.

Main topics covered

- Nature
- Science and creation
- Healing and the sanctity of life
- Kabbalistic views of creation
- Miracles

Nature

The Torah opens with a succinct account of how God created the universe unaided. It follows from this fundamental premise that God has complete control over his creation. Although the Hebrew scriptures do not contain a systematic theological formulation of divine omnipotence, biblical religion is imbued with the conviction that God's power over nature and humanity is absolute in a manner that distinguishes him from mere mortals, even from the delusional claims of mighty kings. The prophets and psalmists make effective polemical use of this truth to mockingly contrast the Lord of the universe with the impotent images of wood and stone that are the objects of adoration by other peoples. The miraculous plagues inflicted on Egypt at the time of the exodus illustrate and confirm the cosmic truth that the God who created nature transcends the laws of nature.

Often, the recognition that a benevolent deity wields unchallenged power over the universe is adduced in order to provide reassurance in times of individual stress or national crisis. Although the forces of adversity might presently appear to be inexorable, God ultimately holds sway over nature and nations, and it is he alone who will determine the outcome. It is common in the discourse of biblical authors to make facile transitions between depictions of the creator of the heavens and earth, and to the supreme judge of nations and individuals.

According to the account in Deuteronomy Chapter 11, as Moses was preparing the new generation to begin their "normal" national life in the land of Israel, he made the following observation: "For the land, which you enter to possess, is not as the land of Egypt, from where you came out, where you sowed your seed, and watered it with your foot, as a garden of vegetables. But the land, which you are going over to possess, is a land of hills and valleys, and drinks water from the rain of the skies; a land which the Lord your God cares for; the eyes of the Lord your God are always upon it, from the beginning of the year to the end of the year." The special religious character of the promised land is thus not to be sought in some intangible mystical aura or in its historical associations, but in the physical climate: unlike the ecology of Egypt, where the dependable flow of the Nile provides the inhabitants with sustenance, conditions in the land of Israel are subject to a fundamental uncertainty. The land's inhabitants can never enjoy full confidence that they will have sufficient rainfall. Consequently, the people's hearts must continually be turned upwards, praying that they will receive sufficient rain. And because it is God who controls the flow of water from the heavens, they will also be mindful that their agricultural abundance will be proportionate to their devotion to the divine commandments. The climatic conditions of the land of Israel, because they make the survival of its residents so obviously dependant on God's generosity, promote an ongoing sensitivity to the quality of their religious lives. The ecological impact on the Jewish religious mentality is evident throughout the Bible and in post-biblical writings. The threat of drought hovers over numerous admonitions to observe the commandments.

On the whole, the classical documents of ancient Judaism, including the Bible and talmudic literature, are addressed to an audience of farmers, and many of the commandments of the Torah can only be observed fully by people who are growing their own food. This is true about the regulations governing charity, most of which are described in terms of portions of various kinds of agricultural produce that should be left for the poor. In fact, much of Jewish practice, symbolism, values and theology is so intimately bound to the specific natural conditions of Israel, and to the types of grains and fruits that grow there, that the transplanting of those laws into other settings can be problematic. The general principle that was adopted by normative Jewish law is that biblical commandments that relate directly to the soil are not in force (at least not by the authority of the Torah) outside the borders of the holy land.

For example, prayers for rain were instituted in the daily prayers, but were ordained by the talmudic rabbis to be recited only during the seasons when rain actually occurs and is beneficial. In the Middle Eastern climate, rain can fall only during the winter, and therefore the designated times for asking for rain are limited to those months, reflecting the agricultural rhythms of the Israeli or Babylonian environments. These dates lost much of their relevance for the Jewish communities that arose in northern Europe, where rain falls, and is welcomed, throughout the year; or in the southern hemisphere, where the summer and winter seasons are reversed.

Science and creation

The Psalmist wrote (19:1) "The heavens declare the glory of God, and the firmament shows his handiwork." The intricate harmony of the universe has provided powerful evidence for believing Jews that the world was designed by a supremely wise and powerful creator. Jewish rationalists insisted that knowledge of God must be founded on an extensive grounding in science. The classic Aristotelian proofs for the existence of God are variations on the idea of positing a first link in the chain of causality. If we accept the assumptions that everything that exists has a cause, and everything that moves had to be set in motion, we must continue to search back as far as we can in order to arrive at the beginning of the process. Because Aristotle insisted that it is impossible to have an infinite series, we are forced at some point to posit an original "uncaused cause" or "unmoved mover"; and that is identified with God. Of course, the God whose existence we have proved in this manner is, at best, a principle of physics or metaphysics; and it is not obvious that it is identical with the Bible's personal deity who revealed the Torah and guides the destinies of human beings.

In spite of the general confidence that Aristotelian philosophy and science were in harmony with the tenets of Hebrew monotheism, a major conflict existed over the creation. Whereas the biblical narrative, as understood by the ancients, speaks of God calling the heavens and the earth into being out of nothingness, Aristotle claimed to have proven that primordial matter had always been in existence.

Maimonides' treatment of this question is very instructive. He begins by expressing his readiness to accept the Aristotelian view, provided that its correctness is irrefutably proven. As to its apparent disagreement with the scriptural account, Maimonides states simply that the Bible is open to non-literal interpretation, and it would be no more difficult to interpret the creation story in accordance with Aristotle than it was to supply metaphoric explanations for the "hand of God" and other blatant anthropomorphisms. At this point, Maimonides launches into a careful critique of Aristotle's thesis, arriving at the conclusion that the arguments are flawed. In fact, Maimonides adds, it appears that Aristotle himself did not make all the claims that were attributed to him by later writers. As long as science is unable to arrive at a conclusive resolution of the question of the universe's eternal existence, there is no objective reason to prefer one opinion to the other. Under the circumstances, Maimonides decides that it is best to uphold the traditional doctrine of creation out of nothing, in keeping with the straightforward meaning of the Bible, because this view has religious advantages in that it reinforces God's total mastery over all of creation. However, he admits that if someone should succeed one day in discovering an irrefutable demonstration of the world's eternity, then he would have no problem revising his views and interpreting the Bible accordingly.

Healing and the sanctity of life

From numerous texts in the Bible and other Jewish works it is clear that God afflicts people with illnesses by way of warning or punishment, even as he cures those people from their sicknesses. Fearsome ailments figure prominently among the punishments that will befall Israel if they violate the covenant. In texts that extol God's power, it is common to mention the fact that he "heals the sick" (Deuteronomy 32:39; Psalms 41:4; 103:3). The same attitude, that health is ultimately under God's control and that sicknesses can be healed through prayer or piety, is prevalent in rabbinic literature as well. The rabbis understood that the skin ailment known in Hebrew as *zara'at*, usually identified with leprosy, whose ritual treatment is described at great length in Leviticus Chapters 13 and 14, was not merely a physiological infection, but rather a divine retribution for the moral transgression of slander.

In light of this correspondence between spiritual and medical well being, it might have been expected that Judaism, like some other religious ideologies, would manifest an essential antagonism to the practice of medicine, insofar as it trespasses onto a spiritual domain. In fact, some traces of this approach may be found in Jewish traditions. The Mishnah relates that King Hezekiah buried a "book of cures," and that the sages of his generation acknowledged the wisdom of his action. The most common interpretation of their motives was that the people were relying on medical cures instead of being moved to religious contrition. This tradition assumes a tension, if not an outright conflict, between the practice of medicine and a proper sense of dependence on the Almighty.

Nevertheless, the dominant approach in Judaism is reflected in sources like the following: "One who goes in for a blood-letting should say: May it be your will, O Lord, my God, that this operation may provide a cure for me, and that you will heal me, for you are the God who heals faithfully, and your healing is true, because men have no power to heal, but it is merely a customary practice among them. Said Abbaye: A man should not say such a thing, because the school of Rabbi Ishmael has taught: 'He shall cause him to be thoroughly healed' (Exodus 21:19) From this we learn that permission has been granted to the physician to heal."

The initial view expressed in the wording of the blessing assumes that human physicians are merely going through motions, while the actual cure is being accomplished by supernatural means. However, the contrary view voiced by Abbaye (a fourth-century Babylonian rabbi) implies that medical care by a physician is really required. Abbaye's approach was accepted unanimously by subsequent authorities on Jewish law. The *Shulhan 'Arukh*, the important sixteenth-century law code, declared: "Permission has been granted to the physician to heal. It is a commandment to do so, and it is included under the general category of saving life. If a person refuses to do so, then he is guilty of shedding blood."

This formulation alludes to an additional principle that is crucial to Jewish values, namely that the saving of human life stands at the top of the hierarchy of ethical priorities. In general, the sanctity of human life overrides all other considerations, even if the benefit or danger is only of a doubtful nature.

This theological premise has been filtered through the scholarly apparatus of Jewish legal discourse to provide very precise guidelines to many questions of medical ethics, including some that emerge from modern technological developments. Predictably, Jewish law forbids suicide and active euthanasia, though it does not necessarily require the artificial prolongation of life. The Mishnah ruled that when a woman's life is endangered by childbirth, then her welfare takes priority over the "potential" life of the foetus, and a therapeutic abortion may be mandatory under such circumstances. The kinds of the ritual objections that some Christian groups have voiced against stem-cell research or blood transfusions have been rejected by Jewish authorities because these procedures prolong life. While organ transplants are generally favored on similar grounds, Jewish law is concerned that the donor's death be established with certainty according to acceptable criteria. Because brain death is currently the recognized standard definition of death in the medical world, and it was unknown in classical talmudic sources (which speak only of respiration and heartbeat), the matter is subject to a controversy among rabbinic authorities.

Kabbalistic views of creation

The question of how the universe emerged from the deity was a central one for the kabbalistic teachers. Their universe was an intricate blending of different, interdependent levels of existence, each with its own logic of creation. The creation of our physical world is arguably the least important and least interesting of these creations. The *Zohar* is more interested in the complex process of development of the *sefirot*, in which the upper ones beget the lower as their offspring following a sexual model that served to transform human sexuality into a mystical reflection of their metaphysical paradigm.

There are, according to this doctrine, four realms or dimensions of creation, in descending sequence of closeness to their origin and their decreasing levels of spirituality. They are: *Azilut* (emanation); *Beri'ah* (creation); *Yezirah* (formation); and *'Asiyyah* (action). The uppermost level retains its intimate connection to the unknowable *Ein-Sof*, whereas the lowest coincides with the physical world in which humans function.

Zimzum: Contraction

Isaac Luria's doctrine of creation began from premises that might be termed "pantheistic": God permeates the entire universe and is found in everything. If that statement were consistently true, then it would make no sense to speak of a "creation," if nothing can exist that is not God. For this reason, Luria taught that an essential precondition for the creation was that the *Ein-Sof*, the infinite God who had not yet been differentiated into the *sefirot*, voluntarily withdraw himself from a portion of the universe in order to make possible the creation of something other than himself. Into this "vacant" space (a tiny point in the totality, though it includes the entire physical universe), God could then exercise his abundant love and generosity. The process of God's contracting himself is designated as *zimzum*. Even after God withdrew from the "point" of empty, primordial space, he left a faint trace of his holy essence to serve as a substratum for creation. At this stage in the process it was possible to create the primordial air and the Primordial Man, which were the vessels into which God would pour his cosmic goodness.

Prior to the act of *zimzum*, the principles of divine mercy and judgment remained undifferentiated. The process of *zimzum* itself required the separation of the forces of judgment from the totality because the principal characteristic of Judgment lies in its making distinctions and drawing borders. It was this aspect of justice that was accomplished in order to make possible the *zimzum*. The first beings to be created in this process were the unformed "primordial air and Primordial Man" (*Adam Kadmon*). Adam Kadmon contained the sefirot in the form of concentric circles, but it afterwards was reorganized in the familiar human form. In its primitive, undifferentiated state, the Primordial Man was capable of containing the divine light that was poured onto it. However, in order to allow for distinct objects to enjoy the light, that light had to be divided into multiple vessels. These vessels, which were fashioned in order to set limits to the infinite light, were fashioned from the substance of divine judgment.

In addition to its intrinsic merits as a way of explaining the monotheistic concept of a world that is allowed to exist outside God, the myth of the *zimzum* provided an attractive solution to the perennial problem of how the good and omnipotent God could allow evil to exist. For Luria, God has voluntarily relinquished his total control over the creation in order to allow the universe to be a beneficiary of his goodness.

The Breaking of the Vessels

Luria's portrayal of the creation had its own dramatic myth to account for the existence of evil. This myth was based on the premise that not all of the vessels in the Primordial Man were solid enough to contain the ray of divine light that issued from *Ein-Sof*. When the light radiated to the lower "limbs" (which would later differentiate into the seven lower *sefirot*), the vessels proved inadequate to contain the light, and therefore they shattered. The result of this catastrophe is that the universe has ever since been a chaotic confusion of the divine light and the broken shards of justice that were left over from the vessels. In the standard terminology of Lurianic Kabbalah, it is these shards or husks, known in Hebrew as *kelippot*, that became the root of evil in the universe. The image of holy sparks scattered and lost in the universe, provided a powerful representation of a primordial state of exile that is intrinsic to God and built into the cosmic fabric; and only afterwards was the state of exile extended to the human situation, especially to the earthly exile of the people of Israel.

This powerful mythic scheme, which seems to imply that the perfect God was guilty of misjudging the strength of his vessels, invites some difficult theological questions. The Lurianic literature is ambivalent about suggesting the possibility that the shattering of the vessels was not really an unanticipated mishap, but a necessary and intentional stage in the creation process.

Miracles

For the simple Jewish believer, it was God's ability to suspend and manipulate the laws of nature that demonstrated his unique greatness. In rabbinic retellings of biblical stories, the preachers would outdo each other in adding wonder upon wonder, and in magnifying the proportions of the miracles, in order to strengthen the people's faith in their God. The perception that God intercedes supernaturally to help the righteous has inspired Jewish hagiographic narratives in all generations. Expressions of popular piety, such as Hasidism, continue to ascribe miraculous abilities to their spiritual leaders.

Several rationalist Jewish thinkers held a different view of the matter, and found the existence of miracles to be fundamentally opposed to their religious outlook. Because one of their most powerful proofs for God's existence was based on the eternal and unchanging laws that govern the universe, leading to the conclusion that it was God himself who established those immutable laws, it would diminish God's might and his wisdom to assert that these laws can be suspended, even by God himself. With regard to those miracles that are explicitly recounted in the Bible, Maimonides, following a talmudic tradition, argued that the exceptions to the normal natural laws were programmed into the structure of the universe from the time of the creation.

As advances in modern science provided rational explanations for many of the phenomena that previous generations had ascribed to miracles, and as the standards of verification made it more difficult to adduce acceptable proof for miracles, Jewish thinkers tended to place less emphasis on God's active intervention in the natural order. Some, like Mordecai Kaplan, founder of Reconstructionism, rejected any kind of "supernaturalism." Others stressed that the difference between nature and supernatural wonders is largely a matter of faith. The devoted believer has the spiritual sensitivity to discern God's hand at work in the very same events that atheists explain scientifically.

Key points you need to know

- Judaism has generally asserted that God is the sole creator of the universe and is not limited by the laws of nature.
- The natural world was created for humans, and Judaism asserts that God sends us natural benefits in proportion to our moral and religious behavior.
- Jewish rationalists believed that God is better exalted as the author of unchanging scientific laws than as a capricious performer of miracles.
- While recognizing that health and healing lie ultimately in God's hands, Judaism has mandated physicians to practice their craft and to cure the sick according to the utmost of human ability.

- Lurianic Kabbalah formulated an elaborate mythical account of how God differentiated himself from the created world and generated a complex reality of good and evil.
- Recent Jewish thought has been less interested in God's involvement in nature or miracles.

Discussion questions

1. Does the traditional Jewish faith in God's mastery over nature allow for satisfactory explanations of disease or natural disasters?
2. In light of Maimonides's aversion to miracles, how do you suppose he would deal with the more obvious supernatural wonders of the Bible, such as the ten plagues of Egypt or the splitting of the Red Sea?
3. How can Maimonides's approach to the problem of the eternity of the universe be relevant to current controversies between science and religion, such as the creation/evolution debate?
4. Can Luria's creation myths be formulated in an abstract or theoretical way that would make sense to modern people?

Further reading

General

Alter, Michael J., *What Is the Purpose of Creation?: A Jewish Anthology*. Northvale, NJ: Jason Aronson, 1991.

Creation in classical Jewish philosophy

Novak, David, and Norbert Max Samuelson, eds, *Creation and the End of Days: Judaism and Scientific Cosmology: Proceedings of the 1984 Meeting of the Academy for Jewish Philosophy*, Studies in Judaism. Lanham, MD: University Press of America, 1986.

Samuelson, Norbert Max, *The First Seven Days: A Philosophical Commentary on the Creation of Genesis*, South Florida Studies in the History of Judaism. Atlanta, GA: Scholars Press, 1992.

—— *Judaism and the Doctrine of Creation*. Cambridge and New York: Cambridge University Press, 1994.

Judaism and medicine

Dorff, Elliot N., *Matters of Life and Death: A Jewish Approach to Modern Medical Ethics*, 1st ed. Philadelphia, PA: Jewish Publication Society, 1998.

Jakobovits, Immanuel, *Jewish Medical Ethics: A Comparative and Historical Study of the Jewish Religious Attitude to Medicine and Its Practice*. New York: Bloch, 1975.

Rosner, Fred, *Modern Medicine and Jewish Ethics*, 2nd rev. and augm. ed. Hoboken, NJ and New York: KTAV and Yeshiva University Press, 1991.

—— *Biomedical Ethics and Jewish Law*. Hoboken, NJ: KTAV, 2001.

——*Contemporary Biomedical Ethical Issues and Jewish Law*. Jersey City, NJ: KTAV, 2007.

—— *Pioneers in Jewish Medical Ethics*. Northvale, NJ: Jason Aronson, 1997.

Rosner, Fred and Moshe David Tendler, *Practical Medical Halachah*, 3rd rev. ed. Northvale, NJ: Jason Aronson, 1997.

Shulman, Nisson E., *Jewish Answers to Medical Ethics Questions*. Northvale, NJ: Jason Aronson, 1998.

Tendler, Moshe David, *Medical Ethics: A Compendium of Jewish Moral, Ethical and Religious Principles in Medical Practice*, 5th ed. New York: Committee on Religious Affairs, Federation of Jewish Philanthropies of New York, 1975.

Kabbalah

Freedman, Daphne, *Man and the Theogony in the Lurianic Cabala*, Gorgias Dissertations. Piscataway, NJ: Gorgias Press, 2006.

Matt, Daniel Chanan, *God and the Big Bang: Discovering Harmony between Science and Spirituality*. Woodstock, VT: Jewish Lights, 1996.

Nigal, Gedalyah, *Magic, Mysticism, and Hasidism: The Supernatural in Jewish Thought*. Northvale, NJ: Jason Aronson, 1994.

Modern views

Kaplan, Mordecai Menahem, *Judaism without Supernaturalism: The Only Alternative to Orthodoxy and Secularism*, 1st ed. New York: Reconstructionist Press, 1958.

Wine, Sherwin T., *Judaism Beyond God*, Library of Secular Humanistic Judaism. Hoboken, NJ and Milan, KS: KTAV and Milan Press, 1995.

10 Israel's sacred history

In this chapter

Biblical religion, in declaring that God is concerned with human morality, also understood that history is religiously significant as a gauge of Israel's fulfillment of their national covenant. Prophetic preaching taught that there is a direction or divine plan to history, and Jewish tradition elaborated their visions of the future into a complex vision of a redeemed world in which Israel would be restored to its sovereignty under an anointed king (messiah) from the house of David and a rebuilt Temple in Jerusalem, when the entire world will submit to divine justice and acknowledge the truth of Israel's God. The literature of Apocalypse envisioned a catastrophic end of history when God will overthrow the evil empires who rule the world and establish the kingdom of God on earth. The medieval philosophical tradition interpreted the traditional eschatological imagery as symbols for an era of universal enlightenment. The Kabbalah equated the redemption of Israel with the metaphysical unification of God with the exiled Shekhinah. In modern times there has been a tendency to abandon belief in a literal messiah who will restore Israel's political sovereignty, in preference for a belief in an age of universal enlightenment. The longstanding tension between the centrality of the land of Israel and the reality of exile injected religious dimensions into the Zionist movement and its project of reestablishing a Jewish national home in the territory of the ancient homeland. Some religious Jews view this development as part of the eschatological redemption and others as an affront to the divine will, with many gradation between those extremes.

Main topics covered

- Judaism and history
- Biblical visions of redemption
- Jerusalem the holy city
- David and the ideal of monarchy
- Apocalypse

- Rationalist eschatologies
- Redemption according to the Kabbalah
- Modern attitudes
- Homeland and exile

Judaism and history

In the western religious traditions, it is often taken for granted that religions are "historical" in the sense that they attach spiritual importance to historical events and to the sequence of revelations and human moral development. This was not always the case. Ancient paganism was concerned largely with understanding or influencing nature. It deified natural forces and phenomena like the sun, moon or seas, which it viewed as instances of eternal, unchanging cycles. It was a revolutionary development when the Hebrews declared that God was concerned with the moral behavior of human beings, and that history was the stage upon which humans acted out their religious faith and values. The conviction that history is religiously meaningful permeates Jewish thought from the earliest strata of the Bible.

As we have observed in preceding chapters, much of the Torah is a story, and its personalities and values, usually filtered through an extensive tradition of interpretation, continue to occupy and define the day-to-day consciousness of Jews. The chronicles of Israel's kings, their successes and defeats as well as their social and religious policies, were imbued with religious significance. Phenomena like political leadership, community, exile and social justice were viewed as crucial theological categories. Already in God's covenant with Abraham, it was stated that God has a plan for history in which the Hebrews were to play a special role. This stimulated Jews over the ages to speculate about the eventual culmination of historical development in the realization of God's ultimate purpose of a redeemed world.

The impact of Judaism's historicism is evident in the way key events from their sacred history, especially from the biblical era, are ritually commemorated and relived in the holiday calendar, as described elsewhere in this volume. The covenantal idea leads to the widespread assumption that there is a divinely ordained direction to historical events, and that God's plan for humanity will culminate in a redeemed and enlightened world.

Biblical visions of redemption

The Hebrew words that are used to designate the religious concepts "redeem" or "redemption" are apparently adapted from the context of civil law where they refer to the restoration to the debtor of an item that was left with the creditor as a security deposit. In an analogous manner, biblical religion trusted in God to rescue individuals, the nation, and perhaps humanity at large, from the perils or oppressions that threaten their welfare. Hebrew prayer, whether in biblical texts like the Psalms or in the later rabbinic liturgies, is often ambivalent about whether a plea for redemption is being expressed on behalf of an individual or the nation. The present discussion will concern itself primarily with Jewish expectations of collective redemption, which usually takes the form of an ideal world that will be established at the end of history (eschatology).

In certain respects, the covenantal framework of biblical religion required that it eventually reach a culmination in which God's historical plan reaches its ultimate goal. Prophetic preaching also contained several components that would be interpreted by later generations as oracles of the end of history.

Since ancient times, the Hebrew singular *navi* has been translated as "prophet," but the convention can be misleading. The English word "prophet" originates in the Greek *prophetes*, which designates an oracle, someone capable of predicting the future. This is not the role of the biblical *navi*. The *navi* was a messenger of God, but the content of the message was not necessarily the foretelling of future events. Because the biblical *navi* was concerned largely with urging the community to be punctilious in obeying the divine will, they often supported their reprimand with threats of the terrible consequences that would result from continued disobedience. Furthermore, in times of national tragedy, defeat and exile, when the *navi*'s role was to provide hope and consolation, this usually took the form of encouraging visions of a utopian future that lay in store for God's faithful if they would maintain their faith under adversity. In their original contexts, such statements about the future were, of course, conditional on the people's behavior. However, after the biblical era, when prophecy ceased to be a living force, Jews would turn to their sacred scriptures in order to find out what God was saying to them. This led to the perception that the words of the *nevi'im* of old had originally been directed towards future generation. This process is probably what induced ancient Greek-speaking Jews to feel that "prophet" was the closest equivalent to the Hebrew *navi*.

The prophets' threats expressed worries that were very real to the ancient Hebrews. Invading armies would carry out widespread slaughter, deprive Israel of the fruits of their soil and exile them to distant and hostile lands. Those threats were fulfilled when the northern kingdom fell to Assyria and Judea to Babylonia. In times of tribulation, the prophets comforted the people with messages of encouragement and consolation, assuring them that all was not lost, that if they now acknowledged the error of their former ways and faithfully followed God's commands, then they would be restored to their former greatness and create an ideal society of spiritual stature and social justice.

After prophecy ceased, later generations began to read the ancient threats and consolations as if they were predictions of the future. For Jews living under the yoke of the Persian, Greek or Roman empires, it was clear that not all those predictions had come to pass, so they must belong to a scenario of complete and final redemption. Imagery from the biblical prophecies was combined in diverse ways, and in varying degrees of literalness, to produce detailed pictures of the culmination of history.

As a general rule, it was assumed that the catastrophic events would come to pass as a prelude to the establishment of the utopian world. Some prophecies spoke of vengeance that would be exacted from the wicked heathen nations who oppressed Israel, while others described how the nations of the world would willingly do homage to God in Jerusalem. It was common for Jews who had recently experienced a great tragedy—such as the Seleucid persecutions, the destruction of the second Temple, the Roman suppression of the Bar Kokhba revolt, the Crusades, the expulsion from Spain and Portugal, the Cossack massacres or the Nazi Holocaust—to regard those events as the fulfillment of the catastrophic prophecies. In rabbinic eschatological discourse it was common to identify the catastrophe with a vivid prophecy from the book of Ezekiel (Chapters 38–39) that described the invasion of Gog, king of Magog, who would lead an alliance against Israel from the north and cause untold death and carnage before ultimately being destroyed. The necessity for such a catastrophe was often justified as a purging of the world's remaining evil, so that the new world can be based on a foundation of pure goodness. Another popular analogy is that of the birth pangs that must precede the creation of something new.

From early rabbinic times, Jewish thinkers argued whether or not Israel would have to repent completely before they would be declared deserving of the redemption. A talmudic tradition stated that "the son of David will come only in a generation that is completely righteous or one that is completely guilty." It would appear that there were few eras in history when Jews did not believe that the redemption would arrive within a generation or two.

The biblical writings contained many specific themes that were incorporated into the standard vision of eschatological redemption. Among the most prominent of these are:

- the ingathering of the exiles to their homeland.
- the rebuilding of Jerusalem and its Temple.
- the restoration of Israel's sovereignty under a king from the line of David, of the tribe of Judah.
- In keeping with the biblical manner of installing kings and high priests, his head would be anointed with olive-oil; hence, he was referred to as a "messiah" (Hebrew: *Mashiaḥ*), an anointed one.
- a society entirely devoted to God.
- all nations will acknowledge Israel's God and worship him.

- The prophet Malachi (4:4) declared: "Lo, I will send you the prophet Elijah before the great and terrible day of the Lord comes." According to the biblical story, Elijah never died, but was elevated to heaven in a flaming chariot. Throughout history, various figures were identified as the "Elijah," the precursor who heralded the arrival of the true redemption.

Jerusalem the holy city

In the book of Deuteronomy and other sections of the Torah ascribed to the same school, we find repeated declarations that formal worship must be carried out exclusively in one locality: "Take heed to thyself that ...in the place which the Lord shall choose in one of thy tribes, there thou shalt offer thy burnt-offerings" (Deuteronomy 12:13–14, etc.). Subsequent Jewish tradition never doubted that the place that was being referred to was Jerusalem. The centralization of Israelite worship was a feature in the reforms instituted during the reign of King Josiah of Judah, following the discovery of a hitherto lost book of the Law of Moses during his time. (Most historians assume that the book, roughly equivalent to the book of Deuteronomy, was actually composed at that time.)

The city of Jerusalem was one of the last parts of the land of Israel to come under Israelite control. According to the biblical account, it remained, even after Joshua's

Figure 10.1 Jerusalem

conquest, in the hands of the Jebusite nation. Until the acquisition of Jerusalem, there were several sites that hosted the Tabernacle, and which thereby were recognized as authorized centers of sacrificial worship.

The Israelite history of Jerusalem, as national capital and religious center, begins with King David. Later biblical tradition suggested an identification of Jerusalem with the land of "Moriah" where Abraham went to sacrifice his son Isaac (see Genesis 22:2 and 2 Chronicles 3:1). At any rate, Jerusalem did not have any major historical or cultic significance before it was chosen by David to be his capital. The name Zion, which originally designated the mountain on which the city sat, or its fortress, later came to be used as a synonym for it. Because David's reign had been marked by wars, he was not deemed the proper person to preside over the construction of the holy Temple. That privilege was to be left to David's son and heir, Solomon, who was not involved in military activities. The name "Jerusalem" includes a cognate of the Hebrew word "shalom," meaning peace.

The religious centrality of Jerusalem to the people at large was underscored by the requirement of the Torah that three of the major annual festivals be observed as times of pilgrimage to the Temple. There were many other kinds of gifts and offerings, whether of the mandatory or free-will kinds, that could be brought to the Temple at other times of the year.

The Bible contains many beautiful passages that extol the unique beauty of Jerusalem. Some of the most moving are in the book of Psalms, in songs that were probably chanted by the pilgrims when they visited the holy city. The destruction of Jerusalem was considered an almost unbearable loss to the Jewish spirit, and all eschatological visions include assurances that the holy city and its Temple will be restored in the future redemption.

David and the ideal of monarchy

It is likely that the term "messiah" first came into use in response to the Hasmoneans' controversial assumption of royal and priestly authority. By applying the word to a future redemption, when God will restore the legitimate lines of the Zadokite priesthood and the Davidic kings, they were calling attention to the fact that the Hasmonean priest-kings could not legitimately hold either office.

The Bible's attitude towards monarchy is ambivalent. In the only discussion in the Torah devoted to the question of what form of political structure Israel should adopt in their land (in Deuteronomy 17:14–20), the tone of the passage seems to be opposed to the institution of monarchy. The prospect is introduced as a possible demand issuing from the people, whose motivation is the result of their desire to be "like all the nations that are around me"; and the text is concerned exclusively with setting strict limits to the king's authority. The general tenor of the passage seems quite antagonistic to the institution of monarchy, with the strongly implied suspicion that, without safeguards and vigilance, the normal tendency of kings is to become tyrants.

A similar negative attitude is evident in the narrative of the book of Samuel, which describes the historical transition of the Israelite nation from a loose alliance of tribes without a permanent political structure to the appointment of their first King, Saul. The prophet Samuel was upset by the people's request for a stable government and turned to God for guidance. The response he received was: "Listen to the voice of the people in all that they say to you; for they have not rejected you, but they have rejected me, that I should not reign over them." The people's perceived need for a mortal king revealed their lack of faith in God. Samuel proceeded to appoint Saul as the first King of Israel. Notwithstanding the charismatic leader's promising beginnings, Saul's reign turned out to be very problematic. Towards the end of his life, he suffered from a severe mental illness that expressed itself in bouts of violent paranoia. He perished brutally in battle with the Philistine armies at Mount Gilboa.

David, who was Saul's successor, arose from humble beginnings, a descendant of the Moabite convert Ruth and the youngest brother in a family of simple shepherds. He achieved popularity when he killed the Philistine giant Goliath. He was a poet (all or most of the book of Psalms in the Bible has been traditionally credited to his authorship) and a musician, as well as a successful military leader. His decision to acquire Jerusalem and build it up as Israel's proud capital city and religious center was regarded with admiration by posterity. David's romantic life, however, led him to some very grave moral offenses, and the tensions among his various wives were reflected in tragic rivalries and general dysfunction among his children. David's infatuation with the beautiful Bathsheba led him to commit adultery and to cause the death of her innocent husband. The consequences of this grave moral lapse continued to trouble him throughout his reign. In his twilight years, he is depicted as a vindictive old man, obsessed with taking revenge on the enemies that he accumulated during his lifetime.

Given the general antipathy towards the institution of monarchy and the specific failings of King David himself, it is not so easy to explain why the Bible and later Jewish tradition nonetheless remembered him in such a favorable light, to the point of idealizing his reign as a virtable golden age. The unique aura that surrounded David's dynasty found its most decisive expression in the divine covenant that was associated with it. The prophet Nathan promised him "your house and your kingdom shall be established forever before you; your throne shall be established forever." Even after the nation was split into the northern ten tribes of Israel and the southern kingdom of Judah, the throne of Judah continued to be occupied by

David's descendants until the kingdom fell to the Babylonians and the last reigning Davidic king, Zedekiah, was taken as a hostage to perish on Babylonian soil. The generations of Jews who lived under foreign domination, without their own king or national autonomy, looked back nostalgically to the reign of David as the archetype of Israelite grandeur and proud independence.

After the destruction of Jerusalem and its holy Temple, the prophets of Israel sought to reassure the dejected exiles that their ancient glory would one day be restored to them. In several of those visions of the future redemption, the reestablishment of David's dynasty played a significant role. Thus, when the prophet Isaiah envisioned a world governed by an enlightened king who would bring idyllic harmony, the subject of his vision was "a shoot from the stock of Jesse" (Jesse was David's father). In some versions of the prophetic eschatology, the reigning king is not just an heir to the Davidic line, but David himself.

Initially, the messiah was viewed as one among several features that will accompany the redeemed future. Possibly under Christian influence, his role was expanded until he was viewed as the actual redeemer. For the most part, Jewish tradition has not understood the messiah to be a supernatural figure.

An interesting concept that appears in rabbinic literature, possibly in the wake of the failed Bar Kokhba uprising, tells that the restoration of the true Davidic monarchy will be preceded by a failed messiah from the tribe of Joseph who will die without achieving the redemption.

Apocalypse

As is discussed elsewhere, the belief in resurrection of the dead was projected to the eschatological future. Most Jewish messianic scenarios include a description of this event.

A distinct variation on eschatological speculation was the genre known as Apocalypse (from a Greek work for "hidden" or "secret") that was very popular in ancient times. According to the standard formula, the hero (often a minor figure from the Bible) is initiated into an esoteric revelation about the imminent climax of history, when the evil empires who subjugate the world and persecute the faithful will be overthrown by God, so that authority can be transferred to the deserving minority who have hitherto been oppressed by the heathens and the heretics. The Apocalyptic authors use striking symbolism to describe the succession of evil kingdoms that have tyrannized the world, the ferocious retribution that will be exacted from them and the magnificence of the heavenly kingdom that will be established in its place. Implicit in the apocalyptic mentality is the belief that there is an inexorable plan for the unfolding of history. It also reflects a perception that the only hope for the triumph of good is if God takes an active hand in the matter. According to their understanding, the evil was so glaring that God had reached the limits of his patience and would act very soon. Apocalyptic ideas had wide following among ancient Jews, especially under the despised rule of the Romans, and similar themes found their way into rabbinic literature.

As was noted elsewhere, several texts in the Dead Sea scrolls, particularly the document known as the "Scroll of the War of the Children of Light and the Children of Darkness," stated that God divided humanity from primordial times into the righteous and the wicked. Accordingly, the scrolls envisage an ultimate apocalyptic battle in which the forces of darkness, who have ruled the world through most of its history, will be decisively vanquished. The "war scroll" actually contains a detailed battle plan for that war, which was expected to occur imminently. The bloody and vindictive tone of these texts, as well as the acrid hostility that is generally expressed towards their opponents, requires us to reconsider the gentle pacifism that characterizes Josephus's portrayal of the Essenes.

Rationalist eschatologies

In Jewish philosophical literature we find diverse attitudes towards the eschatological traditions that they inherited from the biblical and rabbinic eras. In general, the rationalists tended to downplay the more violent descriptions that characterized much of that literature, insisting that the process would be of a more spiritual nature and that the texts should therefore be interpreted as allegories. Some, like Saadiah, were primarily concerned with bringing order to the numerous components, including concepts like the "world to come" that hovered between the realms of eschatology and afterlife. In contrast to the folk imagination that found consolation in exaggerating the wondrous dimensions of the anticipated redemption and the vengeance on their enemies, the rationalists preferred to perceive it as an age of universal enlightenment when all the nations of the earth will finally recognize the one God of Israel. Maimonides noted how Bar Kokhba had been hailed as the messiah by some leading rabbis of his time. This, he insisted, proves that the talmudic sages did not expect the messiah to perform wonders, because no miraculous abilities were attributed to Bar Kokhba.

It is probably significant that Maimonides did not include a discussion of messianic theories in the *Guide of the Perplexed*, though this topic was very much on the minds of his contemporaries and he included belief in the coming of the messiah among the "thirteen articles of creed" that he compiled to serve as a declaration of obligatory Jewish doctrines. His law code, the *Mishneh Torah*, concludes with "Laws relating to Kings and the Messiah." The primary role of the messiah who appears in the *Mishneh Torah* is to restore the political independence of Israel so that the Jews may at long last govern themselves in all aspects of life according to the laws of the Torah. Although Maimonides' treatment of the topic is based on biblical and talmudic sources, it is at times reminiscent of Plato's *Republic*, as the philosopher-king-messiah presides over a rational and enlightened state.

Redemption according to the Kabbalah

The theology of the Kabbalah ascribed the imperfections of our world and the sufferings of the Jewish people to disharmony in the realm of the metaphysical *sefirot*. These calamities were provoked by human sinfulness and heresy. The flow of beneficial forces into our world was interrupted and the Shekhinah was separated from the main body of the *sefirot* structure, paralleling the geographic and spiritual displacement of the Jewish people.

According to Isaac Luria's doctrines, the primordial shattering of the vessels left us with a world in which sparks of holiness and husks of evil (*kelippot*) are strewn together in confusion, and in which the primordial hierarchy of creation has become fundamentally disoriented. In such a world, the ultimate goal to be pursued by humans consists of liberating the holy sparks from among the husks, and elevating them to their proper level of sanctity.

Common to all versions of kabbalistic teaching is the premise that observance of the religious precepts of the Torah is the essential vehicle for bringing redemption. Whenever Jews meticulously follow their religious laws in their daily lives, provided that they do so in full consciousness of the kabbalistic rationales that underlie each act, they are contributing to the hastening of redemption. From the kabbalistic perspective, it is not only Israel or humanity that is being redeemed, but the metaphysical realms as well. This process is perceived as a "repair" of the flawed state of the current world, and in Lurianic Kabbalah it is designated by the word *tikkun*.

For the kabbalists who flourished after the cataclysmic days of the Spanish and Portuguese expulsions of 1492–1496, or the Ukrainian Cossack massacres of 1648–1649, the messianic quest took on a mystical urgency that led to the appearance of several figures who claimed to be the expected messiah, and who succeeded in attracting immense followings.

There are conflicting assessments of the importance of messianic aspirations in the ideology of the Ba'al Shem Tov, the founder of eastern European Hasidism. In a surviving letter that was widely accepted as authentic he expressed his conviction that the spread of his teachings would serve as a prelude to the final redemption. However, some scholars have argued that Hasidism was striving to neutralize the eschatological themes that had caused so much disappointment to previous generations, by reinterpreting them as allegorical expressions of processes that take place within the individual soul.

Modern attitudes

To the extent that messianic hopes occupy a central place in the traditional liturgy and authoritative literature, they continue to dominate the official attitudes of Orthodox Judaism. Nevertheless, there are extreme variations in how the belief

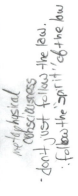
(handwritten margin notes:) metaphysical consciousness - don't just follow the law. Follow the "spirit" of the law

(handwritten annotation:) "elevating of the sparks" → through performance of the commandments

(handwritten annotation:) eschatologic portion

finds actual expression in Jewish religious life. The severe consequences of failed messianic movements, such as those of Shabbetai Zevi and Jacob Frank, persuaded many to oppose subsequent manifestations of messianic enthusiasm. Others, however, have been stalwart in the conviction that this fundamental Jewish value must be cultivated, especially to remedy the despair of persecution and massacres. Many are convinced that the active striving for redemption is itself a means to hasten its coming. Influential segments of the religious Zionist community are convinced that Zionism and the creation of the state of Israel are the fulfillment of the biblical prophecies, with the Nazi Holocaust as its catastrophic prelude.

Among more liberal Jews, there has been a general discouragement of literal acceptance of traditional messianic imagery. The notion of a monarch who will restore the institutions of ancient Israel was antithetical to several cherished values of the Emancipation. Nevertheless, few have been willing to jettison entirely this profound and appealing motif of Jewish thought, particularly when it was also legitimized by the surrounding Christian culture. The modernized Jewish messianic ideologies tend to equate the traditional concepts with faith in human progress, and the "messianic age" has been identified with an assortment of ideologies, such as enlightenment, tolerance or socialism.

Homeland and exile

Although the original covenant between God and Abraham stipulated that the patriarch's descendants would dwell in the land of Israel, since the destruction of the biblical kingdoms of Israel and Judah most Jews have lived outside the boundaries of their historical homeland. In the traditional vocabulary of Jewish texts, there was no question that the this situation is "exile" (Hebrew: *golah* or *galut*), a term that has unmistakably negative connotations. The expectation that the final redemption will include an ingathering of the exiles remained a permanent feature in Jewish eschatological thought and prayers. The tension between the centrality of the holy land and the reality of the exile is a constant theme in Jewish religious thought over the ages. Throughout history, prominent Jewish religious leaders like Judah Halevi and Moses Nahmanides were sensitive enough to the religious imperative of dwelling in the holy land that they forsook comfortable lives and distinguished positions in the diaspora to take on the difficult journey to the land of Israel. There was scarcely an era in Jewish history when Jews were not migrating to the holy land, even if it was only to enjoy the spiritual merit of dying and being buried there.

Under the influence of the European Jewish Enlightenment, as many Jews sought admission into secular societies, all expressions of ethnicity and nationalism were perceived as awkward. The ethnic solidarity among Jews who dwelled in different lands was regarded as incongruous with the demands of patriotism, and questions of dual loyalties were raised. In response, Enlightenment Jewish thinkers tended to stress a more positive interpretation of Jewish dispersion, claiming that its main purpose was to spread monotheism and morality to the previously heathen world.

When the Zionist movement arose in the late nineteenth century, it was a secular political movement whose leadership was largely antagonistic to traditional Jewish religion. Most leaders of traditionalist Judaism were hostile to political Zionism, more because of its anticlericalism than because they disagreed strongly with its key objectives. In fact a few significant Orthodox rabbis anticipated Theodor Herzl in arguing that a sovereign Jewish homeland was the only solution to the urgent social and political perils that were besetting European Jewry. Unlike their secular counterparts, these religious proto-Zionists usually attached eschatological significance to the Jewish national movement. Among the most prominent precursors of religious Zionism were: Rabbi Zevi Hirsch Kalischer (1795–1874); Rabbi Judah Alkalai (1798–1878); and Rabbi Samuel Mohilewer (1824–1898).

Orthodox supporters of Zionism organized themselves as a separate party in the Zionist movement known as the Mizrachi movement (derived from the Hebrew acronym for "Spiritual Center"). The party was founded in 1901 at a conference of religious Zionists convened in Vilnius, Lithuania, by Rabbi Isaac Jacob Reines (1839–1915), who served as the organization's first president. The ideology of the Mizrachi movement saw Jewish nationalism as an instrument for realizing religious objectives, especially of enhancing the opportunities for the observance of the Torah by a Jewish society dwelling on its native soil. In addition to its important network of modern religious schools (which later became the basis for the Israeli State Religious School System), in which spoken Hebrew and biblical studies were taught (unlike the traditional yeshivas), the Mizrachi party participated fully in Zionist congresses and other political activities, and trained its members for agricultural labor in Palestine. Largely through its youth movement, B'nei Akiva, it established communal farms in Palestine, notably in the Beth Shean valley in Galilee.

During the early decades of the twentieth century, the Jewish community in Palestine was polarized between two groups: the "old yishuv (=settlement)," the traditional religious community who lived a religious life of study and prayer in the "holy" towns, subsidized by donations from Jews abroad; and the "new yishuv" consisting of Zionist settlers, largely socialist and anti-religious, who strove for Jewish economic productivity, especially in agricultural settlements.

While the traditionalist leadership, organized politically as the "Agudat Israel" movement, was largely hostile to Zionism as a movement, and argued that the Jews are a religious community defined by Torah and not a normal nation, the establishment of the state of Israel in 1948 made that antagonism largely irrelevant. In Israel the Agudat Israel have represented the interests of the "Ḥareidi" or "ultra-Orthodox" constituency in the national parliament, the Knesset. Owing to the nature of Israel's proportional representation system, the relatively small numbers of Agudat Israel representatives have often been crucial for the survival of government coalitions, and this leverage has allowed them to be very effective in channeling resources towards their yeshivahs and other institutions. They have advocated religious legislation, such as public enforcement of Sabbath and dietary laws, and the rejection of non-Orthodox conversions in the definition of "Jew" for purposes of entitlement to automatic citizenship under Israel's "law of Return."

Polarization between militant secularists and religious communities has remained an ongoing feature of Israeli society. The most intransigent and extreme of the Orthodox anti-Zionist organizations is the Neturei Karta movement, a small but vocal group that was founded in 1935 to promote total separation from the Zionist Jewish community in Jerusalem. The name Neturei Karta, Aramaic for "guardians of the city," was first used in 1938, and alludes to a talmudic statement that religious scholars, not soldiers or police, are the true guardians of a city. Neturei Karta have tried as much as possible to avoid using the facilities of the Israeli state, including courts, identity cards, schools, currency and public utilities. They have been outspoken in propagandizing against the legitimacy of the Jewish state. They have gone so far as to negotiate privately with hostile Muslim states and leaders. There are other Orthodox streams who oppose Zionism on similar religious grounds. The most visible among these has been the Satmar Hasidic sect led by the Teitelbaum dynasty. In more recent years, statements in a similar spirit have been expressed by some exponents of the Sephardic "ultra-Orthodox" faction associated with the Israeli "Shas" movement.

One towering rabbinic leader emerged from the traditionalist world who was determined to overcome the mutual hostility of the religious and secular camps. This was Rabbi Abraham Isaac Kook (1865–1935). Rabbi Kook was born in Latvia where he received a traditional Jewish religious yeshivah education. He went on to achieve prominence in the Lithuania yeshivah world as a brilliant scholar. In 1904 he arrived in Palestine, which was then under Ottoman Turkish rule, and would become a British Mandate after World War I. In 1924 the British appointed him Chief Rabbi of the Ashkenazic community in Palestine.

Rabbi Kook devoted much of his public life to the goal of reconciliation between the Zionists and the religious traditionalists, and even between the leftist and rightist factions of the secular Zionist movement. His halakhic rulings tried to accommodate the needs of the struggling and economically fragile Zionist settlements; notably, by permitting agriculture during the sabbatical year (when Torah law forbids agricultural labor in the land of Israel) by means of a farfetched legal fiction. Rabbi Kook's sympathy for the anti-religious Zionist pioneers was rooted in his conviction that those idealistic atheists were performing a religious mission, even if they were unaware of it. He recognized that their commitment to their cause was fueled by altruistic motives.

Rabbi Kook was motivated by his strong belief in the idea of progress, which asserted that history was moving irreversibly towards the creation of a perfect and enlightened society. His writings, though composed in a flowery rabbinic Hebrew, show unmistakable influences of Hegelian and Marxist ideas, which he integrated with traditional Jewish messianism and kabbalistic eschatological themes. Although historical hindsight now makes his optimism appear pathetic, Rabbi Kook was thoroughly convinced (as were the champions of various secular ideologies at the time) that universal enlightenment would soon cause the world to recognize and support the just Jewish claim to national restoration in their homeland.

Rabbi Kook was disappointed by the positions of his fellow traditionalists. Having abandoned full involvement in day-to-day life in favor of narrowly "religious" pursuits, these people were, in Rabbi Kook's view, products of the anomalous predicament of Jewish exile, and hence their model of Judaism was as inauthentic as that of the atheistic Zionists who desired a physical, national "redemption" devoid of spiritual content. Rabbi Kook argued that the approaching stage of Jewish history would embrace both spiritual and material redemption. The Jewish people would be the vanguard of a universal spiritual revival. However, for this to happen, Judaism itself must undergo an internal spiritual revival. Merely to live according to the commands of Jewish law is no longer sufficient. By the same token, political Zionism must have religious content, and cannot be limited to a narrow, parochial nationalism. His eschatological vision drew from the symbolism of the Lurianic Kabbalah and from Hasidism. Rabbi Kook died before the Nazi Holocaust and before the establishment of the state of Israel. We cannot know how his optimistic outlook would have been affected by these events, or by the resurgence of anti-Semitism at the end of the twentieth century.

In the early decades of Israeli statehood, the mainstream religious Zionist movements encouraged full participation with the secular majority. A prayer for the welfare of the state of Israel was formulated and is recited in many synagogues. It refers to the Jewish state as "the first flowering of our redemption." The Chief Rabbinate (with separate Ashkenazic and Sephardic branches) was appointed by the government and accepted as authoritative by religious Zionists. Under Israeli law, matters of family law (marriage and divorce) and personal status were placed under the exclusive jurisdiction of religious (that is, Orthodox) courts. A special arrangement (*hesder*) was established in order to allow full participation in military service within a program of yeshivah study.

Until 1967 religious Zionists in Israel were marginalized both by the secular majority, and by the more visibly religious groups that seemed to offer a more authentic, uncompromising brand of religion. The place of the religious factions within the Zionist movement and the state of Israel was altered radically by the Six-Day War of June 1967, which resulted in the capture of east Jerusalem (which had been occupied by Jordan in the 1948 War of Independence) and other territories of the biblical land of Israel. The long-range fate of these territories, and of their Arab inhabitants, became a major controversy of Israeli policy makers. From a purely political perspective, the main choice facing the nation was between the military security that was offered by the expanded borders, and the relative demographic stability that would be achieved by excluding a large Arab population from the borders of the Jewish state.

A religious claim provided powerful justification for those who wished to hold on to the occupied territories: if the state of Israel was viewed as the unfolding of a messianic scenario, then the miraculous victory of the Six-Day War was an essential stage in that process. The territories belong to the Jewish people by divine decree, and consequently they may not be handed over to foreign hands. The issue of territories, viewed in its eschatological context, became the defining feature for broad segments of religious Zionism in the post-1967 era. Under the spiritual leadership of Rabbi Kook's son Zevi Judah Kook thousands of modern young religious Jews campaigned actively against any territorial compromise and established numerous settlements throughout Judea and Samaria. Many of these settlements, though originally founded illegally, were subsequently granted official recognition by Israeli governments. The most powerful political voice of the movement against territorial compromise was "Gush Emunim" (the Bloc of the Faithful). However the fundamental values of Gush Emunim filtered down to the mainstream of Israeli society, particularly to religious educational networks, in which a land-centered nationalism was presented as the highest form of religious activism, and the histories of Zionism and the state of Israel were viewed as irreversible steps in the unfolding messianic fulfillment. The aspirations of Gush Emunim were widely respected by much of the Jewish public, especially when Arab intransigence made the return of the territories a far-off theoretical possibility.

When peace agreements with Egypt (1977) and the Palestine Liberation Front (1993) put the return of occupied lands onto the actual political agenda, Gush Emunim found itself in active opposition to the policies and laws of the Israeli government. In the 1990s mainstream rabbis were instructing religious Jews to disobey military commands to evacuate occupied lands, and branding Prime Minister Yitzhak Rabin a "traitor" to the higher Jewish cause. An adherent of these views assassinated Rabin in November 1995. For many Israelis, this event resulted in a sobering realization of the dangers inherent in extreme religious nationalism. However with the breakdown of the peace process, the outbreak of Arab violence (Intifada) against Israeli civilians and the increased popularity of the fundamentalist Hamas movement among the Palestinians, messianic religious Zionism enjoyed a revival, which now pitted them against former allies in the secular right wing parties who had accepted the premise that a democratic Israel could not hold on indefinitely to a large Arab population.

The Gush Emunim movement was generally vague or ambivalent about the long-term status of the non-Jewish residents of the occupied territories. A more extreme position was taken by Meir Kahane, whose banned racist party "Kach" condemned democracy as an un-Jewish import, and advocated laws that would prohibit sexual and social contact with Arabs, actively calling for the eviction of Arabs from territories that belonged by rights to the Jews.

> ## Key points you need to know
>
> - Biblical religion focused on the history of Israel as the unfolding of a divine plan.
> - Post-biblical Judaism evolved diverse expectations about the culmination of history, based on biblical themes and responses to contemporary events.
> - Classic Jewish eschatological concepts include the restoration of the Israelite state to be led by a descendant of King David, the ingathering of the exiles, the rebuilding of Jerusalem and its Temple, the universal recognition of God, and the resurrection of the dead.
> - Medieval philosophers often interpreted the imagery of the earlier sources in a non-literal manner, as metaphors for intellectual wisdom.
> - Kabbalistic writers, especially the Lurianic stream, formulated an intensely metaphysical doctrine of simultaneous national and theological redemption. This approach inspired mystical messianic movements, such as that of Shabbetai Zvi.
> - Non-traditional modern Jewish thinkers downplayed the nationalist elements of Jewish eschatology, but retained a faith in a "messianic age."
> - Some religious Zionists attach eschatological significance to the rebirth of a Jewish state in the twentieth century.

Discussion questions

1. How does Judaism's concern with history find expression in ritual practice?
2. How would Jews who believe that the Bible is the literal word of God account for conflicting eschatological scenarios; for example, that the unbelievers will be violently overthrown and that they will voluntarily come to worship God?
3. How did the obscure title "anointed one" (messiah) become the most common term for designating the future redemption?

Further reading

Jewish historiography

Baron, Salo Wittmayer, *History and Jewish Historians: Essays and Addresses*, 1st ed. Philadelphia, PA: Jewish Publication Society of America, 1964.

Grabbe, Lester L., ed., *Did Moses Speak Attic?: Jewish Historiography and Scripture in the Hellenistic Period*, European Seminar in Historical Methodology. Sheffield: Sheffield Academic Press, 2001.

Kochan, Lionel, *The Jew and His History*. London: Macmillan, 1977.

—— *Jews, Idols, and Messiahs: The Challenge from History*. Oxford and Cambridge, MA: Blackwell, 1990.

Myers, David N. and David B. Ruderman, *The Jewish Past Revisited: Reflections on Modern Jewish Historians*, Studies in Jewish Culture and Society. New Haven, CT: Yale University Press, 1998.

Yerushalmi, Yosef Hayim, *Zakhor, Jewish History and Jewish Memory*, Samuel and Althea Stroum Lectures in Jewish Studies. Seattle, WA: University of Washington Press, 1982.

Jewish eschatology: general

Cohn-Sherbok, Dan, *The Jewish Messiah*. Edinburgh: T&T Clark, 1997.

Greenstone, Julius H., *The Messiah Idea in Jewish History*. Philadelphia, PA: Jewish Publication Society of America, 1906.

Lenowitz, Harris, *The Jewish Messiahs: From the Galilee to Crown Heights*. New York: Oxford University Press, 1998.

Saperstein, Marc, ed., *Essential Papers on Messianic Movements and Personalities in Jewish History*, Essential Papers on Jewish Studies. New York: New York University Press, 1992.

Scholem, Gershom Gerhard, *The Messianic Idea in Judaism and Other Essays on Jewish Spirituality*, 1st Schocken Books ed. New York: Schocken, 1971.

Silver, Abba Hillel, *A History of Messianic Speculation in Israel: From the First through the Seventeenth Centuries*. Boston, MA: Beacon Press, 1959.

Jewish eschatology: Ancient

Charlesworth, James H., Hermann Lichtenberger and Gerbern S. Oegema, eds, *Qumran-Messianism: Studies on the Messianic Expectations in the Dead Sea Scrolls*. Tübingen: Mohr Siebeck, 1998.

Klausner, Joseph, *The Messianic Idea in Israel, from Its Beginning to the Completion of the Mishnah*. Translated by W.F. Stinespring. London: Allen and Unwin, 1956.

Neusner, Jacob, Ernest S. Frerichs and William Scott Green, eds, *Judaisms and Their Messiahs at the Turn of the Christian Era*. Cambridge and New York: Cambridge University Press, 1987.

Jewish eschatology: philosophical

Funkenstein, Amos, "Maimonides: Political Theory and Realistic Messianism." *Miscellenea Medievalia* 11 (1977): 81–103.

—— *Maimonides: Nature, History and Messianic Beliefs.* Tel Aviv: Mod Books, 1997.

Jewish eschatology: kabbalistic

Altshuler, Mor, *The Messianic Secret of Hasidism*, Brill's Series in Jewish Studies. Leiden and Boston, MA: Brill, 2006.

Idel, Moshe, *Messianic Mystics.* New Haven, CT: Yale University Press, 1998.

Kraushar, Alexander and Herbert Levy, *Jacob Frank: The End to the Sabbataian Heresy.* Lanham, MD: University Press of America, 2001.

Mandel, Arthur, *The Militant Messiah: Or, the Flight from the Ghetto: The Story of Jacob Frank and the Frankist Movement.* Atlantic Highlands, NJ: Humanities Press, 1979.

Menzi, Donald Wilder and Zwe Padeh, eds, *The Tree of Life: Chayyim Vital's Introduction to the Kabbalah of Isaac Luria: The Palace of Adam Kadmon.* Northvale, NJ: Jason Aronson, 1999.

Scholem, Gershom Gerhard, *Sabbatai Sevi: The Mystical Messiah, 1626–1676*, Bollingen Series. Princeton, NJ: Princeton University Press, 1973.

Judaism and Zionism

Cohen, Jack. *Guides for an Age of Confusion: Studies in the Thinking of Avraham Y. Kook and Mordecai M. Kaplan*, 1st ed. New York: Fordham University Press, 1999.

Elkins, Dov Peretz, *Shepherd of Jerusalem: A Biography of Rabbi Abraham Isaac Kook*, 1st Jason Aronson Inc. softcover ed. Northvale, NJ: Jason Aronson, 1995.

Gellman, Ezra, ed., *Essays on the Thought and Philosophy of Rabbi Kook.* Rutherford, NJ and New York: Fairleigh Dickenson University Press and Cornwall Books, 1991.

Hertzberg, Arthur, ed., *The Zionist Idea: A Historical Analysis and Reader.* New York: Atheneum, 1972.

Holtz, Avraham, *The Holy City: Jews on Jerusalem*, 1st ed., The B'nai B'rith Jewish Heritage Classics. New York: Norton, 1971.

Ish Shalom, Binyamin, Rav *Avraham Itzhak Hacohen Kook: Between Rationalism and Mysticism*, SUNY Series in Judaica. Albany, NY: State University of New York Press, 1993.

Ravitzky, Aviezer, *Messianism, Zionism, and Jewish Religious Radicalism*, Chicago Studies in the History of Judaism. Chicago, IL: University of Chicago Press, 1996.

Yaron, Zvi, *The Philosophy of Rabbi Kook*. Translated by Avner Tomaschoff, 2nd ed. Jerusalem: Eliner Library, 1992.

11 *Life after death*

In this chapter

Although the Bible says almost nothing about life after death, the topic was of concern to authors during the second Temple era. The Pharisees advocated the doctrine of resurrection into physical bodies, and this became the normative view from the talmudic era and onwards. Alongside the resurrection, which is expected in the messianic era, the rabbis spoke of the "garden of Eden" as a paradise for the righteous and of Gehinnom as the place of punishment for sinners. Some medieval philosophers preferred to believe in a disembodied survival of the intellect, while the Kabbalah formulated a doctrine of multiple reincarnations. Modern Jewish thinkers have generally expressed little interest in the afterlife.

Main topics covered

- The biblical background
- Resurrection and reincarnation
- Medieval and modern views

The biblical background

The Bible did not teach that individuals survive death in any religiously significant way. Although there are several terms and passages in the Hebrew scriptures that could allude to some sort of afterlife conception, and others that would be creatively interpreted in that vein by Jews of later generations, their place in the broader context of biblical world-views is marginal. Assurances of reward or threats of punishment after death do not figure in the preaching of the prophets, nor as incentives for attaining holiness and atonement. Even when the Torah is emphasizing that God's grace or wrath will continue beyond a person's life span, it is referring to future generations rather than to survival in a supernatural afterlife. Some scholars suggest that the Bible's compilers wished to emphasize thereby the absolute value of life in the present world. It is likely that they were repelled by the afterlife conceptions that were prevalent in the ancient Near East, which often involved deification of the deceased or of the rulers of the underworld. Such attitudes were perceived as inherently antithetical to the prophetic ideals of ethical monotheism.

Resurrection and reincarnation

It is only in the latest stratum of the biblical corpus, in the book of Daniel, that the promise of afterlife rewards is invoked to motivate religious devotion, to encourage the faithful to persist in their commitment to God's word. "And many of them that sleep in the dust of the earth shall awake, some to everlasting life, and some to shame and everlasting contempt. And they that be wise shall shine as the brightness of the firmament; and they that turn many to righteousness as the stars forever and ever" (Daniel 12:2–3). A similar theme is found in the non-canonical book of 2 Maccabees that is included among the "Apocrypha." Both these works were composed in the historical setting of the Hellenistic persecutions of the second century BCE

An unusual passage in the Mishnah deals with mandatory articles of belief. Among the heretics who forfeit their place in the world to come, the text includes "one who says that there is no resurrection of the dead." It is evident that this passage must be understood in the context of the sectarian controversies of the Second Temple era.

In his description of the three main Jewish sects, Josephus offered the following information about the Essenes:

> For it is a fixed belief of theirs that the body is corruptible, and its constituent matter impermanent, but that the soul is immortal and imperishable. Emanating from the finest ether, these souls become entangled, as it were, in the prison-house of the body, to which they are dragged down by a sort of natural spell; but when once they are released from the bonds of the flesh, then, as though liberated from a long servitude, they rejoice and are borne aloft…

Of the Pharisees Josephus notes: "Every soul, they maintain, is imperishable, but the soul of the good alone passes into another body, while the souls of the wicked suffer eternal punishment." Concerning the remaining sect, the Sadducees, he reports, "As for the persistence of the soul after death, penalties in the underworld, and rewards, they will have none of them."

The Mishnah's strict insistence on belief in resurrection can therefore be viewed not merely as a theoretical exercise in dogma, but as an identification of sectarian credentials. In this matter, the rabbis of the Mishnah were the successors to the Pharisaic party of the Temple era. The Pharisaic doctrine of resurrection may have originated as a borrowing from Iranian traditions that were absorbed into Judaism during the Persian era. However, there are other factors that could have influenced their position.

Josephus' survey of the Essene attitude suggests an important difference in world-views that is implicit in the dispute over afterlife theories. The Essene commitment to an exclusively spiritual survival goes hand in hand with their negative attitude towards the physical aspects of life, including sexuality and family. The Essene outlook has some similarities with Greek philosophical thinking where the cultivation of the intellect is seen to be in a fundamental conflict with the temptation of the bodily "appetites" that distract the mind from spiritual contemplation. The Pharisaic insistence that the dead will ultimately be restored to physical bodies implies an affirmation of physical existence. In this, it is consistent with the biblical attitude that sees God's creation of the material universe as essentially good, and the ideal model of human religious life as one built on sanctification in the flesh.

Because resurrection does not occur in the observable present, it had to be projected to an unspecified future age. As, such it became a stage in the Jewish eschatological vision, one of the many wonders that would be performed in the redeemed world. Rabbinic sources often refer to the destination of the departed as "the word to come," a term that more often designated the stage after messianic resurrection. This invites the question of what befalls the soul from the moment of death until the resurrection. A widespread notion had it that the disembodied spirits continue to live on individually in a supernatural abode, and several texts seem to apply the term "world to come" to the place that souls inhabit immediately after being severed from their bodies.

In rabbinic discourses about the fates of the righteous and the sinners, the souls of the former inhabit the "garden of Eden" whereas the latter suffer torments in "Gehinnom." In the Bible the garden of Eden was an idyllic paradise from which the first woman and man were expelled after disobeying God. Although some of the rabbinic sources can be interpreted as referring to a terrestrial garden, most seem to speak of it as a supernatural, heavenly paradise. The name Gehinnom is usually traced to the "vale (Hebrew: *gei*) of Ben Hinnom" south of Jerusalem, which had been a notorious scene of a child sacrifice cult during the First Commonwealth era. Not surprisingly, the popular imagination supplied vivid descriptions of both these afterlife destinations. They served preachers through the ages as effective incentives for their congregations to pursue good and eschew evil. When formulating the daily prayers, the rabbis of the Tannaitic era inserted a reference to resurrection in the blessing that speaks of God's power—but not in the blessings that deal with eschatological themes. Similarly, medieval Jewish philosophers often discussed doctrines of the afterlife in connection with the subject of divine justice.

The doctrine of resurrection has implications with respect to certain Jewish observance. Most notably, traditional Judaism requires burial of a corpse and forbids cremation.

Medieval and modern views

Medieval Jewish philosophers encouraged humans to transcend their impermanent physical existence in order to achieve immortality through the intellectual contemplation of eternal, abstract truths. This ideal did not harmonize easily with the belief in a physical afterlife. Maimonides accepted the traditional dogma that in the messianic era, God will resurrect the dead of previous generations in bodies of flesh and blood. However, he went on to declare that the revived people will then live out their normal lifetimes, after which they will again die natural deaths. Although Maimonides enumerated belief in resurrection among the mandatory Jewish dogmas, his sincerity was questioned by some contemporaries, and he composed a special treatise to confirm his commitment to the doctrine.

In the cosmology of the Jewish Aristotelians, a sequence of emanated "separate intelligences," pure disembodied intellects, occupy the continuum between God and our world and are equated with the biblical angels and with the astronomical bodies that orbit the Earth. The lowest of these, the "active intellect," is the power that imprints upon the human mind the capacity to conceptualize universal and abstract ideas that are not mere collections of sense data. The influence of the active intellect on the human mind produces the "acquired intellect" that is the only part of the human being capable of immortality. The Jewish philosophers were not in agreement about whether people retain their individuality, or are subsumed into a cosmic intellect. This approach makes immortality contingent upon rational, rather than moral, perfection. Ultimately it remains an elitist ideal, accessible only to those who possess the requisite intellectual gifts and training.

Although Josephus's account of Pharisaic belief might be construed as a reference to transfer of souls into different bodies, the medieval Kabbalah was the only Jewish movement for which the transmigration of souls ("*gilgul*") was the normative doctrine, a notion which they often combined with belief in the pre-existence of souls (an idea that had roots in rabbinic texts, and may ultimately have derived from Plato). One popular theory spoke of each soul fashioning a spiritual garment composed of virtuous deeds, which it will don when it is finally admitted to God's presence. Early kabbalists envisaged metempsychosis as a punishment, or second chance, for certain transgressions, especially sexual ones. However later sources treat it as a normal process, in which the new bodies are not necessarily human. Variations on the transmigration motif include the belief that a departed soul can enter ("impregnate") a living person in order to fulfill certain missions. Kabbalistic folklore often spoke of possession ("*dibbuk*") by sinful spirits who had forfeited their right to redemptive transmigration.

In modern times, acknowledgment of the principle of physical resurrection continues to be a defining feature of Orthodox Judaism. Most early Reform thinkers felt that a literal belief in resurrection was unacceptable. Many liberal Jews shared the prevalent Protestant conviction that immortality of the soul is rationally demonstrable.

Discussions of the afterlife are almost entirely absent from non-Orthodox religious discourse in recent generations. Jewish representatives are more likely to focus on ethical commitments to this world. Even a philosopher like Franz Rosenzweig, whose theology was responding to the challenges of human mortality, conceived of eternity as a religious dimension of life, not as an afterlife state. Similarly, the important theological responses to the Nazi Holocaust, as formulated by authors like Elie Wiesel, Emil Fackenheim, Richard Rubinstein and others, are rendered more poignant and disturbing by their reluctance to appeal to a supernatural retribution.

Key points you need to know

- Promises of rewards or punishment after death do not appear until the latest strata of the Bible.
- The three Jewish sects of the Second Commonwealth were divided in their views of the afterlife: whether there is no survival after death, whether there is purely spiritual survival or restoration to physical bodies.
- Rabbinic traditions insisted on belief in resurrection, alongside concepts like paradise, Gehenna, and the "world to come."
- Maimonides accepted the rabbinic dogma of resurrection but minimized its importance by depicting it as a temporary episode.
- The kabbalistic doctrine of *gilgul* envisioned souls returning to earth repeatedly until they overcome their sinfulness.
- Recent Jewish thought has been more interested in ethical issues, stressing the importance of goodness in this life.

Discussion questions

1. "Jewish scholarly discussions about the afterlife often approach it from the perspective of divine justice, while popular religion is likely to treat it as an incentive to human behavior." Discuss this statement.
2. The Hebrew liturgy mentions resurrection, alongside rainfall, as an example of God's might, but not in connection with hopes for redemption. Discuss possible implications of this fact.
3. The Essenes (according to Josephus) and Maimonides both believed that people survive death in a disembodied state. What are the main differences between their positions?

Further reading

Gillman, Neil, *The Death of Death: Resurrection and Immortality in Jewish Thought*, 1st ed. Woodstock, VT: Jewish Lights, 1997.

Raphael, Simcha Paull, *Jewish Views of the Afterlife*. Northvale, NJ: Jason Aronson, 1994.

Segal, Alan F., *Life after Death: A History of the Afterlife in the Religions of the West*, 1st ed. New York and Toronto: Doubleday, 2004.

Segal, Eliezer, "Judaism." In *Life after Death in World Religions*. Edited by Harold G. Coward, 11–30. Maryknoll, NY: Orbis, 1997.

Sievers, Joseph, "Josephus and the Afterlife." In *Understanding Josephus: Seven Perspectives*. Edited by Steve Mason, 20–34. Sheffield: Sheffield Academic Press, 1998.

Wolf, Arnold Jacob, "Maimonides on Human Immortality." *Judaism* 15 (1966): 95–101, 211–16, 337–42.

12 The mystic path

In this chapter

The biblical model of holiness was a complex one that encompassed ethical purity rather than spiritual elevation from everyday life. Nevertheless, some schools cultivated disciplines of personal holiness that allowed them to experience mystical ascents to the heavenly realms. The paradigmatic vision was that of the prophet Ezekiel who described a divine being riding on a chariot (*merkabah*) fashioned of angels. The "work of the chariot" was pursued as an esoteric mystical practice during ancient and medieval times. It is not clear whether the Kabbalah should be characterized as mysticism, since its main features involve a description of the divine workings in terms of the ten *sefirot* and a system for eliciting the esoteric meaning of the Bible, but it does not try to achieve unity or intimacy with God.

Main topics covered

- Holiness and the encounter with God
- The work of the chariot
- Heikhalot literature:
- The mysticism of the Hasidei Ashkenaz
- Kabbalah and mysticism

Holiness and the encounter with God

The Bible speaks repeatedly of holiness (Hebrew root: *K-D-Sh*) as a divine attribute and as a virtue to which the Israelites should aspire. The term is employed in an immense variety of contexts, including dietary regulations, sacrificial offerings, ritual and cultic purity (especially by the priesthood), avoidance of incest and other illicit sexual practices, maintaining ethical standards, observance of holy days, and more. The Torah repeatedly exhorts the Israelites to be holy because God is holy. It admonishes the people not to profane the holiness of their land by means of crime, idolatry or unchastity. Thus, it is difficult, and probably misleading, to dissociate the ideal of holiness from other qualities such as justice or piety.

In late biblical and post-biblical texts, the concept of holiness came to be associated especially with intimate experiences of the divine. The scriptural descriptions of prophetic revelations were understood as paradigms of how humans can attain a spiritual state of holiness that allows them to ascend to the celestial realms and experience the divine presence, which was usually portrayed as a royal court populated by an elaborate entourage of angels. The most graphic of those biblical accounts provided the imagery for a tradition of Jewish mysticism.

The work of the chariot

Talmudic literature knew of secret teachings concerning the "account of creation" and the "account of the chariot." This undertaking was regarded as potentially perilous to those who did not have the proper spiritual preparation. It could severely endanger one's mind, faith and even life. Hence, the rabbis generally upheld the secrecy of those teachings, and it is no longer possible to reconstruct their precise content or mystical character. The expression "account of the chariot" indicates that it involved a replication of the experience of the prophet Ezekiel as described in the first chapter of the biblical book bearing his name. There, in dazzling imagery, Ezekiel described a chariot composed of angelic beings that was drawn by supernatural creatures that combine animal and human features. The pinnacle of the vision came when the prophet spoke of the being that was borne on the swiftly moving chariot, a human-like image seated upon an exalted throne:

> … the likeness of a throne, as the appearance of a sapphire stone: and upon the likeness of the throne was the likeness as the appearance of a man above upon it.
>
> And I saw as the color of amber, as the appearance of fire round about within it, from the appearance of his loins even upward, and from the appearance of his loins even downward, I saw as it were the appearance of fire, and it had brightness round about.
>
> As the appearance of the bow that is in the cloud in the day of rain, so was the appearance of the brightness round about. This was the appearance of the likeness of the glory of the Lord. And when I saw it, I fell upon my face, and I heard a voice of one that spake.

Selected verses from this passage, combined with a similar vision of God exalted by angels from the sixth chapter of Isaiah, were adopted into the *Kedushah* ("Sanctification") passages that occupy a central place in the standard Jewish liturgy. We may reasonably assume that the talmudic adepts of "*merkabah* (chariot) mysticism" were striving, by focusing on the relevant biblical passages, to emulate the experience of the prophets who ascended to an exalted spiritual state where they could behold the Almighty from nearby.

Heikhalot literature

During the early Middle Ages, there appeared several detailed descriptions of mystical ascents to the divine throne. The alleged narrators and heroes of these works were prominent rabbis from the talmudic era, notably Rabbi Akiva and Rabbi Ishmael. Although Rabbi Akiva is described in the Talmud as one of the few who successfully mastered the account of the chariot, there is no indication that Rabbi Ishmael was involved in such pursuits. It is therefore to be assumed that the use of these names in the medieval works was pseudepigraphic. The liturgical poets also dwelled lovingly on this experience, and composed powerful elaborations of the Kedushah prayer in which the innumerable kinds of angelic figures were described and augmented in rich detail as they sang the praises of the creator.

An important new metaphor made its appearance in the early medieval mystical texts, that of multiple levels of *palaces*. It was those palaces that give the works their Hebrew name of *Heikhalot*. Before arriving at the level or spiritual state of the throne-bearing chariot, the mystic must ascend through the various palaces. Each level in the ascent is more difficult and more perilous than the previous one. The danger is symbolized by terrifying angels who are posted at each level to keep away mortals who lack the spiritual qualifications to continue the journey. A horrible fate awaits the person who is rejected by the guards. In order to be allowed access to the next level, the mystic must qualify according to religious standards of piety, righteousness and purity. However, there is also a technical aspect to the process, which usually consists of possessing the appropriate "seal," a kind of password. The correct seal normally contains the name of the angel whom one is confronting at that level. When the seal is displayed, the hostile gatekeeper is transformed into an ally who helps the mystic rise to the next level.

Modern scholars are not in agreement about whether the medieval Heikhalot texts can teach us anything reliable about the experiences of the Merkabah mystics during the talmudic era. There is some evidence that motifs appearing in the medieval Heikhalot writings were known during the earlier era. Furthermore, the principal motifs underlying the ascent through spiritual levels, along with the mixture of sublime and magical elements, were characteristic of the ancient religious movement known as Gnosticism, which posited a spiritual goal of secret knowledge of the divinity. At its core, Gnosticism was a form of religious dualism; that is to say, it viewed the world as being embroiled in an eternal cosmic struggle between the powers of good and evil, with good being entirely spiritual in nature, and evil identified with matter and the physical body. A select few have been entrusted with the secret knowledge (*gnosis*) of how to rise above pitiful and depraved physical existence, to eventually arrive at a realm of pure light and spirit.

The mysticism of the Hasidei Ashkenaz

The mystical lore of the medieval German pietists (known as the *Hasidei Ashkenaz*) was derived from diverse sources, not all of which can be identified with certainty. They cultivated the traditions of the Heikhalot mystics, and spoke of the work of creation and the work of the chariot. An important focus of their speculation was the concept of Divine Glory (*kavod* in Hebrew), the spiritual force that is seated, as it were, upon God's throne, and serves as the intermediary between God and the created universe. They frequently referred to the *kavod* (or a particular manifestation of it) as the "special cherub" or the "holy cherub." Their belief in an intermediary between the purely spiritual realm and the physical world was inspired by the philosophical speculations of Saadiah Gaon whose Arabic theological treatise had been translated into Hebrew.

Kabbalah and mysticism

It is common to define Kabbalah as "Jewish mysticism." In fact, this equation is a very problematic one for a number of reasons. If we understand mysticism as constituting an experience of mystical union or intimacy with the divine, then it would appear that very few kabbalists were striving for such an experience. All versions of kabbalistic theology begin with the premise, which they shared with the rationalists, that true knowledge of God as God really is cannot be achieved by mortal humans; and the most we can hope for is some interaction with the lower manifestations of the divine emanations. Even within this more modest formulation of the mystic quest, one finds little evidence in the principal kabbalistic writings that their authors were concerned primarily with achieving an ecstatic encounter with the absolute. Most kabbalistic works are dauntingly theoretical and academic. They attempt to describe the workings of the divine powers in the upper and lower realms, and to discern references to kabbalistic teachings in the sacred scriptures and in the observance of religious precepts. Even the realm that was known as "practical Kabbalah" was not directed towards mystical experience, but to the manipulation of supernatural forces (what in other contexts would be called "magic"). One can think of several major medieval kabbalists who invested extraordinary devotion and ingenuity in the formulation of doctrines, and in the esoteric interpretation of sacred texts, but who provide no indication whatsoever that they had ever had a mystical experience, or were even attempting to have one. By contrast, the medieval Jewish philosophers were more explicit about asserting that they were seeking to achieve, at the end of a long and disciplined regimen of moral and intellectual development, a direct encounter with the divine.

Scholars who insist on equating Kabbalah with mysticism are often forced either to redefine the term "mysticism" in a non-standard way or to assert that the kabbalists were involved in mystical ecstasies, but that they chose not to write about them. Neither of these approaches is very satisfactory or convincing, and they seem to be driven by a determination to force Kabbalah into a conceptual model that is not quite appropriate to the facts. Noted Jewish mystics and mystical movements, such as the *Hasidei Ashkenaz*, the Egyptian school of "Jewish Sufis" whose most distinguished representative was Maimonides's own son Abraham, or Abraham Abulafia, did not follow the classical forms of *sefirot*-based Kabbalah that evolved in Provence and Spain. The quest for ecstatic experience was most pronounced in the eastern European Hasidic movement that arose in the eighteenth century, a movement that blended a popular version of Kabbalah with numerous other ideas and values from Jewish tradition. Aspects of their mystical teachings, especially their doctrines of devotion and ecstasy, are described in the chapter dealing with prayer.

The school of Neoplatonist philosophy had a significant mystical tendency that followed naturally from its fixation on the problematic relationship between the purely spiritual One and the diversity of the physical world. As the Neoplatonists were trying to describe the process of emanation through which the material world emerged from pure spirit, it was also formulating a program through which the philosopher should strive for release from the shackles of gross matter, in order to ascend towards the absolute divine light. The emergence of kabbalistic literature coincided with the eclipse of Jewish Neoplatonism by Maimonidean Aristotelianism, and it appears that some important Neoplatonic themes were sublimated into Kabbalah. This process is most discernible among the earliest generations of kabbalistic authors.

The perception of Kabbalah as a mysticism also derives in large measure from its own claims to be a branch of ancient Jewish teaching. The kabbalistic literature that began to appear from the twelfth century and onward made frequent use of imagery taken from the account of the chariot; and insisted that its own doctrines, which described in meticulous metaphysical detail the emanations of the celestial domains, were a systematic formulation of those same traditions. However, the experiential dimension of the talmudic "account of the chariot" was downplayed by most medieval kabbalists in favor of a theoretical mapping out of the supernatural emanations.

When referring to their own teachings, the kabbalists do not use the term "mysticism" (indeed, there is no real equivalent to that concept in classical Hebrew). Instead, they employ expressions that are translated more accurately as "esotericism" or "secret doctrine." In this respect too we may recall the Talmud's strictures against the public teaching of the works of creation and of the chariot, a policy that was built upon a very real fear that not all people have the spiritual capacity to deal with such teachings and the experience might cause them harm. For the philosophers, the fear was chiefly of falling into heresy. The talmudic mystics entertained additional fears, and told of prominent sages who had become injured (mentally or spiritually), or even died, because of their experiences; in addition to one who "cut the plants" and abandoned Judaism.

The kabbalists took the requirements of esotericism very seriously, at least on a theoretical level. One of the reasons why we know so little about the origins of their doctrines is because the earliest teachers were scrupulous about not putting them into writing. When Nahmanides began to include a few vague allusions to kabbalistic imagery in his commentary on the Torah, of the sort that would make little sense to anyone who had not already been initiated into the intricacies of kabbalistic hermeneutics, he was taken to task by veteran teachers who believed that even this was more publicity than ought to be permitted. However, the secrecy could not be maintained for long, and by the thirteenth century very few limitations still remained in place regarding the public teaching of the doctrine. Quite the contrary, kabbalists were often infused with a missionary zeal that stemmed from their conviction that any form of Judaism that was not motivated by the proper understanding of the commandments was incomplete, a meaninglessly mechanical performance of arid rituals. The perception arose that the ban on public teaching had been intended to apply to former generations, but was now no longer in force, and that the widespread dissemination of the doctrine at a particular stage of history was part of an inscrutable divine plan. Although the inherently academic and theoretical nature of Kabbalah kept it from being fully absorbed by the broad populace, it nevertheless lent itself with surprising ease to popularizations that did attract large followings; and the diverse manifestations Kabbalah have played central roles in Judaism since the Middle Ages.

In the history of world religions, mystics often found themselves at odds with organized institutions and orthodoxies. The administrators of the respective orthodoxies were understandably distrustful of individuals whose claims to unmediated communication with the divine set them above the authority of the imperfect human organizations that were charged with guiding the affairs of the religious communities. And indeed, the mystics themselves were often convinced that normative religious bodies, concerned as they were with external rituals and administrative politics, had entirely missed the point of the true spiritual quest. Mystics were often outspoken critics of legalism and worldliness, both of which were, to varying degrees, essential components of any viable organization. Kabbalah does not fit the standard pattern of tension between orthodoxy and individual spiritual experience. This was not only because they were not striving for unity with God, though that was certainly an important factor that distinguished it from Christian, Muslim or Hindu forms of mysticism. Unlike the mystics who arose in other religions, the kabbalists were not objecting to the legalism of traditional Judaism. On the contrary, one of the central objectives of Kabbalah was to provide a deeper motivation for the performance of the religious commandments as they had been set down in the written and oral Torahs. Treatises devoted to the "rationales for the commandments" are a popular genre of kabbalistic literature. For the most part, the kabbalists accepted as valid the full body of traditional religious law and customs. Their doctrine explained how the observance or non-observance of these religious laws could have cosmic consequences.

For example, the kabbalist Rabbi Moses Nahmanides was one of most respected figures of rabbinic Judaism, the author of celebrated commentaries to the Bible and Talmud. Other leading kabbalists also acquired formidable reputations in more conventional branches of Jewish scholarship. It is interesting to observe how carefully these kabbalists-halakhists insisted on maintaining the distinctions between the different realms of their religious scholarship. There was a widespread understanding that kabbalistic theology should not influence the ultimate halakhic decision-making process. This convention is aptly illustrated in the work of the sixteenth-century sage Rabbi Joseph Caro, a devoted kabbalist who received communications from a supernatural voice (*maggid*), but whose most important contribution to Jewish posterity was his authoritative code of Jewish religious law, the *Shulhan 'Arukh*. In spite of the centrality of Kabbalah to Caro's personal spiritual outlook, there were scarcely a handful of instances where his kabbalistic beliefs impelled him to issue a ruling that contradicted the normal methods of halakhic decision-making.

Key points you need to know

- Ancient Jewish sources speak of an esoteric discipline called the "work of the chariot" about which we have little information.
- Early medieval traditions described mystical experiences in terms of an ascent through levels of palaces (*Heikhalot*).
- Though Kabbalah is commonly equated with Jewish mysticism, it is arguable that medieval philosophy has more explicitly mystical objectives.

Discussion questions

1. Can you find biblical passages other than the visions of Ezekiel and Isaiah that could have served as the basis for mystical interpretation?
2. Why is access to mystical teachings often restricted to a select group? What objections might there be to disseminating them publicly?
3. Historians have noted that until recently we do not know of women who were involved in Kabbalah or Jewish mysticism. What explanations can you think of for this situation?

Further reading

Ancient Jewish mysticism

Arbel, Vita Daphna, *Beholders of Divine Secrets: Mysticism and Myth in Hekhalot and Merkavah Literature*. Albany, NY: State University of New York Press, 2003.

Boustan, Ra'anan S., *From Martyr to Mystic: Rabbinic Martyrology and the Making of Merkavah Mysticism*. Tübingen: Mohr Siebeck, 2005.

Elior, Rachel, *The Three Temples: On the Emergence of Jewish Mysticism*. Oxford and Portland, OR: Littman Library of Jewish Civilization, 2004.

Gruenwald, Ithamar, *Apocalyptic and Merkavah Mysticism*, Arbeiten zur Geschichte des Antiken Judentums und des Urchristentums. Leiden: Brill, 1980.

—— *From Apocalypticism to Gnosticism: Studies in Apocalypticism, Merkavah Mysticism and Gnosticism*, Beiträge zur Erforschung des Alten Testaments und des Antiken Judentums. Frankfurt-am-Main: P. Lang, 1988.

Kuyt, Annelies, *The "Descent" To the Chariot: Towards a Description of the Terminology, Place, Function and Nature of the Yeridah in Hekhalot Literature*, Texte und Studien zum Antiken Judentum. Tübingen: J.C.B. Mohr (Paul Siebeck), 1995.

Scholem, Gershom Gerhard, *Jewish Gnosticism, Merkabah Mysticism, and Talmudic Tradition*, 2nd improved ed. New York: Jewish Theological Seminary of America, 1965.

Swartz, Michael D., *Mystical Prayer in Ancient Judaism: An Analysis of Ma'aseh Merkavah*. Tübingen: J.C.B. Mohr, 1992.

Hasidei Ashkenaz

Dan, Joseph, "The Devotional Ideals of Ashkenazic Pietism." In *Jewish Spirituality*. Edited by Arthur Green, 289–307. New York: Crossroad, 1986.

—— *The "Unique Cherub" Circle: A School of Mystics and Esoterics in Medieval Germany*, Texts and Studies in Medieval and Early Modern Judaism. Tübingen: Mohr Siebeck, 1999.

Grözinger, Karl-Erich and Joseph Dan, *Mysticism, Magic, and Kabbalah in Ashkenazi Judaism: International Symposium Held in Frankfurt-am-Main, 1991*. Berlin and New York: Walter de Gruyter, 1995.

Kabbalah as mysticism

Blumenthal, David R., *Understanding Jewish Mysticism: A Source Reader*, The Library of Judaic Learning. New York: KTAV, 1978.

Cohn-Sherbok, Dan, *Kabbalah and Jewish Mysticism: An Introductory Anthology*, 2nd ed. Oxford: Oneworld Publications, 2006.

Elior, Rachel, *The Paradoxical Ascent to God: The Kabbalistic Theosophy of Habad Hasidism*, SUNY Series in Judaica. Albany, NY: State University of New York Press, 1993.

—— *Jewish Mysticism: The Infinite Expression of Freedom*. Oxford: Littman Library of Jewish Civilization, 2007.

Idel, Moshe, *The Mystical Experience in Abraham Abulafia*, SUNY Series in Judaica. Albany, NY: State University of New York Press, 1988.

—— *Kabbalah: New Perspectives*. New Haven, CT: Yale University Press, 1988.

Marcus, Ivan G., "The Devotional Ideals of Ashkenazic Pietism." In *Jewish Spirituality: From the Bible through the Middle Ages*. Edited by Arthur Green, 356–66. New York: Crossroads, 1987.

Scholem, Gershom Gerhard, *Major Trends in Jewish Mysticism*, Schocken Paperbacks, SB5. New York: Schocken Books, 1961.

Wolfson, Elliot R., *Through a Speculum That Shines: Vision and Imagination in Medieval Jewish Mysticism*. Princeton, NJ: Princeton University Press, 1994.

—— *Venturing Beyond: Law and Morality in Kabbalistic Mysticism*. New York: Oxford University Press, 2006.

—— *Luminal Darkness: Imaginal Gleanings from Zoharic Literature*. Oxford: Oneworld Publications, 2007.

13 *Wisdom and scholarship*

In this chapter

The study of the written and oral Torahs is one of Judaism's most cherished values, and Jewish tradition has encouraged intellectual and scholarly pursuits. This chapter describes achievements of Jewish religious scholarship in the realms of biblical and talmudic studies.

Philo of Alexandria followed an allegorical method of philosophical exegesis of the Bible, and the ancient rabbis developed elaborate methods of halakhic interpretation and aggadic exposition. An innovation of the medieval era was the literal interpretation of the Bible according to critical standards of literary and philological scholarship (*peshat*), an approach that originally took hold under Arabic influence, but also enjoyed a significant following in France. Notwithstanding some opposition to non-traditional readings of scripture, the literal method came to coexist with other methods, such as the midrashic and the specialized hermeneutics that were developed by the philosophers and kabbalists. Some of the most prominent Jewish commentators are surveyed.

Traditionalists and rationalists, especially during the medieval era, disagreed over the question of whether rational explanations should be sought for the laws of the Torah or whether they should be obeyed unquestioningly as expressions of devotion to God. Modern scholars challenged the assumption of the Torah's supernatural revelation at Sinai, and liberal Jews used this evolutionary model of Judaism as a justification for introducing changes to modernize Jewish ritual and theology.

The inherent difficulties of talmudic discourse, and the multiplicity of opinions recorded in it, meant that it could not be used as a guide to practical religious life without some mediation. Towards that end, medieval Jewish scholars studied the Talmud intensively, producing several different genres of specialized literature. Chief among them were: explanatory and critical commentaries; codifications of law; and responsa. Explanatory commentaries, of which the preeminent one was authored by Rabbi Solomon ben Isaac of Troyes ("Rashi") sought to make the text accessible to readers and students; critical commentaries posed questions, resolved contradictions and proposed alternative interpretations. Law codes decided from among the Talmud's conflicting opinions and organized the material topically so that it could be used as a source of practical guidance. Responsa were letters written by leading rabbis in answer to specific questions, thereby enhancing the relevance of the ancient texts to new situations.

Main topics covered

- The centrality of Torah study as a religious value
- Biblical scholarship
- Ancient Jewish exegesis
- Biblical study in the rabbinic era: midrash
- Medieval biblical studies: the rise of literal exegesis
- The Torah and commandments in Jewish thought
- Biblical studies in the modern era
- Talmudic scholarship
- Critical commentaries to the Talmud
- Codes of talmudic law
- Responsa literature

The centrality of Torah study as a religious value

Fundamental to Judaism is the belief that God revealed in his message to the people of Israel through the vehicle of prophecy, and that message is preserved in written form as the Hebrew Bible. The central pillar of the revelation, the Torah, was revealed through the agency of the greatest of prophets, Moses. The study of Torah is arguably the most highly esteemed act of religious piety; and therefore Bible study was incorporated into the structures of Jewish worship. The words, personalities and ideas of the Bible accompany religious Jews through all aspects of their daily lives.

Jews have regarded their scriptures as the products of revelation that were conveyed to the people through the agency of people known in Hebrew as *nevi'im*.

For reasons that are not spelled out explicitly in the documents of the time, there was a widespread perception, at least among later generations of Jews, that prophecy ceased at a certain point in history; that is to say, God no longer revealed his will through chosen human beings, and the last three biblical prophets, Haggai, Zachariah and Malachi lived at the beginning of the Second Temple era. The perceived cessation of prophecy is presumably to be correlated with the fact that the body of sacred scriptures was now considered closed, so that works composed after this time would not be included in the official "Bible." This also signaled a crucial change in the central role that was now assigned to the reading and interpretation of the scriptures. Whereas previous generations were informed of God's will by the divine messengers who dwelt in their midst—the prophets—Jews would henceforth have to seek guidance by reading the messages that God had addressed to previous generations and were preserved in the received scriptures. The teaching, study and exposition of the Torah and other biblical books therefore were elevated to the status of central religious activities in the Jewish religion.

Of course, a religion that is founded on commandments and laws cannot be observed unless the members of the community are aware of those laws. However, Torah study is a key Jewish value that is not merely a means to observance of the commandments. The study of the divinely revealed law grew to encompass topics and approaches that have no obvious relevance to daily life.

The notion that God's Torah is to be studied and taught, as well as obeyed, is found in the Bible itself. The liturgical recitation of the *"Shema' Yisra'el"* is a fulfillment of that obligation, as it commands "And these words, which I command you this day, shall be in thine heart, and you shall teach them diligently unto your children." Philo, Josephus and the rabbinic traditions all testify with pride to the Jews' extensive knowledge of their laws, instilled through instruments like an organized school system and preaching in the synagogue on the sabbath.

Virtually all the forms of Judaism that we know of since biblical times have had a scholarly or bookish quality. This situation appears to derive naturally from the need for the older revelations to be mediated by interpreters who were capable of making the original messages understandable and relevant to new situations. A rabbinic maxim states that "an uncultured person does not fear sin, nor is an ignoramus pious." This observation is true of many aspects of day-to-day Jewish practice. To cite a typical example: rabbinic law requires that blessings be recited before partaking of food, thereby expressing appreciation to God for providing sustenance to his creatures. To fulfill this obligation properly, however, it is necessary to recite the blessing that is appropriate for each specific food. To do so demands considerable expertise not only in the wording of the numerous possible blessings, but also in the biological and agricultural details of how the foods are grown and prepared; how to prioritize which foods should be eaten and blessed first, and how to deal with dishes composed of diverse ingredients. Though occasionally we hear of religious thinkers (as in the Hasidic movement) extolling the simple piety of the illiterate believer, mainstream rabbinic Judaism usually expected quite a high degree of erudition from its adherents.

Biblical scholarship

Much Jewish scholarly energy through the ages was directed towards the interpretation of the sacred scriptures. Even as the biblical corpus was taking shape and taking on authoritative status, sophisticated systems were being evolved for deriving meaning from it. The belief that the Torah was authored by the perfect and omniscient God meant that exegetes could assume that every word and letter had been carefully chosen, and there was not one detail that was not bursting with significance. The belief that the Bible was composed according to standards that differ radically from those of normal human literature often produced a disparity between literal readings and the specialized religious hermeneutics. There was no uniform approach for dealing with the phenomenon of multiple interpretations of sacred texts.

Ancient Jewish exegesis

In first-century CE Egypt, Philo of Alexandria expounded his allegorical method of interpreting the Torah in conformity with Greek philosophy. He insisted nonetheless that his allegorical explanations should not cancel out the literal meaning. In particular, he berated more radical allegorists in his community who argued that there was no longer any reason to fulfill the commandments according to their literal sense, because their ultimate purpose is to symbolically teach us theological truths and moral virtues, and this has already been accomplished. Although Philo accepted the basic logic of that argument, he stated that the philosophically enlightened Jews must nonetheless continue to observe the rituals because to do otherwise would compromise their credibility as role models to the community. The tension between literal and allegorical readings would reappear with the rise of Jewish philosophy in the medieval era.

As we have seen, one of the distinctive doctrines that Josephus ascribed to the Pharisees was their belief in an unwritten ancestral tradition, a doctrine that set them apart from the Sadducees who acknowledged only that which was written in the scriptures. While originally the concept of "oral tradition" might have been used in that limited sense, to contrast it with the Torah or the written scriptures, the rabbis of the talmudic era understood it in a broader sense, as implying not only that its teachings had been transmitted orally, but also that it is positively forbidden to write them down. The only texts that were allowed to be written were (with a few exception) those contained in the Bible, which were read publicly as part of the liturgy. By contrast, any text that was designated as part of the "oral Torah" must never be written.

Unlike written documents, an oral tradition cannot be learned privately. It requires that the student be in personal proximity to a teacher. Indeed, rabbinic literature attached great significance to the institution of discipleship, wherein the student accompanied the teacher through his daily activities and performed menial services for him. What the disciple learns from the master in this way was not confined to the inculcation of facts and texts; by being in the master's presence, the disciple had the opportunity to benefit from the kinds of moral and spiritual guidance that cannot be derived from lectures or books. This convention diminished the danger of

This strict distinction between oral and written components had practical applications in Jewish law. For example, because the prayers were considered part of the oral tradition, prayer books could not be used in worship, even though the rabbinic liturgy was quite elaborate and lengthy. As a result, rabbinic law requires that a prayer leader repeat the prayers after the congregation recites them individually, for the benefit of worshippers who are unable to memorize them. Similarly, in ancient times, it was customary that the public reading of the Bible be accompanied by an Aramaic translation known as a *targum*. Because the targum was considered part of the oral tradition, rabbinic law forbade the person who was reciting it to glance at the biblical scroll while he was doing so, in order to avoid giving the mistaken impression that he was reading the Targum from the written scroll. The same rule applied to people who recited liturgical blessings while participating in the ceremonial reading of the Torah; they had to look away from the scroll, because the blessings belong to the oral tradition, and they must not appear to be reading it from a written text.

training brilliant scholars who were deficient in moral or spiritual stature. In order to properly fulfill the objectives of discipleship, it was usually necessary for the aspiring scholar to spend at least part of his life wandering in search of teachers. Talmudic literature contains some stories that illustrate the difficult stresses that prolonged absence could place on families. Perhaps this was one of the reasons why rabbinic law exempted women from the religious obligation of studying Torah.

Biblical study in the rabbinic era: midrash

During the Yavnean generations, two main systems of midrashic interpretation emerged among the rabbis. Both of them were rooted in a system that had been formulated by Hillel the Elder who taught in Jerusalem around the turn of the millennium. It appears that the differences between the two schools relate in large measure to how they viewed the connection between the written and oral portions of the Torah.

One method was associated with Rabbi Ishmael ben Elisha. On the whole, Rabbi Ishmael respected the simple meaning of the Torah's text, and refrained from reading much more into it than was warranted by the actual language and literary norms of Hebrew. His principle "the Torah speaks in human language" acknowledged that some of the phrasing in the Torah was intended for stylistic or esthetic purposes, and should not be used as a pretext for creative or imaginative interpretation. To many of the Torah's laws Rabbi Ishmael applied a method of analysis that appears to be influenced by the categories of Greek logic. He paid particular attention to patterns of generalizations and particulars, and formulated a set of hermeneutical rules to determine when the scope of the law applied only to the particular examples mentioned in the verse, when they encompassed all instances of the generalization, and when they included items that were analogous to the particular examples. Rabbi Ishmael maintained the integrity of the literal or contextual meaning. For him, the written and oral traditions remained separate entities that should not be intermingled.

A different hermeneutical approach was espoused by Rabbi Akiva. Akiva insisted that the words of the Torah, as an inspired revelation uttered by God himself, could not be reduced to the trivial conventions of human literary expression. Because God does not waste his holy words, every grammatical particle or letter in the Torah teaches something new. The verses that Rabbi Ishmael interpreted according to his "generalization and particulars" method were interpreted by Rabbi Akiva according to a somewhat different hermeneutic involving "inclusions and exclusions," which allowed him to extend the scope of the Torah much farther. By attaching significance to so many incidental features of the biblical text, Rabbi Akiva was able to create links between the written Torah and many of the traditions that had been passed down in the name of the oral Torah. For Rabbi Akiva, the oral and written Torahs were far more unified than they were for Rabbi Ishmael and his school. The schools of Rabbi Akiva and Rabbi Ishmael coexisted throughout the Tannaitic era. Each of the schools produced its own commentaries on the legal sections of the Torah (that is: from Exodus to Deuteronomy). Some of those works have survived in complete form, others as sections of larger works. Others have been partially reconstructed in recent years based on quotations in medieval manuscripts.

The literature of aggadic (non-legal) midrash, most of which originated in the land of Israel during the late classical era, can be classified according to a variety of criteria. A useful distinction is between "exegetical" and "homiletical" works. In the exegetical type, the emphasis is on verse-by-verse interpretation. The comments usually have a moral or theological point. The works of homiletical midrash deal more with general topics and themes that are suggested by the biblical texts—usually by the opening words of the day's scriptural reading. These compilations consist largely of artistically crafted introductions to the readings. The division between exegetical and homiletical collections was determined to a large extent by the nature of the biblical books to which they were attached. A book like Genesis, which consists entirely of narrative, lends itself naturally to exegetical treatment of each verse. The opposite is true of Leviticus whose text is devoted to technical details of law, much of it on topics like purity and sacrificial procedures. It would be difficult for a preacher to find a lot of appropriate material there for sermons addressed to a popular audience. Hence it is understandable that he would confine himself to one or two general themes that can be linked to each reading. Indeed, the classic aggadic midrash collection *Genesis Rabbah* is of the exegetical type; whereas *Leviticus Rabbah* is of the homiletical type.

Medieval biblical studies: the rise of literal exegesis

The ancient Jewish expositors were not concerned primarily with understanding the Bible on its own terms. Although the rabbis occasionally distinguished between literal and homiletical interpretations, at least to the extent of recognizing when their interpretations had strayed from the literal sense, their standards of interpretation fell short of true literal or contextual exegesis.

It is generally assumed that the flourishing of Jewish biblical interpretation during the Middle Ages was inspired by Arabic Islamic models. The Arabic influence made itself felt in a variety of ways. A fundamental prerequisite for good textual interpretation is a mastery of the language's grammar; and the basic structures of Hebrew morphology were probably not known to Jewish scholars until the Middle Ages, when they learned them from the Arab grammarians. Perhaps the most fundamental characteristic of the "Semitic" languages, the linguistic family to which Hebrew and Arabic both belong, is the fact that almost all words are built around three-letter consonantal "roots." Words, verb conjugations and all the manifold building blocks that make up a language are created by adding vowels, prefixes, suffixes and the like to a basic root. In many cases in Hebrew, not all the consonants in the root actually appear in every word form, owing to phonetic factors. Because of this, early Hebrew grammarians and lexicographers were of the opinions that such words had only two (or even one) root letter, which led to some unnecessarily complex descriptions of the language and its grammar. The discipline of scientific grammar was thus pioneered by students of Arabic, and was afterwards applied by Jewish scholars to the Hebrew language.

The spirit of scientific inquiry that infused much of medieval Arabic society led some Muslims to apply scholarly methods to their own scripture, the Qur'an. It was hoped that the appeal to an objective standard of textual interpretation could minimize the number of theological and sectarian disputes to which the Islamic world was susceptible. In their pursuit of rational truth, many Jewish scholars were moved to apply similar approaches to their own Bible. An appeal to a neutral standard of interpretation was important if Jews were to participate in theological debates with representatives of the other biblically based religions.

The Hebrew term that was employed to designate the literal, scientific study of the Bible is "*peshat*." *Peshat* was often contrasted to midrash, or "*derash*," the homiletical or technical interpretations that characterize the ancient rabbinic works.

Not all Jewish scholars were so enthusiastic about subjecting the Bible to critical analysis, even though the medieval commentators did not usually raise the kinds of serious theological challenges that would later be posed by modern academic biblical studies, which called into question fundamental religious doctrines like the unity and Mosaic authorship of the Torah. Conservative religious leaders insisted that the oral tradition underlying the talmudic and midrashic interpretations was as much a divine revelation as the text of the written Torah. Therefore, questioning the received understanding posed a threat to the validity of rabbinic Judaism in its entirety.

Most medieval interpreters took intermediate positions on this question. They acknowledged that certain midrashic explanations were so farfetched that their authors could not conceivably have intended them to be accepted as serious exegesis; rather, they were to be treated as a literary convention employed by the ancient preachers or as possessing a deeper, allegorical significance. At the other extreme, there were certain non-literal interpretations that the tradition took very seriously, elevating them at times to the status of quasi-official dogma. In general, the interpretations of biblical verses that affected practical religious law were treated in a different manner from historical and theoretical passages. Insofar as the *peshat* commentators were traditionally observant Jews, they were not ready to draw conclusions that would affect time-honored religious practice. In some instances, they maintained that, though the traditional interpretation might not reflect the original intent of a given biblical precept, it does faithfully convey the content of the oral legal tradition.

The diversity of exegetical approaches gave rise to the widespread conviction that scripture can be read on numerous levels, a view that had been formulated previously by Christian interpreters and theologians. Although rationalists like Maimonides were uneasy with any text whose meaning was not unambiguous and unmistakable, most Jewish scholars preferred to see the multiple possibilities of interpretations as an indication of the greatness of the Bible and of its divine author. As a thirteenth-century Jewish scholar formulated it, "Do you not see how frequently even a profane author can speak in such a way that his words contain two meanings? How much truer this is with respect to words of wisdom that were spoken under the influence of the Holy Spirit!" In fact, the Talmud spoke of "seventy facets to the Torah."

With the rise of the philosophical and kabbalistic formulations of Judaism, the tendency arose to speak of a hierarchy of four distinct hermeneutical systems. The *peshat* was usually placed at the lowest rung of the scale, followed by *derash*. The allegorical interpretations of the philosophers or the kabbalists were usually assigned a place at the top.

Following is a survey of some of the more influential Jewish Bible commentators.

Rabbi Solomon ben Isaac (Rashi)

The eleventh-century French exegete Rabbi Solomon ben Isaac of Troyes is discussed elsewhere in this book in his capacity as the author of the most successful and influential commentary on the Babylonian Talmud. His commentaries to the Hebrew Bible achieved a similar status. Most works of Jewish biblical exegesis that were published after Rashi's use him as their starting point; and hundreds of works were written explicitly to serve as commentaries (or "supercommentaries") to Rashi's work.

Rashi's commentary to the Torah took an intriguing middle path between the midrashic tradition and philological criticism. He aimed to provide his readers with a tool for moral and spiritual edification as well as an accurate explanation of the biblical text. While it is possible to view this duality of objectives as mere eclecticism, many scholars have sought to discern consistent rules governing when Rashi chooses to cite an accepted rabbinic interpretation, and when he applies critical principles. A widely accepted thesis has it that Rashi cites the midrashic explanations only when they are responding to a legitimate difficulty or anomaly in the Hebrew text. It is indeed likely that Rashi's methodology underwent a transition during the course of his scholarly career, as he progressed from a traditional to a more philological approach. This premise would help explain why his commentaries to biblical books other than the Torah make less use of midrashic interpretations (though we must bear in mind that fewer midrashic materials were available for those books). In fact, Rashi's grandson Rabbi Samuel ben Meir explicitly reported, "Our Rabbi Solomon… took an interest in the literal interpretation of the Bible… He conceded to me that, if he had the time, he should compose different interpretations, after the manner of the new literal explanations that are being discovered every day."

As a work of academic scholarship, Rashi's Bible commentary made valuable contributions to our understanding of Hebrew grammar, lexicography and literary structure. Though he had only limited familiarity with the new studies of grammar that were being produced in Arabic-speaking countries, his powerful intellect and common sense enabled him to produce insightful and valid comments about the structure of the Hebrew language. His intimate familiarity with talmudic Hebrew and Aramaic stood him in good stead when he interpreted rare and difficult words in the Biblical dialect. He made profitable use of the Bible's convention of poetic parallelism (repeating the same idea in different words) in order to identify synonyms.

Similarly, he based many of his lexicographical identifications on the ancient Aramaic targums. He often based his interpretations on a careful study of the traditional accents that guided the chanting and punctuation of the Biblical texts. To facilitate understanding, he included diagrams and many translations of difficult words into French.

Scholars have also noted that Rashi's personality and religious values are frequently in evidence in his biblical commentaries. He tried to discern expressions of God's unconditional love for the Jewish people, a concern that was certainly provoked by the Christian claim that the church had usurped the status as the "chosen people."

Rabbi Samuel ben Meir (Rashbam) and the French *Peshat* school

Rabbi Samuel ben Meir was the grandson of Rashi He lived in northern France sometime between c. 1080 and c. 1160, and was also a prominent Talmud commentator. He appears to have been familiar with Christian interpretations, and may have participated in religious disputations. Arguments directed against the Christian understanding of the Bible appear very frequently in his commentaries. It is possible that Rashbam's choice of method was influenced by his involvement in interreligious disputations; because refutations of Christian theological claims would appear more conclusive and credible if they were based on a neutral, objective reading of the Bible than if they were anchored in the partisan Jewish readings.

Unlike Rashi, Rashbam was completely devoted to the *peshat*. He had no qualms about disagreeing with the midrashic traditions. Although he was fully committed to the authority of rabbinic religious law, he did not necessarily see it as originating in a correct understanding of the written text of the Torah.

Rashbam's devotion to literal interpretation was shared by several distinguished French exegetes of the time, including Rabbi Joseph Kara, Rabbi Eliezer of Beaugency and Rabbi Joseph Bekhor Shor. Each of these scholars produced important commentaries according to the *peshat* method.

Rabbi Abraham Ibn Ezra

In the breadth of his intellectual and literary interests, Rabbi Abraham Ibn Ezra (1089–1164) was an exemplary representative of the "golden age" of Spanish Judaism. He was an accomplished author of Hebrew liturgical and secular poetry, an authority on grammar, a Neoplatonic philosopher, an astronomer, translator and a physician. He spent much of his life as a wandering scholar in a state of constant poverty. His earlier years were spent in Spain and North Africa. At the age of fifty, evidently in response to a personal tragedy, he set his sights towards Italy and France, where he would exert a strong influence on the local scholarly communities. He made the acquaintance of Rashbam's brother Rabbi Jacob Tam. Ibn Ezra composed his works in the course of his travels, and that situation is reflected in the fragmentary and diverse quality of several of his writings. Many of his works are so concise as to appear hopelessly cryptic. He was the first Spanish exegete to compose his Bible commentary in Hebrew.

Ibn Ezra tried to produce a commentary that was primarily literal, but which would also uphold the interpretations of the rabbinic tradition. Underlying his method was an intense polemical dispute with the Karaites, the Jewish movement that denied the authority of the rabbinic oral tradition. Ibn Ezra often indulged in polemics against Karaite scholars, and strove to demonstrate the superiority of the rabbinic interpretations, basing himself on linguistic, grammatical and logical criteria. He argued that without a supplementary interpretative tradition like the rabbinic "oral Torah" it would be impossible to implement the teachings of the Bible. In keeping with the literary conventions of his time, he enjoys conducting lively and witty (and, occasionally, insulting) exchanges with authors of interpretations that he rejects. The greater part of Ibn Ezra's commentary is devoted to detailed grammatical analysis, but he is also very sensitive to the literary and psychological dimensions of biblical storytelling. He liked to derive moral lessons, and often provided illustrations from his personal experiences. He was an enthusiastic advocate of astrology, and often digressed into demonstrations of the numerical or astrological significance of laws or stories in the Bible.

Rabbi Moses ben Nahman (Nahmanides, Ramban)

Rabbi Moses ben Nahman (1194–1270) is also known by the Hebrew acronym "Ramban" and as designation "Nahmanides" (= son of Nahman). He was a resident of Gerona in Catalonia. Nahmanides was a prolific author, producing important Talmudic commentaries and other works on Jewish religious law. He also had a broad education in science, philosophy and languages. He was chosen by the king of Aragon to defend Judaism at the famous religious disputation against the apostate Pablo Christiani. In the wake of his success in defending Judaism against Christian interpretations, he was impelled to fulfill his dream of moving to the holy land, where he spent the latter years of his life. He died in Acre.

Nahmanides' Torah commentary is the mature work of an accomplished scholar. In it he dealt in profound detail with each aspect of the biblical text. He was familiar with the commentaries of Rashi and Ibn Ezra, and he discusses their explanations carefully, often expressing his disagreement. He displayed a solidly conservative leaning, utilizing his formidable erudition and ingenuity in order to support the traditional rabbinic teachings, and severely chastising scholars, like Ibn Ezra, who do not demonstrate proper respect for the received explanations.

Ramban's commentary to the Torah was one of the earliest documents to include references to the teachings of the Kabbalah. He included several kabbalistic interpretations in his commentary, which he introduced as "according to the way of truth." He tried to sidestep the restrictions against public teaching of the doctrine by formulating the passages in such a brief and cryptic way that they could not be understood by anyone who was not already familiar with kabbalistic symbolism.

The Torah and commandments in Jewish thought

From the perspective of Jewish religious historiography, the pivotal and defining event in history was the revelation of the Torah at Mount Sinai. Devotion to the Sinai covenant is manifested chiefly through observance of the commandments as they are defined in the written and oral Torahs. The commitment to religious practice was therefore a categorical imperative that preceded any attempt to provide rationales for the individual commandments or for the legal system as a whole. Religiosity was usually measured not according to the orthodoxy of one's beliefs, nor by the sublimity of one's mystical experiences, but by scrupulous observance of religious law.

Against this traditional approach, the schools of Jewish rationalism posited a Judaism whose ultimate goal was to attain an intellectual understanding of God. Within that context, the life of religious observance serves only as a means towards achieving that end. Viewed this way, the laws that regulate society and prohibit crimes have no inherent value of their own. Their chief purpose is to produce a society in which individuals have the security and physical opportunities for pursuing their philosophical speculations. Many of the Torah's ritual prohibitions are designed to instill discipline, because the intellect cannot reach its full potential if it is distracted and clouded by the temptations of the "bodily appetites." By training us to restrain our sexual desires or other physical urges (for example, by forbidding consumption of certain foods), the Torah is contributing to our intellectual development. Some commandments are designed to teach us correct religious beliefs, or to save us from theological error. This is achieved by internalizing those ideas through the performance of symbolic acts, or through the uncompromising rejection of idolatry and polytheism.

Maimonides and other Jewish philosophers insisted that religious observance must be understood as part of a broader process of spiritual and intellectual perfection. They challenged the views of many Jewish thinkers through history that the performance of a commandment has a greater spiritual value if it has no ulterior purpose but is a pure expression of the believer's submission to God's will. Maimonides was convinced that only an irrational deity could issue laws that were arbitrary or capricious. He did not even entertain the traditional Jewish view that some commandments were incomprehensible to humans owing to our limited intelligence. He tried to show how the benefits of every precept can be understood without resorting to esotericism. In taking this position, Maimonides found himself at loggerheads with several passages in the Talmud that explicitly characterized certain biblical precepts as irrational or incomprehensible. In response, Maimonides offered a limited definition of "irrational," as meaning merely that there is more than one way to implement a rational principal, and that the Torah must sometimes choose arbitrarily from among the plausible options if the law is going to be observed at all. For example, the requirement to worship God through the offering of animal sacrifices can be justified on rational grounds; yet the Torah's designations of the precise animals or methods of sacrifice to be offered on each occasion can, according to Maimonides, be arbitrary. Ultimately, however, Maimonides insisted that it is possible to provide coherent rationales for all the commandments in the Torah.

One of the considerations that had discouraged traditional Jewish thinkers from ascribing rational purposes to the commandments was the prospect that people might find alternative ways of achieving the same purpose, or discard the commandment once the purpose had been achieved. As we have seen previously, this was a dilemma that affected Jewish philosophers since the time of Philo of Alexandria. Indeed, later generations would accuse Maimonides and his disciples of having caused a general weakening in the religious commitments of Sephardic Jewry that culminated in their readiness to accept Christianity, if only outwardly, rather than submit to martyrdom in the days of the Spanish Inquisition.

For rationalists, inasmuch as the truths of philosophy are derived from scientific observation and logical analysis, they should be universally valid; and it is therefore inappropriate to speak of specifically "Jewish" beliefs. This premise calls into question the validity of many aspects of traditional Judaism that focus on the specific history of the nation, or on the climate or geography of the land of Israel. The Jewish philosophers often resolved this difficulty by claiming that the universal truths were being translated into terms and symbols that were specific to the historical experience of the Jewish people. This kind of argument is a natural extension of Maimonides' understanding of "The Torah speaks in human language," as described above.

Biblical studies in the modern era

The first significant modern challenge to the traditional belief that the Torah had been directly revealed by God came from a Sephardic Jew in Amsterdam, Benedict (Baruch) Spinoza (1632–1677). In his "Theological-Political Treatise," Spinoza argued that the Torah was a humanly composed document that had claimed divine authority in order to serve the political needs of imposing obedience on the primitive ancient Hebrews. Subsequent scholarship, especially among liberal Protestants, formulated more compelling theories of a historical development of the Torah and its compilation from an assortment of documents or oral traditions. Even those Jews who acknowledged the historicity of an original supernatural revelation might argue that the scriptures in their current form had been shaped by humans in accordance with their historical realities, and hence specific laws and doctrines could legitimately be changed or rejected to bring them into conformity with more enlightened values. In this way the premises of biblical criticism served the needs of Jewish religious reform.

Moses Mendelssohn, on the other hand, marshaled the principles of enlightenment religion in order to defend the foundations of traditional Jewish life. The prevalent

Figure 13.1 Portrait of Spinoza

Enlightenment view held that the ultimate truths about God, metaphysics and morality are derived through science and logic, which makes the notion of supernaturally revealed doctrines very problematic. Seen this way, theology should lie outside the proper realm of revelation. Mendelssohn equated this position with that of traditional Judaism. Judaism lays no claim to a distinctive theology, but shares the same rational world-view that ought to be evident to all intelligent people. If (as enlightenment religion generally held) universalism is a religious virtue, then Judaism qualifies as a more universalistic system because it does not restrict salvation to members of its own community.

The particularistic character of Judaism is embodied in the Torah's system of commandments and laws. Mendelssohn espoused a very traditional position about their literal revelation by God at Sinai, but asserted that this "revealed legislation" was a particular feature of God's relationship to the Jewish people and had little to do with "religion" as it was understood by the Enlightenment.

In the nineteenth century, a productive alliance arose between the advocates of Jewish religious reform and the pioneers of academic Jewish studies, which was known in German as *Wissenschaft des Judentums*. The most illustrious pioneer of that movement was Leopold Zunz (1794–1886). He was one of the founders of the "Verein für Kultur und Wissenschaft der Juden" (Society for the Culture and Science of the Jews) in Berlin in 1819; and edited its journal, the *Zeitschrift für die Wissenschaft des Judentums* (*Journal for the Science of Judaism*). Although the body of his research was based on sound, ideologically neutral principles, and some of his works are still consulted today, his choice of topics for investigation was often influenced by the ideological needs of the Reform movement, in which Zunz was an ordained rabbi. Thus, he devoted a monograph to the history of Jewish names in which he showed that throughout history Jews had adopted names from the non-Jewish surroundings. His conclusions served to refute the claims of traditionalists that the tendency of Jews in their own times to take on European names was an unprecedented departure from tradition. Similarly, Zunz composed a thorough history of Jewish preaching and biblical interpretation. In addition to the brilliant contribution it made to this important area of Jewish literary history, it also provided a strong justification for the reformers' practice of preaching weekly sermons in their temples.

Another prominent scholar in the ranks of the Reform leadership was Abraham Geiger. Unlike Zunz, whose scholarly interests diverted him from active institutional leadership, Geiger took an active role in the guidance of the Reform movement. He also produced significant works of scholarship, notably a history of ancient translations of the Bible in which he tried to demonstrate that the Hebrew scriptures had undergone considerable editing as a result of the ideological ferment of the Second Temple era. One of his most influential scholarly claims was that the Pharisees were a liberal ideology, whose bold interpretations of the Torah served to make it more humane and compassionate. This portrayal conflicted with the prevailing Christian stereotype of the Pharisees as a group of rigid formalists; at the same time, it established them as a paradigm for the European Reform movement in their commitment to save the Jewish tradition from becoming ossified.

The cultivation of academic Jewish scholarship was of especial relevance to the Positive-Historical school and its American offshoot, Conservative Judaism (as well as the Reconstructionist movement that branched off from it). More than any of the other modern ideologies, they stressed the intimate relationship between the Jewish religion and the cultural history of the Jewish people; and consequently they saw topics like Hebrew literature, art and music as indispensable manifestations of Judaism. Zacharias Frankel was a respected academic scholar of rabbinic literature, and his scholarly interests were embedded into the curriculum of his seminary in Breslau. Under the leadership of Solomon Schechter, the Jewish Theological Seminary of America assembled some of the world's foremost authorities in Bible, rabbinics, Hebrew literature, Jewish philosophy and other academic subjects. Schechter himself forbade the teaching of the "documentary hypothesis" of the development of the Torah; however, after his death, it quickly became the normative approach to the topic at the seminary.

Talmudic scholarship: commentaries

With the acceptance of the Talmuds, especially the Babylonian Talmud, as an authoritative interpretation of Jewish tradition and religious law in the early medieval era, it became a favorite focus for the intellectual energies of advanced students. The combination of the Talmud's authority and the difficulties inherent in understanding its complex discussions generated a rich scholarly literature devoted to interpreting rabbinic texts and applying them to legal issues. In most Jewish circles, mastery of the Talmud and its related works was acknowledged as the foremost sign of status and leadership. In the Ashkenazic milieu, it was often the sole topic of scholarship, to the exclusion of both biblical and secular studies.

There now follows a survey of the main branches of literature that were produced from the Middle Ages and onwards devoted to the elucidation of the Talmud.

Talmud commentaries

The diverse literature of medieval talmudic commentaries may be divided into two main types:

1. explanatory
2. critical.

In general terms, explanatory commentaries aim to make the meaning of the Talmud understandable to students, whereas the critical commentaries seek to identify difficulties and contradictions, which they then propose to resolve.

During the medieval era, it was the Ashkenazic (French-German) scholars who excelled in the writing of commentaries of all sorts, covering all the major works and genres of earlier Jewish religious literature. The rabbis of Arabic-speaking countries were more concerned with the systemization of Jewish law than with the elucidation of the talmudic discussions.

Explanatory commentaries to the Talmud

The Talmud placed many difficulties in the path of its medieval students. It was composed in languages that were no longer spoken, Hebrew and Aramaic. The style was terse to the point of being cryptic. An intricate kind of logical reasoning was central to talmudic argumentation, requiring a demanding level of intellectual subtlety. A successful commentary would have to overcome all those difficulties.

Some fragments of Talmud commentaries have survived from the *Geonim* of Babylonia. The Geonim were the leaders, during the early Middle Ages, of the same academies that had produced the Talmuds, and hence their interpretations are of great importance. However, the commentaries that have survived consist mostly of translations of difficult words, and rarely deal with the full understanding of the argumentation. In many instances we have the impression that these works were not intended as complete commentaries, but were composed ad hoc, in response to students' questions about specific passages, and later collected together.

Most commentaries were composed in the languages of the Talmud itself, Hebrew and Aramaic. In Arabic-speaking lands, some works on talmudic law were composed in Arabic. The most influential rabbinic work to be composed in Arabic was Maimonides' commentary on the Mishnah. Maimonides provided a clear explanation of the text, a summary of the Talmud's explanation, and an indication of which of its opinions are to be followed. The commentary was subsequently translated into Hebrew, making it accessible to Jews throughout the world. It was very popular, and brought about a revived interest in the study of the Mishnah as a separate work; prior to that time, the Mishnah had normally been read as part of the Babylonian Talmud.

Important explanatory commentaries to the Babylonian Talmud were composed in the eleventh century. Rabbi Hananel ben Hushiel, who lived in Kairowan, Tunisia, (c. 990–1050) assembled a paraphrased summary of the discussion, and usually omitted sections that were of a non-legal (aggadic) character. He often indicates which of the opinions cited in the Talmud is the accepted one. A distinctive feature of his commentary is his practice of presenting the parallel passages from the Palestinian Talmud alongside the Babylonian. Although there is much that is valuable in the commentary, it does not address all the difficulties that an average student is likely to encounter, and is best used in conjunction with a more complete commentary. At about the same time in central Europe, there appeared the commentary ascribed to Rabbi Gershom ben Judah and his students (he is generally referred to by his honorific title "the Light of the Exile"). Rabbi Gershom lived in Mainz, Germany, and died in 1028. The Mainz commentary bears a striking resemblance to Hananel's in its methods: it tends towards summaries and paraphrases, rather than precise explanation.

The Commentary of Rabbi Solomon ben Isaac (Rashi)

This is the same Rashi whom we encountered as an influential Bible exegete. As a young man, he pursued his studies in the Talmudic schools of Mainz and Worms, and his teachers included the foremost disciples of Rabbi Gershom. Rashi's Commentary which covers almost the whole of the Babylonian Talmud, has been printed in every version of the Talmud since the first Italian printings in 1484. It deals successfully with all the tasks that confront a commentator. Without sacrificing brevity and clarity, it provides a full and adequate explanation of the words, and of the logical structure of each Talmudic passage. Unlike some other commentaries, Rashi does not paraphrase or exclude any part of the text, but carefully elucidates the whole of the text. Invariably he strives to interpret the Talmud on its own terms, even in matters that might have struck others as theologically primitive or anachronistic, such as the human-like depictions of God, or the fanciful portrayals of demons and folk remedies. In keeping with the Talmud's lack of sequential presentation, an important function of Rashi's explanation is to fill in information found elsewhere in the Talmud or rabbinic literature. This assistance was especially helpful for allowing students to learn Talmud on their own without constant recourse to teachers. Indeed, the publication of Rashi's commentary marked a major milestone in the democratization of Jewish scholarship, in that it prevented the creation of an elite whose authority over the community lay in their exclusive possession of esoteric knowledge.

Though more detailed than the previous commentaries, Rashi remains concise, usually limiting himself to the most straightforward explanation. In most cases (but certainly not all of them), he avoids raising difficulties or contradictions that are not absolutely necessary for a basic understanding of the text. Rashi's commentary presupposes a basic familiarity with the Talmud's language and methods, and cannot serve the needs of a complete novice. It never spoon-feeds the student, but rather provides assistance to a learner who is willing to invest an initial effort. Rashi included descriptions of the *realia*: details of agriculture, architecture, science and other items of material culture that were mentioned in the Talmud. We often have the impression that Rashi was in the habit of observing or consulting artisans or farmers at their labors in order to assist him in picturing the details described by the Talmud. The commentary also compared different manuscripts and paid close attention to determining which readings should be preferred. This is consistent with a general tendency among Ashkenazic scholars to freely emend and tamper with the text. In many places, Rashi provided translations of difficult words into the vernacular, usually French.

It is probably a sign of the success of Rashi's achievement that no subsequent scholar tried to compose another explanatory commentary. Virtually all later explanations of the Talmud use Rashi as their starting point.

Critical commentaries to the Talmud

The purpose of Rashi's commentary was to simplify the study of the Talmud. In that context, he impresses us throughout by his remarkable restraint. In almost all cases he confined himself to presenting a single consistent interpretation of the passage in question, though it is often clear that several different options were available to him. He usually avoids making practical legal decisions (as was the usual practice among Sephardic commentators, who viewed the Talmud chiefly as a code of law), or noting when the current passage contradicts something that was said elsewhere in the Talmud.

The phenomenon of "critical commentaries" only became possible after Rashi had laid his solid foundation for understanding the Talmud text. In many ways, the critical commentaries are the antithesis of the explanatory ones. They thrive on exploring different options, and on weighing the arguments for and against each option. The critical commentaries, as they evolved in France and Germany, encouraged a multiplicity of possible interpretation.

The authors of critical commentaries scanned the entire Talmud—actually, the entire corpus of rabbinic literature—with a view to spotting difficulties and contradictions. Underlying their endeavor was their conviction that the Talmud, in spite of its outward appearance as a patchwork of diverse sources and opinions, was really a single entity, so that all its discordant parts had to be harmonized with one another. In order to resolve the apparent discrepancies, they proposed novel ways of explaining the text, and drew subtle new conceptual distinctions.

The critical commentaries were known as *Tosafot*, "additions," probably because their authors presented them as supplements to Rashi's commentary. The original Tosafot were produced in France, and to a lesser extent in Germany, Italy, England and in Slavic countries. Their authors were from the school of Rashi, and included his grandsons.

In some instances, the stimulus to reinterpret the Talmud lay in the fact that their own local custom contradicted what appeared to be the talmudic rulings. Many of those problematic local customs that had taken root in the Jewish communities of Germany and France actually had their origins in the land of Israel, as preserved in Italy from which the early Ashkenazic settlers had migrated to northern Europe. The Tosafot were thus required to harmonize their older Palestinian practices with the authority of the Babylonian Talmud.

The methods that typify the critical commentaries are in fact the very same ones that the Talmud itself uses in comparing its sources and subjecting them to intensive intellectual analysis. Indeed, it is evident that the critical commentaries were not only *interpreting* the Talmud, but also (and perhaps, primarily) *continuing* to practice the methods of talmudic discourse.

Unlike Rashi, the critical commentaries did not seek to provide a running commentary on the entire Talmud; this was unnecessary now that Rashi had done the job so brilliantly. Now the commentators could choose to concentrate on particular texts that required elucidation or presented exegetical problems.

The most common format for a critical interpretation was to suggest a difficulty or contradiction in the text or in Rashi's commentary, and then to suggest a new explanation of the passage that would resolve the problem. In doing so, the commentator compared the current passage with other passages in the Talmud or elsewhere, suggested alternative interpretations, or ruled on normative religious practice.

Because the composing of explanatory commentaries had functionally ended with Rashi, virtually all exegetical activity that has been carried out since his time has been of the critical kind. The Tosafot constitute a variegated literature, created over a span of two centuries. They originated as notes taken by students at their teachers' lectures. As the students wandered to different schools, they would collect teachings from several teachers. Tosafot have appeared in the margins of almost all printed editions of the Talmud. The fifteenth- and sixteenth-century Italian printing houses who initiated this convention determined that particular versions of the Tosafot would appear alongside each volume of the Talmud; however, dozens of alternative versions exist in manuscript, many of which have been published only in recent years. A similar genre of literature was being produced by Christian scholars of the time who were known as the *Glossatores*, in connection with the study of Roman and Canon Law.

Though the Tosafot format was originally cultivated in France and Germany, it eventually achieved popularity in Spain as well. This process was inspired by the fact that several important Talmud scholars in Spain and Provence studied in France and Germany, and then returned to Spain to instill the scholarly methods and religious values that they had absorbed there. We find the work of the Tosafot being continued in the school of Rabbi Moses Nahmanides.

Another term that is frequently employed for such critical commentaries is "Hiddushim," which means "new interpretations." This term appears to have originated in Spain in the school of Nahmanides. It reflects a belief that novel insights into the original meanings of ancient texts can be uncovered by the scholarship of later generations. Among later authors, the terms Tosafot and *Hiddushim* become interchangeable.

Codes of talmudic Law

The Talmud is a book *about* law, but it is not easy to derive practical rulings from the Talmud because numerous opinions are proposed and defended. The difficulty of the subject matter, the vastness of the literature and the lack of a logical organizational structure all place obstacles in the way of a simple layperson, rabbi or judge who needs to know what Jewish law requires in a given situation. The Talmud itself provides a few general rules for deciding between opposing views. These rules usually ignore the content of the argument, focusing instead on the identity of the rabbis involved.

Shortly after the redaction of the Babylonian Talmud we note the appearance of works designed to facilitate its use as an effective source of law. On the whole, the attempts at codification that were produced during the Geonic era (from the eighth to the eleventh centuries) were little more than abridgements of the Talmud. The earliest of these, though not technically a code, was a work known as the *She'iltot*, ascribed to Rabbi Aha of Shabḥa, a Babylonian scholar of the early eighth century. This work probably originated in sermons or lessons that were delivered in the synagogues or academies, possibly from the talmudic era. Each unit (*she'ilta*) is a discrete exposition, and is related to the biblical text that was read in the synagogue on that Sabbath or festival. Other works from the Geonic era are abridgements of the Talmud. That is to say, they consist of word-for-word quotations of passages from the Talmud, while omitting sections that are not directly necessary for deciding the law.

In addition to these efforts at comprehensive codification, several of the *Geonim* composed monographs devoted to specific topics in Jewish law. These works, written in Arabic, follow a model that had been established in the literature of Islamic law and bear a strong similarity to modern law textbooks. These works follow a rigorously logical arrangement, beginning with basic principles and then methodically outlining all the various sub-categories. Monographs of this sort were devoted to topics like inheritance, gifts, bailments, oaths, deeds, acquisition, contracts, robbery, neighbors, and more.

Rabbi Isaac Alfasi's Halakhot

Arguably the most revered authority on Jewish law in the Middle Ages was Rabbi Isaac Alfasi, who lived in North Africa and Spain during the eleventh century. From his academy in Lucena, Spain, he came to be acknowledged as the leading scholar of Spanish Jewry. Alfasi followed the older model of providing a shortened version of the Talmud, adding legal decisions, and removing "unnecessary" material. The degree to which Alfasi's code dominated the talmudic culture of Sephardic Jewry is nothing short of astounding. It remained the unchallenged source of authority until the sixteenth century, when it was displaced by the *Shulhan 'Arukh* (see below). During the 500 years of its preeminence, worthy rivals arose, especially Maimonides'

Mishneh Torah (see below); and yet Alfasi continued to be the chief authority in almost all communities.

Maimonides' *Mishneh Torah*

Rabbi Moses Maimonides was one of the towering figures in medieval intellectual and religious life. In addition to his law code, which is described here, he excelled in the fields of philosophy, science, medicine, exegesis and communal leadership.

His *Mishneh Torah* was composed in rabbinic Hebrew, and modeled consciously after the style of the Mishnah. It is divided up into fourteen general sections (comparable to the Mishnah's "orders"), each of which is further subdivided into books (corresponding to tractates), and then into numbered chapters and laws. Maimonides's father, Rabbi Maimon, had been a disciple of Alfasi's most distinguished student, Rabbi Joseph Ibn Migash. The strong influence of Alfasi's code is very perceptible in Maimonides's decisions, a fact that he acknowledges with great respect. Maimonides continued to revise and improve the *Mishneh Torah* throughout his life. As he matured and became more independent in his judgments, he felt freer to disagree with Alfasi.

Figure 13.2 Illuminated manuscript of the *Mishneh Torah*

The title "*Mishneh Torah*" ("The Second Law") was derived from the Hebrew name for the book of Deuteronomy, which consists of Moses' summary or review of the rest of the Torah. Similarly, Moses Maimonides's *Mishneh Torah* was intended to be a summary of the entire body of Jewish religious law. The code is sometimes referred to as the *Yad ha-Ḥazaqah*, "the mighty arm." This is a play on the numerological value of the Hebrew word for arm, "*yad*" whose letters add up to fourteen, the number of volumes in the code. The author himself referred to the book as "*Sefer Meḥokek*" ("The Book of Legislation"), a title that is rarely employed.

Some of the distinctive features of the *Mishneh Torah* are the following:

- It encompasses the full range of Jewish law, as it was set out for all ages and places. In this respect it differs from almost all other Jewish law codes, which confined themselves to laws that were in force in their own times and lands. Thus, the Mishneh Torah includes rules that apply only in the land of Israel under an independent Jewish state, and ones that could not be observed following the destruction of the Temple.
- Maimonides's expertise in the full range of rabbinic literature was more extensive than any of his predecessors. He consulted the full range of biblical, talmudic and post-talmudic literature.
- The *Mishneh Torah* completely reorganized and reformulated the laws in a clear and logical system.
- Whereas almost all other codes, both before and after Maimonides, were composed in a mixture of Hebrew and Aramaic as in the Talmud, Maimonides insisted on the consistent use of a single language, an elegant rabbinic Hebrew modeled on the style of the Mishnah.
- The *Mishneh Torah* presents only the normative rulings without discussion or explanation of how the decisions were reached.
- It opens with a section on systematic philosophical theology, derived largely from Aristotelian science and metaphysics, which Maimonides regarded as the most important component of Jewish law and the ultimate end to which all the specific laws are directed. Maimonides's interpretation of Jewish religion in terms of philosophical ideas aroused much opposition.

Maimonides stated openly that in publishing the *Mishneh Torah* his aim was to supplant the Talmud entirely as the practical source of authority in Jewish law. From this point on, most Jews should not have to struggle through the difficult and intricate web of talmudic dialectic, but could learn the law directly from Maimonides's code.

From this description, Maimonides's code emerges as far superior to anything that preceded it, according to every criterion: it was more logically and accessibly organized, more comprehensive in its scope, and clearer in its literary presentation. In fact, it also outdid any subsequent legal compendia in all these areas. Nevertheless, except for the Jews of Yemen, with whom Maimonides maintained a special relationship during his lifetime, no Jewish community ever accepted Maimonides as their primary authority on Jewish law. Throughout the Middle Ages, Alfasi's code continued to hold sway. There is no obvious explanation for this anomaly. Some historians have ascribed the situation to the controversial nature of Maimonides's philosophical views, or his attempt to circumvent the study of the Talmud; however these factors do not seem to provide adequate reasons for the phenomenon. It might all boil down to a basic cultural conservatism in medieval society that discouraged the introduction of far-reaching innovations.

Rabbi Joseph Caro's *Shulhan 'Arukh*

Rabbi Joseph Caro (1488–1575) was born in Spain, but following the expulsion of the Jews from the Iberian peninsula in 1492 he wandered through Turkey, Bulgaria and Greece, settling finally in Safed in the land of Israel. The title of his law code *Shulhan Arukh* means "the set table," and expresses its purpose, to make the whole of Jewish law conveniently available to all seekers. Its arrangement follows the order of an earlier code by Rabbi Jacob ben Asher (c. 1270–c. 1343) of Toledo, Spain known as *Arba'ah Turim* (the four columns). As indicated by its title, the code is divided into four main topics, each of which is subdivided into a sequence of numbered paragraphs. The four "columns" are:

- *Orah Hayyim* ("The Path of Life"; see Psalms 16:11):
  This section deals with worship and ritual observance in the home and synagogue, through the course of the day, the weekly Sabbath and the festival cycle.
- *Yoreh De'ah* ("Teach Knowledge"; see Isaiah 28:9):
  This section deals with assorted ritual prohibitions, especially dietary laws and regulations concerning menstrual impurity.
- *Even ha-Ezer* ("The Rock of the Helpmate"; according to 1 Samuel 5:1 and the Rabbinic interpretation of Genesis 2:18):
  This section deals with marriage, divorce and other issues in family law.
- *Hoshen Mishpat* ("The Breastplate of Judgment"; see Exodus 28:15):
  This section deals with the administration and adjudication of civil law.

The *Shulhan Arukh* is divided up into the same four main topics, with each section subdivided into numbered paragraphs and sub-paragraphs.

The origins of the *Shulhan Arukh* lie in Rabbi Caro's earlier work, the *Beit Yosef* ("House of Joseph"), a detailed commentary to the *Tur* in which he carefully examined every law in the earlier code, tracing its sources in talmudic and medieval rabbinic literature, and comparing the interpretations and rulings of the leading medieval authorities. The *Shulhan Arukh* summarizes the conclusions of the *Beit Yosef.*

In general, Caro based his decisions on three leading pillars of Jewish codification:

- Rabbi Isaac Alfasi
- Maimonides
- Rabbi Asher ben Jehiel ("Rosh," "Asheri"), the father of the *Tur*'s compiler.

In cases of disagreement among those three authorities, Caro usually adopted the majority position. Although many rabbis were initially opposed to basing religious law on a summary code, rather than examining the original sources, the *Shulhan Arukh* rapidly came to be accepted in almost all Jewish communities as the most authoritative statement of normative religious law. In recent generations, acceptance of the *Shulhan Arukh* has come to be regarded as a defining criterion of religious orthodoxy and traditionalism.

Rabbi Moses Isserles's *Mappah* ("Tablecloth")

Rabbi Moses (ben Israel) Isserles (Acronym: ReMA) lived in Krakow, Poland, from 1530 to 1572. His *Mappah* consists of supplementary glosses to the *Shulhan Arukh* in which he cites Ashkenazic authorities who were overlooked by Caro's code. It was evident that, in spite of its great virtues, the *Shulhan Arukh* could not be accepted by Jewish communities in Germany and Poland without some modification. In his glosses Isserles supplemented the rulings of Caro's original *Shulhan Arukh* with material drawn from the laws, interpretations and customs of Franco-German and Polish Jewry. All standard printed editions of the *Shulhan Arukh* include Isserles's note. When people refer to the "*Shulhan Arukh*" they usually have in mind the combination of Caro's and Isserles's works.

Responsa literature

The Hebrew expression underlying "Responsa" means "questions and answers." The term refers, quite literally, to the practice of addressing questions in writing to religious authorities who then reply with a reasoned answer to the question. The origins of the Responsa literature lie in the era of the Babylonian *Geonim*. As Jewish communities arose in numerous lands, and as the major communities produced their own rabbinic scholars and leaders, the practice of writing responsa proliferated in roughly the same fashion throughout the Jewish world, and it still continues to the present day. It became a routine matter for the rabbis to keep duplicates of all their responsa so that they could eventually be assembled into collections. In this way, we now possess responsa by most respected authorities on Jewish law from the beginning of the Middle Ages.

More than any other genre of Jewish legal discourse, Responsa compel the rabbi to cope with social, historical and material realities. Whereas the writing of a commentary or a law code can be an academic exercise that never gets applied to contemporary circumstances, the authors of Responsa do not enjoy that luxury because the choice of topic is not under their control, but is decided by the questioners. The existence of Responsa literature was thus an important catalyst for maintaining the vitality and relevance of the Jewish legal system. The Responsa preserve valuable historical information that would not otherwise have found its way into normal codes and commentaries.

Key points you need to know

- Traditional Judaism has a respect for learning, and sees scholarship as an important criterion for religious leadership.
- Different eras and cultural environments produced diverse approaches to the study of the Bible, including philosophical, midrashic, homiletical and philological.
- The Middle Ages witnessed a particular flowering of Jewish learning. Not only was the Bible interpreted from rationalist and kabbalistic perspectives, but there was a new interest in Hebrew grammar and lexicography and the literal meaning of the text.
- The centrality of commandments to Jewish religiosity leads to conflicting positions on whether it is desirable to seek rational justifications for those commandments.
- Modern challenges to the belief in the Torah's divine revelation were an important factor in the development of non-traditional streams of Judaism.
- The Talmud and its authoritative status generated several genres of scholarship that have occupied the most gifted minds of the Jewish community. Great rabbis composed works designed to explain and analyze the Talmud, as well as to make it into a practical source of legal guidance.

Discussion questions

1. Discuss some common features common to scholarly achievements of Rashi and Maimonides.
2. Suggest some reasons why the medieval era produced a greater variety of Jewish scholarly literature than the talmudic era.

3. In what ways did Ashkenazic and Sephardic Jews differ in their approaches to the study of the Talmud?

4. In what ways did the traditionalist response to modern "academic" Bible scholarship differ from its medieval counterpart? What reasons might account for the differences?

Further reading

Biblical interpretation: general

Faur, José, *Golden Doves with Silver Dots: Semiotics and Textuality in Rabbinic Tradition*, South Florida Studies in the History of Judaism. Atlanta, GA: Scholars Press, 1999.

Greenstein, Edward L., "Medieval Bible Commentaries." In *Back to the Sources: Reading the Classic Jewish Texts*. Edited by Barry W. Holtz, 213–60. New York: Summit Books, 1984.

Simon, Uriel, *Four Approaches to the Book of Psalms: From Saadiah Gaon to Abraham Ibn Ezra*, SUNY Series in Judaica. Albany, NY: State University of New York Press, 1991.

Smalley, Beryl, *The Study of the Bible in the Middle Ages*. Oxford: Oxford University Press, 1983.

Talmage, Frank, *Disputation and Dialogue: Readings in the Jewish-Christian Encounter*. New York: KTAV, 1975.

Walfish, Barry, *Esther in Medieval Garb: Jewish Interpretation of the Book of Esther in the Middle Ages*, SUNY Series in Judaica. Albany, NY: State University of New York Press, 1993.

French biblical exegesis

Blumenfield, Samuel M., *Master of Troyes: A Study of Rashi, the Educator*. New York: Behrman House for the Jewish Institute of Religion, 1946.

Federbusch, Simon, ed., *Rashi, His Teachings and Personality: Essays on the Occasion of the 850th Anniversary of His Death*. New York: Cultural Department of the World Jewish Congress and the Torah Culture Department of the Jewish Agency, 1958.

Ginsberg, Harold Louis, ed., *Rashi Anniversary Volume*. Philadelphia, PA: Jewish Publication Society of America, 1941.

Hailperin, Herman, *Rashi and the Christian Scholars*. Pittsburgh, PA: University of Pittsburgh Press, 1963.

Liber, Maurice, *Rashi*. New York: Hermon Press, 1970.

Lockshin, Martin I., *Rashbam's Commentary on Deuteronomy: An Annotated Translation*. Providence, RI: Brown Judaic Studies, 2004.

Pearl, Chaim, *Rashi*, Jewish Thinkers. London: Halban, 1988.

Shereshevsky, Esra, *Rashi, the Man and His World*. New York: Sepher-Hermon Press, 1982.

Ibn Ezra

Lipshitz, Abe, ed., *The Commentary of Rabbi Abraham Ibn Ezra on Hosea*. New York: Sepher-Hermon Press, 1988.

Shachter, Jay F., ed., *The Commentary of Abraham Ibn Ezra on the Pentateuch*. Hoboken, NJ: KTAV, 1986.

Twersky, Isadore and Jay Michael Harris, eds, *Rabbi Abraham Ibn Ezra: Studies in the Writings of a Twelfth-Century Jewish Polymath*. Cambridge, MA: Harvard University Press for the Harvard University Center for Jewish Studies, 1993.

Nahmanides

Chavel, Charles Ber, *Ramban, His Life and Teachings*. New York: Feldheim, 1960.

—— ed. *Commentary on the Torah*. New York: Shilo Publishing House, 1971.

Twersky, Isadore, *Rabbi Moses Nahmanides (Ramban): Explorations in His Religious and Literary Virtuosity*, Texts and Studies. Cambridge, MA: Harvard University Press, 1983.

Talmudic scholarship

Brody, Robert, *The Geonim of Babylonia and the Shaping of Medieval Jewish Culture*. New Haven, CT: Yale University Press, 1998.

Elon, Menachem, *Jewish Law: History, Sources, Principles*, Philip and Muriel Berman Series. Philadelphia, PA: Jewish Publication Society of America, 1994.

Freehof, Solomon Bennett, *The Responsa Literature and A Treasury of Responsa*. New York: KTAV, 1973.

Groner, Tsvi, *The Legal Methodology of Hai Gaon*. Edited by Jacob Neusner, Brown Judaic Studies. Chico, CA: Scholars Press, 1985.

Jacobs, Louis, *A Tree of Life: Diversity, Flexibility, and Creativity in Jewish Law*, Littman Library of Jewish Civilization. Oxford and New York: Oxford University Press, 1984.

Katz, Jacob, *Divine Law in Human Hands: Case Studies in Halakhic Flexibility*. Jerusalem: The Magnes Press The Hebrew University, 1998.

Maimonides, Moses, *The Code of Maimonides*, Yale Judaica Series. New Haven, CT: Yale University Press, 1949.

Soloveitchik, Haym, "Rabad of Posquieres: A Programmatic Essay." In *Studies in the History of Jewish Society in the Middle Ages and in the Modern Period Presented to Professor Jacob Katz on His 75th Birthday*. Edited by E. Etkes and Y. Salmon, vii–xl. Jerusalem: Magnes, 1980.

Twersky, Isadore, *Rabad of Posquières, a Twelfth-Century Talmudist*, Harvard Semitic Series. Cambridge, MA: Harvard University Press, 1962.

—— "The Shulhan Arukh—Enduring Code of Jewish Law." *Judaism* 16 (1967): 140–58.

—— ed. *A Maimonides Reader*, Library of Jewish Studies. New York: Behrman House, 1972.

—— "Religion and Law." In *Religion in a Religious Age*. Edited by S. D. Goitein. Cambridge, MA: Association for Jewish Studies, 1974.

—— *Introduction to the Code of Maimonides (Mishneh Torah)*, Yale Judaica Series. New Haven, CT: Yale University Press, 1980.

14 *Justice and morality*

In this chapter

Biblical religion recognized that humans should choose to obey God's command-ments, but they inevitably fail to do so completely. Such failures are regarded as sins, and Judaism provided various ways of atoning for sins. Except for the ancient Essenes, Judaism has upheld the principles of moral free will and responsibility. Even the omnipotent God is understood to act according to understandable standards of justice, and correspondingly, human society is expected to be founded on just laws. Biblical and rabbinic law include detailed systems of civil and criminal legislation that were traditionally perceived as crucial to the Jewish religion. Faith in God's fair treatment of humanity, and in the divine covenant with Israel, were severely challenged by the Nazi Holocaust, and Jewish theologians proposed diverse ways, traditional or otherwise, of responding to the trauma. Though clearly placing great emphasis on the ideals of political and domestic peace, Jewish teaching does not reject war, and has expressed differing attitudes towards the acceptable circumstances for waging war, or to the interpretation of the wars in the Bible.

Main topics covered

- Sin, repentance and free will
- Human justice
- Divine justice, theodicy and Holocaust theology
- War and peace

Sin, repentance and free will

A fundamental theme of biblical religion is that humans, though they ought to be striving to follow unswervingly in the path to which God has directed them, are after all imperfect beings who are subject to lapses in the pursuit of moral and spiritual goals. The Torah devotes much space to the different ways in which human sinfulness can be atoned for—such as by undergoing punishment, by offering the designated sacrifices or by observing the annual Day of Atonement. The narratives of the Bible provide many striking examples of the sinners who successfully repented, including King David, and the populace of Nineveh after being admonished by the prophet Jonah.

In Josephus Flavius' survey of the Second Temple Jewish sects, he singled out for mention the disputes over the belief in human free will. The Sadducees maintained that people have freedom of choice, and hence can be held responsible and punishable for their virtuous or sinful acts. At the other extreme, the Essenes maintained that human destiny is entirely predetermined. The Pharisees acknowledged that much of a person's life is determined by forces beyond his or her control. With regard to moral and religious matters, however, we may choose to either obey or transgress the divine commands. Owing to the absence of documents from the Sadducees, we have no direct way of measuring the accuracy of Josephus's description. With respect to the other groups, however, it is possible to compare it with other evidence. One fact that emerges is that, notwithstanding Josephus' determination to present the debate in philosophical terms that would be familiar to his Hellenistic and Roman readership, the views that emerge from Hebrew sources have more to do with the practicalities of religious life and with the authority of the Bible than with abstract philosophical theories.

Indeed, several of the Dead Sea scrolls from Qumran are distinguished by an unmistakable belief that history has been preordained, and that from the beginning of time God assigned future souls to either the righteous, the "children of light," or the wicked, the "children of darkness." The former, restricted for the most part to the faithful members of the Qumran sect itself, can take no credit for their righteousness. Throughout history they have been a persecuted minority, but in the coming cataclysmic battle, they will emerge triumphant to rule the world in accordance with God's true will. Even in the Qumran documents, this position is not espoused with consistency, and the faithful are often exhorted to choose the virtuous path.

To the extent that rabbinic literature preserves earlier Pharisaic ideas, we do find, for example, a rabbinic dictum "everything is in the hands of heaven except for the fear of heaven," a statement that is consistent with Josephus' account of the Pharisaic view. On the whole, it may be said that the rabbis were usually sensitive to the complexity of human freedom and responsibility, though they did not treat it in philosophical terms. In particular, the incongruity between divine foreknowledge and human freedom, which furnished the framework for much of the classic theological formulation of the question, is rarely raised in traditional Jewish sources.

Much of biblical and rabbinic preaching consists of calls to repent. This presupposes that individuals have the power to meaningfully alter their moral habits and patterns, a prospect that would be meaningless in a deterministic framework. In general, Jewish tradition recognizes that humans are imperfect beings and will never be completely sinless. God, however, is compassionate and forgiving, and is happy to forego full retribution provided that we are sincerely willing to improve. This theme is cultivated most intensely in the rituals, liturgy and customs of the New Years and Day of Atonement season, but it permeates all aspects of Jewish religious life. A recurrent motif in midrashic homilies is that, though God is the ultimate judge who can mete out rewards and punishments according to strict standards of justice, he is, more significantly, a loving parent of humanity who would prefer to forego retribution in hope that his children will try to better themselves. Accordingly, the prayers often turn to God beseeching him to judge us according to his "standard of mercy" and not according to the "standard of justice."

Another favorite contrast in midrashic homiletics is the one between the "good urge" and the "bad urge." The former is, of course, the desire to obey God and act morally. The latter is sometimes depicted as a general desire to rebel against the divine will; but more specifically, it is identified with the destructive potential of unrestrained sexual urges. Thus, the "bad" urge is not evil in any absolute theological sense. A talmudic legend describes how the Jewish sages in the early Second Temple era succeeded in capturing the bad urge (personified as a kind of monster). They were on the verge of destroying it entirely when they realized that people were no longer building homes, getting married, siring children, or engaging in commerce. Consequently, they acknowledged that it is a necessary instinct for healthy human survival provided that it is kept under control, which can be effectively accomplished by observing the discipline of the Torah.

Jewish philosophical thinkers have generally agreed that the belief in a God who rewards or punishes his creatures presupposes that humans have the freedom to choose between right and wrong courses of action. To state otherwise would imply that God is unjust in rewarding and punishing people for their moral decisions. As in other religious traditions, Jews had to deal with the apparent philosophical contradiction between human free will and God's knowledge of our future actions.

Human justice

What God revealed at Mount Sinai was not, for the most part, a theological doctrine, nor was its primary purpose to bring the people to a state of mystical intimacy with the Almighty. According to the traditional Jewish understanding, it was an elaborate set of laws. Many of them were of an ostensibly prosaic character, not very different from the ones that we would expect to find in force in any civilized society.

Even before Sinai, the Bible assumes that the establishment of a structure for the administration of civil and criminal justice is a universal obligation of human society, and that it was commanded to the common ancestors of the human race. The rabbis of the Talmud included this requirement in their lists of seven commandments that are incumbent upon all humanity (children of Noah; Noachides). Employing the midrashic modes of biblical interpretation, they found support for their belief that the institution of a legal order is a human norm that is not restricted to the Jews.

The prophet Moses is portrayed in the Torah as a judge who "sat to judge the people, and the people stood by Moses from the morning to the evening" (Exodus 18:13–27) until his father-in-law Jethro advised him to institute a more efficient judicial hierarchy that would deal with most normal questions, leaving only the most difficult cases for Moses's personal involvement. The ancient Israelites took especial pride in their divinely revealed legal system, and when Moses was instructing his people on the eve of his death, he was careful to remind them, "this is your wisdom and your understanding in the sight of the nations who, when they shall hear all these statutes, shall say, Surely this great nation is a wise and understanding people... And what nation is there so great, who has statutes and judgments so righteous as all this Torah!" The ultimate purpose of the biblical legal system is to achieve justice, insofar as that elusive goal can be reached by finite and fallible human beings.

For the most part, the biblical model of justice is not limited to the dutiful obedience to the laws, but involves an active commitment to social values, and must frequently take the form of protest against the political leadership. The classical prophets of Israel were constantly castigating their contemporaries for their complacent assurance that it is enough to observe the technicalities and rituals of the law while the ruling classes continue to oppress the poor and the vulnerable. Nevertheless, the Torah admonished that even the poor should not be favored in judgment.

Rabbinic law translated the general principles of biblical justice into specific procedures for judicial administration. Talmudic law contained detailed regulations designed to prevent expressions of favoritism or intimidation of litigants in the courtroom, and gravely cautioned the scholar-judges to resist pressure from the wealthy or powerful. Traditional Judaism regards adherence to the full system of law, including its criminal and civil components, as a sacred religious obligation; and resorting to gentile courts as a betrayal of faith. In practice, the ability to administer criminal law was lost back in early Roman times, and the rich tradition of Jewish civil law ceased to function significantly, even in strictly Orthodox communities, soon after the Emancipation.

Divine justice, theodicy and Holocaust theology

In the Torah it is assumed that God is subject to expectations of fairness that are analogous to those demanded from his creatures. This attitude finds striking expression in the story of Abraham. When God informed him of his decision to destroy the sinful cities of Sodom and Gomorrah, Abraham was concerned lest innocent people perish because of the divine wrath against the depraved majority. He boldly challenged God: "Will you also destroy the righteous with the wicked?... Far be it from you to act in this manner, to slay the righteous with the wicked... Shall not the judge of all the earth act justly?" God treats Abraham's concerns seriously enough that he engages him in a lengthy sequence of bargaining until Abraham finally concedes that there are not enough righteous people in the wicked cities to justify sparing them. On a number of occasions Moses also argued with God to restrain himself from destroying the sinful Israelites.

Early biblical religion had not evolved a clear sense of individual responsibility, and therefore was not very troubled by instances of collective suffering that could be explained in terms of the sins of the parents being visited on the children, or an entire nation being treated as an organic unit. This approach could be applied to the history of Israel because God's treatment of the people was in proportion to their upholding of the covenant. Nevertheless, the Torah affirmed that "the fathers shall not be put to death for the children, nor shall the children be put to death for the fathers; every man shall be put to death for his own sin."

Some biblical works confronted the question of divine justice, theodicy, more directly. Ecclesiastes went on at length about the meaningless and arbitrary character of the human situation. The book of Job was built on a narrative framework of God inflicting terrible sufferings on a righteous person in order to test the limits of his faith, and concluded that God's reasons exceed the comprehension of mere mortals.

Rabbinic thought tended to take a more simplistic view of such questions, and often assumed that there is no punishment that is not warranted by sin. At any rate, the midrashic collections that are our main source for reconstructing their beliefs originated in sermons, where the preachers' objectives were likely to be more practical than philosophical. The disasters of the past were invoked as object lessons, and the important thing was to learn from those events in order to become better people and observe the Torah more fervently. Their belief in afterlife retribution allowed the rabbis to explain that the wicked are given rewards for their few virtuous deeds during their lifetimes, so that they may be consigned to continual torments in the next world; and that the present sufferings of the righteous are in order to allow them to enter paradise with a clean slate.

An ideology of martyrdom evolved during the early rabbinic era that was likely associated with the widespread consciousness that the world that prevailed under the Roman oppression was fundamentally unjust. Rabbi Akiva, who himself was martyred for continuing to expound the Torah in the face of edicts forbidding it, formulated a mystical ideology of "chastisements of love" according to which God inflicts suffering and martyrdom as a privilege to the most righteous people, thereby providing them with the ultimate opportunity to convey their absolute devotion. Underlying all these views was a strong rejection of dualistic approaches that would ascribe evil to a power outside God. Jewish sources insist that God must be recognized as the source of evil (or, at least, of what appears to us as evil) as well as good.

The medieval Jewish philosophical tradition had relatively little to contribute to the classic formulation of the problem of theodicy: how can an omnipotent and benevolent deity allow evil and suffering to exist in his world? The answers proposed by Jewish thinkers were not much different from those found among other theologians from the monotheistic traditions. The ability of humans to inflict harm on innocent victims is a necessary result of their having free will. As for other forms of suffering, we must acknowledge our limited perspective; God is so vast that we cannot hope to see our sufferings in their complete context. Some Jewish thinkers invoked the argument that evil has no absolute reality, but is nothing more than an absence or dilution of goodness.

These rationalist approaches contrast starkly with that of the Kabbalah, whose explanations of evil and injustice call upon mythological motifs, especially in their vivid portrayals of a demonic realm, the "other side" ruled by Samael and Lilith. Even in kabbalistic texts the evil realm is depicted as being under God's dominion, and it is linked with the divine attribute of judgment that utilizes destructive force to maintain order in the universe. The kabbalistic doctrine of Rabbi Isaac Luria formulated the myth of the "shattering of the vessels," a catastrophe at the beginnings of creation that generated a chaos of holy sparks and evil shards that humans must strive to separate.

Jewish discussions of theodicy attained an unprecedented urgency in the wake of the Nazi Holocaust. Many modern Jews could no longer uphold the simple trust in God's fairness that was fundamental to their grandparents' faith. Many felt that the immense suffering of pious and innocent Jews, including hundreds of thousands of children, could no longer be accounted for within the traditional categories of covenant and retribution. A number of discussions that began to appear in the 1960s established the basis for a distinct discipline of "Holocaust theology."

One of the first to grapple with the issue was Richard Rubenstein, whose *After Auschwitz* and subsequent writings argued that it was no longer possible to believe in the traditional Jewish God who guides history and upholds a covenant with the Hebrew nation. If Judaism is to be perpetuated, it must rediscover the primal nature religion that gives meaning to simple and recurring human activities.

Probably the most influential of the Holocaust theologians was Emil Fackenheim whose ideas stemmed from his conviction that the Holocaust was a unique and unprecedented event in Jewish or human history. It could not be compared with previous massacres and Jewish martyrdoms, because the racialist Nazi ideology did not target Jews as a religious group, thereby depriving the victims of the possibility of turning their deaths into acts of religious martyrdom. Arguably Fackenheim's most significant contribution was his assertion that a "commanding voice" emerges from Auschwitz, a religious imperative comparable in its importance to the 613 commandments of the Torah, forbidding Jews to allow Hitler a posthumous victory by allowing Judaism or the Jewish people to disappear. The correct response to this

614th commandment is to work towards the continued existence of the state of Israel, as well as to maintain Jewish life in all its forms. Several of Fackenheim's premises were questioned by subsequent thinkers. For example, it is very hard to define in what respect Hitler's "Final Solution" is unique when compared with other instances of massive genocide. Furthermore, it is questionable whether a religion or culture can endure purely by the determination to spite its enemies, as Fackenheim appeared to suggest.

Several Orthodox thinkers have tried to respond to the Holocaust in terms of traditional religious categories. This frequently involves attaching some measure of blame to the Jewish victims, and rabbis have singled out specific Jewish groups for blame, such as the modernists or the Zionists. Statements in that spirit usually provoke indignation from those who find the accusations distasteful, or who oppose fanning the flames of communal factionalism. Some religious Zionist ideologues, especially in Israel, have tried to understand the Holocaust in terms of an eschatological scheme in which it served as a necessary stage in the divine plan that leads up to the creation of a sovereign Jewish state, and through it to ultimate redemption.

Eliezer Berkovits, himself a Holocaust survivor, argued for a traditionalist understanding of evil, even the Holocaust, as a necessary corollary of the human freedom to make moral choices. Irving Greenberg, in a remarkable variation on Fackenheim's views about the unprecedented dimensions of the Holocaust, has argued that it was God who failed to uphold the Sinai covenant. Therefore those Jews who nevertheless choose to continue identifying with their people and religion are doing so on a voluntary basis, now that the original covenant can no longer be viewed as coercive or obligatory in the traditional sense. So radical are Greenberg's views that some have questioned whether they can be accommodated within any meaningful definition of Orthodox Judaism.

War and peace

By modern standards, the Bible strikes us at times as disturbingly bellicose in its acceptance, and even encouragement, of war as a means of defending the true faith and aggressively combating idolatry. To be sure, the ancient enemies of God are portrayed as irredeemably evil and perverse; Abraham was not allowed to take possession of the land "for the iniquity of the Amorites is not yet complete," implying that even God cannot declare a war against people who have not incurred punishment by their complete and utter depravity. The conquest of Canaan under Joshua involved the slaying of entire populations (at least, the adult males), as did other biblical military campaigns. The sins of the Israelites were also punished by carnage at the hands of invading armies.

On the other hand, the ideal of peace (Hebrew: *shalom*) is repeatedly stressed as a moral value and as an indispensable quality of an ideal society and a redeemed world.

The Hebrew word derives from a root meaning "whole" or "complete." A survey of occurrences through the Bible indicates that it refers to a state in which there is no conflict. One of the more powerful elements in prophetic visions of the redemption is a complete elimination of wars between nations. Some of the most poignant and best-known depictions of that longed-for situation were uttered by Isaiah: "Nation shall not lift up sword against nation, neither shall they learn war any more."

Jewish religious thought over the ages has tried in diverse ways to account for the incongruous scriptural messages and to formulate coherent responses to actual situations. It is impossible to point to anything approaching a consensus or authoritative statement on these issues, and all we can do here is point out some of the main themes in the discussion.

As regards the biblical wars, rabbinic literature tended to view the circumstances of Joshua's conquest as unique. The brutal elimination of the seven Canaanite nations was a one-time, divinely ordered campaign that cannot serve as a precedent for other situations. The rabbis established a legal discourse to distinguish between commanded wars, obligatory wars and optional campaigns. Because rabbinic literature was compiled in times when Jews did not actually have a government capable of fielding armies, warfare was not a main topic of their discussions. War was most likely to be treated in the context of midrashic reconstructions of biblical exploits, or in eschatological and apocalyptic visions of the future—albeit those visions often involved the violent overthrow of the Roman imperial forces. In midrashic homiletics, it was common to interpret scriptural glorifications of war in a symbolic way, frequently as a metaphor for the animated scholarly debate in the talmudic academies.

The centrality of peace as a religious ideal is evident in ancient Jewish letters and dedicatory inscriptions, which normally conclude with prayers for *shalom*. It is customary to conclude prayers and blessings with Psalms 29:11, "the Lord will give strength unto His people; the Lord will bless his people with peace," or "he who creates peace in the upper realms, may he also create peace over us and over all Israel." Rabbi Simeon ben Yohai inferred that "peace is great because all blessings are contained within it." The blessing recited by the priests, one of the most important liturgical passages in the Torah, is structured so as to reach its culmination in the words "the Lord lift up his countenance upon thee, and give thee *peace*" (Numbers 6:26). In other places, "peace" refers to the general welfare of a person's family, or to a state of security from threat.

The teachings of the talmudic rabbis provide many instructive examples of applications of the ideal of peace to communal and domestic settings. Some interpretations stressed that it is not sufficient to respond peacefully to situations that arise, but rather, one must actively pursue peace and to seek out opportunities to bring it about. Presumably responding to situations of communal or national factionalism, they often contrasted unity and harmony with divisive fanaticism.

The extent to which peaceful resolution is to be preferred to victory—even in a religiously mandated war—emerges from a remarkable retelling of a biblical story, as found in several midrashic compendia. Countering an explicit command from God to wage war against Sihon and the Amorites, the rabbis relate that Moses decided instead to offer the enemy a peaceful resolution. In the end, God was persuaded by Moses's policy, and made it the basis of the laws of warfare in the Torah, where it states that the enemy should be first be allowed the option of suing for peace.

The high priority that Jewish tradition assigned to peace is demonstrated by the way that it overrides other cherished values. For example, the rabbis insisted that it was proper to bend the truth in order to avoid domestic strife. The third-century sage Bar Kappara learned this principle from the narrative of Genesis 18: when Sarah was notified that she would bear a child at the age of ninety, she responded in disbelief: "after I am waxed old shall I have pleasure, my lord [referring to Abraham] being old also?" However, when God reported this conversation to Abraham, he quoted Sarah as having said "Shall I…bear a child, when *I* am old?"—diplomatically omitting the clause about Abraham's age. Bar Kappara inferred from this passage that God himself was willing to take the responsibility for the inaccuracy in order to avoid any friction between a husband and wife.

Key points you need to know

- As a commandment-based religion, Judaism has generally assumed that humans have the freedom to obey or disobey the divine precepts and moral exhortations.
- Though humans are imperfect and subject to the temptations of the "bad urge," Jewish tradition has usually understood that God is forgiving and treats people mercifully provided that there is a sincere desire for improvement.
- The pursuit of justice—including social justice—underlies the Jewish insistence on establishing a proper judicial system. Jewish law deals with this topic in intricate detail.
- Judaism believes that God treats his creatures justly. Belief in retribution in the afterlife helps account for cases when the righteous suffer and the wicked prosper.
- The inexplicable anguish of the Nazi Holocaust stimulated much theological reflection on theodicy, producing both traditional and untraditional or heretical responses.
- Jewish tradition places great stress on the ideal of peace, though it has rarely espoused pacifism.

Discussion questions

1. Can Rabbi Akiva's models of martyrdom and "chastisements of love" be applied to the sufferings of the Holocaust?
2. How does the rabbinic concept of the "bad/evil urge" compare with modern psychiatric views of the libido?
3. Discuss how the belief in a divine covenant with Israel had to be reinterpreted in the wake of the Holocaust.

Further reading

Law and ethics

Borowitz, Eugene B., *Exploring Jewish Ethics: Papers on Covenant Responsibility.* Detroit, MI: Wayne State University Press, 1990.

Dorff, Elliot N. and Louis E. Newman, *Contemporary Jewish Ethics and Morality: A Reader.* New York: Oxford University Press, 1995.

Elon, Menachem, *Jewish Law: History, Sources, Principles.* Philadelphia, PA: Jewish Publication Society, 1994.

Herzog, Isaac, *The Main Institutions of Jewish Law*, 2nd ed. London: Soncino Press, 1965.

Jacobs, Louis, *Jewish Personal and Social Ethics.* West Orange, NJ: Behrman House, 1990.

Levine, Aaron, *Case Studies in Jewish Business Ethics*, Library of Jewish Law and Ethics. Hoboken, NJ and New York: KTAV and Yeshiva University Press, 2000.

Loewenberg, Frank M., *From Charity to Social Justice: The Emergence of Communal Institutions for the Support of the Poor in Ancient Judaism.* New Brunswick, NJ: Transaction Publishers, 2001.

Novak, David, *Jewish Social Ethics.* New York: Oxford University Press, 1992.

Rakover, Nahum, *Ethics in the Market Place: A Jewish Perspective.* Jerusalem: Ministry of Justice and the Jewish Legal Heritage Society, 2000.

Schwarz, Sid, *Judaism and Justice: The Jewish Passion to Repair the World.* Woodstock, VT: Jewish Lights, 2006.

Telushkin, Joseph, *A Code of Jewish Ethics*, 1st ed. New York: Bell Tower, 2006.

Theodicy and Holocaust theology

Banki, Judith Herschcopf and John Pawlikowski, *Ethics in the Shadow of the Holocaust: Christian and Jewish Perspectives*, Bernardin Center Series. Franklin, WI: Sheed & Ward, 2001.

Carmy, Shalom, *Jewish Perspectives on the Experience of Suffering*, The Orthodox Forum Series. Northvale, NJ: Jason Aronson, 1999.

Cohn-Sherbok, Dan, *Holocaust Theology*. London: Lamp Press, 1989.

—— *Theodicy*. Lewiston, NY: Edwin Mellen Press, 1997.

—— *Holocaust Theology: A Reader*. New York: New York University Press, 2002.

Fackenheim, Emil L., *Quest for Past and Future: Essays in Jewish Theology*. Bloomington, IN: Indiana University Press, 1968.

—— *The Jewish Return into History: Reflections in the Age of Auschwitz and a New Jerusalem*. New York: Schocken, 1978.

—— *To Mend the World: Foundations of Post-Holocaust Jewish Thought*. Bloomington, IN: Indiana University Press, 1994.

—— *God's Presence in History: Jewish Affirmations and Philosophical Reflections*, 1st Jason Aronson ed. Northvale, NJ: Jason Aronson, 1997.

Katz, Steven T., *Post-Holocaust Dialogues: Critical Studies in Modern Jewish Thought*. New York: New York University Press, 1983.

—— *Historicism, the Holocaust, and Zionism: Critical Studies in Modern Jewish Thought and History*. New York: New York University Press, 1992.

War and peace

Goldberg, Edwin C., *Swords and Plowshares: Jewish Views of War and Peace*. New York: URJ Press, 2006.

Polner, Murray and Stefan Merken, *Peace, Justice, and Jews: Reclaiming Our Tradition*. New York: Bunim & Bannigan, 2007.

Schiffman, Lawrence H. and Joel B. Wolowelsky, *War and Peace in the Jewish Tradition*, The Orthodox Forum Series. New York and Jersey City, NJ: KTAV for the Michael Scharf Publication Trust of the Yeshiva University Press, 2007.

Part III

Jewish observances and institutions

15 *Jewish education*

In this chapter

The centrality of scripture to Jewish religious life makes it crucial that members of the community have basic literacy skills in the Bible and other authoritative texts. In antiquity, elementary schools were administered by the communities for male pupils of elementary school ages, and some students could pursue more advanced talmudic studies in the *yeshivah*. Both the traditionalist and liberal communities responded to the challenges of modernity by introducing innovations designed to groom Jewish students for coping with the new challenges.

Main topics covered

- Elementary education
- Advanced studies: the yeshivah
- Modern developments

Elementary education

If it were possible to rate the relative importance of different religious precepts in Judaism, then the obligation of religious study ("*Talmud Torah*") would have a strong claim to primacy. This attitude has remained quite constant throughout Jewish history. Prior to modern times, formal education was limited to boys. Talmudic tradition speaks of the establishment of a system of compulsory public education during the era of the Second Temple. Although that narrative should not necessarily be accepted at face value, it likely approximates situations that prevailed during the talmudic era. In medieval times, most Jewish boys were expected to read and write in Hebrew, a requirement that was essential to allow them to fulfill their basic religious obligations of prayer, rituals and participation in the synagogue services.

The Talmud designates five or six years as the youngest age for the beginning of formal schooling, though there is evidence that in medieval French and German

Figure 15.1 Family prayers

communities they began earlier. In talmudic times, the elementary curriculum was geared almost entirely towards training boys to read the Bible, especially the chanting of the Torah. Because at the time there existed no written notation for the vowels, punctuation or cantillation, faithful memorization was crucial for preserving precisely the correct reading of the sacred text. Even after the introduction of written diacritical signs, it remains quite a challenge to master the traditional reading because those signs are not written into the scrolls from which the Torah is read in the synagogue. The objective of teaching children the accurate reading of the Bible was generally achieved in the Arabic-speaking communities. Hebrew grammar was often taught in Spain and Italy, but neglected in Germany and France. Among European Jews, there was a stronger tendency to progress as quickly as possible to the study of the Babylonian Talmud, which was a greater intellectual challenge and carried greater prestige. It was argued that the student would pick up his knowledge of the Bible, along with a traditional interpretation, by means of the many verses that are cited and expounded in the Talmud.

Advanced studies: the yeshivah

The advanced stages of rabbinic study, devoted principally to the meticulous analysis of halakhah (religious law), form the background to the great literary collections of the talmudic era in Babylonia and the land of Israel. Information about the nature of rabbinic education may be culled from the chapters in this book that deal with the talmudic era and its literature. As long as the rabbis maintained their commitment to an unwritten Torah, the life of a student necessarily involved frequent travel in order to study at the feet of their teachers. This convention was probably an important factor in the exclusion of women from the world of traditional Torah scholarship.

In the medieval curriculum, advanced students would progress from their elementary studies to intensive study of the Talmud, along with the dialectical analysis of the critical commentaries (such as the *Tosafot*). Sephardic schools generally took a more practical and systematic approach to religious studies, emphasizing study of the whole Bible (not just the Torah), of the Mishnah and practical codes of Jewish law, preferably Rabbi Isaac Alfasi's compendium. Only a small group of extremely gifted students, if they intended to become full-time rabbis, were encouraged to study the Babylonian Talmud.

Women, who did not participate officially in communal worship, did not normally receive a Hebrew education in either Ashkenazic or Sephardic communities during the medieval era. Their contribution to education was usually as "enablers," creating the conditions that facilitated the studies of their husbands and sons. Nevertheless, records from the Cairo Genizah do contain passing mentions of girls who attended school. More often, girls would be given training in embroidery or some other practical skill, and some rudiments of prayer. Some degree of accommodation of the needs of women's religious education is discernible in the occasional references to translations of biblical readings, prayer books and other texts from Hebrew into the vernacular languages. A handful of women are known to have succeeded in mastering the standard religious academic curriculum. These tended to be daughters of prominent rabbis. In Iraq, the daughter of the Gaon Rabbi Samuel ben Hophni (died 1034) is reported to have lectured on Talmud to male students. A similar tradition existed concerning Dulcie, the daughter of Rabbi Eliezer of Worms (1140–1225), who gave public discourses on the Sabbath.

Depending on the economic circumstances of the family and the scholarly abilities of the student, medieval boys were likely to continue their studies until the age of thirteen or fifteen in schools that were administered by the community, but paid for by the parents. Advanced students would study in a *yeshivah*, a school devoted primarily to the study of the Babylonian Talmud and legal codes. The school day was, typically, very long, extending from dawn until night. Although the Jewish schools in France and Germany focused exclusively on the traditional religious texts, the Spanish and Italian communities encouraged a broader education that might include literature, calligraphy, philosophy, mathematics, natural sciences and medicine.

Modern developments

Demands for educational reform were central to the Enlightenment ideology. There was much criticism of the old-style elementary school (*ḥeder*) and its primitive pedagogical approaches, rote learning and the appalling disrespect for the teachers. The non-traditionalists advocated greater exposure to the Bible and Hebrew grammar at the expense of talmudic dialectics, as well as well as secular studies and vocational skills. The implementation of curricular and pedagogic improvements was not exclusive to any particular denomination.

Although there is no room in this introductory work for a full survey of modern Jewish educational frameworks, a few significant developments are worthy of note:

- *The Lithuanian Yeshivah.* In 1803, Rabbi Hayyim of Volozhin (1749–1821) established what was to become the classic model of the Lithuanian yeshivah, a central institution that was designed not merely to educate local youths, but primarily to attract the finest students throughout the Jewish world. At his "Eẓ Hayyim" ("Tree of Life") yeshivah the students would be exposed to a demanding schedule, and the content of the curriculum emphasized a rigorously logical analysis of the Talmud. The graduates were not usually expected to become professional rabbis (in fact, students who were suspected of studying the practical rabbinic curriculum were frequently looked down upon), but to return to their communities and apply their strong grounding in Judaism to daily pursuits. Rabbi Hayyim's approach exerted a decisive influence on the curriculum of subsequent yeshivas that were established along similar models, sometimes with formal examinations. The growth of the movement in Lithuania was severely slowed by persecutions under the Czarist and Soviet regimes, and was ultimately ended by the Nazi Holocaust. Remnants of those yeshivah communities succeeded in reestablishing branches after World War II, particularly in the United States and Israel, where they have achieved a prominent position in the Orthodox world.
- *The Beit Ya'akov religious schools for girls.* The concept of formal education for Jewish girls was considered a radical and controversial innovation when the first

Beit Ya'akov school was opened in 1917 in Krakow by Sara Schnirer. Since then the Beit Ya'akov institutions, which combine religious and vocational training, have become a common feature of traditional communities worldwide, and their graduates serve as teachers for less traditional schools as well.

- *Supplementary education and day schools in America.* The first generations of Jewish immigrants to North America sent their children to public schools, and Jewish education commonly took the form of after-school or Sunday classes that rarely went beyond the most basic skills at reading (but not necessarily understanding) the Hebrew prayers. It was later realized that this experience exerted a decidedly negative response; and the latter half of the twentieth century was marked by a rapid growth in Jewish day schools in which the curriculum was usually divided equally between secular and Jewish components.

- *The* kolel. Although the concept has roots in nineteenth-century Lithuania, the phenomenon of a *kolel*, an advanced yeshivah for married students, is largely an outgrowth of western affluence and (especially in Israel) the welfare state. Fundamentally, the institution provides stipends for students with wives and children, allowing them to pursue advanced rabbinic studies. In Israel, enrolment in a kolel allows men from non-Zionist communities to avoid compulsory military service. In recent decades in America, a movement of "community kolels" allows its participants to combine their personal studies with educational outreach programs directed to the broader Jewish community.

Key points you need to know

- Organized Jewish elementary education for boys has existed since talmudic times.
- Ashkenazic Jews came to focus almost exclusively on talmudic studies, whereas Sephardic Jews offered a more diverse curriculum of Jewish and secular studies.
- Apart from a few distinguished exceptions, formal education was not extended to Jewish girls or women until modern times.
- Judaism has used diverse kinds of educational reform to adapt to modern circumstances. These include the creation of frameworks for teaching girls and women, intensifying the experience of Talmud study, diversifying the curriculum and making accommodations for secular and vocational studies.

Discussion question

1. The medieval church discouraged literacy among all but the clergy, largely in order to ensure that the clergy control the orthodox interpretation of the Bible. How would you account for the fact that Judaism took the opposite attitude and encouraged Hebrew competence in the Jewish community?

Further reading

Drazin, Nathan, *History of Jewish Education from 515 BCE to 220 CE* New York: Arno Press, 1979.

Eckman, Lester Samuel, *History of the Mirrer Yeshiva: From Its Beginnings Till 1945*. Elizabeth, NJ: Judaic Research Institute, 2004.

Fishman, Isidore, *The History of Jewish Education in Central Europe from the End of the Sixteenth to the End of the Eighteenth Century*. London: E. Goldston, 1944.

Helmreich, William B., *The World of the Yeshiva: An Intimate Portrait of Orthodox Jewry*. New Haven, CT and London: Yale University Press, 1986.

Kanarfogel, Ephraim, *Jewish Education and Society in the High Middle Ages*. Detroit, MI: Wayne State University Press, 1992.

Morris, Nathan, *The Jewish School: An Introduction to the History of Jewish Education*. London: Eyre and Spottiswoode, 1937.

Szajkowski, Zosa and Tobey B. Gitelle, *Jewish Education in France, 1789–1939*, Jewish Social Studies Monograph Series. New York: Columbia University Press for Conference on Jewish Social Studies, 1980.

Wertheimer, Jack, ed., *Family Matters: Jewish Education in an Age of Choice*, Brandeis Series in American Jewish History, Culture, and Life. Waltham, MA and Hanover, NH: Brandeis University Press and University Press of New England, 2007.

16 Places of worship: temple and synagogue

In this chapter

Ancient Judaism assumed that the preferred manner of worship was sacrifice, especially of animals, in the Jerusalem Temple through the hereditary priesthood. Sacrifices took many forms and had diverse functions. The institution was terminated with the destruction of the Temple by the Romans, and Jewish thinkers in subsequent generations have held differing views regarding the relative value of sacrifice and verbal prayer.

Synagogues are first attested in the latter decades of the Second Temple era. The name means a "house of assembly" and they served diverse communal functions, especially for the reading and expounding of the Bible, as well as for public worship. It appears that women originally prayed together with the men, but sexual segregation was introduced in the medieval era and remains the norm in Orthodox synagogues. In congregational prayer, as formulated by the ancient rabbis, there is a distribution of roles between the individual congregants and a prayer leader. Previous generations cultivated the elaborate craft of *piyyut*, Hebrew liturgical poetry. In modern times, the roles of the synagogue and the rabbi have been adapted to make them approximate those of the Christian church and minister.

Main topics covered

- Biblical worship: temple and priesthood
- The origins of the synagogue
- Women in the synagogue
- Aspects of communal prayer
- Piyyut
- The synagogue in modern times
- The modern rabbi

Biblical worship: temple and priesthood

Although the destruction of the Temple brought an end to the biblical sacrificial cult, its fundamental importance to Judaism will be readily apparent to anyone who browses through the numerous passages about the priesthood, sanctuary and offerings that fill the pages of the Torah, Mishnah, Talmud, the prayer book, codes of Jewish law, and other central documents of the Jewish religion. In modern western culture, the notion of burning animals as an act of religious devotion appears peculiar, or even distasteful or immoral. In previous ages, however, the Hebrew sacrificial system was one of the least problematic areas of the religion to justify to outsiders, because similar rites were practiced by most religions in both western and oriental lands.

In a controversial discussion in his *Guide of the Perplexed*, Maimonides suggested that God would have preferred to ordain verbal prayer in the Torah, but that the Hebrews of that generation, freshly liberated from slavery in Egypt, were not sophisticated enough for it; and God knew that they would not accept the monotheistic religion if it did not satisfy their inclination to offer sacrifices. Presumably, the original reason for offering sacrifices was to invoke the gods' good will by feeding them. Some remnants of this attitude survive in biblical idioms like "sweet savor before the Lord," but the prophets, as well as later Jewish authors, made it clear that such expressions were not to be understood literally, and that God has no need for human gifts.

Jewish tradition provides no agreed-upon rationale for the institution of sacrifices. The most common word for sacrifice is *qorban*, from a Hebrew root meaning "near," "close." A well-established Jewish tradition interprets the word in the sense of "bringing one closer to God." Often, the religious impact of sacrifices lay in the fact that the offerers were depriving themselves of the objects that they were devoting to God. With respect to those offerings that were intended to procure forgiveness, it is common to see them as a form of vicarious atonement, in that the animal is being substituted for the sinners who really should have forfeited their lives. The rabbinic tradition understood that the central act of the sacrificial procedures was the pouring out of the blood, because blood holds the soul of a living creature.

The sacrifices can be classified according to several different criteria, including:

1. *Purpose*: as a communal obligation attached to a fixed time or date; thanksgiving; cleansing or sin offering; guilt-offering; purification; fulfillment of a vow; and more.
2. *Material*: sheep or cattle, meal offering, wine or water libation, first fruits, and more.
3. *Mode of offering*: burnt offering (consumed entirely on the altar); portions assigned to the priests; may be eaten by donors.

The regulations are set out in meticulous detail in the Torah, and were expanded in subsequent works.

Sacrifices may be either communal or individual. The communal ones are offered by the priests on behalf of the entire nation. Of especial importance was the *Tamid*, the "continual offering" of a lamb that was burned on the altar every morning and evening. Because they were being offered on behalf of the entire people of Israel, Pharisaic tradition insisted that they be purchased from a special fund to which all the Jews of the world, whatever their economic circumstances, were required to contribute the identical amount annually.

During the eras when no sanctuary existed, sacrificial worship was not carried out, as is the case at present. We know that Jewish temples were erected in Egypt during the Second Temple era, by the military garrison on the island of Elephantine, and later by the priest Onias; however, these endeavors were not sanctioned by later Jewish tradition.

The most essential parts of the sacrificial service can only be performed by priests (Hebrew: *kohen*; plural: *kohanim*). In fact, entry into the inner precincts of the sanctuary, where the altars are located, was permitted only to male priests. The Jewish priesthood is a hereditary caste, consisting of those who trace their ancestry back to the very first high priest, Moses's older brother Aaron. Now, in the absence of a Temple, the sanctity of the priesthood finds expression in a small number of ritual restrictions, obligations and prerogatives. For example, priests may not marry divorcées or converts to Judaism, or come into proximity of corpses; they recite the "priestly blessing" (Numbers 6:24–27) in the synagogue service and are the first to be called up to participate in the liturgical reading of the Torah. However, they have no special position of authority in the community.

In addition to the priests, descendants of the tribe of Levi were also set apart by the Torah to perform quasi-priestly functions, including participation in choirs that chanted psalms to accompany the worship in the sanctuary. Because Aaron and Moses were members of the tribe of Levi, the Aaronide priesthood is actually a subset of Levites. The priests and Levites were not assigned tribal territory in biblical times, and were therefore expected to occupy themselves in religious activities, whether in connection with the actual sacrificial cult or as judges and teachers. The Torah declared that the general Israelite populace is required to set aside portions of their property, especially of their food, for the upkeep of the priests and Levites. Thus, a *terumah* (usually translated as "heave-offering") was designated from produce; a tithe (tenth) should be given to the Levites, out of which the Levites must separate a tenth for the priests. Additional priestly portions were to be taken from bread (*hallah*), meat, wool, and other commodities.

Figure 16.1 Blessing of *kohanim* at Western Wall

The origins of the synagogue

Since talmudic times, the synagogue has been the central and most recognizable religious institution in any Jewish community. The Greek word "synagogue" and its Hebrew and Aramaic equivalents (*beit keneset, be kenishta*) mean "house of assembly," indicating that it served a range of communal functions. Archeological evidence from Egypt reveals the existence of sites designated *proseuche* (place of prayer). It is not clear whether prayer was one of the primary purposes of the Palestinian synagogues when they first made their appearance in ancient times. In talmudic times, communal worship was one of the chief activities to take place inside synagogues, though definitely not the only one.

The synagogues' main functions in antiquity involved the public reading of the Bible—especially, the Torah—on Sabbaths and festivals, and with the preaching of sermons based on the designated biblical sections. The main text for scriptural reading in the synagogue was the Torah, whose five books were read sequentially over a given time-period. The most common cycle was probably three and a half year (that is, twice every seven years), though the custom prevalent in Babylonia, and which subsequently became almost universal in Jewish communities throughout the world, was to complete the reading in a single year. On Sabbaths and festivals, the reading from the Torah was followed by the reading of a passage with a related theme from the books of the Prophets (*Nevi'im*).

According to talmudic law, every adult male is required to participate in at least three prayer services each day: in the early morning, afternoon and night. The morning service is a lengthier one, and on certain days includes the formal reading of the Torah. More elaborate services take place on the Sabbath (extending from Friday evening until Saturday night) and on the many annual festivals. While it is considered preferable to recite one's prayers as a member of the congregation in the synagogue, and certain portions of the service can only be recited in the presence of a community (defined by talmudic law as at least ten adult males), the obligation to pray is a personal one and applies even where the individual is not in a congregational setting.

The physical form of a synagogue is not defined in detail by Jewish religious law. Essentially all that was required was enough space to contain the congregation, the furniture to house the Bible scrolls that are read during the service, and a table or platform on which to read from the scrolls. Synagogues are usually designed to conform to the talmudic requirement that worshippers be facing in the direction of the Temple Mount in Jerusalem.

In theory, traditional synagogue worship was largely "democratic," in that all (adult male) worshippers had roughly the same rights and obligations to lead and participate in the prayers or scriptural readings. While biblical law assigned privileges to the Priests and Levites, these pedigrees were only of minor, ceremonial significance after the destruction of the Jerusalem Temple. Nevertheless, the congregational setting also provided opportunities to underscore inequalities in learnedness, social status and other distinctions. The social hierarchies could make themselves felt when people were called to participate in the ritual reading from the Torah on Sabbaths or festivals, when the rich and powerful members of the community stood a better chance of being called up for the honor than the common folk. Competition over social recognition, and disgruntled complaints about having been slighted by the synagogue authorities, were a frequent source of friction. Some incidents led to deep-rooted feuds, and even to violence.

The Middle Ages introduced the eminently democratic institution of "interrupting the service." The right of mistreated parties to interrupt public worship in order to plead their cases is one that was respected in both European and Middle Eastern Jewish communities. There is reason to suspect that its beginnings can be traced to the land of Israel during talmudic times. In Islamic countries, the right to interrupt services seems to have been based on the legal assumption that the community as a whole, assembled in the synagogue, had the status of the supreme tribunal, in accordance with the biblical notion that "the people shall judge" (Numbers 35:24). Thus, to plead before the congregation was equivalent to addressing the highest court of appeal. A virtually identical procedure was entrenched in the customs of the German and French Jewish communities from the earliest days of their documented history.

Women in the synagogue

The archeological evidence from ancient synagogues provides no physical indications of separate rooms, galleries or other physical divisions that would have been set apart for women, nor are any such divisions mentioned in the abundant literary sources (aside from one unique situation that arose during certain annual festivities in the Jerusalem Temple). When we combine these facts with the testimony of several passages in rabbinic texts that seem to assume that women were present at the prayer services and sermons, the circumstantial evidence suggests that, prior to medieval times, men and women worshipped together in the synagogues. Thus, the separation of sexes in the synagogue appears to be a medieval development. In the Islamic world, this can be easily understood as an adaptation of the prevailing cultural attitudes, because women were generally excluded from the mosques, and only in a minority of instances were they assigned a separate section at the rear of the sanctuary. In Christian lands it is more difficult to account for the transition, since by the Middle Ages it had become normal for men and women to sit together in the churches. Likely, the Jewish convention emulates an earlier phase of Christian practice. It is at any rate consistent with a more general segregation of the sexes that extended to other aspects of social life as well. The separation was intended primarily to keep the worshipper from being distracted by sexual temptations. In Arab lands, the women's section of the synagogue usually took the form of a gallery, from which they

Figure 16.2 Devout women

could hear, though not necessarily observe, the service below. In many European communities, women conducted their own services in separate rooms, officiated by female prayer-leaders.

Aspects of communal prayer

The forms and texts of worship retained a large measure of uniformity throughout the scattered and distant Jewish communities. This was a consequence of the meticulous detail with which these matters were discussed in the Talmud, and of the authoritative "orders of prayer" that were issued by the leaders of the medieval Babylonian academies, the *geonim*. Communal prayers would be led by a prayer leader, the "representative of the congregation." In theory, this function could be performed by any qualified person (that is, an adult male), though in reality the assignment of the duties was likely to involve issues of religious or social status. The pattern that evolved in European communities was that the congregants would read most of the texts quietly by themselves, and the prayer leader recited only the beginnings and ends of assigned passages, in order to maintain synchronization. Among Jews from Islamic lands, it is common for the congregants to chant most of the service in unison.

The talmudic liturgy was formulated on the assumption that the texts of the liturgy were part of the "oral Torah," and hence could not be written down. Owing to the length and complexity of some of the prayers, it was acknowledged that not all Jews were capable of memorizing them, and hence the principal function of the prayer leader was to recite the prayers properly on behalf of the community, so that even the ignorant could fulfill their obligations. This was particularly conspicuous in the case of the *Amidah* ("Eighteen Benedictions"), the lengthy rabbinic prayer that formed the core of the liturgy. Following the talmudic norm, the *Amidah* would be recited quietly by the individual congregants, and afterwards repeated aloud by the prayer leader for the sake of those who were not capable of saying it by themselves.

By the Middle Ages the prohibition against writing oral Torah had been rescinded, and it was now possible to make use of written prayer books. Therefore, the prayer leader's repetition of the Eighteen Benedictions became something of an anachronism, as well as a disruption to the synagogue decorum because people were unlikely to pay proper attention to it, and some were even inclined to use it as an opportunity to conduct private conversations. Some authorities, including Maimonides, were in favor of discontinuing the practice. However, the conservative character of Jewish custom made it impossible to accept such a radical departure from traditional practice.

Piyyut

The precise standardization of the prayers and customs was typical of the Babylonian rite. In ancient Palestine, on the other hand, the prevailing attitudes were more open to improvisation in worship. This phenomenon is most impressively apparent in the development of the genre of *piyyut* (Hebrew plural: *piyyutim*), Hebrew liturgical poetry.

The classical authors of *piyyut* were probably synagogue cantors. Many of their poems were composed as alternative versions of the standard prayers that were recited at the Sabbath and festival services, which were the most widely attended occasions of congregational worship. Many of the *piyyutim* were designed to be recited responsively with the congregation, or to the accompaniment of a choir. The literature of *piyyut* was immense in its volume and magnificent in its literary quality.

A full description of *piyyut* would be impossible within the boundaries of this book. We shall confine ourselves instead to a brief survey of the writings of one of the most important synagogue poets, Yannai. Yannai lived in the land of Israel, probably in the sixth or seventh century. He was the author of a cycle of poetic versions of the Sabbath and festival prayers, known as *kerovah*s. The *kerovah* follows an elaborate form, consisting of eight distinct sections. The *piyyut* uses many inventive poetic devices, including acrostics (making the first letters of the lines spell out the alphabet or the author's name) and rhymes. At specified points, it cites verses from the biblical sections that are read on that day. The *piyyut* is full of allusions to interpretations from the midrash, and presumes extensive familiarity with rabbinic literature. The most elaborate form of *kerovah* was known as the *kedushta*, designed to be recited at the Sabbath or festival morning service in conjunction with the seven-blessing *Amidah* prayer.

The linguistic texture of classical *piyyut* is unique. Generally it attempted to employ a purely Hebrew vocabulary, eliminating the numerous Greek and Aramaic loan words that were so common in rabbinic discourse. The authors utilize the Hebrew elements very creatively, often turning the three-letter roots that are the basis of most Hebrew words into two-letter words. The poets attached novel meanings to the words, based on unusual usages in the Bible. Certain fundamental religious concepts and biblical figures (such as: Torah, Abraham, Moses or Israel) are never mentioned by name in the poems, but are invariably alluded to by means of ingenious epithets. Each *piyyut* is specifically linked to the themes found in the assigned biblical readings for that day, while retaining the themes of the prayer or blessing in which it is embedded. Because the Palestinian rite divided the Torah into approximately 150 sections, to be read over three and a half years, it was an extraordinary challenge to compose a cycle of original *piyyut* that would cover all the Sabbaths as well as annual festivals. Yannai and other classical liturgical poets did precisely that, and with impressive success.

As the Babylonian liturgy became the dominant one throughout the medieval Jewish world, the profile of the *piyyut* in Jewish worship diminished considerably. The Babylonian cycle of reading the Torah was an annual one, and therefore the individual sections that were read each Sabbath were much longer, leaving less time for poetic elaborations. Furthermore, the Babylonian sensibilities were less amenable to replacing the standard prayers with poetic alternatives, or with allowing "interruptions" in the mandatory prayers. The *piyyutim* were now included as additions to the fixed prayer, not as replacements. Nevertheless, the genre of *piyyut* continued to thrive throughout the Middle Ages, and many of the era's most prominent rabbis and scholars, including several who were better known as authorities in talmudic law, made distinguished contributions to the poetic legacy.

In the Enlightenment era, when reformers were looking for ways to shorten the Sabbath and festival synagogue services, the *piyyut* were among the most obvious candidates for deletion because their esoteric learned character was beyond the comprehension of Jews with limited Hebrew literacy and the grammatical underpinnings of the poems diverged considerably from the respectable models of classical biblical Hebrew. Apart from a few solemn holidays, especially Rosh Hashanah and Yom Kippur, the reduction or removal of *piyyut* from the services has become the norm even in Orthodox worship.

The synagogue in modern times

During the Jewish Enlightenment it was common for Jews to reinterpret their values and institutions along the lines of comparable Christian (especially Protestant) ones. A notable example of this pattern was the widespread identification of the synagogue as the central locus of Jewish religious activity, analogous to the role of the church for Christianity. For this reason, the synagogue and liturgy became the key targets for most calls for modernization of Judaism. In the earliest phase of Reform in the late eighteenth and early nineteenth centuries, there were recurring demands for esthetic changes in the forms of worship, usually modeled after the conventions of the churches. Advocates of these reforms were concerned that the synagogue should not appear bizarre or crude according to the prevailing cultural standards. For this reason, they called for the enforcement of decorum during the services, in contrast to the relative informality that often characterized the traditional style of prayer. Instrumental (usually organ) music and choral singing were introduced, following the norms of European classical music. This raised halakhic problems, because the playing of musical instruments on the Sabbath and festivals was prohibited by traditional rabbinic law. Various means were sought to shorten the services, whose traditional versions extended to about three hours, with much of its content beyond the comprehension of the average worshippers. Items were deleted because they were deemed non-essential or obsolete.

Several reforms were introduced to the content of the liturgy on the grounds that the customary prayers expressed values that were inconsistent with modern sensibilities, or were likely to cause embarrassment from the perspective of their gentile neighbors. The reformers removed texts that expressed eschatological longings for the ingathering of the exiles to Jerusalem, the rebuilding of the land of Israel under the Davidic monarchy, and the re-establishment of the sacrificial cult in the restored Temple.

The need to accommodate congregants with limited mastery of Hebrew and traditional practice promoted several additional developments in the structures of synagogues and worships. For example, in traditional services, the person leading the services would face in the same direction of the other worshippers (towards Jerusalem), and the reading from scripture would take place on a platform (*bimah*) situated in the center of the sanctuary. In modern congregations, it is more common to delegate these duties to professionally trained cantors, and the *bimah* is often located at the front of the sanctuary, tacitly lending the experience the quality of a theatrical show in which the cantor is performing for an audience. In some synagogues, the cantor even faces towards the congregation during the prayers. While these practices are more likely to be encountered in non-Orthodox settings, they tend to overlap denominational divisions.

The modern rabbi

Although the functions of the rabbi in contemporary western Jewish communities have come to resemble those of Christian clergy, involving pastoral counseling, preaching, and performing rituals on behalf of the congregation, the rabbi's original role was as an expert in Jewish law (*halakhah*) and the chief judge of the community. In this sense, traditional rabbinic literature recognized, at least theoretically, that women could perform rabbinic functions, because at least one legal ruling is ascribed to a woman named Beruriah in an ancient rabbinic text.

The roles of modern rabbis were now extended to pastoral functions and to the preaching of theology and moral instruction. One area in which the modern rabbi maintains a closer resemblance to his or her ancient counterpart is in the role of a preacher. The weekly sermon, a literary oration in which the rabbi would creatively link the words of the Bible to the concerns of the community, was a crucial part of the Sabbath or holiday synagogue service in ancient times, and forms the basis for much of midrashic literature. In medieval Germany and eastern Europe, the practice fell into decline, and in many localities the community's rabbi was only expected to deliver two sermons during the year: on the Sabbath prior to Passover he would speak about the intricate laws related to the approaching holiday, especially those involving food preparation and the elimination of leaven from the house; and on the Sabbath between the Rosh Hashanah and the Day of Atonement, at the height of the Jewish penitential season, the rabbi would deliver a discourse on the theme of repentance. The deficiency from the side of the community rabbis was often filled by itinerant preachers who traveled from town to town to deliver their homilies. In the eighteenth and nineteenth centuries, when advocates of religious reform demanded the reintroduction of weekly sermons on non-halakhic themes, they were accused of proposing unheard-of innovations. However, the weekly sermon continued to occupy a central role in the synagogue services in southern Europe and in Sephardic communities throughout the Middle Ages. Many examples of the genre were recorded by their authors or students, and sermons lie at the root of several well-known works of moralistic and exegetical literature.

Key points you need to know

- In biblical Israel, worship was usually equated with the offering of sacrifices on the altar of the sanctuary. A priestly caste was charged with administering this cult.
- The synagogue emerged during the late Second Commonwealth as the setting for communal activities like reading and teaching the Torah. Eventually its main role was associated with congregational prayer.
- Distinctive and highly structured formats were developed to accommodate the individual, collective and esthetic aspects of synagogue prayer. The genre of *piyyut* once enjoyed great popularity. The venerable art of preaching fell into neglect in several medieval communities, but was revived in the modern era.
- Largely under Christian influence, modern Jewish communities assigned increased importance to the synagogue as a setting for Jewish religious life. The rabbi, once defined by his authority as an expert in Jewish religious law, took on pastoral or ritual roles resembling those of Christian ministers.

Discussion questions

1. Compare the roles of priests and rabbis in traditional and modern Jewish communities.
2. Discuss some of the features that would be common to a well crafted *piyyut* and a scripture-based sermon.
3. Note some features that were introduced to Jewish practice before the oral Torah was put into writing.
4. To what extent might the distribution of roles in the synagogue reflect views about the fundamental natures of men and women?

Further reading

Synagogue and community

Baron, Salo Wittmayer, *The Jewish Community: Its History and Structure to the American Revolution*, Morris Loeb Series. Philadelphia, PA: Jewish Publication Society of America, 1942.

Finkelstein, Louis, *Jewish Self-Government in the Middle Ages*, 2nd ed., Abraham Berliner Series. New York: Feldheim, 1964.

Liturgy and liturgical poetry

Elbogen, Ismar, *Jewish Liturgy: A Comprehensive History*, 1st English ed. Philadelphia, PA and New York: Jewish Publication Society and Jewish Theological Seminary of America, 1993.

Heinemann, Joseph and Jakob Josef Petuchowski, *Literature of the Synagogue*, Library of Jewish Studies. New York: Behrman House, 1975.

Hoffman, Lawrence A., *The Canonization of the Synagogue Service*, Studies in Judaism and Christianity in Antiquity. Notre Dame, IN: University of Notre Dame Press, 1979.

Idelsohn, A.Z., *Jewish Liturgy and Its Development*. New York: Schocken Books, 1967.

Petuchowski, Jakob Josef, *Theology and Poetry: Studies in the Medieval Piyyut*, Littman Library of Jewish Civilization. London and Boston, MA: Routledge and Kegan Paul, 1978.

Posner, Raphael, Uri Kaploun and Shalom Cohen, *Jewish Liturgy: Prayer and Synagogue Service through the Ages*. Jerusalem: Keter, 1975.

Preaching

Bettan, Israel, *Studies in Jewish Preaching: Middle Ages*, Brown Classics in Judaica. Lanham, MD: University Press of America, 1987.

Saperstein, Marc, *Jewish Preaching, 1200–1800: An Anthology*, Yale Judaica Series. New Haven, CT: Yale University Press, 1989.

——*"Your Voice Like a Ram's Horn": Themes and Texts in Traditional Jewish Preaching*, Monographs of the Hebrew Union College. Cincinnati, OH and West Orange, NJ: Behrman House for Hebrew Union College Press, 1996.

17 *Judaism and daily life*

In this chapter

The diversity of Jewish law and ritual affects all aspects of life. As regards women, traditional Jewish law usually assumes that they are primarily occupied as wives and mothers. Various consequences emerge from that premise that limit their responsibilities in the public sphere. This chapter describes the legal structures of Jewish marriage and divorce as regulated in the halakhah. In the realm of ritual, talmudic law generally exempted women from time-bound ritual performance, but later generations were inconsistent about how strictly to maintain the exemption, or to increase or lessen women's participation in ritual activities. Some central precepts observed in the home were considered the special domain of women. Modern Jewish movements have generally supported equal treatment of women in religious matters.

The daily regimen of traditional Jews is guided by formal prayers that are recited at fixed times of the day, preferably in a congregational setting. The most prominent prayers are the *Shema'*, a declaration of God's oneness; and the *Tefillah*, a composition of blessings on various themes involving praise, pleas and thanks addressed to God. These are organized into three services, in the morning, afternoon and evening. Jewish rationalists, who stressed their belief in an impersonal and unchanging deity, had to reinterpret the function of prayer. Hasidism instilled in its followers a simple faith in God as a loving father figure, and turned prayer into a mystical experience through its teachings about cleaving to God (*devekut*) and ecstatic experience (*hitlahavut*).

Jewish tradition ordains a complex system of restrictions that determine which foodstuffs may be eaten. As with much Jewish ritual, no definitive rationale was provided, and commentators have proposed different medical, moral or symbolic explanations for the laws. The "kosher" laws relate to the nature of the species, the manner in which creatures are killed, the separation of milk and meat, and other factors. The religious status and social context of these laws have undergone much change in modern times.

Main topics covered

- Religion in the daily lives of Jews
- Jewish Women
- Daily prayer
- The *Shema'*
- The *Tefillah* ("Eighteen Blessings")
- Philosophical attitudes to prayer
- Hasidic prayer
- The significance and purpose of the Jewish dietary laws
- Definitions of permissible and forbidden species
- Ritual slaughter (*sheḥitah*)
- Separation of milk and meat
- Tithing
- Modern developments in the Jewish dietary laws

Religion in the daily lives of Jews

Most of the chapters in this book deal with, and derive from, formal works of religious literature. For the most part, these compendia of biblical exegesis, talmudic law and theology constitute the only source that we have for information about the Jewish religion at the time. Though such writings do reveal to us a wealth of information, the picture that they paint will inevitably be an incomplete one. The compilations in question belong to a limited range of literary genres, and only matters that are relevant to those genres are likely to get mentioned. The common occurrences of day-to-day life, the ones that undoubtedly affected the lives of most ordinary Jews, are precisely the ones that tend to be omitted from the standard works of advanced religious scholarship. Furthermore, those works were composed by relatively small circles of male scholars and authors, and deal with academic or institutional topics. Consequently, the religious lives of women, who did not play an active role in the synagogues, academies or institutions of religious leadership, were not described in a systematic manner, leaving major gaps in the information that was preserved about them. Jews in those days did not write memoirs, novels or other genres of personal expression that would provide us with a basis for reconstructing their actions and religious feelings. Legal discussions, in particular, are far more likely to deal with crises and anomalies, rather than with normal situations.

This is not to say that we are completely in the dark about the ordinary religious lives of Jewish men, women and children in former times. The scope of subjects that found their way into the standard literary genres could be surprisingly flexible, so that glimpses of such phenomena occasionally peek through. Particularly valuable from this perspective is the literature of the Responsa that responded to concerns of a living society. Much valuable information of this kind is also preserved in works devoted to the recording of ritual customs.

It is also crucial to keep in mind that the classification of "religious" phenomena is much more extensive in pre-modern Judaism than it is in modern western liberal society. So extensive is the range of human activities that fall within the compass of the *halakhah* that it is hard to identify an activity that a person performs during the day that would be religiously neutral. Thus, for traditional Judaism, the preparation of food according to the complex Jewish dietary laws, or the rhythms of menstruation and sexual relations, constitute religious activities of no less importance than participation in communal prayer or the authoring of learned Talmud commentaries.

Unfortunately, none of this alters the basic fact that the literature in our possession was (with a few interesting exceptions) composed by an intellectual elite, and reflects their own perspectives. The present chapter will not strive for completeness, but merely to present a selection of characteristic phenomena.

Jewish women

The religion of Jewish women did not get recorded in any consistent manner, and we are compelled to extrapolate it from standard works of Jewish law and exegesis and similar documents. Nevertheless, the diversity of the literature touches on many relevant aspects of female religious activity and spirituality. It is typical of Judaism that most of the issues that we think of as defining the "status" of women were carefully demarcated in Jewish religious law. Based on the principles set down in talmudic literature, women were considered to be obligated in the performance of the great majority of the biblical commandments and laws. However, the small number of precepts from which they were exempted included the most visible communal rituals, the ones that western society regards as more definitively "religious." The Talmud's determination of which laws were incumbent upon women and which were not was justified by the rabbis' exegetical reading of various biblical texts, in accordance with the technical methods of midrashic hermeneutics. The ancient sources did not normally justify such rules by ideological or sociological principles. Nevertheless, historians usually presume that, underlying the specific rules was a general, and realistic, assumption that the woman's domestic responsibilities, especially those related to child-rearing, made it unreasonable to impose excessive ritual demands on her time. When examining these phenomena from a modern perspective, it is important to recognize that the assignment of gender roles was, on the whole, not a function of the religious traditions. Rather, the major patterns were determined by basic realities of biology and economics; and religious law merely regulated people's behavior within those parameters.

For the duration of their reproductive years, women would usually be involved in a cycle of pregnancy, childbirth and nursing, a fact that minimized their usefulness as physical laborers, or in other types of work that would take them outside the home. Although Jewish law declared that to "be fruitful and multiply," was an important religious commandment—in fact, the very first commandment to be recorded in the Torah—in practical terms this was not something that was really under people's control prior to the recent introduction of effective contraception. Conversely, men were at a disadvantage as child-rearers if only because of their inability to breast-feed. Therefore, the traditional "patriarchal" model of women working in the home and men outside it was not the result of religious doctrines or edicts.

The society that emerges from ancient Jewish texts is based on heterosexual, polygamous families. The Torah outlawed homosexual relations as an "abomination" and this perspective was not challenged in the classical sources. Jews were aware that their view differed radically from much of Greek thought, where a man's marriage to a wife was dismissed as an unpleasant social obligation while true erotic devotion was directed towards adolescent boys. Notwithstanding the rare case of the Essenes, who eschewed marriage out of misogynistic motives, we find almost no disparagement of sexuality or celebration of celibacy. A Jew was to aspire to marriage and children, if at all possible.

Marriage was regarded primarily as a way to protect women. Much stress was placed on the need for a *ketubbah*, a prenuptial contract that guaranteed the rights of the parties during the marriage, and especially those of the wife after its dissolution. The Torah mentions a procedure for divorce, and though early rabbinic traditions disagreed about the religious desirability of the institution, the view that prevailed was that divorce was a legitimate option with no stigma attached to either party. Arguably, most of the relevant discussions in talmudic literature are concerned with deathbed situations where divorce is to the woman's legal advantage, as a means of exempting her from ritual complications that would ensue if she were left a widow. Although complications resulting from polygynous families were discussed at length in talmudic literature, it appears that most actual marriages were monogamous, if only for economic reasons.

Several of the above assumptions became subject to modification in the Middle Ages, and it is interesting to note how Judaism dealt with those instances. To take one straightforward example, we note that in Christian society several women were able to pursue spiritual and mystical callings by adopting monastic discipline, which freed them from commitments to home-making and child-rearing. This was not an option for Jewish women, because Judaism had a deep-rooted antipathy to voluntary celibacy, which it regarded as a tragic violation of the natural order.

Developments in medieval Jewish society did create limited opportunities for redefining certain aspects of gender roles. For example, the affluence of certain Jewish communities allowed many women to delegate their domestic chores to servants, thereby removing some of the traditional obstacles to participation in religious rituals. Similarly, the fact that many medieval Jews were occupied in commerce rather than in agriculture meant that housewives would frequently take care of a family business, and take on other economic roles that their talmudic ancestors had not anticipated. Their enhanced social status inspired some women to be more assertive in claiming an increased role in religious observance. Furthermore, during talmudic times, when it was forbidden to study oral traditions from written books, it was necessary for scholars to wander from their homes in order to study with their masters, a possibility which effectively ruled out women's participation in religious learning. In the Middle Ages, on the other hand, the Talmud and other works were available in written form, facilitating somewhat women's access to religious education and scholarship.

The leadership role of males in the traditional Jewish community was closely bound to their access to the authoritative texts. Under the threat of the Spanish Inquisition, when communities of "Conversos" attempted to maintain their Judaism in secret while outwardly accepting Christianity, the textual basis of the religion was removed, because Jews were denied access to all works of Jewish literature. Under these circumstances, women, with their experience in maintaining unwritten customs and traditions, emerged as figures of spiritual or charismatic leadership in several crypto-Jewish communities.

The responses of the Jewish religious authorities, and of the women themselves, to these developments varied widely. The rule of thumb that was set down in the Talmud (a rule that admitted of several exceptions) stated that women were exempted from "positive commandments that are time-defined." While this served to include virtually all the ethical and civil laws, it exempted them from many of the rituals associated with the various calendrical cycles. As we shall see, much depended on whether or not the exemption was perceived as precluding or discouraging voluntary performance of the rituals. This issue was discussed by the rabbinical authorities of the eleventh and twelfth centuries, including such eminent figures as Rashi and his grandson Rabbi Jacob Tam; and the scholars responded in different ways. Some permitted the women to perform such rituals as the taking of the "four species" on the Feast of Tabernacles, and to recite the accompanying blessing even though it contained the formula "Blessed are you, O Lord...who has sanctified us through your commandments and commanded us to..."—which was not, strictly speaking, true according to the premise that women are exempt from time-bound precepts. Other authorities regarded this as an unjustified transgression of the Torah's prohibition "Ye shall not add unto the word which I command you" (Deuteronomy

4:2). Even where women were permitted or encouraged to voluntarily adopt time-limited religious practices, the logic of the talmudic reasoning led to the corollary that they could not vicariously represent or lead the community in the performance of those rituals; because they would then be performing the precepts on behalf of people who had a more solid, biblically based, obligation.

In several areas of Jewish observance it is possible to discern a lessening of women's roles *vis à vis* the talmudic era. For example, they were removed from the synagogues into separate sanctuaries or women's galleries. Some other instances that come to mind are:

- Talmudic law places women on an equal footing with men with regards to several prayers and blessings, especially those that were believed to be of rabbinic origin, rather than from the Bible. By the Middle Ages, it was considered unimaginable in some circles that women could participate so actively in organized worship; so the ancient sources were reinterpreted in order to justify the prevailing situation. The most influential rationale was that of Maimonides who ruled that women share the obligation of prayer in a generic sense, but are not required to participate in specific congregational services, or to worship at fixed times.

- Talmudic law gave women an equal status in the public reading of the scroll of Esther, the principal observance associated with the festival of Purim. Because Purim originated in a later book of the Bible rather than in the Torah, it was not necessarily subject to the rule that exempted women from time-defined precepts. The Talmud even ruled that women should be allowed to read the Scroll of Esther on behalf of the congregation. However, the early medieval authorities reformulated the relevant Talmudic passage so as to grant women an equal obligation only in *hearing* the recitation, not in *performing* it.

- The wearing of fringes or tassels (*ẓiẓit*) on the corners of garments, in accordance with Numbers 15:38, is not a time-defined precept in the normal sense of the concept. Nevertheless, because the prevalent position of talmudic law was that nightgowns were not subject to the obligation of fringes, the rabbis debated whether this limitation constituted a sufficient reason to classify the precept as time-defined. Evidently, the dominant view in ancient times was that women were obligated to wear the fringes. Medieval Jewish law unanimously assumed that women were exempt from the practice, and generally discouraged women from taking it on even as an expression of voluntary piety. Nevertheless, there were women who insisted on wearing fringes. Thus, it was reported concerning Rabbi Jacob Moellin (known as "Maharil"), the influential fifteenth-century authority on Ashkenazic customs, that

> he could not fathom why women would want to take upon themselves the obligation of fringes. They asked him why he did not protest against the rabbi's wife known as Bruna who lived in his city [of Mainz], who always wore the

ritually fringed undergarment. He replied: Perhaps she will not heed me; and regarding such situations it says [in the Talmud]: It is preferable that they transgress unintentionally than deliberately.

- The Talmudic sources are unmistakable in stating that the obligation of Torah study applies to males and not to females. As with other such exemptions, it is not as clear whether women are nevertheless permitted, or even encouraged, to pursue religious studies. In a passage from the Talmud that was not necessarily intended to be grasped as a normative legal discussion, Rabbi Eliezer ben Hyrcanus commented that "if one teaches his daughter Torah, it is as if he is teaching her lewdness." Maimonides ruled that women are forbidden to study Torah except for those topics that are necessary for their practical religious lives. Maimonides's view, which is consistent with his own negative assessment of the intellectual abilities of women (and with the attitudes prevalent in the surrounding society), became normative for subsequent legal rulings on the topic, and a large body of literature evolved to define what areas of Torah it is permitted to teach to women.
- The prevailing opinion in the Talmud permitted women to perform circumcisions, and this position was codified in several early compendia of Jewish law. It appears that the original practice in Ashkenazic communities was that the mother took an active and visible role in the circumcision ceremonies of her sons, including holding the baby in her lap during the operation. The Tosafot forbade women to perform the circumcision, claiming that this case constituted an exception to the normal rules governing decisions in talmudic arguments. In the thirteenth century, Rabbi Meir of Rothenburg objected strongly to the mother's holding the child during the circumcision, "because it is not seemly for a lavishly dressed woman to be among the men and before the divine presence." Rabbi Meir's approach, which reflected the contemporary social norms regarding the separation of the sexes, was almost universally adopted by subsequent authorities.

Although the matter requires extensive study, there seems to be a general pattern of women's ritual obligations being diminished as part of the transition to medieval society. The phenomenon was most pronounced in Islamic countries.

There were nevertheless areas of Jewish ritual in which Jewish women were specially subject to certain religious duties. A passage in the Mishnah listed three precepts that were associated most closely with women. In the Middle Ages, these were viewed as prototypes for distinctively female commandments:

The list includes:

- *The kindling of sabbath lamps.* The nature and origin of this practice, which is not technically limited to women, will be discussed in connection with the Jewish ritual calendar. It will suffice for our present purposes to note that rabbis stated that it has a special relevance to women, either because they were most likely to be in the home when the time came to light the lamps, or because of an allegorical association with the sin of the first woman, Eve, when she "extinguished the light of the world" by bringing death to humanity through her disobedience.

- *The dough offering (hallah).* According to Biblical law, during the process of baking bread a portion must be set aside from the dough to be assigned to the priests for their upkeep. Although this ritual was not assigned specifically to women, women were normally the persons involved in baking bread for their household. The concept of *hallah* came to symbolize the full range of religious laws that dealt with the preparation of food and the application of the Jewish dietary laws. In the vast majority of cases, the observance and enforcement of these rules were entrusted to women.

- *Menstrual impurity (niddah).* Biblical law decreed that women are impure and sexually unavailable for one week after the onset of menstruation. A talmudic tradition relates that the "daughters of Israel" were so meticulous in their observance of these rules that, in order to avoid violating the more stringent prohibitions that relate to bleeding outside their normal periods, they took it upon themselves to extend the restrictions through the week following the cessation of their uterine bleeding. At the conclusion of the term of impurity they would bathe in a *mikveh*, a special purification bath, before being allowed to resume marital relations. The *niddah* prohibitions were among the few areas of the biblical purity system to survive the destruction of the Temple; though, strictly speaking, what was being observed was not the purity aspect, but separate prohibitions governing sexual relations. The observance of these rules would obviously have far-reaching effects on the relationships within the family. Although the Torah's concern with menstruation seemed to focus on its effects on the males, the application of the laws rested solidly on the women.

The language of the Biblical purity code normally suggests an association between ritual defilement and physical or moral "uncleanness," conjuring up images of filth and ugliness. The talmudic texts, on the other hand, tend to minimize such imagery, and generally deal with the rules as technical issues that carry no moral stigma, but are a component of the full Jewish religious regimen. Notwithstanding that some talmudic texts ascribe the imposition of these blood-related rules on women as a penalty or atonement for Eve's having "shed blood" and introduced death in the Garden of Eden, menstruation was typically accepted as a natural and healthy part of the biological rhythm, rather than as a demonic taboo. An oft-quoted talmudic tradition explained the menstrual prohibitions as designed to enhance a wife's desirability to her husband. Maimonides pointed out that in all the purity laws, the activities and biological processes that the Torah designated as sources of defilement were not unnatural or immoral ones, but on the contrary, they were the most natural and recurrent stages of the life cycle. For Maimonides, the purpose of these laws was not to discourage or stigmatize those actions or processes, but rather to enhance the sanctity of the Temple and sacred objects by restricting access to them.

We must keep in mind that the average woman prior to modern times probably did not have occasion to menstruate very often during her lifetime. Women would marry shortly after reaching puberty, and most of their childbearing years would be spent pregnant or nursing. Nevertheless, the observance of the rules made considerable demands on a woman. They required periodic self-examination, which included checking for bloodstains on their undergarments. The immersion in the *mikveh* at the conclusion of the term of impurity was governed by diverse regulations, including some that were designed to make sure that her entire body came into direct contact with the water. This involved carefully washing one's hair and unraveling any knots, removing jewelry, rubbing off scabs, and so forth.

The cleansing in the *mikveh*, in the awareness that it would lead to a resumption of marital relations, possesses a powerful erotic as well as a spiritual dimension. Depending on the physical cleanness and comfort of the *mikveh*, the immersion might also be an unpleasant ordeal in settings that do not possess efficient means for heating water or buildings. In small communities, the awareness of who was and was not going to the *mikveh* can provide women with intimate knowledge of each other's sexual lives, pregnancies and the like.

The varied changes that affected the lives of modern women also had an impact on Jewish women, and these changes often defined the borders between liberal and traditionalist communities. Among the earliest enactments of the Reform movements were measures intended to remove the limitations on the participation of women in religious life. Because the Reformers did not subscribe to the doctrine of divinely commanded laws, and did not acknowledge the obligatory status of rituals, they did not normally have to deal with concepts of obligation or exemption from commandments, or with women's status in the civil and criminal law systems. At any rate, the movement, virtually from its beginnings, did support the ordination of female rabbis, though only one woman actually received ordination in Europe before the Holocaust. The ordination of a female Reform rabbi in 1972 initiated a trend that became commonplace in the ensuing decades. Similar developments occurred shortly afterwards in the Reconstructionist movement and, in a decision that proved very controversial and divisive, in the Conservative movement, where women were counted in the required quorum of ten for congregational worship in 1974, and in 1983 were allowed rabbinical ordination. In recent years, even some strands of Orthodoxy in the United States and in Israel have come close to allowing women rabbinic status, in such areas as the training of "rabbinic pleaders" to represent women's interests before religious courts, or in the increasing opportunities available for study of the Talmud and other subjects from which they were previously excluded.

Daily prayer

Underlying the formal institution of prayer is the simple belief that God listens to prayers and responds. The most common Hebrew term for prayer is the root *PLL*, meaning "to judge," suggesting that self-evaluation is an important element in the prayer experience.

While the Bible preserves a rich literature of prayers, texts addressed to God in praise, petition or thanksgiving (including the entire book of Psalms), there is scarcely any mention of a "liturgy" in the sense of standardized texts, prayer times or practices. On the whole, the offering of sacrifices in the Jerusalem Temple was assumed to be the preferred vehicle of worship. The Qumran library preserves numerous prayers and liturgical documents from the late Second Temple era, but scholarship has not had an easy time correlating those texts with the talmudic evidence about the origins of the rabbinic liturgy. The Talmud discusses many details about how to conduct worship, but does not include a full text of the liturgy. It was not until well into the Middle Ages that the words and regulations of the liturgy were systematically set forth in prayer books.

Although there is much debate over the details of the process, scholars generally confirm the talmudic tradition that the main foundations of Jewish prayer as we know it were established by the rabbis at Yavneh following the destruction of the second Temple. There is no agreement as to whether that original liturgy had a precisely defined text, or merely a set of thematic guidelines that left the wording to the individual worshipper or prayer leader.

The standardized prayers deal with the needs and concerns of the entire community. Individual prayer, often characterized as petitions for divine mercy, existed but was not discussed extensively in the literature. Though it is considered preferable to participate in communal worship, the prayers are deemed obligatory even when the person is not in a congregational setting. When recited in a community, one individual leads the prayers on behalf of the others. At appropriate points, the participants respond "amen" to indicate their consent to the leader's words. Certain passages, notably those related to the idea of holiness, are considered so important that they may not be recited in their complete form without a proper quorum of ten worshippers.

The basic unit of rabbinic prayer is the "blessing" (*berakhah*). This consists of a sentence beginning "blessed are you, Lord our God, king of the universe" and concluding with specific content. Blessings are employed in diverse settings. For example, one may recite one before performing an action as a way of indicating that the action constitutes the performance of a religious precept ("…who has sanctified us with your commandments and commanded us to…"); or before partaking of food or some other kind of pleasure, as an expression of gratitude.

The norms that were described thus far were for normal weekday worship. Variations exist for Sabbaths, festivals and other special occasions. Biblical festivals include an "additional" (*Musaf*) service.

The standard daily liturgy is composed of two basic elements:

1. The *Shema'*, recited every morning and evening.
2. The *Tefillah*, recited every morning, afternoon and evening. The times for the *Tefillah* coincide with those of the morning and afternoon daily sacrifices (*tamid*); and the evening or nighttime service corresponds to the overnight burning of the sacrificial leftovers. In practice, the *Shema'* and *Tefillah* are juxtaposed in the morning and evening services, so that on a normal weekday there are actually three prayer services.

The Shema‘

The name *Shema'* is taken from the opening Hebrew word of the scriptural passage (Deuteronomy 6:4–9) "Hear, O Israel, the Lord our God is one Lord." Ancient Jewish tradition understood that there exists an obligation to recite this passage, whether as a declaration of "taking on the yoke of heavenly kingship," or as fulfillment of the precept contained in the passage itself: "these words, which I command you this day…you shall talk of them…when you lie down, and when you rise up."

In addition to this paragraph, the *Shema'* includes two other short sections from the Torah:

- Deuteronomy 11: 13–21, understood by the Mishnah as "acceptance of the yoke of the commandments." This passage deals largely with the rewards and punishments in store for those who obey or disregard the commandments.
- Numbers 15: 37–41, dealing with the commandment to place fringes or tassels on the corners of garments. The passage concludes with the words "I am the Lord your God who brought you out of the land of Egypt" and its recitation was regarded as the fulfillment of a directive to recall the exodus.

When incorporated into the daily liturgy, the Shema' is surrounded by a sequence of blessings. In a congregational setting, the service is preceded by an invitation to prayer recited by the leader: "Bless the blessed Lord!" to which the worshippers respond "Blessed is the blessed Lord eternally!"

The opening blessing of the *Shema'* service relates to the time of day, and expresses the idea that God is the master of nature who (in the morning service) creates light and (in the evening service) brings nightfall. Immediately preceding the biblical *Shema'* passages is a blessing based on the theme that God expressed his great love for Israel by bestowing the Torah upon them. This accords with the premise that the recitation of the *Shema'* functions as the fulfillment of the duty to study Torah. The mention of the exodus at the end of the third paragraph leads to a blessing on the theme of redemption, as exemplified by the exodus from Egypt, which prefigures the future redemption. The evening service contains an additional blessing asking for divine protection from the dangers of night.

The Tefillah ("Eighteen Blessings")

The Tefillah portion of the liturgy is often referred to as the "eighteen blessings" (*Shemoneh Esreh*), though the current weekday version actually consists of nineteen blessings. The name reflects its older structure in the Palestinian rite. In the prevailing Babylonian rite, the original blessing for the house of David and the restoration of Jerusalem is divided into two separate blessings. Although its format and much of its phraseology derives from biblical models, especially from Psalms, the text is a rabbinic creation.

The Talmud observed that the structure of this prayer is modeled on the way that a subject should approach a mortal king with a plea: open with words of praise; then present the petition; and then conclude with an expression of gratitude. Accordingly, the first three blessings consist chiefly of praises of God, the last three of thanksgiving, while the intermediary paragraphs contain an assortment of requests for divine assistance. For the most part, the petitions are for the welfare of the people of Israel, including hopes for national and religious restoration. On Sabbaths and holidays, when the appropriate mood is one of satisfaction and wellbeing, the petitions are omitted and replaced with a blessing related to the themes of the holy day.

The *Tefillah* is recited while standing; hence its alternative name, the *Amidah* (standing). Worshippers are supposed to face and direct their prayers towards the site of the Temple in Jerusalem. When recited in a congregational setting, the worshippers first recite the *Tefillah* quietly by themselves, after which the prayer leader repeats it—a practice that originated in an era before the introduction of written prayer books.

Philosophical attitudes to prayer

The impersonal divinity that was contemplated by the Jewish rationalists was very different from the God of traditional religion. There appears to be no obvious purpose in pouring out one's heart in prayer before such an unchanging deity or in expecting the heavenly father to be overcome with compassion. That God is self-contained and invariably does what is just and rational. It is therefore illogical to imagine that he responds to reminders or persuasions from mortals. Viewed this way, prayer and worship can only affect the worshipper as a form of self-examination or a statement of belief. Because all verbal discourse about God is ultimately inadequate and misleading, Maimonides stated that the highest form of worship is not prayer, but silent contemplation.

Maimonides spoke of "love of God" and "fear of God"; however he interpreted both concepts as purely intellectual categories. Fear refers to the existential feeling of awe that overcomes us when we contemplate how infinitely great God is in comparison with our puny selves. "Love" is the corresponding drive to draw as close as is humanly possible to the experience and understanding of God.

Hasidic prayer

More than any other Jewish religious movement, Hasidism stresses the importance of sincere prayer as an activity that can elevate the soul of the worshippers towards their creator and invoke divine blessings. The Ba'al Shem Tov's doctrine of prayer imbued it with two essential mystical ideals:

- *Devekut* (literally: "clinging"; constant devotion): the unceasing consciousness of God's presence.
- *Hitlahavut* ("bursting into flame"; ecstatic enthusiasm): the experience of spiritual exultation as the soul is elevated towards God.

Hasidic prayer developed a reputation for disregarding the technical regulations and ritual formalities imposed by Jewish law, especially the fixed times for prayer services. It celebrated the sincere devotion of the unlettered—even by means of simple whistling or recitation of the Hebrew alphabet—rather than the learned and precise recitation of the liturgy. Hasidism also encouraged the participation of all limbs of the body and forms of expression in worship: through gesticulation, dance and acrobatics. This feature was singled out for special condemnation by he movement's early opponents. Some features that were once distinctive to Hasidic prayer, particularly the incorporation of moving and spirited singing, have now achieved widespread acceptance in the broader Jewish community.

DIETARY LAWS

The significance and purpose of the Jewish dietary laws

The Bible and later Jewish traditions pay careful attention to food in relation to its origin, manner of preparation and the method of its consumption. The familiar English word "kosher" originates in the Yiddish pronunciation of the Hebrew *kasher*, "fit," a term that originally did not relate specifically to the permissibility of food. The full observance of these standards, as customary among Orthodox Jews today, extends to the instruments and equipment with which the food was prepared. In practice, Jews who observe these regulations strictly may only eat any cooked or processed food in other observant Jewish homes, or establishments that are under authorized supervision.

As with many other biblical rituals, the ancient sources do not provide consistent rationales for the existence of dietary regulations, allowing the Jewish commentators to suggest a variety of possible reasons. The Torah subsumes the dietary laws under the ideal of achieving "holiness," a concept that was associated, among other things, with the separation of Israel from the pagan world. Indeed, adherence to dietary restrictions has the effect of minimizing social interaction in venues where food is served, and it therefore diminishes the likelihood of intermarriage with gentiles. Moralistic thinkers have stressed that, by compelling Jews to refrain from eating many foods, the dietary laws strengthen the quality of moral self-discipline. Some authors, notably Maimonides, pointed out that there are health-related advantages to the Jewish diet, in that it excludes foods like pork that often caused trichinosis. Most recent commentators, however, have avoided such explanations, because they might be taken to imply that the rules need not apply where there are no health issues—and in fact, some liberal Jewish movements have invoked such arguments to justify the elimination of dietary observances. It is common to point out the moral symbolism of the fact that predatory birds and beasts are forbidden by Torah law, and that the slaughtering process should minimize the animal's suffering.

There are a number of different criteria that affect the ritual permissibility of food. Chief among them are:

Definitions of permissible and forbidden species

The Torah provides specific definitions for different types of creatures:

1. "Beasts of the earth" (quadrupeds). Permitted animals must have cloven hooves and chew their cuds. According to this criterion, sheep, cattle, goats and deer are allowed; while carnivorous beasts are prohibited.
2. Aquatic creatures must have both fins and scales. Shellfish, shrimps, eels, lobsters, and other such species are forbidden.
3. The Torah provides lists of forbidden birds, but does not specify criteria or rationales for their exclusion; though all of the birds on that list are predators or scavengers. Theoretically, Jewish law understood that any bird not on the forbidden list should be permitted. However, because we are no longer able to identify the biblical names with certainty, it is generally required that permissibility be supported by a local tradition. Among the permitted fowl are: chicken, geese, ducks and (according to most authorities) turkey.
4. "Winged swarming things" (winged insects). The Torah provides a definition that includes locusts and grasshoppers as permitted. In practice, however, there are currently very few Jewish communities that eat these species.

Ritual slaughter [sheḥitah]

The permitted mammals and birds must be slaughtered in accordance with Jewish law. The person who performs the slaughter is called a *shoḥet*. The method of slaughter is a single quick, deep stroke across the throat with a perfectly sharp blade with no nicks or unevenness. Maimonides claimed that this is the most humane, cost-effective method of slaughter.

Examinations are made to establish that the animal or bird was not subject to physical disqualifications. The Torah prohibits animals that died of natural causes, that suffered from fatal illnesses, or that were killed other than by proper slaughter.

Removal of blood

The Torah prohibits the consumption of blood. Therefore the blood must be left to drain after slaughter. Afterwards, the remaining blood is removed by means of absorption through coarse salt, or by broiling.

Removal of the sciatic nerve

The Torah tells an enigmatic tale about the patriarch Jacob's struggle with a supernatural being who injured his thigh. The passage concludes, "Therefore to this day the Israelites do not eat the thigh muscle that is on the hip socket, because he struck Jacob on the hip socket at the thigh muscle." In accordance with that story, the sciatic nerve must be removed from meat before it may be consumed.

Separation of milk and meat

Based on threefold repetition of the precept "thou shalt not boil a kid in its mother's milk" in the Torah, the Jewish oral tradition prohibits eating meat and dairy together. The rabbis extended this prohibition to include poultry (which has no mother's milk), though it does not apply to fish, which is not considered meat at all (it is also exempted from the requirement of slaughter). The separation extends to utensils and equipment in which meat and dairy foods are prepared, eaten, and washed. Though some kinds of vessels can be cleansed between dairy and meat use, it is usually more practical for Jewish households to keep separate sets or dishes. It is required that one wait after eating meat before one may eat dairy foods. There are varying local customs with regard to how long the interval must be, ranging from one to six hours; these are based on differing views about the precise purpose of the delay.

Tithing

Whether according to biblical or rabbinic law, portions of food and produce must be set aside for the sake of the priests, Levites or the poor. The food remains forbidden until this is done. Traditional interpretation held that most of these rules apply (at least, by the authority of the Torah) only to produce that was grown in the land of Israel.

Modern developments in the Jewish dietary laws

In keeping with their generally negative attitude towards ritual, the classic Reform movement rejected the principle of dietary restrictions, though the movement later adopted a more sympathetic attitude, recognizing some of the benefits of the practices. Of course, they treat the restrictions as optional customs and traditions, not as obligatory laws. There is a general tendency to stress the ethical rationales for the laws, and some authorities in Conservative Judaism have gone so far as to declare veal forbidden because of the inhumane treatment of the animals.

While traditional dietary laws presuppose that most food preparation (including the slaughter) took place in the home, modern food production is now done on a mass industrial basis. Technological changes also mean that the food is subjected to assorted chemical and biological additives whose precise contents are known only to experts. The upshot of all this is that many of the detailed regulations described in the preceding paragraphs are no longer observed actively within the household. Instead, Jewish communities and organizations maintain agencies that inspect the manufacturers or caterers, and issue certifications of their kosher status; these often take the form of symbols printed on the labels. Under these circumstances, the role of the observant Jewish consumer is relegated largely to checking the labels of the retail products they purchase.

Key points you need to know

- In traditional Jewish societies, religion permeated all aspects of daily life, affecting such features as food, dress and family relationships.
- As defined by ancient Jewish sources, women were presumed to be mothers and homemakers, and were therefore exempted from many time-defined or public obligations that would have impeded their domestic functions. These limitations were sometimes augmented or diminished in response to social changes.

- Traditional Judaism sees marriage and children as the preferred state of religious and social fulfillment.
- Some important religious precepts were considered the special province of women.
- Traditional Judaism contains an obligatory daily liturgy that consists of morning, afternoon and evening services.
- The *Shema'* recited in the morning and evening, contains passages from the Torah that speak of God's oneness and sovereignty, the commitment to obey his commandments, and other key religious themes. It is embedded in a framework of blessings.
- The *Tefillah* or "eighteen benedictions" is recited at all three daily services. It consists largely of petitions on behalf of the community, and includes pleas for eschatological redemption.
- The rationalist conception of an omniscient and unalterable God can lead to a discouraging of petitionary prayer and an emphasis on meditation and self-examination.
- Hasidism teaches that prayer should be an emotional and mystical experience of intimate conversation with a compassionate father in heaven.
- Traditional Jewish law contains complex and specific rules governing the acquisition, preparation and eating of food. No single agreed-upon reason is provided for those laws.
- The Torah identifies certain species of animals, fowl, sea creatures and insects as permissible and others as forbidden.
- Meat must be slaughtered in a specified manner, and subjected to inspections and the removal of blood and other forbidden portions.
- The principle of separating meat from milk has far-reaching implications that relate to the structure of a family's kitchen and the possible range of social interaction.
- The industrialization of food preparation has had an impact on the observance and religious significance of the Jewish dietary laws.

Discussion questions

1. What are some of the pitfalls involved in reconstructing the religious experiences of common people from official documents?
2. In what ways have Judaism and Jewish law defined the roles assigned to women, and to what extent did they merely accept or regulate the existing social norms?
3. Can Judaism's patriarchal division between public masculine and domestic feminine domains be harmonized with egalitarian principles?
4. Discuss how the experience of prayer might differ for a talmudic scholar, a philosopher and a follower of Hasidism.

5. If the Jewish dietary code is designed to achieve "holiness," how might the nature of holiness be affected by modern developments in food preparation and kosher observance?

Further reading

Religion and daily life

Abrahams, Israel, *Jewish Life in the Middle Ages*. New York: Atheneum, 1969.

Ben-Sasson, Haim Hillel and Samuel Ettinger, *Jewish Society through the Ages*. New York: Schocken Books, 1971.

Ben-Sasson, Menahem and Stefan C. Reif, *The Cairo Genizah: A Mosaic of Life*. Jerusalem: The Israel Museum, 1997.

Fine, Lawrence, ed., *Judaism in Practice: From the Middle Ages through the Early Modern Period*, Princeton Readings in Religions. Princeton, NJ: Princeton University Press, 2001.

Goitein, S. D., "Religion in Everyday Life as Reflected in the Documents of the Cairo Geniza." In *Religion in a Religious Age*. Edited by S. D. Goitein, 1–18. Cambridge, MA: Association for Jewish Studies, 1974.

Goitein, S. D. and Jacob Lassner, *A Mediterranean Society: An Abridgment in One Volume*. Berkeley, CA: University of California Press, 1999.

Heilman, Samuel C., *Synagogue Life: A Study in Symbolic Interaction*. Chicago, IL: University of Chicago Press, 1976.

—— *The People of the Book: Drama, Fellowship, and Religion*. Chicago, IL: University of Chicago Press, 1983.

Metzger, Thérèse and Mendel Metzger, *Jewish Life in the Middle Ages: Illuminated Hebrew Manuscripts of the Thirteenth to the Sixteenth Centuries*. New York: Fine Art Books, 1982.

Pollack, Herman, *Jewish Folkways in Germanic Lands (1648–1806); Studies in Aspects of Daily Life*. Cambridge, MA: MIT Press, 1971.

Trachtenberg, Joshua, *Jewish Magic and Superstition: A Study in Folk Religion*, Temple Books. New York: Atheneum, 1970.

Jewish women

Baskin, Judith R., "Jewish Women in the Middle Ages." In *Jewish Women in Historical Perspective*. Edited by Judith R. Baskin, 94–114. Detroit, MI: Wayne State University Press, 1991.

—— "From Separation to Displacement: The Problem of Women in *Sefer Hasidim*." *AJS Review* 19, no. 1 (1994): 1–18.

Baumgarten, Elisheva, *Mothers and Children: Jewish Family Life in Medieval Europe*, Jews, Christians, and Muslims from the Ancient to the Modern World. Princeton, NJ: Princeton University Press, 2004.

Falk, Ze'ev W., *Jewish Matrimonial Law in the Middle Ages*. Edited by A. Altmann and J. G. Weiss, Scripta Judaica. Oxford: Oxford University Press, 1966.

Fram, Edward and Agnes Romer Segal, *My Dear Daughter: Rabbi Benjamin Slonik and the Education of Jewish Women in Sixteenth-Century Poland*. Cincinnati, OH: Hebrew Union College Press, 2007.

Friedman, Mordechai A., "The Ethics of Medieval Jewish Marriage." In *Religion in a Religious Age*. Edited by S. D. Goitein. Cambridge, MA: Association for Jewish Studies, 1974.

Friedman, Mordechai Akiva, *Jewish Marriage in Palestine: A Cairo Genizah Study*. Tel-Aviv and New York: Tel-Aviv University Chaim Rosenberg School of Jewish Studies and the Jewish Theological Seminary of America, 1980.

Greenberg, Simon, ed., *The Ordination of Women as Rabbis: Studies and Responsa*, Moreshet Series. New York: The Jewish Theological Seminary of America, 1998.

Grossman, Avraham, *Pious and Rebellious: Jewish Women in Medieval Europe*, 1st ed., Tauber Institute for the Study of European Jewry Series. Hanover, NH: University Press of New England for Brandeis University Press, 2004.

Grossman, Susan and Rivka Haut, *Daughters of the King: Women and the Synagogue: A Survey of History, Halakah, and Contemporary Realities*, 1st ed. Philadelphia, PA: Jewish Publication Society, 1992.

Romer Segal, Agnes, "Yiddish Works on Women's Commandments in the Sixteenth Century." In *Studies in Yiddish Literature and Folklore*. Jerusalem: Hebrew University, 1986.

Prayer and liturgy

Benor, Ehud Z., "Petition and Contemplation in Maimonides' Conception of Prayer." *Religion* 24, no. 1 (1994): 59–66.

Buxbaum, Yitzhak, *Jewish Spiritual Practices*. Northvale, NJ: Jason Aronson, 1990.

Carmy, Shalom, ed., *Worship of the Heart: Essays on Jewish Prayer by Rabbi Soloveitchik*. Hoboken, NJ: KTAV for Toras Horav Foundation, 2003.

Dan, Joseph, "The Emergence of Mystical Prayer." In *Studies in Jewish Mysticism*. Edited by Joseph Dan and Frank Talmage, 85–120. New York: KTAV, 1982.

Donin, Hayim, *To Pray as a Jew: A Guide to the Prayer Book and the Synagogue Service*. New York: Basic Books, 1980.

—— *To Be a Jew: A Guide to Jewish Observance in Contemporary Life*. New York: Basic Books, 1991.

Elbogen, Ismar, *Jewish Liturgy: A Comprehensive History*, 1st English ed. Philadelphia, PA and New York: Jewish Publication Society and Jewish Theological Seminary of America, 1993.

Green, Arthur and Barry W. Holtz, *Your Word Is Fire: The Hasidic Masters on Contemplative Prayer*, 1st Schocken pbk. ed. New York: Schocken, 1987.

Hartman, David, "Prayer and Religious Consciousness: An Analysis of Jewish Prayer in the Works of Joseph B Soloveitchik, Yeshayahu Leibowitz, and Abraham Joshua Heschel." *Modern Judaism* 23, no. 2 (2003): 105–25.

Heinemann, Joseph and Jakob Josef Petuchowski, *Literature of the Synagogue*, Library of Jewish Studies. New York: Behrman House, 1975.

Heschel, Abraham Joshua, *Man's Quest for God: Studies in Prayer and Symbolism*. Santa Fe, NM: Aurora Press, 1998.

Hoffman, Lawrence A., *The Canonization of the Synagogue Service*, Studies in Judaism and Christianity in Antiquity. Notre Dame, IN: University of Notre Dame Press, 1979.

Idelsohn, A. Z., *Jewish Liturgy and Its Development*. New York: Schocken Books, 1967.

Jacobs, Louis, *Hasidic Prayer*, pbk. ed. London and Washington, DC: Littman Library of Jewish Civilization, 1993.

Dietary laws

Berman, Jeremiah Joseph, *Shehitah, a Study in the Cultural and Social Life of the Jewish People*. New York: Bloch, 1941.

Blech, Zushe Yosef. *Kosher Food Production*. Ames, IO: Blackwell, 2004.

Central Council of Jewish Religious Education in the United Kingdom and Eire. *The Book of Kashrut*. [England]: Central Council of Jewish Religious Education in the United Kingdom and Eire, 1948.

Greenspoon, Leonard J., Ronald Simkins and Gerald Shapiro, eds, *Food and Judaism*, Studies in Jewish Civilization. Omaha, NE and Lincoln, NE: Creighton University Press, 2005.

Karo, Joseph ben Ephraim, *The Kosher Code of the Orthodox Jew*. Translated by Solomon Isaac Levin and Edward Allen Boyden. Minneapolis, MN: University of Minnesota Press, 1940.

Kraemer, David Charles, *Jewish Eating and Identity Throughout the Ages*, Routledge Advances in Sociology. New York: Routledge, 2007.

Levinger, I. M., *Shechita in the Light of the Year 2000: Critical Review of the Scientific Aspects of Methods of Slaughter and Shechita*. Jerusalem: Maskil L'David, 1995.

Wagschal, S., *The Practical Guide to Kashrus*, rev. and expanded ed., Practical Halacha Series. Brooklyn, NY: Judaica Press, 2003.

Welfeld, Irving H., *Why Kosher? An Anthology of Answers*. Northvale, NJ: Jason Aronson, 1996.

18 *The sacred calendar*

In this chapter

Jewish life is enhanced by a very elaborate rhythm of holy days. This chapter describes the structure of the Jewish lunar-solar year and the major holidays. The Sabbath is the weekly day of rest and spiritual regeneration. The three annual pilgrimage festivals of Passover, Tabernacles and Weeks commemorate events in Israel's sacred history as well as the agricultural seasons. The penitential season that radiates from Rosh Hashanah and the Day of Atonement is a time of repentance, introspection and forgiveness. Other fasts and days of commemoration have been introduced over time to mark important events in Jewish history.

Main topics covered

- The structure of the Jewish calendar
- The Sabbath
- The three pilgrimage festivals (Passover, Shavuot, Sukkot)
- The penitential season (Rosh Hashanah, Yom Kippur)
- Minor holidays (Purim, Ḥanukkah, fifteenth of Shevat)
- Modern days of commemoration
- Fast days

The structure of the Jewish calendar

The Bible sets out an elaborate sequence of holy days and festivals most of which are identified by days of the month. Nowhere, however, do we find a precise definition of what constitutes a month. Documents from the Second Temple era reveal that the structure of the calendar was a major point of contention between rival Jewish sects. The controversy occupied a prominent place in the Qumran scrolls and is hinted at in rabbinic tradition. The Qumran community advocated a 364-day solar calendar consisting of twelve thirty-day months with four extra days inserted between the quarterly seasons. The fact that 364 is evenly divisible by seven meant that the annual holidays would fall on the same day of the week every year. Holidays could never occur on Saturday, allowing them to avoid conflicts between the restrictions of the Sabbath and the requirements for observing the festivals.

The Pharisaic calendar, which became the basis for the subsequent rabbinic tradition, was based on the actual astronomical cycles of the moon. Because the moon goes through its phases in approximately twenty-nine and one half days, and months are measured in whole days, the year should theoretically consist of alternating months of twenty-nine and thirty days. Nevertheless, talmudic law required that the matter be determined every month by the central religious court (Sanhedrin) on the basis of the testimony of witnesses who had actually seen the new moon appear in the heavens. The rabbis also made certain adjustments in the calendar in order to avoid certain unwanted situations, such as the Day of Atonement falling in direct proximity to the Sabbath, on a Friday or Sunday.

A year composed of twelve alternating months of twenty-nine and thirty days adds up to 354 days, which is eleven and a half days shorter than the solar year of 365 and a quarter days. This creates a problem for the Torah's stipulation that Passover must fall in the springtime (referring to a stage in the ripening of the grain crops), as well as for several other annual festivals that correspond to stages in the agricultural year that is determined by the solar cycle. The rabbinic calendar, like the Babylonian, resolved this problem by periodically adding a thirteenth month. In ancient times this intercalation would be determined by the Jewish court on the basis of astronomical, climatic and economic factors.

In the fifth century, owing to the pressures that were placed on the Palestinian Jewish leadership by the Roman authorities, a permanent calendar was promulgated, and the procedure of hearing testimony about the new month was discontinued. The resulting sequence of seven thirteen-month years out of every nineteen is equivalent to the "Metonic" system developed by the Babylonians and Greeks. This change greatly simplified the observance of holidays in Jewish communities throughout the diaspora.

During the tenth century, the Palestinian Patriarch Ben Meir attempted to restore the traditional prerogative of his office by reviving the old practice of determining the new months on the basis of testimony. The ensuing dispute was part of a larger rivalry between the Babylonian and Palestinian religious authorities. He was opposed by Saadiah Gaon, and the calculated calendar has remained in effect among Rabbinite Jews ever since.

Under the older system for determining new moons, the decision had to be communicated every month to Jewish communities around the world. Until notification was received from the Sanhedrin in the land of Israel, Jews elsewhere could not know whether the new month commenced on the twenty-ninth or thirtieth day after the beginning of the previous month. The notifications were sent by means of messengers who might require almost a whole month to reach some of the far-flung Jewish centers. This was primarily of importance when it came to the observance of the festivals. If people observed the holidays on the wrong date they would be in violation of grave biblical prohibitions. The solution that was introduced in ancient times was that all communities to whom the notification had not yet arrived had to observe each of the Torah holidays for two days, in order to avoid committing any such transgressions. With the adoption of a calculated calendar, the rationale for observing the extra festival days no longer existed. Nevertheless, the Babylonian Talmud (which was completed after the institution of the fixed calendar) stated that Jews should continue to observe the extra days out of respect for ancestral custom. The only exception that was made was for the Day of Atonement, because a two-day fast was felt to be an unreasonable burden. This remains the practice among traditional Jews outside Israel, though liberal denominations have done away with the second days of festivals.

The Sabbath (Shabbat)

The Jewish week is built around the Sabbath, which is observed every Saturday.

Two main reasons are given in the Torah for the institution of the Sabbath:

1. Exodus 20:10: "For in six days the Lord made heaven and earth, the sea, and all that in them is, and rested the seventh day: wherefore the Lord blessed the sabbath day, and hallowed it."
2. Deuteronomy 5:15: "And remember that thou wast a servant in the land of Egypt, and that the Lord thy God brought thee out thence through a mighty hand and by a stretched out arm: therefore the Lord thy God commanded thee to keep the sabbath day."

The Torah repeats in many places that no "work" or "labor" should be performed on the Sabbath—but does not define precisely what actions are included under the prohibition. The Mishnah provides a list of thirty-nine basic categories of prohibited activities. Additional restrictions were added by the rabbis. In addition to some of the more obvious actions associated with earning a livelihood or physical exertion, the forbidden activities include: kindling and extinguishing fires, cooking, carrying objects outside the house, writing, the handling of money and any kind of commerce.

Like all dates in the Hebrew calendar, the Sabbath is measured from sundown on the previous day (Friday) until nighttime the next day (Saturday). As regards its official communal observance, the Sabbath is distinguished by a more elaborate order of prayers than on weekdays, and by increased attendance at the congregational worship in the synagogue. Of equal importance to the public prayers are the rituals that are celebrated in the home, such as the mandatory festive meals, the "sanctification" blessing (*Kiddush*) recited at the beginning of the Sabbath, and the "separation" blessings (*Havdalah*) recited at its conclusion.

A conspicuous feature of Sabbath observance is the ritual lighting of candles on Friday evening to mark the onset of the holy day. Strictly speaking this is not a commandment, in that it was not ordained by the Torah. Nonetheless, the talmudic rabbis attached great importance to having light available before the Sabbath because the Torah prohibited the kindling of fire on the day of rest itself. Hence, if a lamp were not prepared beforehand, then the household would remain shrouded in darkness, leading to general discord. Thus, the principle underlying this obligation is the promoting of domestic harmony. Although the lighting of the candles was not assigned exclusively to women, the talmudic and medieval sources recognized that, in practice, it was usually the woman performed it. Maimonides states simply that it is the woman who is most likely to be at home at the appropriate time. The popular perception of candle lighting evolved until it came to be viewed as a ritual act in its own right.

Many other intricate procedures are required in order to prepare a household for the day of rest. These include the cleaning of the house, the family members and their clothing, and the preparation of food. Because cooking and other everyday activities cannot be performed on the Sabbath, most of the menu would have to be ready before sundown on Friday.

The three pilgrimage festivals

The Torah instructed that three annual holidays should be observed at the holy Temple in Jerusalem. These festivals combine elements of historical commemoration and thanksgiving for the natural bounties of the agricultural season.

Pesah (Passover)

Pesah, observed from the fourteenth day of the first month (Nissan) and extending for seven days (eight outside Israel), commemorates one of the central events in

Jewish sacred history, the exodus from Egypt when Israel was liberated from slavery. The holiday's name is derived from an episode in the Torah's narrative of the event. God inflicted ten miraculous plagues on the Egyptians in order to force Pharaoh to free the Hebrews. The last of these involved the deaths of the Egyptians first-borns. As death visited the Egyptian houses, the Hebrews were instructed to mark their doorways with the blood of a sacrificial lamb as God "passed over" their dwellings. In ancient times, the cornerstone of the celebration was the sacrifice of a lamb on the first evening. According to a widespread Jewish interpretation, this act symbolized the Hebrews' confident defiance of their oppressors, because sheep were an object of worship for the Egyptians.

Passover is also the festival of spring and marked the beginning of the grain harvest in Israel. The holiday is also designated "the feast of unleavened bread." This alludes to the biblical story about how *matzah,* unleavened bread, was taken by the Hebrews as they hastened out of Egypt at God's abrupt notification, because their dough would have no time to rise. Therefore matzah came to commemorate the liberation. By extension, no leavened items may be eaten or be found in one's possession for the duration of the holiday. This requires that a careful search be conducted in the days preceding the holiday of any rooms where leavened items might have been found. Vessels or appliances that were used with leaven must be thoroughly cleaned, where possible. Separate dishes and equipment are usually set aside exclusively for use on Passover. In order to avoid financial hardship, the rabbis devised a mechanism for selling one's leaven to a non-Jew for the duration of the Passover, after which it reverts to the possession of the original Jewish owner. A ritualized search for leaven is conducted on the evening preceding the holiday, following which any remaining leaven is burned or otherwise destroyed.

Figure 18.1 Matzah

Figure 18.2 An illuminated Passover *Haggadah*

The most conspicuous ritual of Passover is the meal that is held on the first night. It has come to be known as the *seder* (order) because of the detailed order of rituals that are performed. While the Temple existed, the main component was the actual roasting and eating of the sacrificial lamb by family units. The Passover seder is the occasion for fulfilling the biblical command to tell the exodus story to one's children. Accordingly, much of the meal consists of a liturgical recitation, known as the *haggadah* (telling). The standard text of the haggadah was compiled in early medieval times, based on talmudic guidelines, and consists of midrashic expositions of biblical passages about the exodus from Egypt and its significance. Where possible, the telling is initiated by a child asking four questions about the peculiar features of the holiday meal; and many features of the meal are designed to provoke the children's curiosity and maintain their alertness.

Various features of the seder were designed to symbolize either the wretchedness of slavery or the joy of freedom. Thus, the Torah commands that the sacrifices be eaten with *maror*, a bitter herb or vegetable, as a reminder of how the Egyptians embittered the lives of the Hebrew slaves. To represent the experience of freedom, the rabbis constructed the meal on the pattern of an aristocratic Hellenistic banquet or symposium. For this reason, the main meal was preceded by an assortment of hors d'oeuvres, and the participants would recline on sofas as they ate (now it is common to lean in one's chair). The redemption from Egypt is perceived as a paradigm for the ultimate future redemption.

As with other Jewish rituals, important sections of the seder service are marked by drinking cups of wine. During the meal the cup will be filled four times. The rabbis attached various symbolic meanings to the number. The most popular of these is that it corresponds to four promises made by God to Israel in the Torah (Exodus 6:6–7): "[1] I *shall take you out* from under the burdens of Egypt; [2] I *shall rescue you* from their service; [3] I *shall redeem you* with an outstretched arm and with great judgments. [4] I *shall take you* to me for a people and I shall be a god to you..." One opinion in the Talmud requires five cups. In most communities, an additional cup is filled and reserved for Elijah the Prophet.

Shavuot, the feast of Weeks

After enumerating the laws of Passover, the Torah goes on to prescribe an offering of an "*omer*," a sheaf of grain (identified as barley) that is to be offered to God "on the morrow of the sabbath." This offering initiates a process of counting seven weeks, at the conclusion of which there is a festival known as the feast of Weeks (Shavuot). According to the straightforward meaning of the text, the counting always begins on a Sunday, so the feast of Weeks will invariably fall on a Sunday. The Qumran scrolls speak of the sheaf being brought on the first Sunday after the conclusion of the Passover week. However, according to the interpretation advocated by the Pharisees and talmudic rabbis (and embedded into the Greek text of the Septuagint), the seven weeks are counted from the beginning of Pesah until the feast of Weeks, Shavuot—with "sabbath" understood here as a day of festival rest, not necessarily a Saturday.

In the Bible, the offering of a measure of barley meal, as well as the special offering of wheaten loaves offered on Shavuot, commemorate the new barley and wheat crops, as well as the beginning of the season for bringing the first fruits of summer. However, according to the rabbinic calculation, the date of Shavuot coincides with the anniversary of the revelation of the Torah at Mount Sinai; and this theme came to dominate the interpretations of the festival rituals. Accordingly, the preceding period of counting seven weeks was understood as an expression of the spiritual anticipation that connected the Exodus to the revelation.

During the medieval era, the period between Passover and Shavuot acquired a morose character that commentators associated with a plague or massacre that occurred at that season in the days of Rabbi Akiva and the Bar Kokhba uprising; and which was intensified when the venerable Rhineland Jewish communities of Speyer, Worms and Mainz were ravaged by crusader mobs in 1096.

Sukkot, the Feast of Booths (Tabernacles)

The biblical festival of Sukkot celebrates both the ingathering of the crops and the historical commemoration of the booths in which the Israelites dwelled during the forty years of their wandering in the wilderness after leaving Egypt. It is observed in the fall, commencing on the fifteenth day of the seventh month (Tishri) and lasts seven days (eight days outside Israel).

Among the many unique rituals of this weeklong holiday, we may mention:

- the obligation to dwell in a *sukkah*, a temporary booth, throughout the days of the festival.
- the procession with "four species", which were identified in rabbinic tradition as:
  a *lulav*, an unopened date-palm leaf;
  an *etrog*, citron;
  hadas, branches of myrtle leaves;
  aravah, willow branches.

These are carried in processions and are subject to numerous symbolic interpretations. In ancient times, the locus of the "four species" procession was in the Jerusalem Temple, but it was subsequently transferred to the synagogues. Rabbinic Judaism celebrated Sukkot as a water festival in anticipation of the middle-eastern rainy season that is so crucial for sustenance.

Figure 18.3 The "four species" of Tabernacles

Shemini Azeret (Eighth Day of Assembly)

The day immediately following Sukkot is understandably treated as the holiday's conclusion. Technically, however, it is a separate festival on which the rituals of the *sukkah* and the four species are not observed. A poignant rabbinic tradition depicted how God was reluctant to dismiss his beloved celebrants, and therefore he added an extra day to ease the transition.

Simḥat Torah (Rejoicing of the Torah)

In ancient times, the liturgical reading of the Torah was conducted according to two different systems: In the land of Israel, the text was read consecutively over a period of about three and a half years. In Babylonia, on the other hand, larger weekly portions allowed the cycle to be completed within the span of a single year. During the medieval era, as the Babylonian practice prevailed, it become common to celebrate the annual completion and recommencement of the reading cycle. Ultimately, the date that attained universal acceptance was the "extra" day that is appended in diaspora communities to the Eighth Day of Assembly. The day was transformed into Simḥat Torah, "the Rejoicing of the Torah." In the contemporary observance of Simḥat Torah, the most conspicuous feature of the ceremony is the *hakkafot* (circuits) when the Torah scrolls are carried in a procession seven times around the synagogue. In many communities this has been extended into spirited dancing, singing and spontaneous forms of rejoicing.

The penitential season

The penitential season is built around the New Year (Rosh Hashanah) and the Day of Atonement, both of which occur in the seventh month of the Hebrew year.

Rosh Hashanah

The Torah (Leviticus 23:24) ordains a holiday on the first day of the seventh month whose only distinctive feature is that it is "a memorial of blowing of trumpets." The rabbinic oral tradition developed this idea into a dramatic narrative according to which humanity stands in judgment before the supreme judge who reviews each person's deeds of the previous year and determines their fate for the coming year. The underlying assumption is that all mortals are sinners, and that if we were judged according to what we really deserve, we would all be found wanting. However, because God is perceived as a merciful parent as well as an all-knowing and all-powerful judge, the worshippers appeal to him for a second chance. God concedes to make this judgment a conditional one, so that if they determine to sincerely repent of their sinful ways, then he will discard it and forgive them.

The biblical precept of "blowing of trumpets" is observed in the form of the sounding of the *shofar*, an instrument fashioned from the horn of a ram.

The Additional (*Musaf*) service on Rosh Hashanah contains three special liturgical sections, reflecting the holiday's key themes.

1. *Malkhuyyot* (kingship): God is affirmed as sovereign of the universe. According to the dominant tradition, Rosh Hashanah is the anniversary of the creation of the world and of the first humans.
2. *Zikhronot* (remembrance): God is depicted as the absolute judge who recalls the deeds of all his creatures.
3. *Shofarot* (trumpeting): This blessing invokes the rich imagery of the ram's horn and its many associations with revelation and redemption.

White clothing and synagogue decorations are donned as symbols of innocence and a reminder of death. In most congregations, the Torah scrolls and the arks that house them are covered with white cloth during the penitential season. At the festival meals it is customary to eat foods that symbolize the themes of the day, particularly the hope for a favorable judgment and a happy year. A widespread custom is to dip food in honey.

Figure 18.4 Shofar

Jewish tradition found numerous symbolic allusions and associations to the shofar. Among the most prominent are:

- It is part of the coronation ceremony in which God is proclaimed as the king of the universe.
- Its tone stirs the heart to repentance and emulates the sobbing of a contrite heart.
- When the patriarch Abraham was ready to obey God's commandment to sacrifice his beloved son Isaac, God provided him with a ram to offer up instead. By sounding the ram's horn, the worshippers invoke the merit of Abraham's righteousness, in hope that it will be credited to his descendants when they themselves are not fully deserving of divine forgiveness.

Days of repentance

The days extending from Rosh Hashanah to Yom Kippur constitute the "ten days of repentance," a season of introspection, forgiveness and moral improvement. The Hebrew term for repentance "*teshuvah*" literally means "return," a turning away from sin back to the path of Torah and righteousness. As formulated by Maimonides, the process should include an honest examination of the self, a rejection of the evil ways of the past and the determination not to repeat one's offences.

The start of the penitential season has expanded to include the month preceding Rosh Hashanah (Elul). The resulting forty-day period corresponds to the forty days when Moses pleaded for the people's forgiveness after they worshipped the golden calf. From the beginning of Elul, the shofar is sounded every morning to call all worshippers to repent. Sephardic Jews add special penitential prayers known as *Seliḥot*, while Ashkenazic Jews begin the recitation of *Seliḥot* at a somewhat later date. Based on a tradition that God will not grant forgiveness to people unless they themselves have forgiven their fellows, it is common for people to seek reconciliation from one another during this season.

Yom Kippur, the Day of Atonement

As described in the Torah, Yom Kippur originated as a ceremony to atone for cultic impurity in the Temple, but was expanded into an annual day, observed on the tenth day of the seventh month, devoted to the forgiveness of sin. A striking feature of the Temple ceremony was the "scapegoat." The high priest would confess the sins of the people, and symbolically place them on the head of a goat who was then sent off to perish in the wilderness.

Following the rabbinic interpretation, "fasting" includes refraining from various physical pleasures, including:
1. Eating and drinking
2. Bathing
3. Anointing with oil
4. Wearing shoes
5. Sexual relations

The Torah commands that people "afflict their souls" from nightfall to nightfall, and accordingly the Day of Atonement is observed as a fast in order to enhance the day's mood of spiritual introspection.

The liturgy of the Day of Atonement incorporates repeated recitations of confessions for sins, which are expressed in the plural form, indicating that the individual is sharing in the responsibility of the entire community. Seliḥot penitential prayers are included in most Yom Kippur services. They are based on the "thirteen attributes of mercy" (Exodus 34:1–7) that God instructed Moses to recite in order to invoke divine forgiveness after Israel's sin of worshipping the golden calf.

In most rites, a solemn ceremony known as the *Kol Nidrei* is performed on the afternoon just before the onset of Yom Kippur. *"Kol nidrei"* is the Aramaic opening of a legal formula for the annulment of religious vows. During the medieval era, the ceremony was inserted at the beginning of the evening service, because of the widespread fear that divine forgiveness might be impeded by the fact that people might inadvertently have failed to fulfill all their vows.

In the traditional observance of the Day of Atonement, virtually the whole waking day is spent at prayer in the synagogue. A fifth service is added to the four services of the normal festival liturgy. This is known as *Ne'ilah* and occurs at twilight, which evokes the solemn atmosphere of the closing of the heavenly "gates of repentance." In spite of the sober imagery of final judgment, Yom Kippur has a joyous tone to it, especially at its conclusion. This reflects the profound confidence that God is, after all, a merciful and loving parent who can be relied upon to grant forgiveness. Thus, the worshippers should emerge from the intense experience with the feeling that they have been spiritually and morally cleansed and are ready to face the new year with confidence.

Minor holidays

The concept of "minor holidays" is used to designate festivals that are not commanded in the Torah; though some of them originate in other books of the Bible.

Purim (the Feast of Esther)

This holiday is observed on the fourteenth or fifteenth of Adar, the twelfth month (late February or March). It recalls the rescue of the Jews of the Persian empire from a threatened genocide as described in the biblical book of Esther. Regarding the days of the celebration, the Bible ordained (Esther 9:22, 28) "...that they should make them days of feasting and joy, and of sending portions one to another, and gifts to the poor...And that these days should be remembered and kept throughout every generation." This was interpreted by the Talmud as involving four main forms of observance:

- The ceremonial reading of the Book of Esther
- Partaking in a festive meal
- Exchanging gifts of foodstuffs
- Giving charity ("gifts to the poor").

The Babylonian Talmud states: "on Purim a person is required to get so drunk that he cannot distinguish between 'Cursed is Haman [the villain of the story]' and 'Blessed is Mordecai [the hero].'" Although the obligation to become intoxicated was included in all the official codes of Jewish law, not all the religious authorities were inclined to accept it at face value. Maimonides, for example, paraphrases the passage as follows: "One drinks wine until he becomes inebriated enough to doze off." Nevertheless, in the popular consciousness Purim took on a unique tone of exceptional frivolity to the point of rowdiness, which made it unique among the festivals of the Hebrew calendar. Furthermore, popular practice evolved an imaginative variety of customs through which Jews could symbolically "blot out" Haman's name in fulfillment of the Torah's command to "blot out the remembrance of Amalek from under heaven" (Deuteronomy 25:19), because Haman was believed to be a descendant of Israel's old nemesis, the Amalekites who had attacked them shortly after their departure from Egypt. The use of special noisemakers became widespread among Ashkenazic Jews. In Catholic lands in Europe, several practices associated with Christian carnivals were adapted by Jews as part of their Purim celebrations. The Jewish Purim incorporated such practices as masquerading, first reported in Provence in the early fourteenth century. The Purim celebrations engendered an entire culture of parody that was directed against institutions of their own religion and society. Among Ashkenazic Jews, a tradition of *Purim-Shpils*, dramatic productions based on the book of Esther or other biblical themes, became a standard part of the holiday celebrations.

Ḥanukkah

The post-biblical festival of Ḥanukkah, observed for eight days in winter (beginning on the twenty-fifth day of Kislev, the ninth month), memorializes the Jewish victory

Figure 18.5 Ḥanukkah oil lamp

over Hellenist oppressors in 168 BCE and the rededication of the Jerusalem Temple. The word "Ḥanukkah" means "dedication." According to a tradition found only in the Babylonian Talmud, the festival celebrates the miracle of a one-day's amount of oil miraculously burning in the Temple candelabrum for eight days until a new supply of undefiled oil could be brought.

According to the standard practice, one candle is lit on the first night of the festival, with an additional candle being lit each of the eight nights. Because of the association with oil lamps, it is common to serve foods that are fried in oil. Ashkenazic Jews eat potato pancakes, while Sephardic Jews eat donuts.

The Fifteenth of Shevat

In the Talmud, this date in mid-winter was designated a "new year for the trees" merely in order to identify the agricultural year to which a fruit crop belongs for purposes of tithing regulations. Gradually during the Middle Ages, it was identified as a joyous day on which penitential prayers should be omitted. The kabbalists, especially Rabbi Isaac Luria's circle in sixteenth-century Safed, found profound mystical symbolism in the fruits of the holy land; and eventually formulated special liturgies for eating fruit on the pattern of the Passover seder. With the rise of the Zionist movement, the fifteenth of Shevat was chosen as an appropriate occasion for expressing the deep connections between the people of Israel and their native soil, and for celebrating the virtues of agriculture and conservation. It has thus taken on the status of a minor holiday in its own right.

Modern days of commemoration

During the Middle Ages it was common for Jewish communities to institute local days of thanksgiving, usually to memorialize rescue from a dire threat of persecution. The turbulent historical events of the twentieth century led to the creation of three new commemorative days. These were not established by religious bodies, and they have not been universally accepted as religious holy days.

- *Yom ha-Sho'ah: Holocaust Remembrance Day.* This day originated in 1959 as a civic commemoration decreed by the State of Israel. The date was chosen to coincide with the anniversary of the Jewish uprising in the Warsaw Ghetto; however, because the event occurred on Passover, the commemoration was moved a week later. Reluctant to introduce a new holiday to the ritual calendar, some Jewish religious groups have preferred to acknowledge the Sho'ah on existing fast days.
- *Yom ha-Azma'ut: Israel's Independence Day* is celebrated on the 5th of Iyyar (late spring) on the anniversary of the signing of Israel's Declaration of Independence in 1948. Although primarily an Israeli national holiday, many Jewish communities and denominations celebrate it in a religious manner with the recitation of thanksgiving psalms and the relaxation of mourning customs that would otherwise be in force during the *"Omer"* season.
- *Yom Yerushalayim: Jerusalem Unification Day.* This is the anniversary of the reunification of Jerusalem in the 1967 Six-Day War. It is celebrated largely by politically right-wing religious groups in Israel who have elevated it to a status higher than that of Yom ha-Azma'ut.

Fast days

The characteristic way to commemorate tragedies and disasters is by means of fasts. A normal ("minor") fast involves refraining from food and drink during daylight hours, as well as reciting penitential prayers. The most serious fast requires more extensive self-denial, and extends through a complete day from evening until nightfall the next day (similar to Yom Kippur). In addition to the fast days that are fixed on the calendar, Jewish tradition allows for ad hoc fasting when a community is faced with a specific threat, such as drought or war; and individuals may take on fasts for appropriate religious reasons.

The traditional Jewish calendar includes a number of annual fasts that commemorate historical events related to the destruction of the first Temple. They include:

- *Tenth of Tevet* (in winter) marking the beginning of the siege of Jerusalem by the Babylonians.
- *Seventeenth of Tammuz* (in summer) marks the beginning of the destruction of the walls of Jerusalem.

- *Fast of Gedaliah ben Ahikam* (on the third of Tishri, the day following Rosh Hashanah) commemorating the assassination of the last Jewish governor of Judea after the Babylonian conquest.
- The major fast is the *Ninth of Av* (in summer), the anniversary of the destructions of the first and second Temples, as well as several other national catastrophes through history. It is a full twenty-four-hour fast, and also incorporates a variety of customs normally associated with individual mourning.

The three weeks between the seventeenth of Tammuz and the Ninth of Av are observed as a time of quasi-mourning, especially the last week or nine days.

A fast for firstborns is widely observed on the day before Passover in acknowledgment that the Hebrew firstborn children were saved from the plague that killed their Egyptian counterparts. This custom is first mentioned in a medieval work, and in standard practice it is usually superseded by partaking in a meal with a religious purpose (such as for the completion of the study of a talmudic work).

Another customary fast of obscure origin is the Fast of Esther, which evokes the biblical queen's three-day fast before approaching the king, as recounted in the biblical story. This fast is observed on the day preceding Purim.

Key points you need to know

- The standard Jewish calendar calculates months according to the phases of the moon, but periodically inserts a thirteenth month to synchronize with the solar year.
- The Sabbath, observed every Saturday, commemorates God's creation of the world and the freedom from slavery by refraining from acts of creative work, and through many special prayers and rituals.
- The three biblical pilgrimage holidays commemorate historical as well as seasonal events. As historical festivals, they recall the exodus from Egypt, the revelation of the Torah and the Israelites' wanderings in the desert. As agricultural festivals, they celebrate the springtime, the grain and fruit harvests, the ingathering of the crops and the approach of the rainy season.
- The Torah's "day of blowing trumpets" and the Day of Atonement were developed by Jewish tradition into a complex season of penitence. It is viewed as the time when humanity stands in judgment before God and we strive to improve ourselves in order to be forgiven.
- Throughout history, and until very recently, Jews have commemorated important historical events by declaring "minor holidays." Disasters have typically been observed as public fast days, in which people deny themselves physical pleasures and pray for divine compassion.

Discussion questions

1. What might the structure of the Jewish calendar indicate about the relationship of God to nature and to history?
2. What connection can you find between the Jewish Sabbath restrictions and the theme of liberation?
3. Compare the Torah's description of the main holidays (for example, in Leviticus Chapter 23) with the descriptions in the present section, and consider the extent of the impact of the oral tradition on the biblical sources.

Further reading

Agnon, Shmuel Yosef, *Days of Awe* New York: Schocken Books, 1975.

Domnitch, Larry, *Jewish Holidays through History*. Northvale, NJ: Jason Aronson, 1999.

Gaster, Theodor Herzl, *Festivals of the Jewish Year: A Modern Interpretation and Guide*. New York: W. Morrow, 1972.

Glatzer, Nahum Norbert, *The Passover Haggadah*, 3d rev. ed. New York: Schocken, 1979.

Goodman, Philip, *The Passover Anthology*, 1st pbk. ed, JPS Holiday Anthologies. Philadelphia, PA: Jewish Publication Society of America, 1993.

—— *The Shavuot Anthology*, 1st ed. Philadelphia, PA: Jewish Publication Society of America, 1974.

—— *The Sukkot and Simhat Torah Anthology*, 1st ed. Philadelphia, PA: Jewish Publication Society of America, 1973.

—— *The Purim Anthology*. Philadelphia, PA: Jewish Publication Society of America, 1973.

—— *The Yom Kippur Anthology*, 1st ed. Philadelphia, PA: Jewish Publication Society of America, 1971.

—— *The Rosh Hashanah Anthology*, 1st ed. Philadelphia, PA: Jewish Publication Society of America, 1970.

—— *The Purim Anthology*. Philadelphia, PA: Jewish Publication Society of America, 1960.

Greenberg, Irving, *The Jewish Way: Living the Holidays*, 1st Touchstone ed., Touchstone Books. New York: Simon & Schuster, 1993.

Harris, Monford, *Exodus and Exile: The Structure of the Jewish Holidays*. Minneapolis, MN: Fortress Press, 1992.

Heschel, Abraham Joshua, *The Sabbath: Its Meaning for Modern Man*, 1st Shambhala Library ed. Boston, MA: Shambhala, 2003.

Isaacs, Ronald H., *Sacred Seasons: A Sourcebook for the Jewish Holidays*. Northvale, NJ: Jason Aronson, 1997.

Pollack, Gloria Wiederkehr, *The Jewish Festivals in Ancient, Medieval and Modern Sources*. Brooklyn, NY: Sepher-Hermon Press, 1997.

Stern, Sacha, *Calendar and Community: A History of the Jewish Calendar, Second Century BCE–Tenth Century CE*. Oxford: Oxford University Press, 2001.

Segal, Eliezer, *Holidays, History and Halakhah*. Northvale, NJ and Jerusalem: Jason Aronson, 2000.

Strassfeld, Michael, Betsy Platkin Teutsch and Arnold M. Eisen, *The Jewish Holidays: A Guide and Commentary*, 1st HarperResource Quill pbk. ed., HarperResource Book. New York: Quill, 2001.

Rubenstein, Jeffrey L., *The History of Sukkot in the Second Temple and Rabbinic Periods*, Brown Judaic Studies. Atlanta, GA: Scholars Press, 1995.

Schauss, Hayyim, *Guide to Jewish Holy Days: History and Observance*. New York: Schocken, 1962.

Sperber, Daniel, *Why Jews Do What They Do: The History of Jewish Customs Throughout the Cycle of the Jewish Year*. Hoboken, NJ: KTAV, 1999.

19 Life cycle observances

In this chapter

This chapter describes some of the major laws and customs that accompany transitions between different stages of the life cycle, from birth through puberty, marriage, death and grieving.

Main topics covered

- Jewish life cycle events and rites of passage
- Birth: initiation into the covenant of Abraham
- Redemption of the firstborn
- Adulthood: bar mitzvah/bat mitzvah
- Marriage, wedding and family
- Death and mourning

Jewish life cycle events and rites of passage

Jewish tradition possesses rituals and observances that are performed on several of the transitional stages of life. It is questionable whether these observances fit the definition of "rites of passage" as understood by anthropologists. Each of them has its own history, rationales and status within the broader system of religious law. Their functions do not necessarily correspond to those of comparable rituals in other cultures. In particular, the Jewish perception of religious acts as divine commandments lends a distinctive context to its rituals. Nevertheless, the dubious category of "life cycle events" provides a convenient rubric under which to collect a diverse collection of Jewish religious practices.

Birth: initiation into the covenant of Abraham

Circumcision is designated in the Torah as the sign of the seal of Abraham's covenant with God, and is required of Abraham's male descendants. In Hebrew, the ritual is termed *berit milah* (covenant of circumcision). The person who performs the circumcision is known in Hebrew as a *mohel*. The Torah narrative describes in detail how Abraham performed the operation on himself and on the males of his household. Later, it was included among the commandments to be observed by the nation of Israel. As with most biblical rituals, scripture provided no explicit rationale for circumcision, leaving room for later exegetes to propose diverse interpretations. Some of the more influential explanations include:

- It represents the inter-generational continuity of the Jewish people.
- It diminishes the distractions of the sexual drive, thereby strengthening the spiritual or intellectual faculties.
- It is hygienic and prevents certain diseases. As with other health-based explanations for religious rituals, most recent authorities have discouraged attempts to reduce the practice to a medical procedure.

According to biblical law, the circumcision is to be performed on the eighth day after a boy's birth. In theory, the father is supposed to circumcise his own son, but this duty is usually delegated to a qualified *mohel*. Rabbinic interpretation held that the obligation overrides the restrictions of the Sabbath or festivals on which cutting and elective medical activities would normally be prohibited. Nevertheless, the circumcision is postponed if there are problems with the child's health on the eighth day, and it is not performed at all on hemophiliacs.

Circumcision is also a normal part of the conversion procedure for male proselytes to Judaism.

The Talmud ordains a poetic blessing to be recited at the circumcision, but has little else to say about the liturgical details of the ceremony. Later custom, especially in medieval France and Germany, elaborated the ceremony with numerous customs, many of which have gained widespread acceptance throughout the Jewish world. Some examples are:

- It is the occasion when the child is assigned his Hebrew name.
- Guests are honored by involving them in the ceremony, mostly by passing the baby to one another as he is carried in and out. In the prevalent custom, those participants are referred to as *kvaters* (for males) or *kvaterins* (females) from the German *gevater*.
- A special honor is assigned to the man who holds the baby during the circumcision. He is referred to as the *sandak*, probably from the Greek *suntekos* (companion) or syndikos (patron).
- The chair on which the sandak holds the baby is designated the "chair of Elijah," because of a legend that the biblical prophet of that name attends every circumcision.

There is no traditional ritual of comparable importance to commemorate the births of girls. In traditional communities, the father is called to the reading of the Torah shortly after the daughter's birth, and on that occasion, as blessings are recited for the health of mother and child, the newborn is given her name. In recent generations, attempts have been made to devise birth ceremonies for girls; but none has achieved widespread acceptance.

For the most part, male circumcision has remained one of the most widely observed Jewish rituals, even among individuals who are otherwise non-observant. To be sure, there have been exceptions to this pattern. Jewish Hellenists found it objectionable to tamper with the natural human form, especially in a culture that encouraged public nudity in the gymnasium. A radical Reform wing in nineteenth-century Frankfurt sought the abolition of circumcision as a primitive rite, and even sought to have it outlawed under secular law. In recent years, it has been challenged in various Jewish circles as a violation of the child's human rights.

Redemption of the firstborn

According to the biblical account, worship was originally supposed to be led by the firstborn males, but that duty was subsequently reassigned to the tribe of Levi. Therefore the Torah requires that the parents of firstborn boys (if they are not of priestly or Levitical descent) formally "redeem" the child by the symbolic payment of a quantity of silver to a priest (kohen). The ceremony should normally be performed when the child is thirty days old.

Adulthood: bar mitzvah/bat mitzvah

Talmudic law acknowledged various ages at which a person might be considered an adult, depending on the particular context. For most purposes, it was equated with the attainment of physical puberty. The rabbis estimated that females mature by the age of twelve years and one day, and males by thirteen years and one day, though ancient Jewish texts know of no ritual to mark this transition. From the perspective of traditional Judaism, the main significance of maturity is that the adult is personally responsible for observing the religious commandments. For this reason, it is common to refer to a Jewish adult as a *bar mitzvah* (male) or *bat mitzvah* (female), meaning: one who is subject to the commandments.

The earliest known reference to holding a festive meal to celebrate a youth's reaching maturity is from the early thirteenth century. Eventually, especially in Ashkenazic communities, a set of practices was devised to give ritual expressions to the occasion. In general, the observances involve the public performance of liturgical functions that they could not perform while they were still children. These included:

- the first wearing of *t'fillin* (phylacteries). Originally, this was not associated with a particular age, but simply when the child was capable of keeping his body clean.
- the first time that the youth is called to participate in the formal reading of the Torah in the synagogue.
- the recitation of a special blessing by the parents to God for releasing them from responsibility for the child's offenses.
- it is also common for the youth to deliver a discourse on a religious topic that demonstrates his learning.

Insofar as the celebration of the child's assumption of adulthood largely involves a public exhibition of scholarly and liturgical skills, it is understandable that pre-modern Jewish practice produced no equivalent observances to mark a young woman's coming of age, because even adult women were excluded from such roles

Figure 19.1 Bar mitzvah

as leading worship and Torah study. By the twentieth century, as participation of women in the general culture and economy expanded into new domains, and as the male *bar mitzvah* celebration achieved greater prominence in the American synagogue, there was a perceptible demand to introduce similar ceremonies for young women. This occurred first in non-Orthodox denominations. In 1922, Mordecai M. Kaplan, founder of the Reconstructionist movement, held a bat mitzvah ceremony for his daughter Judith. Such ceremonies quickly became common in liberal Jewish communities (even though such movements often denied the concept of *mitzvah* in its basic sense of "commandment"). To the extent that those movements advocate egalitarian assignment of synagogue roles, there is no particular problem in observing similar ceremonies for bar mitzvah and bat mitzvah; though there has been some reluctance to accept the traditional age of twelve years, an age that modern society clearly classifies as childhood. Many modern Orthodox communities have also adopted some sort of ceremony for young women, involving religious activities that fit within the patterns of the traditionalist division of sex roles. Much of the traditionalist resistance to such a practice stems from its association with the non-Orthodox.

Objecting to the traditional view that a Jewish child reached religious adulthood at the age of twelve or thirteen, the early Reformers instituted a ceremony at a later age, modeled after the Christian Confirmation. The ceremony was often marked by a catechism-like statement of beliefs presented in a question-and-answer format.

Marriage, wedding and family

Virtually all forms of Judaism have regarded marriage and procreation as basic expectations of religious life. Though Josephus reported that the Essenes did not marry, he did not ascribe that policy to an idealization of celibacy or to a condemnation of sexuality, but rather to their suspicion of women as seductresses (hence the Essenes did not accept even celibate women to their community). Even Jewish philosophical or moralistic schools that espoused dualistic views about the conflict between body and spirit did not infer from this that celibate or monastic life was a superior path to spirituality. The normative Jewish attitude held that purity and holiness can only be achieved by people who have a sanctioned outlet for their sexual urges; otherwise the minds and spirits will be confounded by constant distractions and unholy thoughts. The kabbalists teach that marital sex is a mystical act in which humans emulate the harmonizing unity of the celestial spheres.

Jewish marriage according to both biblical and rabbinic law was polygynous; that is, a husband could have several wives, though a woman could be married to only one husband. Adultery is a grave crime, and is defined as having sexual relations with a married woman.

Though talmudic texts deal at length with complications resulting from polygamous relationships, there are few known examples of actual polygamous marriages during the talmudic era. By the tenth century, Ashkenazic Jewry issued an enactment, ascribed to Rabbi Gershom ben Judah, officially prohibiting polygamy, and this enactment has been universally accepted by the Jewish communities in Christian lands. In Muslim countries, on the other hand, where the majority culture practices polygamy, the Jews also continued to do so. Most of the Arab Jewish communities were expelled in the mid-twentieth century and relocated to western societies, especially the state of Israel, where polygamy is outlawed.

Betrothal and wedding

In ancient Judaism, as codified in rabbinic law, a marriage was preceded by a stage of betrothal (known in Hebrew as *kiddushin* or *erusin*) that was a fully binding relationship in terms of civil, criminal and ritual law. The betrothal could only be terminated by a formal divorce, and infidelity during the betrothal was considered adultery and subject to capital punishment. Nevertheless, the couple were not usually living together as man and wife. In order to avoid the grave legal complications that can result from suspicions of infidelity during this period (normally one year, in order to allow the bride time to assemble her trousseau), most communities have in effect eliminated the betrothal period by postponing the formalities until immediately before the wedding ceremony. The betrothal goes into effect when the groom transfers to the bride an object of some value. In theory, the object can be a small coin, but it is common to use a ring for this purpose. In addition to its legal significance in defining the new relationship between husband and wife, the betrothal is a religious ceremony sanctified by blessings.

The wedding ceremony itself is held under a canopy—known in Hebrew as *huppah*. In ancient sources, this term probably referred to the actual entry of the couple into their new home. Now the canopy is a symbolic ritual item, often a piece of cloth attached to four posts that are held up by guests who are being honored. Seven blessings (Hebrew: *sheva berakhot*) are recited over cups of wine at the wedding, and repeated at wedding festivities throughout the following week. The ancient rabbis ordained that a prenuptial marriage contract (*ketubbah*) must be given to the bride. It defines the mutual obligations of the couple, and guarantees support for the wife upon termination of the marriage, whether through divorce or death.

Figure 19.2 An illuminated *ketubbah*

Divorce

The Torah (Deuteronomy 24:1–4) briefly mentions a procedure for divorce. As understood by the rabbis, it must formally be contracted through the conveying of a proper document of divorce (*get*) by the husband to the wife. Early interpreters disagreed about what is considered a legitimate cause for divorce, and the accepted view is that any dissatisfaction may serve as an acceptable justification. In spite of the formal requirement that the husband must be the one to grant the divorce, in practice the court has the authority to compel the husband to so following a request by the wife.

Death and mourning

Ancient Jewish tradition evolved an elaborate sequence of practices to deal with disposal of a corpse and with the various stages of grieving. The subsequent evolution of mourning practices combined theological factors, local customs, influences from the surrounding cultures and the psychological needs of the mourners.

In keeping with the normative Jewish belief in an eventual physical resurrection, Jewish tradition requires that dead bodies be buried if at all possible. Cremation is forbidden, as is embalming. Talmudic sources speak of a two-stage process. First, the corpse was given a temporary burial for a year to allow the flesh to decay. Then the bones were placed in a chest (ossuary) that was usually interred permanently in a family cave. This practice fell into disuse with the decline of Jewish settlement in Judea, and all communities now practice straightforward burial in the earth. It is preferable to hold the funeral as soon as possible after the death unless there is a compelling reason for a delay.

Participation in a funeral is considered an especially pious act, because the beneficiary will not be able to reciprocate the kindness. It is common for Jewish communities to maintain a voluntary burial society (often known as a *hevra kaddisha*, holy association) to deal with the cleansing of the corpse (*taharah*, "purification"), the arrangements for the burial, and the various ritual requirements. The corpse is covered in a simple white linen shroud. Customs differ with respect to the use of caskets. People attending the funeral are expected to participate personally in covering the corpse with earth.

Mourners are required to tear their garments upon hearing of the death of a close relative, a teacher, community leader or another person for whom mourning is required. The community offers consolation to the mourners. The standard formula for this is: "May the Almighty comfort you among all the mourners for Zion and Jerusalem."

Jewish law recognizes a sequence of phases of mourning, gradually diminishing in the intensity of the grief and of the corresponding restrictions:

1. *From death until the burial* (*aninut*): at this point the mourners are expected to be entirely concerned with arranging the burial. As such, they are exempted from the performance of normal religious obligations including prayer.
2. *First seven days* (*shivah*): following the funeral, the mourners spend a week in their own homes, removed from normal responsibilities, as they are cared for by others. In particular, the first meal they eat upon returning from the cemetery should be prepared by friends or neighbors; and the normal religious services are conducted in the house of mourning rather than in the synagogue. Throughout the week, visitors come to offer consolation and support. In antiquity the mourners would usually sit on inverted beds; though it is now more common to sit on low stools or chairs. Shoes are not worn and activities that focus on one's appearance are avoided.

   Widespread customs observed during the shivah include: lighting of lamps, symbolizing the human soul; eating eggs, symbolizing the cyclic character of life and death; mirrors are covered.
3. *First month* (*sheloshim*): following the conclusion of the *shivah* week, the mourner resumes normal daily life while continuing some of the mourning practices, such as refraining joyful gatherings, shaving or haircuts.
4. *First year*: for the entire first year after the death of a close relative, the mourner continues to avoid public displays of joy.

Apart from the obligatory practices set down in the Bible and Talmud, diverse mourning customs have been introduced through history, especially in medieval Europe communities. These include:

Recitation of Kaddish

The Kaddish is a prayer affirming one's faith in God that is recited between portions of the liturgy and has no intrinsic connection to death or mourning. An apocryphal legend that was in circulation in medieval Europe told about a deceased man whose torments in the next world could be lessened if his son led the communal recitation of the Kaddish. Based on the tradition that the otherworldly punishment extends for up to a year, the custom arose of mourners reciting Kaddish on behalf of their close relations through the year following the death. Because it would be inappropriate to suggest that one's parents were deserving of the maximum penalty, one ceases reciting the mourner's Kaddish after eleven months.

Yahrtzeit: the anniversary of the death

This popular custom was likely copied from Christian precedents. The anniversary of the death is observed by the mourners, usually through the lighting of a twenty-four-hour candle and recitation of Kaddish. Some Hasidic communities treat it as a happy occasion on which the virtues of the deceased are recalled.

Yizkor: holiday memorial prayers

In the Ashkenazic rite, special prayers in memory of the dead are incorporated into the synagogue services on several festivals, including the Day of Atonement. The Hebrew name is taken from the opening words "May God remember…" The Yizkor service includes both communal prayers and an opportunity for individual worshippers to memorialize their own loved ones.

Key points you need to know

- The Torah commands that Jewish boys be ritually circumcised on the eighth day of their lives as an indication of the covenant of Abraham.
- A "redemption" ceremony is often held in which a month-old boy is acquired from a kohen (priest).
- The ritual commemoration of a youth's achieving religious adulthood (bat / bar mitzvah) at the age of twelve / thirteen is a relatively recent development that has become very popular in America.
- Judaism strongly encourages marriage and family life. Marriage is defined by precise legal parameters, and the wedding is an elaborate ceremony.
- Traditional Judaism requires burial of a corpse. The mourning practices reflect a psychological sensitivity to the gradual easing of the grief from the moment of the death.

Discussion questions

1. Which of the "life cycle" rituals described in this chapter can be properly considered "rites of passage" in the anthropological sense of marking a change in a person's social or sexual status?
2. Discuss the differing positions of men and women as reflected in selected Jewish life cycle ceremonies.
3. In what ways do theological beliefs about the afterlife influence the Jewish practices related to death and mourning?

Further reading

The Jewish life cycle

Cardin, Nina Beth, *The Tapestry of Jewish Time: A Spiritual Guide to Holidays and Life-Cycle Events*. Springfield, NJ: Behrman House, 2000.

Donin, Hayim, *To Be a Jew: A Guide to Jewish Observance in Contemporary Life*. New York: Basic Books, 1991.

Fine, Lawrence, ed., *Judaism in Practice: From the Middle Ages through the Early Modern Period*, Princeton Readings in Religions. Princeton, NJ: Princeton University Press, 2001.

Geffen, Rela M., *Celebration and Renewal: Rites of Passage in Judaism*. Philadelphia, PA: Jewish Publication Society, 1993.

Goldberg, Harvey E., *Jewish Passages: Cycles of Jewish Life*. Berkeley, CA: University of California Press, 2003.

Goldman, Ari L., *Being Jewish: The Spiritual and Cultural Practice of Judaism Today*. New York: Simon & Schuster, 2000.

Gutmann, Joseph, *The Jewish Life Cycle*. Leiden: E. J. Brill, 1987.

Isaacs, Ronald H., *Rites of Passage: A Guide to the Jewish Life Cycle*. Hoboken, NJ: KTAV, 1992.

Marcus, Ivan G., *The Jewish Life Cycle: Rites of Passage from Biblical to Modern Times*, The Samuel and Althea Stroum Lectures in Jewish Studies. Seattle, WA: University of Washington Press, 2004.

Pollack, Herman, *Jewish Folkways in Germanic Lands (1648–1806); Studies in Aspects of Daily Life*. Cambridge, MA: MIT Press, 1971.

Vainstein, J., *The Cycle of Jewish Life: A Summary of Basic Laws and Customs from Judaism's Traditional Sources*. Jerusalem: Eliner Library, Dept. for Torah Education and Culture in the Diaspora of the World Zionist Organization, 1990.

Weinberg, Fred, *The Jewish Life Cycle: Illustrated with Selected Ceremonial Objects from the Beth Tzedec Museum and Private Collections*. Toronto: Koffler Gallery, 1984.

Birth

Cohen, Shaye J. D., *Why Aren't Jewish Women Circumcised? Gender and Covenant in Judaism*. Berkeley, CA: University of California Press, 2005.

Hoffman, Lawrence A., *Covenant of Blood: Circumcision and Gender in Rabbinic Judaism*, Chicago Studies in the History of Judaism. Chicago, IL: University of Chicago Press, 1996.

Mark, Elizabeth Wyner, *The Covenant of Circumcision: New Perspectives on an Ancient Jewish Rite*, Brandeis Series on Jewish Women. Hanover, NH: Brandeis University Press, 2003.

Silverman, Eric Kline, *From Abraham to America: A History of Jewish Circumcision*. Lanham, MD: Rowman & Littlefield Publishers, 2006.

Weddings

Bar'am-Ben Yossef, Noam, *Brides and Betrothals: Jewish Wedding Rituals in Afghanistan*. Jerusalem: The Israel Museum, 1998.

Grossman, Grace Cohen, *Romance and Ritual: Celebrating the Jewish Wedding*. Los Angeles, CA: Skirball Cultural Center, 2001.

Olitzky, Kerry M., *The Jewish Wedding Ceremony*. Hoboken, NJ: KTAV, 1996.

Death and mourning

Deitsch, Elka, *From This World to the Next: Jewish Approaches to Illness, Death and the Afterlife*. New York: Jewish Theological Seminary of America, The Library, 1999.

Glick, Shmuel, *Light and Consolation: The Development of Jewish Consolation Practices*. Jerusalem: The Ori Foundation and the Schocken Institute for Jewish Research of The Jewish Theological Seminary of America, 2004.

Goldberg, Hayim Binyamin ben B. P., Shlomo Fox-Asheri and Meir Zlotowitz, *Mourning in Halacha: The Laws and Customs of the Year of Mourning*, 1st ed., Artscroll Halachah Series. Brooklyn, NY: Mesorah Publications, 1991.

Goldberg, Sylvie Anne, *Crossing the Jabbok: Illness and Death in Ashkenazi Judaism in Sixteenth- through Nineteenth-Century Prague*, Contraversions. Berkeley, CA: University of California Press, 1996.

Hachlili, Rachel, *Jewish Funerary Customs, Practices and Rites in the Second Temple Period*, Supplements to the Journal for the Study of Judaism. Leiden and Boston, MA: E. J. Brill, 2005.

Kraemer, David Charles, *The Meanings of Death in Rabbinic Judaism*. London and New York: Routledge, 2000.

Kolatch, Alfred J., *The Jewish Mourner's Book of Why*. Middle Village, NY: J. David, 1996.

Lamm, Maurice, *The Jewish Way in Death and Mourning*. New York: J. David, 1969.

Rabinowicz, Harry M., *A Guide to Life: Jewish Laws and Customs of Mourning*, 2nd ed. London: Jewish Chronicle Publications, 1969. Riemer, Jack, *Wrestling with the Angel: Jewish Insights on Death and Mourning*. New York: Schocken, 1995.

Weiss, Abner, *Death and Bereavement: A Halakhic Guide*. New York: Union of Orthodox Jewish Congregations of America, 1991.

Wieseltier, Leon, *Kaddish*. London: Picador, 1998.

Appendix 1

Guide to pronunciation and transliteration

The language of most Jewish religious discourse is Hebrew, which has a different phonetic structure from European languages. Many words from Hebrew, especially proper names, have become part of English through the medium of the standard Bible translations (notably the "King James" version (KJB)). Even among Jews, differing traditions have evolved of how to pronounce certain elements in the language. Thus, even a precise phonetic transliteration system, replete with exotic-looking diacritic marks, would not guarantee a "correct" or authentic pronunciation for readers who are unfamiliar with Hebrew in the first place. For this reason, I have abandoned any hope of applying scholarly transliteration standards in a work that is, after all, an introductory textbook for an English-speaking audience.

The following are the "rules" that were applied to the rendering of Hebrew words in this book.

- Names that appear in the Hebrew Bible were presented as they appear in the King James editions, without diacritical signs. Most of these names have acquired familiar pronunciations in English that are, in fact, quite different from the way they were spoken in Hebrew, or in English at the time the translation was originally prepared. Several of the familiar English versions of biblical names are based on the Greek, which did not have letters to represent certain Hebrew sounds that can be represented in English (notably: *sh* and *h*). Some English Bible editions indicate accents and vowel lengths for transliterated words, but that information is not included in this book.

- For most other Hebrew words, I have taken as my model the *Encyclopaedia Judaica* (*EJ*), whose editors devised a usable compromise between philological precision and usability. In general, this system includes English equivalents for the consonants and the basic vowels, with the exception of vowel lengths, accents and certain other features. The recently published second edition of the *EJ*[1] is considerably

---

1   Berenbaum, Michael and Fred Skolnik, *Encyclopaedia Judaica*, 2nd ed. 12 vols. Detroit, MI: Macmillan Reference USA in association with the Keter Publishing House, 2007.

less consistent on these points, and evidently did not impose consistency on the authors or section editors. At any rate, seeing as it will likely remain the standard reference work on Judaism for several years to come, I have chosen to use it as my guide on most matters of transliteration.

- Ashkenazic Jews pronounce several of these Hebrew consonants and vowels in ways that differ from the descriptions provided here, and those variants are in some cases more familiar to English-speaking readers. For example, "kosher" is more familiar than "kasher," or "bris" (covenant of circumcision) than "berit." I have nevertheless followed the *EJ* standards, even in cases where this produces anomalies (for example, Rabbi Moses Schreiber would likely have referred to himself as *Chassam Soyfer*, and not "Hatam Sofer" as in this book).
- Hebrew has no upper-case (capital) and lower-case forms. The use of upper- and lower-case forms in transliterated words reflects the conventions of English grammar.

The following are some specific comments about the pronunciation of translated Hebrew.

- *Word accents (stress)*: as indicated, these are not indicated here. However, most words have their accents on the final syllable. The others are accented on the penultimate syllable. The accent can never be before that.
- *Vowels*: The English letters used to indicate vowels should be pronounced according to their "short" versions; though as in English, this does not necessarily reflect their actual length. Thus, *a* is as in "man"; *e* as in "bed"; *i* as in "fit"; *o* as in "for"; *u* as in "jug."
- *Vowel length*: biblical Hebrew grammar distinguishes between long, short and clipped vowels; though the differences between long and short have not been maintained by most Jewish communities. The distinction between "clipped" and normal vowels is, however, maintained; though it is not indicated in the transliterations employed in this book. More technical works would convey that information through the use of superscripts or apostrophes.
- *alef and ayin*: classical Hebrew, like other languages in the Semitic family, maintains a clear distinction between two consonants that have no clear equivalents in English. The *alef* is a glottal stop (or simply not pronounced) at the beginning of a word, or between two vowels. The *ayin* is a guttural sound pronounced from the back of the throat. The *ayin* is not pronounced by most Ashkenazic Jews, though it is in most other traditions. Following the rather inconsistent practice of the *EJ*, the two sounds are not distinguished here. When they appear at the beginning of a word (always followed by a vowel), no special sign is provided. When they appear between two vowels, they may or may not be indicated by an apostrophe (depending on the usage in the *EJ*). On a very few occasions, the *ayin* is represented as a reverse apostrophe (= opening single quotation mark) [ʻ].

- *Doubled consonants*: doubled consonants are usually indicated in vocalized Hebrew by a dot inside the letter. Ashkenazic and spoken Israeli dialects are quite lax about pronouncing the doubling, and this is reflected in inconsistencies in the *EJ* transliterations used here.
- *Hard and soft consonants*: certain classical Hebrew consonants were pronounced in either vocalized or non-vocalized (or hard or soft) variations, depending on where they appear in the word or phrase. These include *b* (vocalized as *v*); *d* (vocalized as a soft *th* sound, as in "the"); *g* (probably softened to a *j* sound); *k* (softened as *kh* as in a Germanic or Scottish "ch"); *p* (*f*); and t (a hard *th* as in "thud"). Although all these variations are still part of the formal grammar, standard modern Hebrew pronunciaiton only maintains the distinctions with respect to *b*, *k* and *p*. The KJB translation indicated the soft or vocalized forms only through diacritical signs that are not usually reproduced. Similarly, technical transliterations indicate the distinctions through the use of diacriticals or an added "h."

  Following the *EJ* convention, based on modern Israeli pronunciation, soft *b* is usually printed here as *v*; soft *k* as *kh*, and soft *p* as *f*. There are some exceptions based on the usages in the KJB (e.g. "Hop*h*ni") or the *EJ* (e.g., "Merka*b*ah" rather than "Merkavah").
- *b and v*: Hebrew has two phonetically unrelated *v* sounds, one related to the *b* and one to the *w*. Both are rendered here simply as *v*.
- *h at end of word*: as in English, Hebrew often indicates a vowel at the end of a word with an "h" that is not actually pronounced. On rare occasions, however, it is intended to be pronounced. Vocalized Hebrew has ways of indicating the difference, but it is not reflected in my transliterations. On such occasions, assume that the "h" should not be pronounced.
- *ḥet* (Ḥ, ḥ): Hebrew has a guttural sound for which no equivalent exists in English, and is usually pronounced as an aspirated "h." This sound, indicated by the Hebrew letter ḥ, may be indicated in biblical names (which the KJB transliterated from the Greek) as either an "h" or a "ch," reflecting an older dialect of Hebrew that distinguished (as Arabic still does) between hard and soft variants of the letter. The *EJ* is inconsistent when it comes to rendering it sometimes as *ḥ* and sometimes as *h*.
- *t*: Hebrew has two different letters (*tet* and *tav*) that are equivalent to the English "t." In classical Hebrew, the "tet" is pronounced more emphatically (as in Arabic), and technical English transliterations indicate it with a diacritical dot underneath it. The distinction is not rendered at all in this book.

Appendix 2

Timeline of the history of Judaism

BCE	c. 1900	1600	Patriarchal era
	c. 1725	c. 1250	Exodus
	c. 1250	c. 1200	Conquest of Canaan, Joshua
	c. 1020	c. 922	United monarchy
	c. 922		Divided monarchy
	722		Assyrians destroy northern kingdom
	587–586		Babylonians destroy Jerusalem and First Temple, exile Judeans
	538		Edict of Cyrus permits Judeans to return to Jerusalem
	515		Completion of Second Temple
	c. 450	c. 440	Return to Zion under Ezra and Nehemiah
	175	167	Hellenistic decrees provoke Hasmonean revolt
	c. 310		Beginning of Hellenistic era
	164	63	Hasmonean era
	63		Beginning of Roman rule
CE	c. 50	c. 220	Tannaitic era
	66		Beginning of Great Revolt
	70		Destruction of Second Temple
	132	135	Bar Kokhba uprising
	c. 210		Completion of Mishnah
	c. 210	c. 500	Amoraic era
CE	c. 450		Completion of Jerusalem Talmud
	c. 550	c. 700	Savoraic era
	c. 600		Completion of Babylonian Talmud
	c. 700	c. 1250	Era of Geonim
	882	942	Saadiah Gaon
	c. 765		Rise of Karaism
	c. 912	1090	Golden Age of Spanish Jewry
	1096		Massacre of Rhineland communities in Crusades

1041	1105	Rashi
1135	1204	Maimonides
c. 1174		Publication of the *Bahir*
c. 1270		Publication of the *Zohar*
1391		Forced conversions of Jews in Castile and Aragon, creation of Conversos
1492		Expulsion of Jews from Spain
1488	1575	Joseph Caro, author of *Shulhan 'Arukh*
1534	1572	Isaac Luria
1626	1676	Shabbetai Zevi
1700	1760	Israel Ba'al Shem Tov
1726	1791	Jacob Frank
c. 1780		Beginning of Enlightenment
c. 1800	c. 1840	First (lay) phase of German Reform
1729	1786	Moses Mendelssohn
1794	1886	Leopold Zunz
1807		Napoleon's "Sanhedrin"
1845		Zacharias Frankel secedes from Reform movement, establishes Positive-Historical school
1865	1935	Abraham Isaac Kook
1881	1983	Mordecai Kaplan, founder of Reconstructionism
1808	1888	Samson Raphael Hirsch
1884	1846	Reform synods
1897		Theodor Hertzl convenes First Zionist Congress
1885		Pittsburgh Platform of American Reform movement
1902		Establishment of Jewish Theological Seminary in New York under leadership of Solomon Schechter
1942	1945	Nazis' systematic murder of European Jews
1948		Establishment of State of Israel
1967		Six-Day War
1983		American Conservative Judaism allows ordination of female rabbis
1983		Reform movement adopts policy of identifying Jews by patrilineal descent.
1983		Jewish Theological Seminary agrees to ordain women as rabbis

CE

Glossary

Account of creation: An esoteric tradition of expounding the biblical creation story. The Mishnah forbids teaching this publicly.

Account of the chariot: An esoteric tradition of expounding Ezekiel's vision of a chariot composed of angelic beings. The Mishnah forbade public dissemination of this mystical discipline.

Aggadah (English adjective: aggadic): The component of the oral tradition that is not concerned with the technical study of religious law. It consists largely of homiletical expositions of the Bible.

Agudat Israel: An association representing the interests of traditionalist Orthodox ("haredi") groups.

Agunah: An "anchored woman"; one who is unable to remarry because she cannot obtain a divorce from her first husband, or because his death cannot be satisfactorily established.

Amidah: "The standing (prayer)" another name for the Eighteen Benedictions, which is recited while standing.

Amora: A rabbi from the third to fifth centuries, whose views are cited in the Talmud or contemporary rabbinic works.

Aninut: The initial and most intense stage of grieving, from the moment of the death until the burial.

Apocalypse: A popular genre of ancient Jewish literature, especially during the Roman era, in which the hero, usually a figure from the Bible, receives a graphically symbolic vision of a catastrophic future when God will overthrow the forces of evil and institute his kingdom on earth.

Apocrypha: Works that were included in the Greek corpus of Jewish scriptures, but not in the Hebrew Bible,

Aramaic: A Semitic language similar to Hebrew that was spoken by Jews from the Second Temple era, especially in the Galilee and Babylonia.

Aravah: Willow, one of the "four species" that is carried during the rituals on the feast of Tabernacles (Sukkot).

Ashkenaz: The Hebrew name for Germany, used to refer to Jewish communities that originated in central Europe, or to the Jews of Christian Europe in general.

'Asiyyah: Hebrew: "action"—the last of the four worlds according to kabbalistic teaching, the one that converges with the physical world.

Attributes of action: In the thought of Maimonides, these are descriptions of God that are to be understood metaphorically, as analogous to the frame of mind that would have produced a certain result if a similar effect has been produced by a human being.

Avot/Pirkei Avot: A tractate in the Mishnah consisting of adages and other non-halakhic traditions. It opens by describing the sequence of transmitting the Torah from Moses via the "fathers of the world" until their own time.

Azilut: Hebrew: "emanation"—the highest of the four planes of reality according to the Kabbalah.

Ba'al Shem: "Master of the name"—a practitioner of magic and healing by means of the kabbalistic manipulation of the names of God.

Bad urge: In rabbinic homilies, the aspect of the human personality that seduces people to sin. It is equated with the sexual urge, and therefore is essential for human survival.

Bahir: The earliest known document containing the teachings of the Kabbalah, the symbolism of the ten sefirot. It first appeared in the twelfth century in Provence, and takes the form of a pseudepigraphic rabbinic midrashic exposition whose main protagonist is Rabbi Nehunya ben ha-Kanah.

Bar Kokhba, Simeon: Leader of a failed Jewish revolt against Rome between 132 and 135 CE. Rabbi Akiva and others believed he was the messiah.

Bar mitzvah: "Subject to the commandments"—a Jewish male who has reached the age when he is legally responsible under Jewish religious law; equated with the attainment of puberty, which is assumed to have occurred by the age of thirteen years and one day.

Bat mitzvah: "Subject to the commandments"—a Jewish female who has reached the age when she is legally responsible under Jewish religious law; equated with the attainment of puberty, which is assumed to have occurred by the age of twelve years and one day.

Beit keneset\be kenishta: "House of assembly," the Hebrew and Aramaic terms for synagogue.

Beit Ya'akov: A network of Orthodox schools for girls founded by Sara Schnirer in 1917.

Berakhah: A blessing, a liturgical formula beginning "Blessed are you, God…"

Beri'ah: Hebrew: "creation"—the second of the four planes of reality according to the Kabbalah; the realm of the highest angels.

Berit milah: "The covenant of circumcision," the ritual circumcision performed on Jewish males, usually on the eighth day of their lives; or as part of a religious conversion procedure.

Bi'ur: A commentary and German translation of the Bible (in Hebrew letters) by Moses Mendelssohn.

Bimah: The elevated platform of a synagogue, used principally for the reading of the Torah.

B'nei Akiva: The youth movement of the Mizrachi religious Zionist movement.

Breaking of the Vessels: In the kabbalistic teachings of Rabbi Isaac Luria, the myth that explains the origins of evil in the universe, caused when the vessels created by God to receive the divine light were unable to contain it and shattered, leaving a mixture of holy sparks and evil shards.

Cairo Genizah: A repository for discarded documents in a synagogue in Fustat (Cairo), Egypt that preserved hundreds of thousands of texts from the early medieval era, and is a key resource for the study of Jewish society, literature and religion.

Canaan: The name for the land of Israel prior to its conquest by Joshua.

Canaanites: The peoples who inhabited the land of Israel prior to its conquest by the Israelites.

Central Conference of American Rabbis: The association of rabbis affiliated with the American Reform movement.

Chair of Elijah: A chair that is customarily set aside for the biblical prophet Elijah at circumcision ceremonies.

Chariot mysticism: See "account of the chariot."

Children of darkness: Those who do not follow God's ways, according to the teachings of the Qumran documents.

Children of light: Those who faithfully follow God's true law, according to the teachings of the Qumran documents.

Columbus Platform: A policy statement issued by American Reform Judaism in 1937, expressing more traditional positions on certain issues

Committee on Law and Standards: The body of Conservative Judaism that makes policy decisions on major questions of Jewish religious law.

Conservative movement: The American incarnation of Positive-Historical Judaism, espousing an approach that tries to accommodate modern values within the structures of traditional Jewish law.

Conversos: Jews who converted to Christianity under compulsion during the time of the Spanish Inquisition.

Council of Torah Sages: An assembly of rabbis who have supreme authority over decisions of the Agudat Israel movement.

Covenant: In Jewish belief, a mutual agreement that defines the relationship between God and the people of Israel. Hebrew: *Berit*.

Daniel: A book included in the *Ketuvim* section of the Bible, purporting to tell the story of the eponymous hero, a Jew who lived during the Babylonian exile and was able to interpret apocalyptic visions of the future.

Day of Atonement: Annual holy day designated by the Torah for forgiveness and atonement of sins. It falls on the tenth day of the seventh month, Tishri, and is observed through fasting and prayer.

Dead Sea scrolls: A library of ancient Jewish texts written during the Second Temple era discovered in caves near Khirbet Qumran in the Judean desert.

Derash: Interpretations that follow the methods of rabbinic midrash.

Devekut: "Cleaving"—the Hasidic ideal of maintaining uninterrupted consciousness of God, especially during prayer.

Diaspora: The Jewish communities scattered outside the land of Israel.

Divided Monarchy: In biblical history, the era during which Israel was divided into two states: the northern ten tribes of Israel, and the southern kingdom of Judah.

Doenmeh: A sect of adherents of Shabbetai Zevi, they accepted Islam while secretly maintaining their faith in Shabbetai Zevi's eventual reappearance.

Eighteen Benedictions: The central prayer of the rabbinic liturgy, whose original structure consisted of a sequence of eighteen blessings (*berakhot*) of praise, petition and thanksgiving. The current version contains nineteen blessings.

Ein-Sof: Hebrew: "The Infinite"—in the Kabbalah, the most exalted level of the godhead, entirely beyond the grasp of human understanding.

Emancipation: The extending of citizenship and civil rights to Jews in modern societies.

Enlightenment: The movement calling for adapting Jewish culture and religion so as to facilitate participation in modern society.

Epicurean: In rabbinic terminology, the most common designation for a heretic, presumably referring to the Greek philosopher Epicurus who denied God's active involvement with the created world.

Erez Yisra'el: Hebrew: "the land of Israel"—the historic Jewish homeland.

Erusin: Hebrew: "betrothal"—a formal stage in the Jewish marriage process, in which the couple are legally bound to one another but do not yet live together.

Essenes: A Second Temple Jewish movement that removed itself from Jerusalem and inhabited separate communities where they observed their distinctive standards of piety and purity. Most scholars identify them as the authors of the Dead Sea scrolls from Qumran.

Etrog: A citron; the "fruit of a goodly tree" that is included among the "four species" used in the rituals of the feast of Tabernacles.

Exodus: The second book of the Torah, describing the enslavement of the Hebrews in Egypt, their miraculous liberation (exodus) by God, and the receiving of the Torah at Mount Sinai.

Ez Ḥayyim: The kabbalistic compendium by Rabbi Hayyim Vital containing his version of the teachings of Rabbi Isaac Luria.

Ezra-Nehemiah: A book in the *Ketuvim* section of the Hebrew Bible (now usually divided into two books) that describes the return of the Jews to Jerusalem following the Babylonian exile.

Fifteenth of Shevat: A date in the winter used for measuring the ages of fruit trees for purposes of various agricultural regulations. Mainly among the kabbalists and Zionists it has taken on the status of a holiday celebrating the land of Israel and its produce.

Four species: Plants that are carried in ritual processions on the feast of Tabernacles as commanded in the Torah. Rabbinic tradition identifies the species as: date-palm frond (*lulav*); citron (*etrog*); myrtle branches (*hadas*); willow branches (*aravah*).

Gaon (plural: *Geonim*; English adjective: geonic):   From a Hebrew word meaning "pride"; the title given to the heads of talmudic academies, especially in Babylonia, after the talmudic era.

Galilee: The northern district of the land of Israel. It became the center of Jewish religious and communal life in the second century CE following the decline of Judea.

Garden of Eden: The paradise in which the first man and woman were place until they were banished for their disobedience. In traditional Jewish thought, the term is used to designate the abode of the righteous in the afterlife. Hebrew: "Gan Eden."

Gehinnom: A notorious and cursed site of heathen child sacrifice in biblical times, it later became identified with the place where sinners suffer torments in the afterlife.

Genesis Rabbah: A work of aggadic midrash on the book of Genesis.

Genizah: A repository for discarded sacred texts, which according to Jewish law may not be actively destroyed.

German pietism: Hebrew: "*Hasidut Ashkenaz*"; an influential mystical and moralistic ideology that arose in the Rhineland in the twelfth and thirteenth centuries.

Get: A Jewish bill of divorce.

Gezerah shavah: A method of midrashic exegesis in which analogies are drawn based on the appearance of a similar expression in two biblical passages.

Ghetto: A neighborhood in which Jews were forced to live. The term was probably taken from the restricted Jewish quarter of Venice, established in 1516, that was situated near a foundry (ghetto).

Gilgul: Reincarnation or metempsychosis into a different body in the next life, according to the doctrines of the Kabbalah.

Gog and Magog, war of: A catastrophic war described in the book of Ezekiel (Chapters 38–39) in his vision of the end of days. This war became a standard component of Jewish eschatology.

Golah or *galut*: Exile, the state of removal from the homeland as punishment for sins.

Golden Age of Spanish Jewry: A blossoming of Jewish cultural and religious creativity in Spain, especially during the eleventh century.

Good urge: In rabbinic homilies, the aspect of the human personality that tends towards virtue and obedience to God.

Great Revolt: The failed uprising against Rome in 66–73 CE that culminated in the destruction of the Second Temple in the year 70.

Guide of the Perplexed: The philosophical masterpiece by Moses Maimonides in which he attempted to reconcile traditional Jewish beliefs with Aristotelian science and philosophy.

Gush Emunim: Hebrew: "bloc of the faithful"—an Israeli religious and political movement that is concerned with maintaining Jewish settlement in territories acquired in the 1967 Six-Day War.

Hadas: Hebrew: "myrtle"— one of the "four species" carried in processions on the feast of Tabernacles.

Haggadah: Hebrew: "telling"—the liturgy for the traditional Passover night meal (*seder*) in which the liberation of the Hebrews from Egyptian slavery is recounted. The reciting of the haggadah is seen as the fulfillment of the precept (Exodus 13:8) "And you shall tell your son on that day."

Hagiographa: Greek for "holy writings"—see "Ketuvim."

Halakhah: The component of the Jewish oral tradition that deals with matters of law.

Hallah: A portion of dough that must be set aside and given to a priest according to Torah law. In colloquial usage, it has come to designate an ornamental loaf of bread eaten on the Sabbath or festivals.

Ḥanukkah: The "feast of Dedication" commemorating the purification of the Jerusalem Temple after it had been used for pagan worship during Antiochus IV's persecutions. The holiday lasts eight days in the winter and is celebrated by lighting lamps every night.

Ḥaredi: Hebrew for "those who tremble"—a term used to described the most conservative type of traditionalist Jews in terms of their dress, observance, devotion to full-time religious study and insulation from the modern world.

Hasid: From a Hebrew word meaning "pious," the term has been applied to several Jewish pietistic ideologies through history, particularly to the movement established by Rabbi Israel Baal Shem Tov in the eighteenth century that advocated a popular mystical devotion based on serving God in joy.

Hasidut Ashkenaz: See "German pietism."

Haskalah: The Hebrew name for the "Enlightenment."

Hasmoneans: The priestly family who led a successful revolt against the Hellenistic persecutions of Antiochus IV, and subsequently established themselves as the political and priestly leaders of Judea.

Havdalah:　Hebrew for "separation"—a ceremony marking the conclusion of the Sabbath or festivals.

Havurah:　Hebrew for "fellowship"—a name used for various Jewish communal groupings through history, including the Havurat Shalom, an American movement of small, non-institutional communities and prayer groups that were prominent in the 1960s and 1970s.

Hebrew:　The Semitic language in which most of the Jewish Bible is composed, as is most subsequent Jewish religious literature. A revived, modernized version of Hebrew is the spoken language in the state of Israel.

Hebrew Bible:　The sacred scriptures of the Jews, traditionally believed to have originated in divine revelation or inspiration. In old Jewish sources it is referred to as *Miqra* ("that which is read aloud"). According to the conventional classification, the Hebrew Bible is divided into three sections:　Torah, *Nevi'im* (Prophets) and *Ketuvim* (Hagiographa), comprising twenty-four books.

Heder:　Hebrew for "room"—used to designate the traditional European Jewish elementary schools that were often criticized for their primitive pedagogy.

Heikhalot:　Hebrew for "palaces"; a genre of Hebrew mystical literature involving the ascent through multiple levels of palaces that are guarded by angels.

Herem:　A ban of excommunication or ostracism, the most effective sanction for enforcing the authority of the rabbi and communal institutions in pre-modern Jewish society.

Hesder:　Hebrew for "arrangement"—an option that allows religious soldiers in Israel to combine religious study with their military service.

Hevra kaddisha:　Aramaic for "holy society"—a voluntary burial society.

Hiddushim:　Hebrew for "new things"—used to designate critical comments on the Talmud or other rabbinic works.

Hitlahavut:　Hebrew for "bursting into flame"—the Hasidic ideal of religious ecstasy or fervor, especially in prayer.

Holocaust:　Originally a Greek term for a burnt sacrificial offering; standardly used to refer to the murder of millions of Jews by the Nazis and their collaborators during World War II. See "Shoah."

Holy cherub:　In the mysticism of the German pietists, a manifestation of divine glory.

Huppah:　Canopy under which Jewish wedding ceremonies are conducted, symbolizing the household now shared by the newly married couple.

Israel:
  1. The name given to the biblical patriarch Jacob after wrestling with a mysterious being in Genesis 32:28: "for you have striven with God and with men and have prevailed."
  2. The entire nation descended from Jacob and his twelve sons ("children of Israel"; "Israelites").

3. During the era of the divided monarchy, Israel was the northern kingdom consisting of ten tribes.

4. In Jewish texts written in Hebrew, Jews almost invariably refer to themselves as "Israel."

5. The modern Jewish state founded in 1948.

Jerusalem Talmud: A commentary on the Mishnah compiled from the discussions of rabbis from the third to fifth centuries in the land of Israel. (This title is not quite accurate, since Jerusalem did not exist at that time.)

Jewish Renewal: A contemporary Jewish religious movement that incorporates elements of Hasidism, Kabbalah, meditation and various New Age concepts.

Job: A book in the Ketuvim section of the Hebrew Bible that explores issues of theodicy and suffering in the framework of a story about a man named Job who is tested by God with terrible afflictions.

Kabbalah: A medieval system of Jewish esoteric teaching based on the doctrine of the ten *sefirot*. Kabbalah includes a theological or theosophic theory about the relationship between the divinity and the created world, as well as a symbolic exegetical system for reading the Bible.

Kach: An illegal ultra-nationalist religious movement in Israel founded by Meir Kahane and advocating the removal of Arabs from Israel.

Kaddish: A prayer consisting of praises of God that is recited at the conclusions of units of the liturgy or of religious study. Since the Middle Ages it has been customary for mourners to lead certain instances of the Kaddish during the first eleven months after the death or on the Yahrtzeit.

Kalam: A Muslim school of theology that influenced Jewish thinkers, it applied rational methods to the analysis and clarification of religious beliefs.

Karaites: A movement that arose in the Middle Ages, whose adherents reject the rabbinic oral tradition and acknowledge only the authority of the Bible.

Kavod: Hebrew: "(Divine) glory"— a spiritual force that serves as the intermediary between God and the created universe in the mystical speculations of the Hasidei Ashkenaz movement. See "holy Cherub."

Kedushah: Hebrew: "sanctification"—the third section of the Eighteen Benedictions prayer (see "*Amidah*"). When recited in a congregational setting it incorporates verses from the chariot visions of Ezekiel and Isaiah.

Kelippot: Hebrew: "husks" or "shards"—in the kabbalistic doctrine of Rabbi Isaac Luria, these are the remains of the shattered vessels that could not contain the divine light. They are the metaphysical source of evil in the world.

Kerovah: An elaborate form of liturgical poetry designed to accompany the recitation of the *Amidah* prayer.

Ketubbah: A Jewish marriage contract, whose main purpose is to guarantee the support of the wife in the event of divorce or widowhood. It also outlines the couple's mutual obligations during the marriage.

Ketuvim: Hebrew: "(sacred) writings"—see "Hagiographa."

Khazars: A seminomadic Turkic nation whose royalty and nobility converted to Judaism in the late eighth or early ninth century.

Kiddush: Hebrew: "sanctification"—a liturgical ceremony, usually recited over a cup of wine, inaugurating the Sabbath or a festival.

Kiddushin: Hebrew: "sanctifications"—a term for betrothal. See "*erusin*."

Kohen (singular); *kohanim* (plural):   A priest. In Judaism, all priests are patrilineal descendants of Aaron, Moses's brother, who was designated the first high priest.

Kol Nidrei: Aramaic: "All the vows"—a ceremony for the cancelation of vows, recited before the evening service of the Day of Atonement.

Kolel: An institution for advanced talmudic studies for married students.

Kosher: Hebrew (according to Ashkenazic pronunciation): "fit"—colloquially applied to foods that are prepared according to the Jewish dietary regulation.

Kvater (masculine); *kvaterins* (feminine):   Yiddish: "godfather"—an individual who is honored by being asked to carry the baby in to a circumcision.

Law of Return: A law passed by the Israeli parliament in 1951 recognizing all Jews as Israeli expatriates and allowing them automatic citizenship.

Levirate marriage: A biblical law requiring a childless widow to marry her late husband's brother, or to undergo a ritual ceremony of release.

Levites: One of the twelve tribes of Israel, descended from Jacob's son Levi. The Levites were designated a holy tribe without a territory, and were to be supported by tithes.

Leviticus Rabbah: A work of aggadic midrash on the book of Leviticus.

Lilith: In folklore and kabbalistic traditions, a female demon, usually the queen of the demons, who threatens newborn infants.

Logos: Greek: "word" or "reason"—in the philosophy of Philo of Alexandria, the rational principle of the universe that serves as an intermediary between God and the physical world.

Lulav: The green, closed frond of a date palm. It is one of the "four species" taken in the ritual processions of the Feast of Tabernacles.

Lurianic Kabbalah: The interpretation of the Kabbalah taught by Rabbi Isaac Luria in sixteenth-century Safed.

Maccabee: Epithet attached to Judah son of Mattathias, the first military leader of the Hasmonean uprising against the Hellenistic forces. The word means "hammer" and may refer to his might, or perhaps to a physical feature. The books about the uprising were titled "Maccabees."

Malkhuyyot: Hebrew: "kingship"—the theme of the first section of the Additional Service for Rosh Hashanah, stressing the theme of God's absolute sovereignty over the universe.

Maror: Hebrew: "bitter herb"—a required food at the Passover seder, symbolizing the bitterness of the slavery in Egypt.

Marranos: A derogatory term for Conversos—probably from a word meaning "pigs."

Mashiaḥ: Hebrew: "anointed one"—a legitimate king or priest who has been installed through the biblical ceremony of anointing the head with olive oil. As an eschatological concept, it refers to the future restoration of the legitimate Davidic monarchy and Zadokite priesthood.

Masorti movement: Hebrew: "traditional"—the name used by Conservative Judaism in Israel and some other localities.

Massekhet: Hebrew: "tractate"—a section of the Mishnah or Talmud, usually dealing with a specific topic. Tractates are divided up into chapters, and several tractates make up an order (*seder*).

Matrilineal descent: The rule in rabbinic law that counts as Jewish a person who is born of a Jewish mother.

Matzah: Unleavened bread, eaten at Passover to recall how the Israelites left Egypt in haste and their dough did not have time to rise.

Megillah: Hebrew: "scroll"; especially the scroll of the book of Esther that is read ritually at Purim.

Merkabah **mysticism:**   Hebrew: "chariot"—an esoteric mystical discipline based primarily on the prophet Ezekiel's vision of a chariot composed of angelic beings bearing a mysterious human-like figure.

Messiah: Widespread English rendering of "*Mashiaḥ*."

Messiah son of Joseph: In some Jewish eschatological scenarios, a figure who will try to redeem Israel but will fall before achieving his mission. The ultimate messiah will be from the house of David.

Midrash: Rabbinic teachings related to the Bible.

Mikveh: A pool of water used for purification.

Min: In rabbinic literature: a heretic.

Minor Prophets: A volume in the *Nevi'im* section of the Bible containing twelve shorter works that are treated as a single book.

Mishnah: From a Hebrew root meaning: "to recite from memory."
1. The title of an authoritative collection of Jewish oral traditions, mostly of legal matters, and organized by subject; compiled by Rabbi Judah the Patriarch in the early third century CE.
2. An individual unit or paragraph in the Mishnah.
3. The genre consisting of oral teachings that are not connected to scripture.

Mishneh Torah: Hebrew: "second Law"—the Hebrew term that is rendered in Greek as "Deuteronomy" (the book in the Torah consisting of Moses's review of his life). The title was adopted to designate Maimonides' comprehensive code of Jewish law.

Mizrachi movement: Hebrew abbreviation for "spiritual center"—religious Zionist movement.

Mohel: One who performs circumcisions.

Moriah: The location of the mountain where Abraham was commanded to sacrifice his son; traditionally identified with the Temple Mount in Jerusalem.

Musaf: Hebrew: "additional"—the additional sacrifices offered on Sabbath and festivals; by analogy: the additional prayer services on those days.

Nasi: Hebrew: "prince"; title given to the communal and judicial head or patriarch of the Palestinian Jewish community.

Navi: Hebrew: "prophet"—one who was chosen to deliver messages from God.

Negative theology: In Maimonides's philosophy: the belief that the use of attributes in the Bible does not convey positive information about God, but serves to deny any deficiencies.

Neo-Orthodoxy: The interpretation of traditional Judaism associated with Rabbi Samson Raphael Hirsch, advocating active involvement with modern western culture.

Neoplatonism: A philosophical approach based on the teachings of Plato and Plotinus that stresses the existence of the transcendent One from which emanated the diversity of the material world.

Neturei Karta: Aramaic: "guardians of the city"—a traditionalist religious movement that virulently opposes Zionism.

Nevi'im: Hebrew: "prophets" (see "*Navi*")—the second division in the Jewish classification of the Bible.

New Christians: Jews who converted to Christianity at the time of the Spanish Inquisition.

Niddah: A menstruating woman, or one who has not become purified of the impurity caused by menstruation.

Ninth of Av: The date of an annual day of fasting and mourning for the destruction of the two Jerusalem Temples and several other national catastrophes.

Noachide commandments: Seven moral and religious obligations that are considered binding on all of humanity (all of whom are descendants of Noah).

Odes to Zion: Poignant Hebrew poems about Jerusalem authored by Judah Halevy

Old Testament: The Christian term for the Hebrew Bible.

Omer: Hebrew: "sheaf"—a sheaf of barley offered up on the second day of Passover, thereby beginning a count of seven weeks until Shavuot, the Feast of Weeks. By extension, the term is used to refer to the process of counting the seven weeks, and to the period during which the counting takes place.

Orthodox Union: The main organization of modern or centrist Orthodox congregations in America.

Orthodoxy: The modern Jewish movement that advocates traditional Judaism.

Other Side: In the Kabbalah, the realm of evil. Aramaic: *"Sitra Aḥra."*

Palestine: The name give by the Romans to the land of Israel.

Palestinian Talmud: See "Jerusalem Talmud."

Passover: The springtime festival commemorating the liberation of the Israelites from slavery in Egypt. The name is taken from the biblical story of how death "passed over" the Israelite dwellings when slaying the Egyptian firstborn. The Hebrew term is *"Pesaḥ."*

Patriarchal era: The generations of Abraham, Isaac and Jacob, the biblical ancestors ("patriarchs") of the Jewish people.

Patrilineal descent: According to a 1983 decision of the American Reform movement, children of a Jewish father should be accepted as Jewish even if the mother was not Jewish.

Pentateuch: Greek: "the five books (of Moses)"—the Torah.

Pesah: Hebrew: "Passover."

Peshat: Hebrew: "simple"—literal or contextual exegesis.

Pesher: Hebrew: "interpretation"—a genre of literature found at Qumran in which biblical texts are interpreted with reference to recent events or the specific history of the Qumran sect.

Pesiqta: Aramaic: "division"—midrashic expositions for "special" occasions, such as festivals and other days that are not part of the sequential cycle of readings from the Torah and Prophets.

Petihah/petihtah: Hebrew/Aramaic: "opening"; "introduction"—a rhetorical structure for introducing midrashic homilies, especially by commencing with a verse from another part of the Bible, and developing a sermon that culminates with the beginning of the passage that is read that day in the synagogue.

Pharisees: From Hebrew: "separate"—a Second Temple movement that encouraged Torah scholarship as a religious value, and maintained strict standards of purity and dietary observance.

Pittsburgh Platform: Policy statement of the American Reform movement in 1885, expressing strong opposition to Jewish peoplehood, ritual and other features of traditional Judaism.

Piyyut: Hebrew liturgical poetry.

Positive Historical Judaism: An evolutionary cultural conception of the Jewish religion advocated by Zacharias Frankel.

Practical Kabbalah: The use of kabbalistic principles in order to manipulate reality, a form of magic.

Priest: See *"kohen."*

Primordial Man (*Adam Kadmon*):   A form of kabbalistic symbolism according to which the *sefirot* are configured as limbs of a human form.

Psalms: A book in the *Ketuvim* section of the Bible consisting of poetic prayers, most of which are traditionally attributed to King David.

Pseudepigrapha: Ancient Jewish texts, many of them of an apocalyptic nature, that claimed to be written or revealed by biblical figures.

Purim: Hebrew: "(feast of) lots"—a holiday commemorating the events recounted in the book of Esther, when the Jews of the Persian empire were saved from Haman's plot to murder them. Also referred to as "the feast of Esther."

Purim-Shpils: Yiddish: "purim plays"—theatrical productions traditionally enacted on Purim.

Qorban: Hebrew: "sacrifice."

Qumran: An archeological site in the Judean desert near the Dead Sea where a library of manuscript scrolls was discovered from the Second Temple era. It is widely believed that Qumran was the site of an Essene community.

Ra'aya Meheimna: Aramaic: "faithful shepherd"—a kabbalistic work by an unknown Spanish author published in standard editions of the Zohar, and purporting to contain teachings of Moses (the shepherd), the prophet Elijah, and Simeon ben Yohai about the secret meanings of the commandments.

Rabbi: Hebrew: "my teacher"—the title given to a recognized authority on Jewish law. In modern times, the position is often perceived as a type of clergyman or woman.

Rabbinites: Jews who accept the authority of the rabbinic oral tradition; usually used as contrast to Karaites.

Rashi: Acronym for Rabbi Solomon ben Isaac (1041–1105) of Troyes, France, the foremost Jewish commentator on the Bible and Talmud.

Redemption of the firstborn: A ritual in which the firstborn son is redeemed from a *kohen* for five silver shekels in order to formally release him from his obligation to serve in the Temple. The ceremony is usually conducted when the boy is one month old.

Reform Judaism: The Jewish movement that advocated introducing changes into traditional Judaism in order to accommodate modern values and ideas, and to facilitate participation in post-Emancipation society.

Responsa: In Hebrew: *"she'elot utshuvot"* (questions and answers); replies written by prominent rabbis to questions about Jewish law and other topics.

Resurrection: The belief that the dead will be restored to life in physical bodies.

Rishon le-Zion: Hebrew: "First to Zion" (Isaiah 41:27)—the official title given to the Sephardic Chief Rabbi of Israel.

Rosh Hashanah: The Jewish New Year, a biblical holiday celebrated on the first day of the seventh month (Tishri). It is portrayed as a solemn day of divine judgment.

Sabbath: The weekly day of rest observed from sundown on Friday until Saturday night in commemoration of God's completing the six days of creation. Hebrew: *"shabbat."*

Sadducees: A Second Temple Jewish movement that upheld the ideals of the traditional Zadokite high priesthood.

Safed: A town overlooking the Sea of Galilee that became a preeminent center of kabbalistic activity in the sixteenth century.

Samael: In Jewish folklore and Kabbalah, the king of the evil demons.

Samaritans: A religious community who observe the Torah. According to the biblical account, they are descended from foreign peoples who were transferred by the Assyrians to Samaria after the exile of the northern Israelite kingdom.

Sandak: Probably from the Greek: "suntekos": "companion of child"—the person who holds the baby during the circumcision ceremony.

Sanhedrin, Syhedrion: Greek: "council"—a Jewish high court and rabbinical council during the Second Temple and rabbinic eras.

Satan: The angel charged with entrapping, accusing and punishing sinners.

Savora'im: The rabbis who were active in Babylonia between the end of the talmudic era and the beginning of the geonic era, sometime between BCE 500 and 700 according to various calculations.

Scapegoat: In the Day of Atonement observances in the Temple, a goat was chosen by lot, then the high priest symbolically placed the sins of the people on its head and sent it to perish in the wilderness.

Scroll of Esther: The book of Esther handwritten on a parchment scroll, especially for liturgical reading on the holiday of Purim. See *"Megillah."*

Second Commonwealth: The era in Jewish history extending from the return of the Babylonian exiles until the destruction of the Second Temple of Jerusalem, roughly 530 BCE–70 CE.

Second Temple Era: Equivalent to "Second Commonwealth," viewed from a religious perspective.

Seder: Hebrew: "order"—
1. One of the six main topical divisions of the Mishnah
2. The procedures for the ceremonial meal on the first night of Passover; or by extension, the meal itself.

Sefer Hasidim: Hebrew: "the book of the pious"—an important compendium of lore from the *Hasidut Ashkenaz* movement of the twelfth and thirteenth centuries.

Sefer Yezirah: Hebrew: "the Book of Creation"—a short and enigmatic treatise describing how God created the world by means of combinations of the ten decimal numbers and the twenty-two letters of the Hebrew alphabet.

Sefirah (singular); *Sefirot* (plural): Ten emanated powers of God symbolically identified with divine attributes, according to the central doctrine of the Kabbalsh.

Selihot: Hebrew: "forgiveness"; penitential prayers recited during the Rosh Hashanah season, on fast days and other occasions.

Semites: Supposed descendants of Shem son of Noah, identified as the Middle Eastern peoples. The term is used most accurately as the name of the language family to which Hebrew, Aramaic and Arabic belong.

Sepharad: Hebrew: Spain.

Sephardic: Adjective referring to:

1. Jews of medieval Spain.
2. Jewish communities in Arab and Islamic lands.
3. Jews refugees from Iberia since the time of the Inquisition.

Septuagint: Greek: "seventy"—the old Alexandrian Greek translation of the Torah (and the rest of the Bible). According to legend it was composed by seventy Jewish elders.

Seventeenth of Tammuz: A fast day held in the summer commemorating the breach of the walls of Jerusalem by the Babylonians as well as other national catastrophes.

Shabbat: See "Sabbath."

Shabbateans: Followers of the seventeenth-century messianic pretender Shabbetai Zevi.

Shalom: Hebrew: "peace."

Shas: An Israeli political party representing a Sephardic Haredi constitutency.

Shavuot: Hebrew: "(feast of) weeks"—a biblical pilgrimage festival observed fifty days after the beginning of Passover. The Torah depicts it as a time of agricultural thanksgiving, and the rabbinic tradition identified it as the anniversary of the revelation of the Torah at Mount Sinai.

Shehitah: Ritual slaughter of animals or fowl.

Shekhinah: The divine presence in the world.

Sheloshim: Hebrew: "thirty"—the first thirty days of mourning.

Shema' (or: *Shema' Yisra'el*):   A central component of the daily liturgy, containing Deuteronomy 6:4–9, 11:13–21, and Numbers 15:37–41, embedded in a framework of blessings. The Hebrew name consists of the opening words, "Hear O Israel…"

Shemini Azeret: Hebrew: "eighth day of assembly"—the day following the feast of Tabernacles (Sukkot), which is celebrated as a separate holiday.

Sheva berakhot: Hebrew: "seven blessings"—seven blessings, several of them poetic celebrations of marriage, that are recited at a Jewish wedding and during the subsequent week of festivities.

Shivah: Hebrew: "seven"—the first week of mourning, when the mourners remain at home and are consoled by the community.

Sho'ah: Hebrew: "destruction"—used to designate the murder of 6 million Jews by the Nazis and their collaborators; an alternative term for "Holocaust."

Shofar: A trumpet made from a ram's horn, sounded especially on Rosh Hashanah.

Shofarot: Hebrew: "trumpeting"—the third theme of the additional (*Musaf*) service of Rosh Hashanah, dealing with diverse occasions of the sounding of the shofar.

Shulhan Arukh: Hebrew: "set table"—an influential sixteenth-century codification of Jewish law by Rabbi Joseph Caro (with supplement by Rabbi Moses Isserles).

Sh'virat ha-kelim: See "breaking of the vessels."

Simhat Torah: Hebrew: "rejoicing of the Torah"—a celebration of the completion of the cycle of reading the Torah and the commencement of a new cycle. It is standardly observed on the second day of Shemini Azeret (the day that is added in diaspora communities).

Sinai: The mountain on which the Torah was revealed to Israel through Moses, according to the biblical account. By extension, the name may be applied to the event itself.

Song of Songs: A book in the *Ketuvum* division of the Bible consisting of sensuous love poetry. Traditionally, it is understood as an allegory for the relationship between God and Israel. It is ascribed to King Solomon, and hence is often referred to as the Song of Solomon. Its Hebrew title is *Shir ha-Shirim*.

Special cherub: See "Holy cherub."

Sukkah: Hebrew: "tabernacle"; "booth"—the temporary structure in which one dwells during the feast of Tabernacles, in commemoration of the wanderings of the Israelites in the desert after the exodus from Egypt.

Sukkot: A seven-day pilgrimage festival held in the fall (commencing on the fifteenth of Tishri) commemorating the ingathering of the crops and the sojourn of the ancient Israelites in the Sinai wilderness.

Synagogue: Greek: "assembly"—a place where Jews assemble for the reading of scripture, prayer and other religious and communal functions.

Tabernacles, feast of: See "Sukkot."

Taharah: Hebrew: "purification"—especially the cleansing and preparation of a corpse for burial.

Talmud: One of two (Israeli and Babylonian) collective interpretations of the Mishnah composed between the third and seventh centuries, consisting largely of intricate debates and analysis on technical issues of religious law.

Talmud Torah: Study of the Torah, as a religious activity and value. The term is also used to designate a Jewish elementary school.

Tamid: Hebrew: "continual offering"—sacrifices offered every morning and evening on behalf of the community.

TaNaKh: An acronym for the three divisions of the Hebrew Bible: Torah, *Nevi'im* and *Ketuvim*.

Tanhuma: A family of aggadic midrash known for the frequency of the introductory formula "Thus began Rabbi Tanhuma"; and for its propensity for fashioning the individual statements of earlier traditions into continuous narratives and homilies.

Tanna (singular); *tannaim* (plural); **tannaitic** (English adjective):   Aramaic: "recite from memory"—

1. A functionary in the amoraic schools responsible for memorizing and reciting earlier traditions.
2. A sage whose views are cited in the Mishnah or other works from the first to early third centuries.

Targum: Hebrew: "translation"—the Aramaic translation that used to accompany the liturgical scriptural reading in the synagogue, for the benefit of those who were not fluent in Hebrew.

Teacher of righteousness: A revered figure mentioned in the Qumran scrolls, who is widely assumed to be the founder of the sect.

Tefillah: Hebrew: "prayer"—the term is used to designate prayer in general; or as the standard Hebrew designation for the Eighteen Benedictions/*Amidah*.

Ten days of repentance: The period extending from Rosh Hashanah to the Day of Atonement, when Jews repent their sins with a view to attaining divine forgiveness.

Ten lost tribes: The tribes of the northern kingdom of Israel during the era of the divided monarchy, who were conquered and exiled by the Assyrians, and subsequently lost to Judaism.

Tenth of Tevet: A minor fast day observed in the winter to commemorate the beginning of the siege of Jerusalem by the Babylonians.

Terumah: Hebrew: "that which is taken up"; "heave offering"—a proportion of produce that is set aside for the priests, and must be consumed in a state of purity.

Tetragrammaton: The holy four-letter name of God that is not pronounced by Jews, and is usually replaced by an epithet meaning "Lord."

T'fillin: Passages from the Torah that are written on pieces of parchment and inserted in leather boxes that are strapped on the arm and forehead, in fulfillment of the biblical precept "it shall be for a sign for you upon your hand, and for a memorial between your eyes."

Tiferet: Hebrew: "beauty"; "glory"—in Kabbalah, the central *sefirah* that embodies the perfect balance of justice and mercy.

Torah: Hebrew: "teaching"; "guidance"; "instruction"—

1. The first five books of the Hebrew Bible, believed to have been revealed by God through Moses.
2. More generally, the teachings of Judaism, or some portion thereof.

Torah im Derekh Erez: Hebrew: "Torah with worldly culture"—the ideology advocated by Rabbi Samson Raphael Hirsch of integrating traditional Jewish belief and observance with involvement in secular culture.

Tosafot: Hebrew: "supplements"—critical comments to the Talmud, especially those produced in medieval France and Germany.

Tosefta: Aramaic: "supplement"—a tannaitic collection organized like the Mishnah and containing alternative or explanatory traditions.

Usha: A village in the Galilee that was a center of rabbinic leadership in the mid-second century CE.

Wissenschaft des Judentums: German: "Science of Judaism"—the scientific or academic study of Judaism, especially as it developed in eighteenth- and nineteenth-century Germany.

Yahrtzeit: German: "anniversary"—the anniversary of the death of a loved one, commemorated through the recitation of Kaddish and other observances.

Yavneh: A coastal town in Judea that was the center of rabbinic leadership during the generations following the destruction of the second Temple. By extension, the term is applied to those generations (c. 70–135 CE).

Yeshivah: An institution for advanced talmudic studies.

Yezirah: Hebrew: "formation"—the third of the four worlds according to the Kabbalah; the realm of the lower angels, the souls and of Paradise.

Yiddish: The vernacular language of Ashkenazic Jewry, consisting chiefly of a German dialect (written in Hebrew letters), with elements of Hebrew, Aramaic and other languages absorbed in the course of the community's migrations.

Yishuv: Hebrew: "settlement"—a Jewish community in the land of Israel.

Yizkor: Hebrew: "May God remember"—title and opening word of the memorial prayer for the dead, recited on some Jewish holidays.

Yom ha-Azma'ut: Israeli Independence Day, celebrated on the fifth of Iyar (in April or May).

Yom ha-Sho'ah: Memorial day for the Holocaust.

Yom Kippur/*Yom ha-Kippurim*: See "Day of Atonement."

Yom Yerushalayim: Hebrew: "Jerusalem Day"—Annual commemoration of the reunification of Jerusalem on 28 Iyyar (June 7) 1967.

Zaddik: Hebrew: "righteous one"; a charismatic leader embodying the values of Hasidism.

Zadok: High priest appointed by David, and the ancestor of the dynasty ("Zadokites") that occupied the high priesthood until the Hasmonean era.

Zealots: A Jewish group committed to violent resistance against the Romans, motivated by their conviction that their sole allegiance should be to God.

Zikhronot: Hebrew: "remembrance"—the theme of the second section of the Additional Service for Rosh Hashanah, stressing the theme that God recalls and judges all the deeds of his creatures.

Zimzum: Hebrew: "contraction"—in the kabbalistic doctrines of Rabbi Isaac Luria, the idea that God intentionally withdrew himself from a part of the universe in order to enable the existence of something other than himself on which he could bestow his blessings.

Zion: The name of a mountain in Jerusalem; by extension, an epithet for Jerusalem.

Zionism: Political movement, founded by Theodor Herzl in the late nineteenth century that advocated the establishment of a national home for the Jewish people in its historic homeland.

Zizit: Hebrew: "tassle"; "fringe"—knotted strings attached to the corners of a garment as a reminder of the commandments, in fulfillment of Numbers 15:38.

Zohar: Hebrew: "brilliance"—the name of the most influential compendium of kabbalistic teachings; composed in thirteenth-century Spain in the style of a rabbinic midrash whose central figure is Rabbi Simeon ben Yohai.

Index